Praise for *Landscape and Englishness* by David Matless

'*Landscape and Englishness* is an essential read for anyone interested in why some kinds of interaction with nature are celebrated and others are frowned on. Drawing on a huge diversity of sources books, films, preservationist tracts, walking guides, novels, music-hall songs, Ministry of Information pamphlets, maps and festival guides Matless reveals how our assumptions about landscape and national identity were forged in the decades between the Great War and the 1950s, and how deeply they've been shaped by history, class and politics ... a revelation.'
— Helen Macdonald, *The Guardian*

'The best book so far on the interpretation of landscape in the middle years of the twentieth century.'
— *Architects' Journal*, Books of the Year

'Creates a convincing portrait of the changing meanings of the English landscape in the twentieth century ... This book is filled with enjoyable cameos of writers, painters, poets and naturalists, but it is also a thoughtful portrayal of the city and the shifting ideology of modernity.' — *TLS*

'Cultural history at its best, subtle, multi-layered and full of new ideas and insights ... this book is a must.'
— *Contemporary British History*

'Always fascinating, the story of what we have done with our countryside, the towns we have expanded and the places we have plundered is well told and extremely well referenced ... Matless tells a good story and marshals his enormously rich research so that it is immediately accessible ... We owe him a great deal for letting us understand so much more clearly what has more recently made us English.' — *Country Life*

'An interesting book, full of intriguing material, subtle arguments, illuminating insights. There is a wealth of illustrations and the book is very well produced ... it is a work of real importance ... it reads as much a work of the heart as well as the mind.'
— *Geography*

ABOUT ENGLAND

DAVID MATLESS

REAKTION BOOKS

To Edwyn

Published by
Reaktion Books Ltd
Unit 32, Waterside
44–48 Wharf Road
London N1 7UX, UK
www.reaktionbooks.co.uk

First published 2023
Copyright © David Matless 2023

All rights reserved

No part of this publication may be reproduced, stored in a retrieval system or transmitted, in any form or by any means, electronic, mechanical, photocopying, recording or otherwise, without the prior permission of the publishers

Printed and bound in Great Britain by TJ Books Ltd, Padstow, Cornwall

A catalogue record for this book is available from the British Library

ISBN 978 1 78914 691 2

CONTENTS

1 Six Decades in England 7

PART I: GOING ABOUT
2 England in Prospect and Retrospect 26
3 English Pastoral 43
4 England Shaken 72

PART II: ENGLISH PLACES
5 English and Suburban 118
6 English Particulars 155

PART III: ENGLISH TIMES
7 English Heritage 202
8 The English Modern 254

9 Concluding 288

REFERENCES 295
SELECT BIBLIOGRAPHY 331
DISCOGRAPHY 344
FILMOGRAPHY 346
ACKNOWLEDGEMENTS 348
PHOTO ACKNOWLEDGEMENTS 349
INDEX 350

1
Six Decades in England

What's It All About?

When I was young, the daily regional commercial television news programme was called *About Anglia*. The 'Anglia' part referred both to Anglia Television, the regional ITV company, and to the region covered, East Anglia. Anglia, the medieval Latin name for England, migrated to the television age, and *About Anglia* ran daily on weekdays between 1960 and 1990, against its BBC rival *Look East*. The title captured both its regional subject-matter, as a programme about East Anglia, and its mode of operation, with outside broadcasts going about Anglia in search of stories.

Surfacing decades on, this multivalent childhood memory may have shaped the title of this book. *About England* examines the England of the late twentieth and early twenty-first centuries in various ways: by attending to commentary 'About England', whereby people have sought to say something about a country, even claiming to speak for it; by going 'About England', to sites deemed to say something about the country, whether from symbolically standing out of the ordinary or by being symbolic in their ordinariness; in finding estimates 'About England', approximations of something hard to pin down, elusive in its meaning, with, for some, Englishness marked out as being never quite definable; and in finding a country 'going about', as if a yacht sailing, either changing a planned course or tacking back and forth to continue in an intended direction, steadily buffeted, negotiating wind.

About England pursues commentary, journey, estimate and manoeuvre over six decades, to open up English questions, and to show how English identity has been asserted, pondered, challenged, parodied, even made preposterous, in a country of contested variety.

Navigating *About England*

About England navigates the country through thematic chapters investigating the past six decades. Questions of landscape, place and geography, and of time, history and heritage, run throughout. *About England* largely sidesteps issues of agriculture, nature and spirituality, which will be addressed in a companion volume, *England's Green*. The book is divided into three parts, including seven chapters following this introduction, before a short conclusion reflects back across the book.

Part One, 'Going About', explores projections of England and their contestation. 'England in Prospect and Retrospect' opens the exploration through the work of recent prospectors of Englishness, cultural practitioners who in photography, literature, history, poetry, ceremonial and government initiative have sought to lay out prospects for the future, and have prospected for national cultural treasure, often through retrospective accounts of the English past. 'English Pastoral' follows, examining the comforts and anxieties of pastoral evocations of England in music, documentary, academic analysis, film, photography and political commentary, with attention to pastoral as a focus for arguments over a racialized Englishness. 'England Shaken' highlights the ways in which dramatic events have unsettled senses of English identity over the past six decades, through war and its remembrance, fears of nuclear catastrophe, political upheaval within the UK and in its relation to Europe, and pandemic. Part Two, 'English Places', considers select sites where Englishness has been located. 'English and Suburban' explores the ways in a which a specific place, suburbia, has been promoted and critiqued for its supposed English qualities, in documentary film, political campaigning, situation comedy, painting and photography. 'English Particulars' considers the meeting point of Englishness and claims for local character in architecture and design, local history, television, environmental campaigning and the particular English 'local', the pub. Part Three, 'English Times', explores the place of the past in recent definitions of England. 'English Heritage' examines architectural heritage as a focus for argument over national identity, and the ways in which the national has been interwoven with the local and global, whether in the country house, in conflicts over townscape, in contests over the term 'heritage' or in the valuing of the industrial past. 'The English Modern' explores late twentieth-century enthusiasm for modernism as a valued architectural heritage, and as a sign of a post-war social democratic past, yet also its rejection. The English motorway, embraced by some as a novel space for modern living, is rejected by others as a force of environmental and cultural destruction. The chapter thereby looks forward to things picked up in *About England*'s companion volume, *England's Green*, notably the place of England in the Anthropocene, with the coal-fired power station a site for reflection on the modern. A concluding chapter then looks back across *About England*.

The Sixty-Year Present

About England moves thematically in each chapter across six decades, between the early 1960s and the early 2020s, and the book is premised on a sense that this time period denotes a sixty-year present. The argument of *About England* is that assumptions still prevalent concerning Englishness, place and landscape were significantly shaped in the 1960s and '70s. *About England* follows on chronologically from my previous book *Landscape and Englishness*, first published in 1998 and reissued in 2016, and shares many of its concerns.[1] The final chapter of that book crept into the 1960s to explore how dominant assumptions shaped in the interwar period and through war and reconstruction began to break down, and *About England* steps off from this shift. War had made planning politically hegemonic, the obligation of the state, but from the late 1960s a number of factors chipped away at this as part of wider changes in England, the UK and the world. Environmentalism, an increasing suspicion of science and critiques from right and left of the authority manifest in modernist planning undercut a country of planned progress. By the late 1960s the post-war end of empire diminished national global self-importance, while new migrations made a postcolonial England. The politics of English nationhood was then as now contested, and the 1973 accession to European political structures further altered the terrain. The England of the late twentieth and early twenty-first centuries is shaped by such shifts, and all register in *About England*. Much of the book in effect sets up a dialogue between the present and the past, whether the 1960s and '70s or in other fields the 1980s, and conversation flows freely.

Looking back sixty years also, however, highlights the proximity of the 1960s to the Second and indeed the First World War. The theme is discussed further in Chapter Four, but the career of a globally famous English musician can be illustrative here. David Bowie is predominantly recalled today as a future-oriented figure from the 1970s, leaving a suburban London youth to be a Starman, but his late 1960s records carried a music-hall air, with a vocal style borrowed from Anthony Newley and a subject-matter happy to invoke the past. The song 'Little Bombardier', from the 1967 *David Bowie* album, tells of a soldier turned loser in peacetime, trying to cope with life and to find happiness, but hounded by authority for innocently befriending children. Bowie's Little Bombardier is as much an outsider as Ziggy Stardust, but with a strangeness derived from wartime scars. The aftermath of war overhangs the 1960s, twenty years on.

And war too overhangs the 2020s, eighty years on. Wartime keeps returning as a meaningful past, as the COVID-19 pandemic demonstrated. Whenever England is shaken, war memories seem to be triggered, and the temporal migration of historic frames of reference runs through *About England*.

How England Calls

From 2011 the census in England and Wales included an English box in the national identity question, inviting reflective and/or instinctive responses. Respondents were allowed to select more than one label, so could choose both English and British. In 2011, 37.6 million (67.1 per cent) ticked English, with 32.4 million (57.7 per cent) ticking this as a sole identity. The figure was highest at 81 per cent in the northeast, lowest at 44 per cent in London. The next lowest was 73 per cent in the west Midlands and the southeast, indicating London as an outlier in England. The British box was ticked by 16.3 million (29.1 per cent), with 10.7 million (19.1 per cent) identifying as British only.[2] The 2021 census results were to be released in early summer 2022, after the text for this book was completed.

England's 2011 census presence matches wider diagnoses of an upsurge in reflection on and identification with England. The census is an unusually meaningful box-ticking exercise, and *About England* reflects on the cultural and political context for its high English return, with events since 2011 – tensions within the United Kingdom, the departure of the UK from the EU, the COVID-19 pandemic – heightening rather than diminishing England as a meaningful cultural and political unit. In 2021 Ailsa Henderson and Richard Wyn Jones indeed argued that Englishness was 'The Political Force Transforming Britain'. Drawing on the 'Future of England Survey' conducted since 2011, Henderson and Wyn Jones found Englishness 'the motor force' in the remaking of British politics.[3] The outcome of that remaking is unclear, and the fuel for the motor various. Early twenty-first-century English outlooks range from expansive nationalistic pride, through patriotisms self-consciously modest, to patriotisms self-consciously progressive, to affectionate Angloscepticism and fears of exclusion from an aggressive insularity. Such potentially contradictory outlooks define contemporary Englishness, as they defined historic Englishness, and the task is less to separate them off in order to identify or sympathize with one against the other, but to recognize the complex singularity entailed.[4]

National cultures may be regarded as never straightforward singularities, existing only in a deconstructive state, affirming their singular nature while at the same time revealing their relationships with elsewhere, their internal heterogeneity and their contradictions. None of which makes national singularity false but describes its condition, its predicament.[5] The predicament of Englishness derives in part from the complexities of geographical scale and from internal varieties. The national refracts with the international and imperial, the local and regional; with the county, the city, the suburb and the country; with towers and houses old and new; with coastal cliffs and ancient sites. Such things are never simply national, but find themselves in a national predicament, which enables as it confines. All that said, in answer to the question 'Are you English?', whether in census or conversation, I couldn't help but say yes, by descent and experience, living in and through England, with never more than a month at a time out of the country. And however complex and hybrid an individual's ancestry and biography might be, however mobile and multiple their life, the answer to the English question can be a straightforward, unreflective, ordinary yes.

In 2001 Julia Bell and Jackie Gay compiled *England Calling*, a set of short stories on England at the millennium. The collection and its framing serves as an indicative example of the complexities of twenty-first-century reflection on how England calls. In keeping with other explorations of the national, Bell and Gay open up the territory by listing variety:

> Writing about landscape inevitably raises political and social questions, because social change is writ large in the topography

of England. Here we have history jostling with industry, towerblocks and cob-walled cottages, pubs and Euro wine-bars, claustrophobic suburbia, the weather, the sea, the moors, the roads and nuclear reactors. Cities and whole swathes of countryside are modified and reconstructed so quickly that they become unrecognisable almost overnight.[6]

Bell and Gay posit that in this changing England a 'generational shift' had made 'Punk and Thatcherism' rather than the Second World War the 'key cultural and historical reference points for many English people'.[7] As noted above, the twenty-first century has shown that war is hardly dead as an identity marker, but Bell and Gay highlight how the 1970s and '80s could also act as a historic watershed. Their introduction opens with a quote from the Sex Pistols' 1977 song 'God Save the Queen', 'There is no future in England's dreaming', a line whose cultural standing had been codified by Jon Savage's influential 1991 account of punk, *England's Dreaming*.[8] *England Calling* sidesteps official national dreams to explore other possible futures for a 'turbulent, rebellious, mongrel nation'.[9] Stories are presented as 'peeling back the layers of Englishness' through the contradictions of present and past: 'before we know what we want, we have to know who we are'.[10] The self-knowledge of the collection is explorative rather than definitive, its stories tending to the inconclusive, their situations unresolved, various Englands left hanging.

The title of *England Calling* itself indicates facets of twenty-firstcentury national identity. In one sense the 'calling' of the phrase has become quickly historic, the collection's millennial stories conveying an England before the common possession of the smartphone. English people communicated back then by speaking face-to-face, or by calling on the mobile, in a world before apps and social media. Very quickly, a 2001 collection comes calling from another time. There might be more distant historic echoes in the title for those who do habitually think back to the Second World War, of the BBC's 'London Calling' signature phrase and in the 'Germany Calling' response call sign of William Joyce, 'Lord Haw-Haw', broadcasting enemy messages to Britain in wartime. Claims to speak for the nation can mark out treacherous ground, and should always be heard with care.

The 'Calling' of the collection also, however, denotes an ongoing geographical story about the relationship between England's constituent parts. Bell and Gay present *England Calling* as going beyond London:

'We may not yet have the cultural confidence of our neighbours in Scotland, but the possibility of the whole of England becoming a country of discovery, to be reclaimed and revitalised by its writers, is the premise for *England Calling*.'[11] London provides two out of 24 stories, while 22 points north, south, east and west register their non-metropolitan Englands. For a collection framing itself via an assumed punk familiarity, the title calls up 'London Calling' by The Clash, a dystopian 1979 song, also the title of an LP, with its opening rallying cry calling to faraway towns. In *England Calling* the faraway towns call back, or rather call across, their voices directed not to London but through a national network that is multi-nodal.

In its emphasis on landscape, politics and social change, *England Calling* is keen to mark itself out from supposed comfortable English cliché. Bell and Gay state that 'The identities revealed may not be comfortable ones, or even very secure, but here English writers have the confidence to examine who they are, to question it, rather than mourning the loss of an Arcadian vision they never felt part of in the first place.'[12] *About England* also reflects on the insecurities of Englishness, but will find these within as well as beyond the Arcadian, as Chapter Three, on 'English Pastoral', explores. It would take only a minor amendment of punctuation in *England Calling*'s title, or indeed in the title of this chapter section, 'How England Calls', to call up such sensibilities. Add an exclamation mark, and England entrances, readers swooning. How England Calls!, whether in home thoughts from abroad, or holiday dreams.[13] Old dreamings, Arcadian or otherwise, carry their own cultural and political complexity and, as this book will show, continue to shape definitions of England.

Nationally Sourced

About England selects its source material from things which have claimed to say something about England, or that have been defined as somehow English. There is a parallel here with Peter Mandler's 2006 study of *The English National Character*, attending to explicit statements on national character as things worth analysis in their own right, and as ways into wider arguments about nationhood.[14] The criterion for inclusion in *About England* is that qualities of Englishness have been discerned or claimed in a place, a building, a poem, a photograph, a painting, a political speech, a television programme or any of the other objects considered in this book. With the exception of the final section of this introduction, which discusses the particular part of England I happen to inhabit, *About England* proceeds through things which have claimed, engaged with or been given an English label. Why things have been labelled as such, and the consequences of that labelling, is one of the themes of this book.

About England demonstrates variety in the nationally sourced, and also moments of delimitation, where labels have a policing role and boundaries are asserted. Many kinds of material are considered, but attention to one medium can conclude this section, and give an indication of the variety of modes in which a national subject-matter can be approached, sometimes directly, sometimes less so. *About England* features a number of musical references, compiled in a concluding discography, music carrying cultural significance in a country claiming global popular musical stature over the past six decades. Music carries messages direct and oblique about England, and to signal such variety, two tracks from around forty years ago here form a putative English double A-side.

The Clash's 1980 triple album *Sandinista* closes its first side with 'Something about England'. The song's words reflect on war and patriotism, undercutting those claiming all would be well if England were for the English. A destitute old man speaks to the singer, of how new problems echo the old, with childhood post-1918 sorrows, five years of combat in the Second World War and a return home to neglect, the architects of a rebuilt world uncaring. England is still marked by class division, and old memories are not good memories, are even hellish. The world turns away, and the old man, representing old England, is all alone. The words are printed within an album lyric sheet illustrated with Steve Bell cartoons, and given a catalogue number 'FSLN 1' after the Spanish acronym for the revolutionary Sandinista movement then governing Nicaragua, and threatened by the USA. The pullout sheet is titled 'The Armagideon Times no3', Armagideon invoking a gloomy mood, 'Something about England' sitting alongside songs about superpower rivalry, nuclear fear, record industry cynicism, government corruption, futile war and tower block misery.[15]

As a 36-track triple album, *Sandinista* was either praised for its eclecticism or criticized as a mess of uneven quality, but 'Something about England' is an orthodox, coherent ballad, a relatively stately narrative on England's state. Amid the cares and fears of a superpower-dominated world, the former superpower sits alone, dependent, diminished, anxious, failing. Those who thrash at the migrant neglect the veteran, and something about England is not right. 'Something about England' signals themes that will recur in *About England*, especially in the fourth chapter, around war and memory, but also points to the ways in which English concerns can migrate politically. The song's sentiments form part of a radical stance critiquing hypocrisy and wary of patriotism, but elements of 'Something about England' echo or anticipate more conservative critiques, as when in the 1970s and '80s the architecture of the post-war peace was damned as a betrayal of wartime sacrifice by defenders of a neglected heritage (as discussed in Chapter Seven below), or when in the twenty-first century a popular military patriotism urged 'Help for Heroes' against governmental neglect of veterans. 'Something about England', like other Clash songs, is nothing if not direct, but its message might be taken in different directions.

Messages about England can also be oblique. In 1987, on the LP *The Guitar and Other Machines*, The Durutti Column included 'English Landscape Tradition', a canonical title lent to an instrumental track. Since 1978 The Durutti Column has been the work of guitarist Vini Reilly, with some regular accomplices, and 'English Landscape Tradition' was written by Reilly with viola player John Metcalfe. The 1987 LP, like those before it, was issued on Manchester-based Factory Records; indeed Reilly was a distinctive voice within a Manchester music scene. On 'English Landscape Tradition' guitar, keyboard, sequencer, drum and viola move for 4 minutes and 49 seconds in a consistent rhythm, steady if not quite stately, the melody elaborated but never departing from the pattern laid down early on, the track's form in traditional mode, if tradition denotes something ever in evolution. 'English Landscape Tradition' may here be a matter of descent, and a point of departure. Titles for instrumental tracks can be incidental, glanced over on a sleeve, but here 'English Landscape Tradition' opens up a field of hearing, the title more than arbitrary. The just under five-minute stretch to the fade out suggests a certain temporality, and a keyboard underlay and guitar harmonics convey broad ease, melody in different instrumentation giving a landscape palette. Pastoral had been a reference before in the group's work, with the first track on their 1980 debut LP, *The Return of the Durutti Column*, entitled 'Sketch for Summer', opening with birdsong effect. The 'English' in

'English Landscape Tradition' locks reference to a particular place, and to sensibilities of pastoral and design.[16]

The Durutti Column's oblique deployment of an English label sits in counterpoint to the directives of The Clash. Musical variety appears in *About England*'s discography, but a double A-side of 'Something about England' and 'English Landscape Tradition' would signal a country at once stark and opaque, bombastic and modest, arresting and lulling. Which side to play? On the record, the two are conjoined.

A Not Uncommon England

About England will go about England in part via accounts of places deemed to say something about a country. To end this introductory chapter, however, an account of a not uncommon place in the Midlands, familiar from my daily round, somewhere not necessarily deemed especially English, but which will open up themes in the rest of the book: claims to local character, legacies of war, heritages industrial and modern, signs of geopolitics, elements of pastoral, forms of suburban living.

The suburban town of Beeston and the neighbouring village suburb of Attenborough are on the western side of Nottingham. Things in this geographically and socially middling place can convey an England of the early twenty-first century.[17] The experience of the middling everyday was perhaps heightened by the COVID-19 pandemic, lockdowns bringing a sense of what is lost when the taken-for-granted is forbidden. The resumption of things – walks to and from a primary school, watching children's sports training – highlighted an ordinary less taken for granted, and some things were spotted anew. What emerges from such a daily round about England?

Beeston is a place name not uncommon, with several Beestons around England (Cheshire, Norfolk and so on), Anglo-Saxon nomenclature for a settlement in bent grass. The town's pedestrianized high street moots another derivation via some pleasantly literal public art, with a sculpted concrete bee-man, seated with bees around. Topography inclines south from the town centre, down Station Road across the railway to the Rylands estates and the town's meadow-name origin. Fields still edge the Trent, parts of the town on the flood plain, the undefended parts unbuildable. One of the bigger English rivers, flowing from the Staffordshire moors to the Humber estuary, the Trent is often held to mark the edge of English north and south. If England is divided that way, Beeston is barely northern, as geographically middling as you can get.

From the Station Road railway bridge the eastern view shows the Boots complex, a major employer and pharmaceutical producer, the site established by Nottingham pharmacist turned entrepreneurial industrialist Jesse Boot between the wars. The 1930s Beeston factories, designed by Owen Williams, were for Nikolaus Pevsner in his 1951 'Buildings of England' *Nottinghamshire* guide 'a milestone in modern architecture', and are now Grade 1 listed as a modernist icon, old futures turned historic.[18] Boots is no longer a Nottingham firm, ownership moving across the Atlantic in the twenty-first century, the HQ in Illinois.

The walk to school goes north along Station Road, flattish, but with the beginnings of a slope. The Trent's valley side eventually rises 100 feet beyond the town centre, through the posher end of town to the golf course. Vary the school route a little and another country appears, street names signalling other national pasts. A little further along Queens Road, a turn to the north shows Waverley Avenue, and on to Melrose Avenue, past Scott Avenue. Names of romantic Scottish nationhood mark an Edwardian and interwar housing development, to sell in suburban England, Walter Scott's 'Waverley' novels a popular reference. Street names lift suburbia just out of the ordinary. Family homes settle for romance.

The geopolitical past, recent and distant, comes into view in the daily round. At the end of Melrose Avenue, across the open grass of Dovecote Park, twelve trees circle the bandstand, planted in 1993 to mark the then twelve member states of the European Community. Decent growth since has made eleven of the trees nearly twice the bandstand height, though one, a later replant, is shorter. Up Dovecote Lane, past The Willows open space, for youth relaxation and dog exercise, to the war memorial. Another route would have found a Boer War memorial in Broadgate Park, recalling 'the cause of a United Empire', but the Dovecote Lane memorial followed the First World War, Beeston in common with almost every English settlement. A Celtic cross of Portland stone stands on a stepped base set up in the 1920s at a junction where road layout and building type make Beeston's village past evident; this 'West End' of Beeston was designated a Conservation Area in 1976. A 'GR' postbox is set in the wall near to the memorial, the absence of a number after the 'G' implying the reign of George V

(1910–36) rather than George VI. Wartime letters from Beeston to the front may have been posted here.

On the west side of the memorial, facing the going down sun, is stated: 'In Grateful Memory of Those Who Gave Their Lives in the Great War 1914–18'. First World War commemoration ('By Their Own Great Valour And The Grace Of God They Won') was supplemented twenty years on, the north face reading: 'World War 1939–1945'. Wreaths are laid each November, staying for several months against winter weather, mostly general in their dedications but with one for a named individual killed in twenty-first-century conflict, his photograph displayed.

Past The Crown public house, and up to the churchyard, another memorial appears, to another conflict, one of only four public monuments in the country to the Crimean War. If the world war cross stands for the general fallen (world war names are listed on a memorial inside the church), here, on a plinth beneath a small obelisk, is a personalized monument to Anglo-Russian conflict. From a non-conscript war, with fewer casualties, there is space for the 1854 death stories of four Beeston

Post box, junction of Dovecote Lane and Middle Street, Beeston, Nottinghamshire.

men. One died in England, in a hospital in Plymouth, from the effects of leg amputation after battle. The others died in Crimea, though not all were killed in action. One was 'slain in the cavalry charge at Balaclava', but two (one of whom had survived the Balaclava charge) 'died of diarrhoea at Scutari hospital'. Graphic details of deaths hardly heroic. Walk across the churchyard, over the tram tracks laid in the 2010s, and a pub shows more memorialization. The Last Post, opened in 2000, is not, however, a military allusion but a Wetherspoon's pun on the pub's former use as postal sorting office.

Up to the primary school, and across the playing field another industrial heritage appears, older than Boots' modernism, the Victorian Gothic of the Anglo-Scotian mills, converted for flats in the twenty-first century. Leaving school, and back to the town square, on which the 1979 revision of the Pevsner *Nottinghamshire* guide notes: 'A shopping centre completed in 1973 involved the demolition of one of Boots' first shops ... It was of 1908, in their prestige half-timbered style ... By *A. N. Bromley*, with statues, heraldry, and stained glass by *Morley Horder* depicting local history.'[19] Some heritage is preserved, some adapted, some let go.

A return route home down Station Road's gentle Trentward incline passes more public art. From 2018 Beeston Civic Society sponsored a brightening up of a long shopside wall as part of the Beeston Street Art Project. What to show? Who to commemorate?[20] Three famous figures with local connections were chosen, painted by street artist Zabou, all of whom say something about Beeston, and perhaps about England. On the left on the wall, fashion designer Paul Smith (b. 1946), born in Beeston, known and knighted for his presentation of Englishness as stylish; Smith's painted chin has corrugations from a shop wall delivery door. On the right, singer Edwin Starr (1942–2003), the American soul artist, who ended up in nearby Chilwell, signalling England as accommodating, international. Starr's hits included the 1970 U.S. number 1 'War', which asked what war was good for, and concluded absolutely nothing. Chilwell is the site of a barracks. In July 1918 an explosion at the Chilwell munitions factory killed 139 mostly female workers, commemorated by wall art further down Station Road; a blue plaque in nearby Attenborough churchyard marks their mass graves. On the middle mural, between Starr and Smith, Richard Beckinsale (1947–1979), an actor typically described as 'much loved', who died young and nationally famous,

Mural of Paul Smith, Station Road, Beeston, Nottinghamshire, painted in 2018 by Zabou.

known for his TV roles in *Porridge*, a classic 1970s BBC prison comedy of incarceration, and *Rising Damp*, a classic 1970s ITV domestic comedy of misery and bigotry.

Round the back of the square, a Civic Society map shows where blue plaques to notables might be found, including Beckinsale at his nearby junior school. Trams pass, each with a famous Nottingham name, dead or alive, some Beeston-connected, as when road cyclist Sidney Standard passes the cycle shop he once owned. Actor Vicky McClure goes by, born in nearby Wollaton, making her name in part by starring in *This Is England*, a series of films by Beeston resident Shane Meadows. Born in 1972, Meadows grew up in Uttoxeter, before moving to Nottingham at the age of twenty; his films are chiefly set in the Midlands and reflective of his experience. *This Is England* appeared in 2006, set in 1983, and with three spin-off Channel 4 television series, set in 1986, 1988 and 1990. Beeston houses the maker of a notable critical exploration of English nationalism, showing skinhead cultures torn between the embrace and rejection of diversity. The young lead, Shaun, is drawn into nationalist culture, in part via allusions to his father's death in the Falklands, but ultimately rejects it, throwing his St George's flag into the sea, one national symbol enveloped and subsumed by another.

Mural of Richard Beckinsale, Station Road, Beeston, Nottinghamshire, painted in 2018 by Zabou.

Mural of Edwin Starr, Station Road, Beeston, Nottinghamshire, painted in 2018 by Zabou.

Another mural just along from Starr-Beckinsale-Smith on Station Road shows reeds and water and bees, a picture of the nature reserve at Attenborough, in flooded former gravel pits along the Trent. Attenborough is the next place along the river, and the next station on the railway line, an old village grown to suburbia. Here is another stop on the daily round, for youth cricket. Attenborough cricket club's ground is The Strand, and underneath the turf you would find a gravelly, sandy Trent beach. The ground's boundary wall was raised in 2012, part of flood defence works after the river spilled over the nature reserve into the village in 2000. Substantial characterful houses overlook the ground, and the church spire is over the way. Bell-ringing practice soundtracks Friday training, and bells for church accompany Sunday morning games. The visitor could delight in English clichés while watching a notable cultural mix at play.

By Attenborough church, outside Ireton House, is a Civic Society blue plaque: 'General Henry Ireton. Lawyer, confederate and son-in-law of Oliver Cromwell born here 1611 died Limerick 1651.' A flag of St George flies in Ireton House's back garden. Up the road is Ireton Grove, and there is an Ireton Street in Beeston. Henry Ireton, English Civil War victor, and 'chief theoretician of the revolutionary army', registers in the locality. English republicanism grew here, Ireton seeking 'a godly commonwealth in England' and signing the king's death warrant. Buried in Westminster Abbey, Ireton's corpse was exhumed and posthumously executed at the Restoration.[21] Robert Ramsey's 1949 biography of Ireton began: 'The village of Attenborough on the confines of Nottinghamshire and Derbyshire, where the Erewash falls into the Trent, cherishes as its claim to notice that it was the birthplace

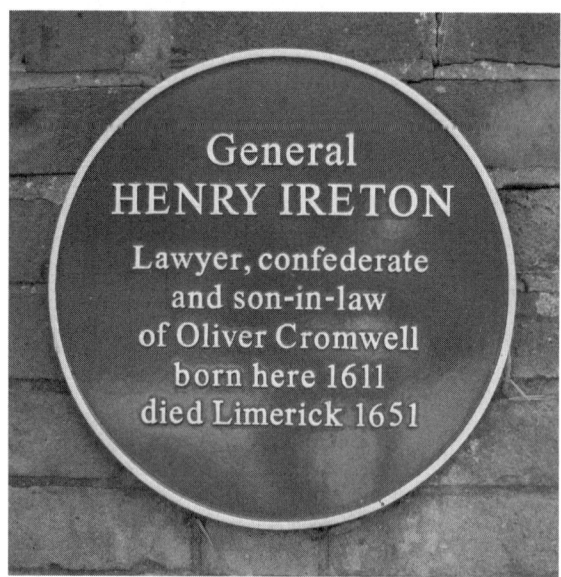

Memorial plaque to Henry Ireton, Attenborough, Nottinghamshire.

Attenborough church and Ireton House, Attenborough, Nottinghamshire.

of Henry Ireton.'[22] Depending on the English perspective, Ireton represents the right or wrong side in the English Civil War. The death place on the plaque denotes another geographical angle, from uncivil war in Ireland, where Ireton acted as Lord Deputy, commanded the New Model Army and accumulated estates. Ireton died of a fever after the siege of Limerick. If a few hundred yards south the Trent flows as an English north–south marker, here is another sign of England divided, unsettled in itself and unsettling others.

This geographical description of a not uncommon piece of England signals many of *About England*'s themes. There are pieces of pastoral, as the bells ring bowling changes at The Strand, yet division accompanies harmony, Ireton's plaque by the church. Unsettled Englands appear, with Beeston's European Community tree circle and war memorials as reminders of continental and global entanglements. Beeston and Attenborough carry suburban qualities, though the suburban here, as elsewhere, blends with town and village. The particulars of the place are valued, promoted in public art and listed as heritage, with the valued past taking various forms: the Victorian industrial, the modernist industrial and in conservation areas nurturing villageness. Pasts are apparent, and elsewheres too, a part of England defined in its relation to other times and places, from the Anglo-Saxon to the modern, Ireland to Crimea. A local excursion goes a long way. Geographical description here, as elsewhere, triggers connection, and says something about England.

PART I:
GOING ABOUT

2
England in Prospect and Retrospect

Scenes and Treasures

In John Drinkwater's 1937 novel *Robinson of England*, Robinson Dare imagines a prospect:

> Robinson often imagined himself to be far up in the air, looking down upon England spread out in gigantic shape, the familiar little map of the school atlases come to life. And there he saw, not a lesson in geography, but the story of a thousand years, moving miraculously with all ages in one, set in a vast scene of hills and woods and rivers and towns, with millions of people who came and went, and suffered and rejoiced, and grew always in number and yet were always the same, contending, overcoming, bewildered, but governed by some purpose that steadily formed the character which made an Englishman something different from any other man on earth.[1]

Robinson of England sees Uncle Robinson take his niece and nephew from his Cotswold base on instructive tours of England. Prospect and retrospect entwine as the children are shown hunts, football matches, industrial districts, market towns. Back in 1909 Robinson had published *The Influence of Landscape upon Character*, and concluded of England: 'The character was in perfect harmony with a landscape that was moderate also.'[2] J. H. Dowd's cover illustration showed Robinson's Cotswold cottage and his frontispiece Robinson's motivation, Dare in an armchair, looking at a wall map: 'He was in love with England.'

This chapter examines the ways in which landscape has been the site for reflections on and investigations of England and Englishness in recent decades, sometimes echoing Drinkwater's Robinson, sometimes

He was in love with England

Cover and frontispiece of John Drinkwater, *Robinson of England* (1937), illustrations by J. H. Dowd.

at odds with presumptions of national unity and continuity. The term 'prospect' brings together the landscape view, the optimistic or pessimistic prognosis and the search for treasure by prospectors of cultural gold. As with Robinson, prospects connect to retrospects, looks forward shaped by backward surveys and glances. This chapter examines notable recent prospectors and retrospectors, opening up the kinds of place stories that will run through *About England*. Photography, national celebration, cultural policy, history and archaeology, poetry and literature are all shown taking stock. The examples here are mostly from the present century, a time of prolific, if not always confident, examination of England.

We English

In photographer Simon Roberts's *We English* (2008), pictures and commentary examine the country. Roberts developed the theme of national identity from his previous Russian study, *Motherland* (2007), via a newly distinctive and consistent style, pictures taken from elevated viewpoints, often the roof of the Roberts family motorhome as they toured

England in the summer of 2008. *We English* offers prospect views, in compositional style but also in asking what England's prospects might be, a theme continued through Roberts's subsequent work gathered in the 2017 collection *Merrie Albion: Landscape Studies of a Small Island*.[3] *We English* concentrated on leisure and landscape, a series of 'tableaux' presenting 'the idea of the collective, of groups of people populating the landscape'.[4] Large-format images invite detailed scrutiny, ostensibly plain pictures of people and places displaying signs of social distinction, pleasures and tensions, a country which may or may not be at ease with itself.[5] Roberts notes the painterly influence of Dutch landscape and the Victorian scenes of William Powell Frith, notably his *The Derby Day*; Roberts's own Epsom image – of picnics and fairground, hot dogs and ices – offers a 'contemporary recreation of Frith's scene'.[6]

In the commentary section of *We English* Roberts sets out his own English biography, his consciousness shaped by places which might be deemed 'quintessentially English': born in 1974 in Croydon, Londoner father, mother from Cleator Moor, Cumbria, formative years in Oxted, Surrey, holidays in Lakeland or in grandparental Angmering on the Sussex coast, now resident in Brighton. Roberts also notes a university 'formal training as a cultural geographer', via a geography degree at Sheffield, a particular intellectual outlook shaping his photography.[7] *We English* shows the landscape cultures of seasides and riversides, ancient sites and folk games, rambling viewpoints and sporting grounds. If on one level all Roberts's pictures show groups of people occupying space, their differing social geography is immediately legible. Birdwatchers meet on a Norfolk beach; bikers stop for Uncle Sam's Ices at Blackgang Chine, Isle of Wight; stepping stones are navigated at Skipton; home fans walk in Sunderland; people wander on Blackpool beach or at the polo club. The viewer spots the social difference. Roberts also finds multicultural English encounters by Derwent Water, on Lindisfarne, at a Cheshire car boot sale and on the beach at Woolacombe Bay. Formal images show casual demotic cohabitation. A vernacular less than spectacular characterizes this English tour: 'I wanted to produce a body of work that was beautiful, where England was rendered in an unashamedly lyrical way, even if the landscape depicted was somewhat banal.'[8]

When Roberts comes to the Cotswolds, he first photographs Cirencester Park Polo Club but the next day heads not to the classic stone villages but the Cotswold Water Park, a Thames Valley leisure space of flooded gravel workings. Two images are shown from 11 May

2008, one of bathers bobbing, the other of 'Keynes Country Park Beach', grass and a bit of sand, a place of extraction turned to safe relaxation. Groups take their patch, keeping their close distance, and no one heeds the photographer. Roberts notes of his large-format 5×4 camera that 'by the time I'd finished setting up, any curious onlookers had lost interest and turned away.'[9] Barbecues are brought, inflatables are inflated, clothes are off for when the sun might break through and something is clearly happening on the water, although the expressions don't suggest any emergency. A warm upper Thames May, in the early twenty-first century.

In 2017 Roberts's *Merrie Albion* collection would emphasize the tensions in English landscape and society in the twenty-first century's second decade, and such images are returned to elsewhere in *About England*. *We English*, however, shows people getting along together, if not rubbing along together. From these images much English leisure (with the exception of some sporting crowds) involves cohabitation at

Simon Roberts, 'Keynes Country Park Beach, Shornecote, Gloucestershire, 11 May 2008', pigment print.

a careful distance, each person or group marking out their blessed plot, walking their allotted path, a collective only in passing. Of the hundreds of people pictured in *We English*, few touch one another. With the exception of the unruly scrum at the January Lincolnshire open-air folk game the Haxey Hood, even the crowd scenes are spaced. One couple walk hand-in-hand by Scarborough's ruined castle, and there is some parental affection displayed, but in photographic technique and content *We English* presents the opposite of, say, Robert Doisneau's famous Parisian photographic kiss, and people seem happy for it.

Summer Olympic Glory

We English as a national photographic collection helped Roberts take on national photographic roles, appointed as an official photographer for the 2010 general election and the 2012 Olympics. *Merrie Albion* includes the equestrian arena at Greenwich, with show-jumping fences designed from national landmarks including Stonehenge, and the Olympic opening ceremony, Roberts photographing the moment when pastoral England transformed to workshop of the world.[10]

The 2012 Olympics offered a moment of national projection, English iconography prominent within the United Kingdom broadcast to the world. The opening ceremony presented a national story, stadium and broadcast spectators seeing the national past enrolled into national prospects, for an optimistic, outward-looking future. The ceremony – 'Isles of Wonder', devised by Danny Boyle and Frank Cottrell-Boyce – was self-consciously progressive, temporally and politically. The opening broadcast film began at the source of the Thames, moving rapidly downriver and entering the stadium to find a rural English landscape, with 'Jerusalem' sung by a solo boy. Rustics played cricket; a maypole stood; a tree topped a green hill, with a hint of Glastonbury Tor. Kenneth Branagh as Isambard Kingdom Brunel surveyed the scene, recited Caliban's 'isle full of noises' speech from Shakespeare's *The Tempest* as Elgar's 'Nimrod' played, and the land was transformed. Roberts's photograph shows industrial chimneys emergent. The green peeled back, and the workshop of the world appeared. The industrial section of the ceremony was entitled 'Pandemonium', after documentary film-maker Humphrey Jennings's compilation *Pandaemonium 1660–1886: The Coming of the Machine As Seen by Contemporary Observers*.[11] Then it was hats off to remember war

Simon Roberts, 'London 2012 Opening Ceremony, Olympic Stadium, Stratford, 27 July 2012', pigment print.

dead, before all sorts walked on: Beatles, Jarrow marchers, Windrush migrants, Pearly Kings and Queens. A film clip of the Queen and James Bond preceded royal arrival in the stadium, the union flag was raised on the slope of the surviving green hill, Mike Oldfield played *Tubular Bells*, NHS personnel danced in celebration of the welfare state (leading some right-wing commentators to complain that the ceremony was politically left-wing) and more variety (children's literature, comedy, music, television) saw the ceremony to a close, the torch arriving to a mix of jollity and solemnity.

The ceremonial pandemonium included a mock-forging of the Olympic rings, rising above the arena. In its ring-making, its green hill, its spectacle, the ceremony might have reminded viewers of Tolkien, a vision of England itself gone global via Peter Jackson's 2001–3 film trilogy of *The Lord of the Rings*. Five rings to inspire them all, and a green shire where hobbits might feel at home. Tolkien's attempt at an English mythology via Middle Earth, with its dramatizations of rural virtue and industrial threat, wartime horror and the fragile joy of peace,

Model of set for 2012 Olympic opening ceremony.

J.R.R. Tolkien, 'The Hill: Hobbiton-across-the-Water', 1937.

anticipates the opening drama of 2012, although Tolkien would have stepped back from the ceremony's celebration of the modern. In *The Lord of the Rings* the rural Midland England-inspired Shire is usurped by evil for industry, though redeemed once evil is conquered. The Shire nonetheless resonated in the stadium, the Olympic green hill bearing a striking resemblance to Tolkien's own colour drawings of Hobbiton. A 1937 drawing of 'The Hill: Hobbiton-across-the-Water' could be a set design for London 2012.

English Icons

The 2012 Olympic ceremony bombarded the world with English and British iconography, projecting a distinctive, globally significant and globally engaged country, although save for the Windrush migrants there was barely a hint of the imperial past. Workshop of the world yes, colonial governor of most of it less worth a boast. Empire seemed either an achievement which couldn't be celebrated or a guilt which couldn't be faced.

The identification and deployment of English icons had marked earlier twenty-first-century national initiatives. In 2008 Bill Bryson edited *Icons of England*, issued in support of the Campaign to Protect Rural England, of which Bryson was president. The book was reissued in expanded paperback in 2010, displaying a cultural and ethnic variety as 95 contributors identified favoured things and places. The Prince of Wales provided a foreword: 'What greater icon could we have than our countryside, which I have always believed helps to define our identity as a nation?'[12] Bryson's book echoed the Labour government's 'Icons: A Portrait of England' project, commissioned via the Department of Culture, Media and Sport's 'Culture Online' in the early 2000s. The government 'Icons' anticipated the Olympic ceremony, enrolling the past into future prospects, but also reflected Labour anxieties about whether, having granted devolution to Scotland and Wales, the party could connect to English identity. The project proposed symbols for a multicultural, pluralist and open-minded country, proud of many pasts and open to the world. The dozen opening selections, announced in January 2006, were Stonehenge, Jerusalem, Holbein's portrait of Henry VIII, the King James Bible, SS *Empire Windrush*, Punch and Judy, *The Angel of the North*, the FA Cup, a cup of tea, *Alice in Wonderland*, the Spitfire and the Routemaster Bus.

The bus had indeed made a global appearance at the closing ceremony of the 2008 Olympics in Beijing, with a waving London mayor, Boris Johnson, ushering the world on to 2012. The national flag, despite its wider public appearance following the European Football Championships in England in 1996, did not make the first Icons list, though it was one of 21 items added to the list in 2006. Other additions included morris dancing, the miniskirt, Constable's *Hay Wain*, cricket, Brick Lane, Blackpool Tower and the Notting Hill Carnival. A subsequent public vote produced a top 100, alphabetically from Coronation Street to York Minster. Up and down the country, expressing many enthusiasms, England in most of its varieties.

'Icons: A Portrait of England' was put on hold after the 2010 general election returned a Conservative/Liberal Democrat coalition, although the Environment Agency continued an 'Icons of the Environment' scheme, with the hedgehog voted number one. A seemingly dormant 'Icons of England' website was maintained for a decade at www.icons.org.uk, a digital fossil of post-millennial culture, though by early 2022 this had become untraceable. Olympic 2012 indeed now appears the last hurrah of a millennial moment where governmental narratives projected a country officially open, tolerant and cosmopolitan.

Before the Conquest

'Icons of England' picked and mixed from the recent and distant past, with the effect an official controlled eclecticism. Diverse items marked stories of diversity, although temporal coverage was skewed to the modern. In the initial list, beyond Henry VIII as obligatory Tudor, there was nothing further back until Stonehenge. A thousands-of-years gap leaped over times often deemed formative in England, not least in stories presenting an Anglo-Saxon land overtaken by conquest. England pre-1066 has been long been claimed for English and British nationalism, not least in Victorian eulogies of Alfred the Great as foundational monarch, but recent decades have seen other senses of England alighting on the Anglo-Saxon as a site of complexity and diversity. Here is a foundational England made from regional identities, with a mix of migration and settlement.

By 1982 XTC were a semi-famous pop group, with some hits on a major label, a dedicated following and a persona bound to their unusual pop origins in the Wiltshire railway town of Swindon. Early 1982 brought their highest chart placing, reaching number ten with the single 'Senses Working Overtime', from the LP *English Settlement*. Those hooked by the single to buy the album would have reached the record shop and found pre-Conquest England on the sleeve. *English Settlement*'s cover showed the chalk-carved white horse of Uffington, on the downs near Swindon, an unlikely image to lure the purchaser.

The Uffington horse is now held to be prehistoric, but had long carried associations with Alfred and the Anglo-Saxon, not least via G. K. Chesterton's 1911 'The Ballad of the White Horse', where it watched over victory against the Danes and was re-scoured as the sign of an ancient enduring England: 'Before the gods that made the gods/ Had seen their sunrise pass,/ The White Horse of the White Horse Vale/ Was cut out of the grass.'[13] The Uffington white horse, not the most obvious pop sales hook, matched XTC's contrarian take on the record industry but also as a 'local badge' signalled a regional identity, and a lyrical and musical attention to England.[14] The 'settlement' evoked by the LP's songs was hardly comfortable, however; indeed it matches a strand discussed in this book whereby place is as much about anxiety as about security. Tracks on war and racist violence suggest a country hardly at ease. But there were also songs against redevelopment in Swindon ('Ball and Chain'), and evoking church bells softly chiming ('Senses Working Overtime'), all presided over by the old

Cover of XTC, *English Settlement*. The LP was released in 1982; this image shows the cover of the 2016 CD reissue. The original LP included the band name and record title above the Uffington white horse design.

horse. Later XTC LPs such as *Mummer* (1983), *Skylarking* (1986) and *Oranges and Lemons* (1989) would develop XTC's English pastoral. In 'Chalkhills and Children' (1989) singer and songwriter Andy Partridge found value in family, and in old tracks, children placed alongside a Wiltshire Roman road as things anchoring his feet, bringing him back to earth and to an eternal Ermin Street.[15] In the 1970s and '80s pop music could often be the portal to extra-musical cultures – existentialist literature, deconstructionist philosophy – but here pop led to pre-Conquest England, in country music of another kind. The Uffington white horse didn't make the top 100 'Icons of England' as voted by the public, but its appearance on a record sleeve indicates the seepage of older signs into modern life.

Pre-Conquest scholarship has also shaped stories of the settled or unsettled English. In August 2021 Ian Hislop's Radio 4 series *This Union: The Ghost Kingdoms of England* looked back to the period between 410 and 1066, with a programme each on East Anglia, Northumbria, Mercia and Wessex, asking how and whether their ghosts were still felt, and concluding they were strongest in Northumbria, weakest in Mercia.[16] Hislop examined how England emerged from this regional variety as 'a workable diverse but unified country', and one of his expert voices was the historian and broadcaster Michael Wood, who in the television age has done as much as anyone to broadcast popular historical stories of England. For his contribution to Bryson's *Icons of England* Wood chose Athelney in the Somerset Levels, the hideout of Alfred from the Danes, as 'one place that stands for the whole tale of this island nation ... the most resonant landscape in our nation's history'.[17]

Wood worked for the BBC from 1976, his *In Search of* ... series including *In Search of the Dark Ages*, whose accompanying 1981 book ends:

> It was the Anglo-Saxon achievement to build England; it was left to the Normans and their successors to make Great Britain. And now, when one considers the vicissitudes of the later history of Britain and Ireland, it is tempting to think that they have not yet succeeded so well.[18]

Wood has written and broadcast around the world, but has consistently returned to England as a meaningful scale for reflection, using the past to think through England's particularity. Wood's 1999 *In Search of England* took its title from H. V. Morton's 1927 travelogue, Wood concerned for 'the Matter of England' and emphasizing the creation of 'the English state' in the ninth and tenth centuries.[19] Wood's tone may differ from Morton's clichéd joviality, but he shares Morton's attention to history's resonance. If, however, Morton asserted the virtue of a gentle and unified English nationhood after war, Wood considers the reassertion of 'older regional identities' and the making of 'new myths' as 'Great Britain begins to recede'.[20] Wood begins his reflection on 'When was England England?' with comment on recent devolution, England's place in Britain in question, in what might be 'the last days of the British state'. The idea of England as an old stable state, pre-Conquest, grounded in administrative units of hundred, shire and borough, provides 'something real to go back to', as 'a workable conception of society, of order and of mutual obligations'. Great Britain is one thing, but 'The Anglo-Saxons created England': 'England . . . is the creation of the Old English.' Wood acknowledges millennial arguments that the future might be one of a 'global culture', where 'We will be living After England', but his fascination for England suggests at least ongoing resonance.[21] When Wood addresses his readership as 'us', the us is English.

In 2010 Wood produced *The Story of England*, a book and TV series on the village of Kibworth in Leicestershire, tracing 'the interaction of the local with the national narrative' and stating: 'this is about England, and there need be no apology for that.'[22] The Midland location, without any claim to historical exceptionalism, ordinary then and ordinary now, is deliberate: 'It is Middle England, geographically and historically.'[23] A 2009 archaeological participatory 'Kibworth Big Dig' and 'History Day' enrolled residents, opening a story from prehistory through Roman times. The English settlement from AD 500 was revealed by a fragment of early Anglo-Saxon bone comb 'under the car park of the Coach and Horses pub on the A6'.[24] On through the Anglo-Scandinavian Danelaw, the tenth-century emergence of an English kingdom and culture, the Conquest and 'Norman Yoke', and the ownership of much of the parish from the 1270s by Merton College, Oxford, whose archive offers the material for the Kibworth story. The Black Death burial field, where over half the residents were interred, 'is still unploughed today'.[25] Lollardry, city connections (to Leicester and Coventry), commercial farming, schooling, civil war, dissent, coaching inns and railways, canals and enclosures, framework knitting and imperial service, all shape Kibworth. Wood's local history renders the story of England.

Wood's method is to look, converse, read and excavate, finding novelties alongside 'deep-rooted ideas and habits': 'identity doesn't come from the top down at all, it is not genetic, it is not fixed, safe and secure, for it can be reshaped by history and culture; so it is always in the making and never made; but it is the creation of the people themselves.'[26] The geography of identity here is complex, localness not suggesting inwardness, as external forces shape place. Empire days are celebrated, heretical parsons removed and men called up by monarchs and governments to fight abroad. Middle England and the earth's ends enfold, in retrospect and in prospect.

Mercia upon Us

Midland England before the Conquest was poetically enfolded into the present in Geoffrey Hill's 1971 *Mercian Hymns*.[27] Thirty short prose poems invoke Offa, king of Mercia from 757 to 796. The sequence includes Offa's naming, crowning, childhood, laws, coins, sword, bestiary, kingdom, journey to Rome and death. English particularity and what counted as global for the eighth century link in linguistic make-up. For Seamus Heaney, Hill places 'the Latinate and the local ... hand in glove'.[28]

Time hops around this Mercia. Hill's 'Acknowledgments' state: 'The Offa who figures in this sequence might perhaps most usefully be regarded as the presiding genius of the West Midlands, his dominion enduring from the middle of the eighth century until the middle of the twentieth (and possibly beyond).'[29] Offa is thus 'overlord of the M5'; his coronation is celebrated in 'the car-park of "The Stag's Head"' and his Mercia is marked by 'desirable new estates' and 'Cohorts of charabancs'.[30] The 'suburban dwellings' of this 'Coiled entrenched England' are named after battles from the eighth to tenth centuries; Hill's notes state that his suburban house names of '"Ethandune", "Catraeth", "Maldon", "Pengwern"', derive from Edington (878), Catterick (late sixth century), Maldon (991) and Shrewsbury (779).[31] Contemporary popular Anglo-Saxondom also features in Hill's amused acknowledgement for Hymn IV: 'To the best of my recollection, the expression "to invest in mother-earth" was the felicitous (and correct) definition of "yird" given by Mr Michael Hordern in the programme *Call My Bluff* televised on BBC 2 on Thursday January 29th 1970.'³² Hill's precise dating of the wordplay panel game gives the note an ironic equivalence to weightier others, and inscribes a popular cultural archaeological record for the future reader. The cited scholarship on myth and coinage might have been followed up without too much trouble, but in the era before the digitization of the *Radio Times* archive such TV ephemera would have been hard to pin down.³³

In 1978, in 'An Apology for the Revival of Christian Architecture in England', Hill hymned a 'Platonic England'.³⁴ England as a resort of ideal, transhistorical form need not imply present inferiority. For Heaney, 'Offa's story makes contemporary landscape and experience live in the rich shadows of a tradition', and Hill's modern Mercia of entrenched, coiled settlement is less a place of diminished cliché than one of pointed domestic nomenclature.³⁵ When in the first hymn Offa is deemed both 'King of the perennial holly-groves' and 'overlord of the M5', 'contractor to the desirable new estates' and 'the friend of Charlemagne', he is, in the round, appreciative: '"I liked that," said Offa, "sing it again."'³⁶ And so the sequence proceeds. Other meeting points of *Mercian Hymns* and the Midlands of the 1970s are noted in Chapter Three below.

In Hill's 2002 collection *The Orchards of Syon* the penultimate poem circles 'Heathrow on hold', over Windsor's Legoland 'scaled-down perfect replicas', visible in descent, and Sussex: 'dormant, rippling with shadows of airflow'. Here is a return to 'our chequered country'. Hill's 'chequered' is characteristically multivalent: a visible patchwork of fields, a moral mixed bag of the glorious and the grim, and chequers, a crafty board game and grace-and-favour residence for political intrigue: 'This much is allowed/ us, forever tangling with England in her quiet ways of betrayal.' Hill approaches 'this autumnal land' in autumnal mood, and *The Orchards of Syon* is a seasonal sequence: 'hermeneutics of autumn, time's continuities tearing us apart.'³⁷ England, in descent, ever falling for its past.

Mildew on the Crop

Past and present sometimes find happy resonance but can also jar, and another trope of England in retrospect is the unease felt when ostensibly pleasant byways unnerve. Melissa Harrison's 2018 novel *All Among the Barley*, the UK winner of the European Union Prize for Literature, just before the UK left the building, closes this chapter and signposts the next, with its treatment of English pastoral's blemished crop.[38]

Harrison is known as a nature writer, her 2020 *Times* 'nature diary' collection, *The Stubborn Light of Things*, covering the period before and after her move from London to Suffolk in 2017. Harrison's Suffolk village with Norman church shows 'a lasting partnership of people, place and nature, and to me there is something deeply moving – almost sacred – about that'.[39] Harrison's nature diary for 16 November 2019 wanders the lanes at dusk: 'Political and social nostalgia may be dangerous, but ecologically it's unavoidable. At dusk – if only briefly – one can imagine that the world is still unharmed.'[40] England is a meaningful frame of reference for Harrison, her 2016 book *Rain* detailing 'four walks in English weather': 'rain is as essential to our sense of identity as it is to our soil.'[41] Harrison's nature diary features a motorway drive where 'watching England unfold' shows 'the past coexisting with the present; the England that existed for so long and exists no longer haunting the modern landscape, almost close enough to touch'.[42]

National nature, and connections between London and Suffolk, also shape *All Among the Barley*, but the effect here is to at once evoke and disturb English pastoral. The novel, set in the summer of 1934, is narrated by adolescent Edith Mather, a farm daughter whose Suffolk life is altered by the arrival from London of Constance FitzAllen, well off, intellectual, mannish in dress and writing articles about traditional ways. Constance mixes a progressive femininity (which attracts Edith) with far right views on farming as the neglected backbone of England, and writes for 'The English Pioneer'.[43] Late in the novel a speaker from the Order of English Yeomanry (which Edith's father has signed up to, and is modelled by Harrison on 1930s movements of similar name) comes to the village, and rows ensue. A complex familial plot gives *All Among the Barley* tension and poignancy, but Harrison makes this more than just an everyday story of country folk through the character and beliefs of Connie, a kind of feminist fascist whose attraction–repulsion for the intellectually curious Edith (who is reading Sylvia Townsend Warner's 1926 feminist witchcraft novel *Lolly Willowes*) drives the narrative.[44] Farm horseman John Hurlock, himself part of the familial plot, is the voice of scepticism as well as intuitive knowledge, critical of Connie's fascism and of her fanciful ideas of tradition. The reader sees events through Edith's narration,

'All Among the Barley: Dawn', poster by Lewis Heriz, produced to accompany Melissa Harrison, *All Among the Barley* (2018).

which turns out to be adult recollection from an asylum at the age of 70, the drama of adolescence having triggered breakdown and incarceration (soon to be concluded as the asylum is set to close). *All Among the Barley* sets up a dark side for English pastoral, the links between interwar agrarianism and organicism and the far right given popular literary form to jar any assumptions of cosy country Englishness.[45]

All Among the Barley echoes Henry Williamson's 1942 *The Story of a Norfolk Farm*, where the Mosleyite author of *Tarka the Otter* told of his own pre-war efforts to rescue farming at Stiffkey in Norfolk, with fascist campaigner 'Lady Sunne' signalling the way forward for rural England. Sunne leaves Williamson some pamphlets, and he joins her party: 'A nation that neglected its soil, neglected its soul; and its people would perish.'[46] *All Among the Barley* was launched with accompanying posters by Lewis Heriz, four prints in the style of 1930s travel posters, 'All Among the Barley: Dawn/ Noon/ Dusk/ Midnight', depicting the book's Suffolk landscape, and with quotes from FitzAllen's 'Sketches from English Rural Life' articles in 'The English Pioneer':

'Strength, Health, and Husbandry and Love of the Natural World'
'Work Performed in Nature Purifies the Spirit'
'Here Beats the Heart of Our Nation, Hale and Lusty'
'Only From Nature Can the Truth Arise'[47]

The poster quotations could almost be from Lady Sunne; indeed one quote – 'Only from Nature could the truth arise' – is given by Connie as derived from Williamson.[48] The phrases echo other organicist writers of the 1930s and '40s, such as the organicist founder of the Kinship in Husbandry, H. J. Massingham, also cited in *All Among the Barley*, or Jorian Jenks, Mosley's agricultural adviser and first editor of the Soil Association's journal *Mother Earth*.[49]

All Among the Barley carries an epigram from William Morris on the past living within us, being alive in 'the future which we are now helping to make'. Reading Harrison's novel, with its careful citation of interwar organicism and fascism, and perhaps with one of Heriz's pastiches on the wall, enlivens the past in distinctive fashion. Here is a story of settlement which may unsettle the sense of the past, make future-building a little more reflexive and, in retrospect and prospect, give any English 'us' pause.

3
English Pastoral

Metaphors and Challenges

This chapter explores the properties of English pastoral, its emotional landscape of comfort and anxiety, and the ways in which pastoral has served to demarcate boundaries of belonging. Pastoral pops up here across source material including music, documentary, literature, photography, poetry and political speech. English pastoral may evoke a gentle world lost in time or extant elsewhere in space, yet pastoral also carries unease, fear, guilt. As in the Classical pastoral trope of 'Et in Arcadia ego', that even in Arcadia death is present, idylls turn out to be troubled. The late twentieth century also saw the development of a critical language of pastoral which itself becomes part of the English cultural story, entangling stories of class and race in the greenery.

At times, though, English pastoral seems far from care; indeed the past six decades show examples where uncomplicated promotions of the idyllic life happily transmit cliché, and become popular for it. Thus in *The Darling Buds of May* (1991–3), a television adaptation of H. E. Bates's novel series of 1958–70 about the Larkin family, any social complexities in Bates's 1950s stories of rural Kent were smothered by an overcompensating jollity, the 'perfick' pastoral bucolics of lead character Pop Larkin. Played by David Jason, a national figure from his ten years portraying lovable rogue Derek Trotter in the London-set comedy *Only Fools and Horses* (1981–91), Pop was a full-cream version of Delboy transplanted down the A2.

The Darling Buds of May was a ratings hit for ITV, immensely popular, indicating the resilient popularity of English pastoral. By the 1990s, however, a series of analytical works had puzzled over pastoral's staying power, and the ways in which it offered metaphors, however escapist, for England. For some writers bucolic joys signalled not pleasant consolations but a cultural problem, and this chapter begins with one influential account from ten years before ITV's *Darling Buds*, Martin Wiener's 1981 *English Culture and the Decline of the Industrial Spirit, 1850–1980*. Wiener gathered English pastoral into an influential analysis of cultural history, and his work opens up key themes of this chapter, the kinds of England evoked by pastoral, the motivations for its scrutiny and the complexities entailed. *English Culture and the Decline of the Industrial Spirit* also shows how scrutiny of pastoral could itself becoming part of English political culture.

For Wiener a study of the preceding century showed English progress deflected. The Victorian period had seen an accommodation between bourgeois and landed capital, with an 'industrial spirit' constrained through 'the gentrification of the industrialist'.[1] Wiener identified 'the Janus face of modern English culture', with the rural and the pastoral facing backward and stability valued in a dominant version of Englishness which 'virtually excluded industrialism'.[2] For Wiener pastoral was a core component of a 'southern metaphor' of Englishness, the term taken from Australian commentator Donald Horne's analysis of Britain in his 1969 *God Is an Englishman*:

> In the *Northern Metaphor* Britain is pragmatic, empirical, calculating, Puritan, bourgeois, enterprising, adventurous, scientific, serious, and believes in struggle ... In the *Southern Metaphor* Britain is romantic, illogical, muddled, divinely lucky, Anglican, aristocratic, traditional, frivolous, and believes in order and tradition ... In both metaphors it was assumed that *Britain is best*, but in the contest as to what Britain was best *at* it was, on the whole, the Southern Metaphor that won.[3]

Like Horne, Wiener interchanges England and Britain in his presentation of Englishness as force for 'decline': 'One of the most striking features of modern British cultural history has been the resilience, the staying power of this view of the nation and of the good society. In this way, the English countryside became a social and cultural force.'[4]

Wiener's book title invoked the analysis of British 'decline' associated with historian Correlli Barnett and others, and scrutiny of pastoral thereby became a political task. *English Culture and the Decline of the Industrial Spirit* concludes:

At the end of the day, it may be that Margaret Thatcher will find her most fundamental challenge not in holding down the money supply or inhibiting government spending, or even in fighting the shop stewards, but in changing this frame of mind. English history in the eighties may turn less on traditional political struggles than on a cultural contest between two faces of the middle class.[5]

Keith Joseph, Secretary of State for Industry until September 1981 (and after that Education Secretary), gave a copy of Wiener's book to fellow members of Margaret Thatcher's cabinet. Whether *English Culture and the Decline of the Industrial Spirit* was read or not, the gesture shows scrutiny of pastoral becoming a political act, in this case from the right, although as discussed below the political left also challenged English pastoral. Thatcher's own actions would signal further complexities of national identity, conservatism and pastoral, with conventional variants of patriotism readily deployed, not least during and after the Falklands War (as discussed in Chapter Four below), alongside assertions of entrepreneurial spirit. Wiener's 'two faces of the middle class' were in evidence within government, historical tensions between the entrepreneurial and the landed playing out within 1980s Conservatism. Some figures, such as Michael Heseltine, sought to personify both traditions, and the play of varieties of conservatism will feature at a number of points in *About England*.

Wiener's presentation of pastoral as in effect a culturally conservative force downplayed other readings which found in pastoral something radical and utopian. Melissa Harrison's *All Among the Barley* would explore such visions on the historic political right, yet Harrison's allusions to William Morris also register a powerful left pastoral radicalism.[6] Wiener acknowledged pastoral's political varieties, but ultimately gathered them around a narrative of cultural conservatism focused on the 'historic and comfortably domesticated rusticality of the South'.[7] Others, however, have taken pastoral to different ends, sometimes via different types of country, southern and northern metaphors cut across by other cardinal orientations, and by things coastal and midland. English pastoral turns out, for all its supposed comforting gentility, to be a challenging mode.

From Gardens Where We Feel on Edge

Suffolk, near enough to London to be connected yet far enough away to seem separate, was Harrison's chosen location for *All Among the Barley*, with its exploration of English pastoral beauties and anxieties. Suffolk has long been a site for reflection on pastoral, with the most notable late twentieth-century example being Ronald Blythe's 1969 'Portrait of an English Village', *Akenfield*.[8] Blythe mixed oral history, social survey, local history and personal vision in presenting a renamed east Suffolk village and the testimony of renamed villagers, Akenfield grounded in the particular but standing for the general 'English village'.[9] Tradition and continuity are emphasized, but in *Akenfield* the agrarian meets the adventitious, Blythe finding different affinities to place of long-standing and new residents, indeed different senses of village 'happiness': 'two contrasting conceptions of this happiness, the new – i.e. the literate and informed – and the old – i.e. the mysterious and intuitive – are now existing side by side in Akenfield, and with scarcely any awareness of each other.'[10] Blythe, as a non-judgemental reader of place, conveys both through personal testimony, Akenfield a ground of contrasting convictions.

Blythe is reflective on the conventions through which lives are lived, including the ways in which assumptions concerning the Englishness of the English village shape the present:

> The new villager's attitudes are deeply coloured by the national village cult. In Akenfield, evidence of the good life, a tall old church on the hillside, a pub selling the local brew, a pretty stream, a football pitch, a handsome square vicarage with a cedar of Lebanon shading it, a school with jars of tadpoles in the window, three shops with doorbells, a Tudor mansion, half a dozen farms and a lot of quaint cottages, is there for all to recognize. Akenfield, on the face of it, is the kind of place in which an Englishman has always felt it his right and duty to live. It is patently the real country, untouched and genuine. A holy place, when you have spent half your life abroad in the services ... So powerful is this traditional view that many people are able to live in the centre of it for years and see nothing more.[11]

Blythe carefully itemizes elements of the village: buildings, institutions, spirituality, childhood, land, produce, and, with the services reference, an imaginative enfolding into global connections. Blythe deploys cliché not to traduce its sentiment but to explore how stories about England shape the country, and how Akenfield, 'on the face of it', rubs up against other senses of place. The complexity of *Akenfield* is indicated by the way in which it has been cited both as an example of English pastoral and as a critical reflection on pastoral convention. In 1974 Peter Hall adapted *Akenfield* for the cinema, drawing out further complexities, and *Akenfield* on screen is discussed further in Chapter Four. Here, though, Blythe's scrutiny of Suffolk is a point of departure for the media through which English pastoral has been invoked, and for critical accounts of the interweaving of pastoral, class and race.

We begin in rural Oxfordshire, in 1983, with birdsong, oar splash, owl hoot, gate creak and bells. Virginia Astley's 1983 LP *From Gardens Where We Feel Secure* mixed piano with sound effects recorded in 1982 around Moulsford, in the Oxfordshire Thames Valley, ambient instrumentals evoking the countryside of Astley's childhood. Astley made an unusual independent chart hit from what Michael Bracewell terms 'the shock of the old (an English speciality)'.[12] The LP was released on Rough Trade records, a seemingly unlikely home for English pastoral, the country on sale in the record shop. *From Gardens Where We Feel Secure* made number 41 in the *New Musical Express*'s 1983 albums of the year, lodged between Dolly Parton and the Marine Girls. The album was divided between 'Morning' and 'Afternoon' sides, track titles conveying the progress, or rather the settled languor, of a pastoral day: 'A Summer Long Since Passed', 'Hiding in the Ha-Ha', 'It's Too Hot to Sleep', and (named from an Auden poem) 'Out on the Lawn I Lie in Bed'. Recording dates and times on the sleeve take the listener to rural England: 'churchbells and children Sunday morning 2nd May Moulsford', 'swing gate 2.30 pm Sunday 25th April South Stoke', 'owl, clock, night noises, Sunday night, 16th May, Moulsford'. In *Akenfield*, itemizing the 'village cult', Blythe commented: 'Its very sounds are formal, hieratic; larks, clocks, bees, tractor hummings. Rarely the sound of the human voice.'[13]

From Gardens Where We Feel Secure shows the complex temporality of pastoral. The bells, the clock, the creaking gate are resonant markers, securely repetitive, the gate-creak comforting rather than eerie, the owls lulling rather than haunting. The album was released in 1983, but the childhood evoked is of the 1960s (Astley was born in 1959), in a mode very different from the '60s Britpopular nostalgia of ten years later. Astley translates the kind of country hippies might have searched for, a place beyond pop culture, into early 1980s independent sound. Astley continued to mine pastoral, in the 1990s writing a musical based on Thomas Hardy's *The Woodlanders*, acting as writer-in-residence at Hardy's home of Max Gate in Dorchester in 2017, and in 2018 publishing *The English River: A Journey down the Thames in Poems and Photographs*, concentrating on the upper river, drawing in part on work as a lock-keeper's assistant, and mixing gentle evocation with memory and grief, with Moulsford again 'my remembered landscape'.[14] Many of the *From Gardens* sounds are invoked, and at Kelmscott, the former home of William Morris, upstream from Oxford, and the end point of Morris's revolutionary utopia *News from Nowhere*, 'time is somehow thinner.'[15] Barring four London and estuary poems, *The English River* brings further news from Astley's somewhere.

From Gardens Where We Feel Secure indicates too pastoral's preoccupation with security. Might that creaking gate need oiling? Or perhaps the creak usefully alerts residents to any visitor, welcome or unwanted. We feel secure in this garden, but are we *really* secure? Pastoral defences might be fragile, and anxieties spring from gardens where we feel on edge.

Moving from the upper Thames into the Cotswolds, we find English village imagery deployed for other ends, and a harder edge to English pastoral. In 2010 the UK passport was redesigned, formerly plain interior papers replaced by landscape scenes of a 'Scenic United Kingdom'.[16] Pictures of complex grain were there in part to hamper forgers, but they also set out a country's landscape culture, showing reed beds, coasts, canals, mountains, village greens, landscape types based on identifiable spots around the four constituent parts of the United Kingdom. There was a fishing village, but not a city in sight, nor a factory, an office, a retail park, a motorway. The UK is not short of urban, industrial and commercial icons, which might be made equally unforgeable, but here was an official statement of, and revelling in, the mythic qualities of rural landscape, for all corners of the UK. Another passport redesign in 2015, on the theme of 'Creative United Kingdom', emphasized the urban and industrial, though Constable's Suffolk *Hay Wain* was there to represent art.[17] From 2010 to 2015, though, a row of Cotswold cottages, Arlington Row in Bibury, stood below the passport

UK passport illustration, 2010, featuring cottages at Bibury, Gloucestershire.

Her Britannic Majesty's Secretary of State Requests and requires in the Name of Her Majesty all those whom it may concern to allow the bearer to pass freely without let or hindrance, and to afford the bearer such assistance and protection as may be necessary.

statement that 'Her Britannic Majesty's Secretary of State Requests and requires' free movement of the bearer.

Here was the latest hard edge to English pastoral, green pleasantries shadowed by twenty-first-century state efforts to deny movement to others, with immigration a newly brutal focal point for national argument. The free movement of labour in an expanded European Union, and Islamist conflict within and beyond the UK, had made 'border control' an acute political issue. While an image of Cotswold pastoral backed free movement for the UK citizen, the UK worried over the free movement of others, those who might aspire to a green and pleasant passport, a document for a better life.

In January 2017 Bibury displayed other anxieties, when English pastoral ideals provoked a parking dispute. Retired dentist Peter Maddox of Arlington Row had regularly parked his yellow Vauxhall Corsa outside his cottage, but the vehicle's brightness annoyed visitors, prompting social media anger, conspicuous colour spoiling photographs of a classic cottage row. A classic country row ensued, escalating when 'move' was scratched on to the yellow car bonnet. Triviality gets serious. Owners of yellow cars drove through Bibury in sympathy, but Maddox decided in the end to replace the scratched car with a grey model.[18] The offence given by the yellow Bibury car indicates some of the qualities of English pastoral. Arlington Row is a group of seventeenth-century weavers' cottages owned by the National Trust, one of which is a holiday cottage but the rest tenanted. Conservation value is here part of a valuing of environment which, in the Cotswolds, becomes also a story of property, conservation regulations linked to a defence of amenity which also in effect protects property values. A bright car interrupts the mutual appreciation of residential and touristic value. Since the late nineteenth-century discovery of arts and crafts traditions in the region by William Morris and others, Cotswold architecture has been seen as organically connected to the land in its local stonework, harmonious in what interwar regionalist H. J. Massingham termed a 'garden of stone'.[19] Where bus services are infrequent, and car ownership essential for those who can afford it, yellow cars become, visually, the wrong machines in the garden, class and pastoral meeting in an acute version of a story found across rural England. Beauty and conservation, property and planning, shape a Cotswold life on edge.

A Different Class of Pastoral

Blythe's 'village cult', Bibury 2017, the 2010 passport, Astley and garden security offer recent iterations of long-standing pastoral joys and anxieties, policing and critique. *Akenfield* indeed emerged in a moment of landscape and environmental questioning which produced influential analyses of English country and class, pastoral and politics.[20] Since the 1960s critical accounts of connections between pastoral and property, and questions of physical and cultural access to the country, have shaped English landscape understandings. The terms of critique were set out in the late 1960s and early 1970s, and continue to frame debate about England.

In 1967 John Berger and Jean Mohr produced their documentary work *A Fortunate Man: The Story of a Country Doctor*, based on the life of the GP John Sassall, in an unspecified area of rural England, though the photographs suggest it is relatively upland, and the area is termed

English Pastoral

'the Forest', Sassall working in the Forest of Dean.[21] Over two opening photographs, of a daytime river with fishermen and a gloomy scene with buildings' brightness illuminated, Berger writes:

> Landscapes can be deceptive.
> Sometimes a landscape seems to be less a setting for the life of its inhabitants than a curtain behind which their struggles, achievements and accidents take place.
> For those who, with the inhabitants, are behind the curtain, landmarks are no longer only geographic but also biographical and personal.[22]

Berger's words and Mohr's photographs move behind the curtain, and follow the doctor. Authorial and medical eyes practise analytical observation, whether on the patient's body or the wider world. Berger would echo the role, minus the medicine, when he moved to the French Alps, producing accounts of peasant life such as *Pig Earth* (1979).[23]

A Fortunate Man, like Berger's Alpine work, moved between labour and the aesthetics of sensory experience. One of Mohr's pictures shows a car on a country lane, woods around, and Berger's facing text states:

> English autumn mornings are often like mornings nowhere else in the world.
> The air is cold.
> The floorboards are cold.
> It is perhaps this coldness which sharpens the tang of the hot cup of tea ... Outside, there is sunlight which is simultaneously soft and very precise. Every leaf of each tree seems separate.[24]

A version of pastoral inhabits *A Fortunate Man*, alongside the work of Sassall, helping to frame life with all its ailments.

In 1973 Raymond Williams's *The Country and the City* paralleled Berger's critical language through a historical survey of literary renditions of urban and rural. Williams presented literary conventions as articulating values of property and overwriting a real history of labour, such that, in a phrase commonly cited in academic commentary, 'A working country is hardly ever a landscape. The very idea of landscape implies separation and observation.'[25] Williams made this comment in discussing the eighteenth-century elite definition of 'pleasing prospects', and the related separation of the aesthetic and practical, of consumption and production, separations able to be made from a position of social dominance. Williams's was not a transhistorical point – indeed he states that 'we can be certain that many more men than writers have looked with intense interest at all the features and movements of the natural world' – but for some this became a shorthand principle used to critique landscape per se.[26] Thus in 1983 the photographic journal *Ten:8*'s special issue on 'Rural Myths' presented pastoral convention, 'deep within the national consciousness', as essentially an outside, bourgeois view, deliberately or blithely concealing various realities.[27] Pastoral obscured the labour producing the landscape, its ownership structures, the proprietorial barriers to access and 'the land as a place to live and work'.[28] The imbrication of labour and sensory pleasure in Berger's work is bypassed, as pastoral, and its accomplice the picturesque, becomes an essentially reactionary mode, presenting a 'Fantasy Island' disengaged from modernity.[29] Criticizing a photographic turn to spiritual themes in the 1970s, Paul Lewis commented: 'What about the vast areas so tenaciously owned and exhaustively farmed which cover the British Isles? Who provided the visual equivalent to Blythe's *Akenfield*?'[30]

Blythe is here placed on the side of documentary against fantasy. *Akenfield*, however, like the work of Berger and Williams, carries a complexity belying easy distinctions. Stephen Daniels argues that the analytical and fictional writings of Williams and Berger demonstrate landscape's 'duplicity', its capacity to move across different modes of affinity and belonging, whether the proprietorial, the unpropertied dweller, the visitor enjoying the view or the worker in the fields, who might also take pleasure in surroundings. Earth and scenery, financial and emotional value, depth and surface, lend landscape analytical potential, 'not despites its difficulty as a comprehensive or reliable concept, but because of it': 'we should beware of attempts to define landscape, to resolve its contradictions, rather we should abide in its duplicity.'[31]

The 1970s as a moment of pastoral reflection registers too in the work of John Barrell. In 1974 Barrell and John Bull edited *The Penguin Book of English Pastoral Verse*, emphasizing pastoral as a mode of power rather than a genteel retreat from the world: 'At the outset, the Pastoral is a mythical view of the relationship of men in society, at the service of those who control the political, economic, and cultural strings of society.'³² Pastoral, with its 'tension between the mythical and the naturalistic', contains contrasting impulses, allowing for 'a direct opposition to social change, a reactionary clinging to a static present, and an often desperate belief in future improvement', with a frequent trope of 'attacking contemporary abuses obliquely, by reference to an idealized version of what life in the country was like'.³³ Barrell and Bull effectively, in Daniels's terms, abide in pastoral's duplicity. Alluding to William Empson's classic 1935 study *Some Versions of Pastoral*, a section of their anthology gathers 'Some Versions of Anti-Pastoral', including John Clare, Oliver Goldsmith and George Crabbe. Barrell and Bull take issue with Williams's idea that, while the Suffolk poet Crabbe confronted 'real history', Clare and Goldsmith were deceived by pastoral. For Barrell and Bull, 'the conventional nostalgia of the Pastoral became the entirely appropriate expression of agricultural discontent.'³⁴ Considering a possible pastoral revival in the 1970s, though, Barrell and Bull found it inadequate for the modern world.³⁵ The late twentieth and early twenty-first centuries, however, would see a renewed fascination with pastoral, for its associations of nature and/or farming. Thus James Rebanks could entitle his popular 2020 account of Lakeland sheep farming *English Pastoral*, the phrase evoking literary convention, yet at the same time asserting the realities of pastoral (that is, non-arable) farming.³⁶

Barrell's anthology editorship followed his 1972 study of John Clare (1793–1864), *The Idea of Landscape and the Sense of Place, 1730–1840: An Approach to the Poetry of John Clare*.³⁷ Clare would become the poetic touchstone for those seeking English landscape beyond the elite prospect, for attention to nature, anger at enclosures of common land and a biographical connection of political economy and personal trauma. In 'The Village Minstrel' (1821) Clare had presented enclosure traducing England:

O England! boasted land of liberty,
With strangers still thou mayst thy title own,
But thy poor slaves the alteration see,
With many a loss to them the truth is known.³⁸

For Williams, Clare was 'a deeply significant figure, for in him there is not only the literary change but directly, in his person and his history, the inwardness of the social transformation'.³⁹ Barrell explored the intricate geographies of Clare's work, his 'desire to write locally', in both vocabulary and syntax, with place as 'a manifold of images, not of visual images only, and not only of topography but of the people and living things that work and live in the place'.[40] The enclosed landscape of agricultural improvement, transforming Clare's Northamptonshire home parish of Helpston from 1809 to 1820, prompts a counter-language of descriptive appreciation: 'This sort of concentration, this sense of place, was inevitably opposed to enclosure, which sought to de-localise, to take away the individuality of a place.'[41] A way of organizing landscape derived from one mode of social organization, taken for granted by those growing within it, is erased, the new landscape symbolic of and sustaining capitalist farming. Barrell, who devotes a detailed appendix to the effects of enclosure in Helpston, does not enlist Clare in a retrospective anti-enclosure campaign. Barrell also notes the nuances of 'place', in 1972 'a modish term in literary criticism', distinguishing Clare as having:

> nothing in common with the 'sense of place' of any number of writers from Wordsworth to, say Charles Olson, who attend to one place, and then perhaps another, with care and in detail, but who are, wherever they are, at the end of the turnpike or the freeway to somewhere else, and can choose to be in this place, or that one.[42]

Clare, with a seemingly true-to-life pastoral-from-below, has been a reference point for aesthetic projects radical and conservative, whether Iain Sinclair's 2005 psychogeographic tracing in *Edge of the Orison* of Clare's 1841 walk from an Epping Forest asylum to his Northamptonshire parish of Helpston or John Betjeman's 1964 comparison of Clare to the 'tenderly observant' Philip Larkin in his review of the latter's *The Whitsun Weddings*: 'He is the John Clare of the building estates, and as true to them as was Clare to the fields and trees of Northamptonshire.'[43] Simon Kovesi, for whom Barrell's book was a 'watershed moment' in Clare commentary, suggests that in later work 'the historicised and aesthetic sensibility of Barrell to place is lost, in the rush to deploy Clare's place to certain contemporary ends', whether the 'eco-pompous' or the casting of enclosure as a plain eco-social evil.[44] Kovesi also highlights Clare's enlistment for heritage and environmental ends, noting that 'Clare as green protest poet and ecocriticism itself were formations born at the same time', and with the 2007 lottery-funded development of Clare's cottage in Helpston as a museum signalling Clare's status in folk, rural and literary histories.[45] From cottage museum to psychogeography to ecocriticism, Clare's work becomes 'more present than ever in contemporary literary culture'.[46]

The scrutiny of pastoral and enclosure shaped a notable twenty-first-century cinematic treatment of England, Patrick Keiller's 2010 film *Robinson in Ruins*, the last of Keiller's Robinson trilogy after *London* (1994) and *Robinson in Space* (1997). In all three a narrator tells of Robinson, a rather different man from John Drinkwater's *Robinson of England*. *London* and *Robinson in Space*, narrated by Paul Scofield, are voiced from the perspective of an acquaintance and ex-lover, while in *Robinson in Ruins* narrator Vanessa Redgrave speaks of the former narrator as her 'ex-beloved'. Keiller's Robinson investigates English landscape, in *London* 'the problem of London' via cultural history and present politics, and in *Robinson in Space* 'a peripatetic study of the *problem* of England', of 'a particularly *English* kind of capitalism', via a regional tour of cities and country, ports and industry.[47] Throughout the trilogy narration proceeds over static camera shots, English landscape the films' only actor. Theory and droll anecdote mix, to the benefit of both.

Robinson in Ruins was filmed as the 2008 economic crisis proceeded, produced as part of a project with Patrick Wright and Doreen Massey under the Arts and Humanities Research Council's 'Landscape and Environment' programme. The film also informed a 2012 Tate Britain installation and book on *The Possibility of Life's Survival on the Planet*. The British Film Institute issue of the film includes essays by Keiller, Massey and Mark Fisher, the latter's entitled 'English Pastoral'.[48] *Robinson in Ruins* is structured around south-central England excursions from Oxford, into Oxfordshire and Berkshire, examining contemporary infrastructures of power (of political authority, of energy distribution), utopian possibilities (Robinson proposes an 'experimental settlement') and the history of agrarian capitalism.[49] Speenhamland, near Newbury, the original site of a system of poor relief enabling labour mobility, and the landscapes of agricultural enclosure (and accompanying protests, at Otmoor in 1830 and in the 'Oxfordshire Rising' of 1596, in the name of customary rights), focus Robinson's enquiry. Keiller's narrator ponders 'the transformative potential we attributed to images of landscape'.[50] Keiller elsewhere writes of his own aim as 'to promote political and economic change by developing the transformative potential of images of landscape'.[51] There are quirky sites here, akin to the attraction to the eccentric found in John Piper's *Oxfordshire* Shell Guide of 1938, but what seems eccentric is pursued such that political and historical logic emerges. The sensibility of *Robinson in Ruins* matches that of a Shell Guide as if co-authored by Piper and E. P. Thompson, in collision if not collaboration. Keiller also makes agricultural enclosure resonate with the prominence of 'enclosure' in early twenty-first-century critiques of neo-liberalism, manifest from 2011 in the Occupy movement. Rural England then and now is shaped by forces beyond itself, for the benefit of the powerful, within and beyond the country.

The meditative style of Keiller's film, allowing viewers to scrutinize a close-up of lichen on a road sign, a waving foxglove or a harvest scene, allows for critical reflection and reverie. The lichen, which appeared on the cover of Keiller's Tate exhibition book, was found above the 'u' in 'Newbury' on a road sign at the Kennington roundabout near Oxford. Keiller focuses, and finds a head shape, which Robinson imagines as that of Goethe, or a Speenhamland magistrate. If nature imitates a human, the human sign also echoes natural structure, the paintwork around the lichen showing in close-up a honeycomb pattern, green on black and, for the lettering, white on grey. The narrator states that Robinson inclines to 'biophilia', and an

Patrick Keiller, 'Detail of lichen on road sign near Oxford', photograph.

anti-neo-Darwinian emphasis on symbiosis over competition, with lichen a sign of 'mutualism'. Elsewhere in the film a breezy foxglove bobs in and out of a static shot for over two minutes, ducking and weaving like Mr Punch, or a boxer.

Cowslips, roses, orchids, teasel, lords and ladies (the plant not the people), are given similar portrait-long scrutiny. Long set images, whether of nature detail or wider landscape, offer something to question, yet are also allowed their own aesthetic power. As combines and tractors proceed for a minute or more across the screen to gather the harvest, and the narrator's commentary covers wheat commodity prices and the advance selling of crops, the viewer might well reflect on enclosure yet also appreciate a spectacle, the process of farming offering a compelling scene, much like foxgloves or lichen. Viewers might even get a touch of agrophilia among the biophilia. Farming and ecology are intertwined, here as in other variants of English pastoral, and while the common assumption in recent decades is that one has eroded the other, the cinematic technique of *Robinson in Ruins* presents both for equivalent view.[52] The overriding narrative theme of economic and financial crisis steers the reader, however, to distaste for competitive commerce, lichen's mutualism at odds with the modern rural.

Babbling Brooks and Rivers of Blood

From Bibury's yellow car across the Cotswolds to Keiller's Oxfordshire, via Berger and Williams, Barrell and Clare, class and pastoral entwine. From the late 1960s critical analysis itself becomes part of the cultural story, English pastoral begging questions as much as offering reassurance. And over the same period connections of pastoral and class run alongside entanglements of pastoral and race, the interwar links invoked in Harrison's *All Among the Barley* carried through to the present.

The magazine *This England*, with its motto 'for all who love our green and pleasant land', was first issued in spring 1968 by Roy Faiers. From his north Lincolnshire base Faiers was owner and editor of the magazine until 2009, when D. C. Thomson publishers (best known for the *Beano*) took over, moving production to Cheltenham with editor Stephen Garnett, and then in 2018 shifting to the company's Dundee base, Garnett and colleagues leaving.[53] Faiers died in 2017, but until 2018 *This England* retained his distinctive mix of gentle country pastoral, English history, military heroes, Christian heritage and editorial polemic on modern English ways. Thus the winter 2018 issue, with readers' tribute letters to Faiers, showed support for a proposed festival to celebrate post-Brexit Britain, awarded the magazine's 'Silver Cross of St George' to UKIP MEP Roger Helmer, and in the short opinion pieces of 'Nelson's Column' expressed scepticism over Islamic values, transgender rights and smart meters.

Gentle nostalgia and harder politics characterized *This England* from its foundation in the late 1960s. There was variety, as when, in the summer of 1973, readers would have opened the cover (showing a flock of sheep passing thatched cottages) to find an editorial against planners, profiteers and politicians, recommending support for Friends of the Earth as well as the Council for the Protection of Rural England, and prefaced with a quote from William Blake: 'England! awake! awake! awake!'[54] Further on in the issue Wyn Daniels presented (a year after Barrell's book) an approving profile of 'John Clare: Poet and Peasant', though enclosure was not mentioned, and the 'peasant poet' tag here suggested contentment.[55] Politically *This England* tended to the right, and sometimes the far right. In 1993 Patrick Wright highlighted the magazine as a meeting point of pastoral and race, noting Faiers's long-standing concern over immigration, and recent regular 'Forever England' columns by Stuart Millson against the EU and multiculturalism. Millson had also contributed to British National Party publications, and was photographed in 1991 presenting French far-right leader Jean-Marie Le Pen with a copy of *This England*.[56] Millson's autumn 1993 column, after enlisting Tony Hancock and Arthur Lowe into a eulogy of English humour, attacked the Channel Tunnel and the creep of 'political correctness' into youth movements: 'If the Scouts and Guides reflect "white Christian" values it is surely because England is just that – basically white and Christian!' The supposed 'culture wars' of three decades on are prefigured: 'The dogmatists try to make us feel guilty about our colonial past; they try to portray national pride as hatred and dislike of others; and they try to make cultural differences between people seem like cultural friction.'[57] For Wright such connections showed the need for 'an increase in the English sense of national identity', for a countervailing 'open and contemporary patriotism': 'So there is England's best-selling heritage quarterly – a thatched cottage, a green field, and an open sewer spewing up just where the picture ends.'[58]

This England was founded in 1968, a notable year for connections of race, patriotism and pastoral in England. In Geoffrey Hill's 1971 *Mercian Hymns*, Hymn XVIII, the second of the hymns entitled 'Offa's Journey to Rome', ends: 'He set in motion the furtherance of his journey. To watch the Tiber foaming out much blood.'[59] Hill's poem 'Acknowledgments' states it is 'adapted from Vergil', but the British, indeed Mercian, reader in 1971 would probably hear another echo, of Enoch Powell's 'Rivers of Blood' speech, made on 20 April 1968 in the Midland Hotel in Birmingham, which famously deployed the same quotation. William Wootten reads Hill against a background of Powell, the MP for Wolverhampton South-West, who styled himself as a voice for the region. In *Mercian Hymns*, pre-Conquest England and post-war England converse in anxiety, oratory, prophecy and warning. 'I am the King of Mercia, and I know,' writes Hill in the eighth hymn, 'Offa's Leechdom'.[60] Borders and peoples, constitutions and institutions, configure Hill's version of Offa's Mercia, and were Powell's political preoccupations. Offa, Wootten notes, is remembered for the 'eponymous dyke which separated the Welsh and English and consolidated the borders of the Anglo-Saxon people'.[61] Classical and demotic, Latinate and vernacular met in Hill, and in Powell. And pastoral too shaped Powell's England, a sense of urban crisis cast against a vision of nation that was at heart pastoral. Powell's 1968 speech gave voice to a fearful Englishness which, jolted by his language, in turn became something feared, Powell proving the capacity for rhetoric to move some to violence. For its political influence, and its particular combination of considered analysis and gut polemic, Powell's England warrants scrutiny.[62]

In his January 1979 essay 'The Great Moving Right Show', identifying political shifts which would produce the first Thatcher government, Stuart Hall noted 'the magical connections and short-circuits which Powellism was able to establish between the themes of race and immigration control and the images of the nation, the British people and the destruction of "our culture, our way of life"'. Hall argued that 'this populism is operating on genuine contradictions, and it has a rational and material core. Its success and effectivity does not lie in its capacity to dupe unsuspecting folk but in the way it addresses real problems, real and lived experiences, real contradictions.'[63] Hall elsewhere noted the arrival of the *Empire Windrush* in 1948 as a 'hinge between the large numbers of black men and women already represented in many walks of British social life before the war ... and the later arrival (in significantly enlarged numbers) of black people as an identifiable group, to live, work and settle on a permanent basis'.[64] Post-war migration produced a non-white ethnic minority population of around half a million by 1962, a million by 1968, different in scale, industrial labour and settlement geography from the earlier Black population, with concentration in specific urban areas. For Powell, new settlement unsettled England, as he spoke in April 1968 to Conservative activists of 'areas undergoing the total transformation to which there is no parallel in a thousand years of English history', where the 'existing population ... found themselves made strangers in their own country'.[65] In February 1967 Powell had drawn a parallel between immigration and destructive urban renewal, where 'entire areas were transformed by the substitution of a wholly or predominantly coloured population for the previous native inhabitants, as completely as other areas were transformed by the bulldozer.'[66] There goes the neighbourhood. The best Powell could hope for was, by the end of the century, the presence of 'fixed and almost traditional "foreign" areas in certain towns and cities, which will remain as the lasting monument of a moment of national aberration'.[67]

Powell emphasized the need for immigration control after the Conservatives lost office in 1964, expressing a distinctive variant of Conservatism, on the one hand facing up to a post-imperial world, on the other reasserting and defending English identity. The England Powell defended had a pastoral core, babbling brooks feeding rivers of blood. Powell's own poetry, collected in *Dancer's End and The Wedding Gift*, took its cue from A. E. Housman, whom Powell had long admired for his *A Shropshire Lad*, as well as for his classical scholarship.[68] Poem XXVI of *Dancer's End*, written in wartime, travels through Northamptonshire, where Powell was stationed at Guilsborough barracks in 1940–41. 'From Guilsboro' to Northampton', under 'a full red August moon', Powell senses 'living presences', the 'ghosts/ Of the old English' rising, who, 'hovering in the fields they once tilled,/ Brooded on England's destiny'.[69] On 22 April 1961, addressing the Royal Society of St George, Powell brooded further on the old English, suggesting an identity submerged through the imperial period but now re-emergent: 'we today at the heart of a vanished empire, amid the fragments of demolished glory, seem to find, like one of her old oak trees, standing and growing, the sap still rising from her ancient roots to meet the spring, England herself.'[70] Powell had by 1961 turned from his earlier fervent belief in empire, and now found that, unlike other empires, for England 'the nationhood of the mother country remained unaltered through it all', indeed somehow 'underwent no organic change as the mistress of a world empire'. For Powell, 'our generation is like one which comes home again after years of distant wandering', with 'the curiosity of finding ourselves once more akin with the old English', who in stone and effigy might 'whisper to us the secret of this charmed life of England'.[71]

Powell's England is therefore a postcolonial place not only in the presence of new migrants but in the re-emergence of older identities. Powell was known in politics for his analytical argument, marshalling factual evidence, but could shift into magic, mythic mode, in keeping with his tenet, expressed in a speech at Trinity College Dublin on 13 November 1964, that 'The life of nations, no less that of men, is lived largely in the imagination.'[72] The somehow intact survival of an older England, popping out the other side of empire, had a clear political message, Powell arguing in a 1957 position paper on challenges for the Conservative Party that 'the Tory Party must be cured of the British Empire', with a patriotism grounded in 'this England' acting as 'a salve to the wound of Suez'.[73] In Dublin in 1964 Powell criticized the myths informing diagnoses of British decline, both of which he traced to the late nineteenth century, namely that Britain possessed a glorious global empire and that Britain was the workshop of the world. For Powell these were myths serving turn-of-the-century political ends, and if 'a nation lives by its myths', Britain was living in error: 'If Britain could free herself from the long servitude of her seventy-year-old dreams, how much that now seems impossible might be within her power. But that is another story, which has not yet begun.'[74] Powell would add in 1969: 'Two myths beyond all others – Britain as an imperial power, and Britain as the workshop of the world – have stood between the British and the necessary recognition of realities. Such myths have to be fought and defeated on their own ground.'[75]

Babbling brooks, and rivers of blood, were imaginative weapons for the fight, and Powell couched the predicament of England in terms not only of imperial history but of the transatlantic present. The Birmingham speech was made in the context of a Labour government Race Relations Bill extending anti-discrimination law, and was delivered two weeks after the assassination of Martin Luther King Jr. To the Eastbourne Rotary Club on 16 November 1968 Powell foresaw that

'With the lapse of a generation or so we shall at last have succeeded – to the benefit of nobody – in reproducing "in England's green and pleasant land" the haunting tragedy of the United States.'[76] Powell's Offa-like 'judgment' was 'the people of England will not endure it.'[77] In searching for new stories of Britain, and specifically England, after empire, Powell can be termed, as Camilla Schofield suggests, a postcolonial nationalist.[78] The 'Rivers of Blood' speech of April 1968 appears as a statement of a particular variant of English postcolonialism, and part of a wider postcolonial pastoral, albeit with sentiments rarely associated with that term. 'Rivers of Blood' became shorthand for the speech, although the phrase itself was not used, Powell foreseeing the 'horror on the other side of the Atlantic' coming to England, and quoting Virgil's *Aeneid*: 'As I look ahead, I am filled with foreboding. Like the Roman, I seem to see "the river Tiber foaming with much blood".'[79] The term 'rivers of blood' carries a twisted pastoral, the arteries of a nation stained. In 1961, speaking to the Royal Society of St George, Powell had imagined that the old English 'would tell us, surely, of the rivers, the hills, and of the island coasts of England', rivers then unsullied.[80]

Powell presented himself as a tribune to the English, his Birmingham speech quoting letters received, granting the unheard voices of private correspondence a public anonymized hearing. After the speech Powell's postbag swelled, with estimates of between 43,000 and 100,000 letters received in the following fortnight, the vast majority supportive. In London, East End dockers and Smithfield meat porters marched in protest at Edward Heath's dismissal of Powell from the Shadow Cabinet. Bill Schwarz judges that the 'huge majority' of Powell's letters were from women, many concerned for housing and home, the rights to the former and the vulnerabilities of the latter: 'The letters created a new affective nation, for whom Powell was spokesman and for which the neighbourhood worked as principal axis. In so doing they devised a peculiarly homely racism.'[81] A domestic pastoral of settled homes under threat involved a gendered story of domesticated Englishness threatened by migrant masculinity, with a hard-working class no longer benefiting from the welfare state after wartime sacrifice.

For Schwarz, Powell shows how 'At the very moment of decolonization, a language of racial whiteness assumed a new prominence *at home*.'[82] In contrast to another 1960s trait whereby 'symbols of the imperial past increasingly appeared a matter for satire or comedy', here a 'reracialisation of the old metropole produced a politics of great emotional charge'.[83] And if Powell had turned from Britain's imperial role, its former dominions offered him a potent reference point. Schwarz notes that Powell's anecdote on a constituent, 'a decent, ordinary fellow-Englishman', who tells him that 'In this country in fifteen or twenty years' time the black man will have the whip-hand over the white man,' is proceeded by the man's wish to see all his children 'settled overseas'.[84] The 'overseas' allusion is to the old imperial white dominions of Australia, New Zealand and Canada, white Britishness sustained across the globe if not at home. The story of post-war immigration here runs alongside a less-remembered story of post-war emigration, with moves from the UK to Australia peaking at 80,000 in 1969. The emotional charge of these other migrant stories registers in my own family history, as at the end of the 1960s my mother's best childhood friend, her bridesmaid in 1955, moved from Norwich to Melbourne in Australia. They kept in touch every Christmas, with occasional crackly phone calls, but never saw one another again.

One of the lasting effects of Powell's English variant of 1968 has been to close down elaborations of the relationship between English identity and white identity, such that making any connection can spark violent assertion or rejection. But, in the aftermath of Schwarz's 'reracialisation' of identity, for many people whiteness might have become a significant lived dimension of Englishness, without any assertion of pride in some 'white identity', or claim to Englishness as somehow inherently white, with whiteness the English be-all or end-all. Powell's England was clearly, however, a white England, and many would keep their distance. At Eastbourne in November 1968 Powell stated: 'The West Indian or Asian does not, by being born in England, become an Englishman. In law he becomes a United Kingdom citizen by birth; in fact he is a West Indian or an Asian still.'[85] The effect is to align whiteness with closure and clarity, grey areas not permitted. For Powell it is the non-white, rather than, say, the white Australian settler in England, who sets things off.

The dazzle of Powell's brilliant whiteness did not, however, prevent critical scrutiny. In 1973 Ann Dummett, in *A Portrait of English Racism*, noted how 'Enoch Powell, ... by referring to England's green and pleasant land as under threat, can rouse feelings instantly.'[86] Dummett, who had worked on behalf of minorities as Community Relations Officer in Oxford from 1964 to 1968, and would later head the Runnymede Trust, reflected on 'Englishness and Whiteness'. Starting from the point that 'What is it to be English?' will mean 'quite different things to different groups of people in England', including by class and region, Dummett noted that 'The notion of what it is to be English, and of what it is to be a white man are distinct notions, although in many ways closely intertwined.'[87] Dummett's book was prescient in its analysis of 'institutional racism', a 'process that ensures racial inequality without wilful, conscious effort': 'Institutional racism works quietly: its effects may shout loud to black people but they are obscure whispers in the ear of the white population.'[88] For Dummett, 'English people are used to thinking of racism as a Bad Thing, but they are convinced that it is always happening somewhere else,' yet England carried racism in its past and present: 'None of us can speak or act towards other people of a different colour as though there were no America, no South Africa, no Wolverhampton, no history of slavery. All these things are present in every encounter, whether we want them to be there or not.'[89] Dummett noted that the 'real truth' about empire was unpalatable because it conflicted with ideas of British decency, making it 'almost impossible for English people to accept or understand the truth about their country's past'. People knew that England abolished the slave trade, but not that it first grew rich from it: 'To accept and understand the ugliness of the truth ... would, for many, tear apart their sense of personal and national identity.'[90] Dummett wondered if 'our whiteness may be our winding-sheet if we continue policies so sure to lead to hatred, bitterness and retaliation'.[91] Her book ended, however, with a hint of hope, looking to 'a racially mixed, racially equal society, where Englishness connotes not your looks but your sense of decency, humour and independence, into the new kind of world that is surely coming, in which white supremacy will be as dead as Babylon'.[92]

Open Country?

In 1973 Ann Dummett suggested that 'once England has become a recognizably racist country, which it now is', to tell Black people 'that they do not belong here' meant saying 'they cannot be expected to identify themselves with England in any way or consider themselves English.'[93] In 1999 Stuart Hall, noting that the democratization of heritage had 'so far stopped short at the frontier defined by that great unspoken British value – "whiteness"', argued for 're-imagining "Britishness" or "Englishness" itself in a more profoundly inclusive manner'.⁹⁴ For Hall, all had 'a stake' in 'what I might call "the post-nation". But only if it can be re-imagined – re-invented to include us.' Hall concluded, however, that '"British" most of us were, at one time ... "English" we cannot be.'⁹⁵

The last decades have chipped away at Hall's 'cannot be', such that a Black Englishness can be an accepted part of the everyday scene, as people born into it, no longer a migrant group. The conditions of prejudicial migrant labour exploitation that produced accounts such as dub poet Linton Kwesi Johnson's 1980 'Inglan is a Bitch' may still persist, but the relation to England shifts.⁹⁶ Johnson's refrain on the condition of England, that there's no escaping it, and his final question of what's to be done about it, are answered in part through such refiguration. Michael Kenny notes in surveys of twenty-first-century non-white ethnic minorities 'a precarious, but increasingly meaningful, sense of identification with England as a place – if not with Englishness as an identity imagined in relation to ancestry and ethnicity'. Kenny suggests that 'English identity is becoming a much more unstable compound, a simultaneous source of admiration and fear, and a point of identification that a wider range of English people are drawn to explore.'⁹⁷ English landscape, and English pastoral, are parts of this new compound. In his 2008 photographic collection *We English*, Simon Roberts included a picture of a Muslim couple from Leicester at Stanage Edge in the Derbyshire Peak District on a walking holiday, who 'spoke of feeling completely at ease in the area'.⁹⁸ The relatively small scale of the figures in Roberts's image means that they register first as a couple walking down a path, with closer scrutiny showing Muslim dress, people part of the scene with identity retained.

Paul Gilroy has been a significant commentator on, in the title of his 1993 essay, 'The Peculiarities of the Black English', paraphrasing E. P. Thompson's 1965 essay 'The Peculiarities of the English', making Englishness more capacious.⁹⁹ In different vein the title of Gilroy's first book, the 1987 *There Ain't No Black in the Union Jack*, challenged a far-right slogan to make space for the non-white. Gilroy entitled his 2002 introduction to a reissue of the 1987 book, 'Race is Ordinary', finding hope in 'the country's wary movement towards racial conviviality', which if 'self-consciously' adopted would make racism unacceptable and 'incompatible with the local understanding of civilisation'.

Gilroy looked to stories 'defined by a liberating sense of the banality of inter-mixture and the subversive ordinariness of this country's convivial cultures in which "race" is stripped of meaning and racism just an after-effect of a long gone imperial history'.[100] Gilroy would present his 2004 book *After Empire: Melancholia or Convivial Culture?* as representing 'the flowering of my ambivalent love of England'.[101]

More recent events, however, have reactivated Gilroy's hoped-for 'long gone'; indeed just as in 1968 Powell worked a transatlantic seam to demonize asserted Blackness, so from 2020 transatlantic currents promoted a re-examination of racism and imperial legacies. If for Gilroy in 2002, 'The symbolic and linguistic system in which political Blackness made sense was a phenomenon of assertive decolonisation and is now in retreat,' the 2020s prompted another kind of step forward.[102] Any revived polarization nonetheless runs alongside a persistent ordinary conviviality, manifest in mainstream forms, Gilroy's hopes still registering in the trivially popular. Thus Black Englishman Dion Dublin, universally popular as a footballer either side of the millennium for his skill, commitment and fair play, diversified from football punditry in 2015 to present the BBC's home-buying/home-making programme *Homes under the Hammer*. Dublin was born in Leicester a year and two days after Powell's 'Rivers of Blood' speech. Fifty years on, a Black man genially oversees worries over the English home. We are a long way – more than a simple cross-Mercian journey – from Powell's Wolverhampton.

In 1993 James Garo Derounian estimated a Black residential presence of 137,000 in rural England and Wales in the 1991 census, his *Another Country: Real Life Beyond Rose Cottage* reporting a mixture of stories, including harmonious coexistence, the interweaving of race into general patterns of wariness to incomers, and open hostility and abuse and presumptions of white supremacy in predominantly white country.[103] The book's subtitle played on the supposed pastoral idyll of a dwelling in the radio serial *The Archers*, though events in fictional Ambridge often hardly support rosiness, and indeed since the 1990s have featured storylines around race. The undermining of assumptions of English country whiteness has come in part from the work of Black cultural practitioners. Derounian drew on the work of Julian Agyeman, Chair of the Black Environment Network (BEN), established in 1988 with a remit of 'working for ethnic minority participation in the environment'.[104] BEN challenged assumptions that the English country was a white space, through campaigns around accessibility and the whiteness of official bodies' promotional imagery, the questioning of ecological assumptions concerning hierarchies of 'native' and 'alien' via an educational 'cultural ecology', and the deconstruction of alignments of race and pastoral. For Agyeman, processes of exclusion diminished the country: 'We need to make the most of the world within Britain.'[105]

BEN's management committee included photographer Ingrid Pollard, who was born in Guyana in 1953 and moved to London in 1956. Pollard's *Pastoral Interludes* exhibition, first shown in 1987, became an influential take on race and English pastoral. Five colour pictures showed Black figures in rural landscapes, with accompanying text conveying feelings of exclusion and histories of violence and enslavement, the 'Atlantic Triangle' central to English history. In the first image a woman sits on a stone wall, a barbed wire fence behind, a wary look to one side, with the caption: 'it's as if the black experience is only lived within an urban environment. I thought I liked the LAKE DISTRICT, where I wandered lonely as a black face in a sea of white. A visit to the countryside is always accompanied by a feeling of unease, dread.'[106] Pollard's photographs were hand-tinted, to evoke watercolour and postcard imagery, the medium invoking nostalgia, the message in stark counterpoint. Postcard conventions are subverted too in Pollard's 1993 photo-essay 'Another View', where Black hands write postcards ('the weather couldn't be better I've got quite a tan') showing Black figures in English tourist landscapes: 'Historic Hastings', 'Beautiful Dorset', 'Best Wishes from London', 'Wordsworths Lakeland'.[107]

In 1992 Pollard produced a photographic work, 'Wordsworth Heritage', as part of the BBC's Billboard Arts Project.[108] The image, displayed on 25 sites around the UK, showed Black walkers, including Agyeman, occupying the romantic Lakeland scene. The postcard form carries a cod-period caption: 'After reaching several peaks, Ms Pollard's party stops to ponder on matters of History and Heritage.' The phrasing is finely judged, the 'Ms' inserting what in 1992 was a distinctly feminist term into the text, the capitalized 'H' words signalling big ideas to be questioned. Scenes surround an outline of Wordsworth's head which challenge yet also inhabit convention. Pictures of Black hikers assert a right of cultural access. If expressions and gestures ask 'How do I make my way in a place I am entitled to be?', these are nonetheless hikers, well kitted out for the scene, equipped for the Lakes. In that sense these are figures less incongruous than, say, white people in the then popular shell suit. Pollard steps across one fracture of belonging through sartorial convention, sidestepping other cultural divides. Consulting maps, waterproofed for English weather, Pollard's figures work with the grain of English landscape, their challenge thereby readily comprehensible, and perhaps more readily accepted. Paul Gilroy, writing in 2022 on the 'dignity and complexity' of the range of Pollard's work from the 1980s onwards, concludes that:

> Her loving recuperation of England's landscapes and its insides – wallpapers and curtains, tools and teacups – shows the country's cultural fibres being unpicked and thoughtfully recycled. This body of work speaks not for hybrids, but for remixes. We are being urged to find, and even to celebrate, the nation's innermost workings. This is done not for her own benefit, but for ours and for England's sake.[109]

Are Pollard's images from 1987 and 1992 still 'contemporary' images, or several decades on are we in another country? Corinne Fowler, in her 2020 book *Green Unpleasant Land*, notes how in the intervening years, 'By embracing romantic ideals of nature as a healing force ... black Britons have reformed the English pastoral.'[110] Fowler's postcolonial pastoral starting point is V. S. Naipaul's 1987 novel *The Enigma of Arrival*, where the Naipaul-like narrator stays in a cottage in rural Wiltshire and reflects on journeys to and between Trinidad and London.[111] Naipaul accounts for migration and provisional settlement through a to and fro of landscape imagery, the English landscapes informing the narrator's colonial educational upbringing encountered in the country. Salisbury Cathedral is familiar from a schoolbook Constable painting, and the postcolonial traveller finds historic depth in Wiltshire, an England of ancient monuments, estate farming and cottage life. Dominic Head notes Naipaul challenging the 'apparent divorce between landscape and migrant identity', with 'enigma' signalling a literary and cultural ambivalence: 'The canon is extended by Naipaul's wishing to join it, much as the English landscape, always in flux in any case, is altered by his integration within it. What appears to be a kind of capitulation is really a subtly radical challenge to codes of Englishness that can seem impregnable.'[112] Pervading *The Enigma of Arrival* is the possibility of meaningful connection, however tentative, as the narrator walks, observes, becomes accustomed. One autumn day, with winter not far off, he reads *Sir Gawain and the Green Knight* on 'the bus back' (though not the bus home) from Salisbury: 'So in tune with the landscape had I become, in that solitude, for the first time in England.'[113]

Heritage and conservation bodies have gradually turned to BEN's thirty-year-old message of making the most of the world within Britain, allowing stories of the Black presence in the English past and present to converse. A key focus has been the country house, an iconic rural landscape discussed further in Chapter Seven below, but which can conclude this chapter's consideration of race and English landscape. In 2013 English Heritage produced *Slavery and the British Country House*, with essays tracing links between British country house owners and the Caribbean, the multiple sources of wealth shaping the country house, including plantation profit. If country house heritage has been upheld as globally significant, 'an iconic signifier of national identity', with designed English landscape a model for the world, other forms of global connection are now illuminated.[114] Landscape is a matter of cultural and economic import–export, with the terms of trade uneven. Empire enabled English country-house landscapes to be transplanted across the world, the home country in replica, while imperial trade shaped the English home. Landscape follows the money, and while landed wealth came from many sources, including landownership, agricultural production, international trade, mineral extraction and manufacturing, cultures of gentility played down rough connections, including connections to slavery. The aspiration to a country life on the part of the newly wealthy placed them at a distance: profits flowed to them, whatever their source, yet they could live a life upstream.

In 1969, in *God Is an Englishman*, alongside the northern and southern metaphors of Britishness and Englishness, Donald Horne noted the 'Imperial Metaphor', with the conceit that Britain's self-interests were also those of humanity. Horne called for English self-examination, a facing up to empire's loss through acknowledgement of empire's reality, 'an honest recognition of the guilt of Britain's history. Only this might set English conceit free for new action.' Horne's 1969 commentary anticipates arguments fifty years on:

> To believe that Britain can forget its history is to believe that Russians should not discuss the crimes of Stalin nor Germans the crimes of Nazism. There is not yet in Britain any institutional

reminder of the guilts of Empire; the builders of the Empire are still the great men of the history texts, and monuments still stand to them in London – but where is the monument to the 'natives' out of whom they constructed their pride? . . . There is a need for a re-writing of history, for a purging of some guilt by its contemplation.[115]

Empire haunts English heritage, and English Heritage and other conservation bodies now reflect on what it means for such stories to be brought to light, not without controversy, as when the National Trust's 2020 report on country houses and colonialism touched raw nerves on what Fowler terms 'sensitive terrain'.[116] Does history become a site for accusation, guilt, denial, reparation, reconciliation? Are country houses sites where histories of a Black British presence might be uncovered, in the process highlighting and challenging the implicit whiteness of such social spaces? The essays in the 2013 English Heritage collection are notably nuanced, acknowledging 'the risk of tarring a property with the "slave taint" if we treat all connections as equivalent'.[117] The history of slavery indeed reconfigures heritage in ways both simple and complex: simple for the brute nature of an ongoing historical phenomenon, and complex for the intricate economic and cultural relationships within which slavery was entangled. In 1993 Julian Agyeman suggested that 'Slavery can be the focus for reconciliation between white and black British heritage, if dealt with sensitively by a multicultural group.'[118] Above or below stairs in the country house, an expanded English story results.

The concluding chapter of Michael Wood's 1999 *In Search of England*, on 'An English Family', discusses Dodington Park in Gloucestershire, a country house whose archive was sold by the owner, Sir Simon Codrington, in 1980 through Sotheby's to an anonymous financier with Antiguan oil interests. The Antiguan government was priced out of bidding; the story is covered further in *Slavery and the English Country House*.[119] For an epilogue to his English search, Wood traced the papers to a warehouse near Heathrow, in the process emphasizing connections to a distinctive history of slavery in Barbuda, which the Codrington family owned for two hundred years. Workers sent to Barbuda from Gloucestershire married slaves. Post-1945 Barbudans moved to Leicester, some carrying earlier Gloucestershire surnames back to England. Searching for England entails attention to the Caribbean, to Ghana and to the Barbudan centre in Leicester, with its coach trips to Dodington Park. One photograph from 1975 shows members with Codrington, at the 'house paid for by the labour of their ancestors'.[120] Wood concludes: 'This is a story about Afro-Caribbean history, but it is also about the English; the Leicester Barbudans' ancestors were African, and Caribbean, but also English – as are their children.' The history of Codrington and Barbuda shows for Wood the error of 'Powell's fantasies of Englishness':

> the English are a nation of immigrants. Every wave has added to it and taken on the culture and language of the nation, from the Vikings to the Kenyan Asians. The new generation of Englishmen and women, in their teens and twenties, born and brought up in this world, are capable of taking on more than one history.

Multiplicity here does not imply division, Wood invoking 'a common sense of culture, custom and language' which 'in an open society . . . can be wide and inclusive. It is always in the making, never made.'[121] Opening the English past might shape an open English future.

4
England Shaken

Unsettlement

The sense of England as a settled place is easily undermined by political anxieties and dramatic events. Concerns chip away, with occasional blasts. Moments of danger shake England, sometimes prompting reconfiguration, though sometimes, as with a snow globe, the shaking is followed by resettling, with barely any sign of disturbance. This chapter considers war, pandemic and political upheaval as forces unsettling the country and provoking reflection about England. Late twentieth- and early twenty-first-century unsettlement was prompted by the Falklands War of 1982, fears over nuclear conflict, the COVID-19 pandemic, the reconfiguration of UK political geography and the UK's joining of and departure from the political structures of Europe. The chapter begins by considering how memories of an earlier conflict, the First World War, have shaped stories about England since the 1960s.

A Hundred Years War

Ronald Blythe's 1969 Suffolk village study *Akenfield* made occasional reference to the First World War, most prominently in the first chapter, 'The Survivors', though the title here denotes age rather than battle. Leonard Thompson, a farmworker aged 71, tells of joining up to escape the hardship of land work just before the war, the army offering better prospects than rural Suffolk. Thompson found horror on the Dardanelles: 'I knew the next sentry up quite well. I remembered him in Suffolk singing to his horses as he ploughed. Now he fell back with a great scream and a look of surprise – dead.' Despite it all, patriotism remained: 'We were fighting for England. You only had to say "England" to stop any argument.'[1]

Akenfield is largely a present-day story: the 1914–18 war seldom appears after the first chapter. In Peter Hall's 1974 film adaptation of the book, though, the First World War is a pervading memory, a continuing presence, overshadowing the century. Hall, himself from Suffolk, directed a film billed as 'Made by People of Suffolk', the actors all amateur and dialogue improvised, with local farmworker Garrow Shand playing three parts: present-day farmhand Tom Rouse, his Second World War father Tom Rouse, and his First World War grandfather Tom Rouse. The credits listed the host Suffolk villages: Burgh, Charsfield (where Blythe lived), Clopton, Debach, Henley, Hoo, Letheringham, Monewden.[2] Blythe produced the synopsis around the village funeral of a First World War veteran, the film mixing contemporary scenes with period reconstruction, a memorial structure personified by Shand's cross-generational playing. The second war is present, father Tom meeting his wife at a dance, only to die in conflict, and with his widow, Dulcie, played by Peggy Cole, the film's other chief character. The first war, however, at greater distance, casts a longer shadow. In period scenes corn is scythed, song accompanies harvest and soldiers sing in church before going to war.

In *Akenfield* the movie, English settlement is defined by death, and by attempts to leave. Thompson's testimony of escaping to the army from being worked to death on the land, only for Suffolk to seem a happy place from the Dardanelles, frames the film. The voiceover includes Thompson's sentry death story, his account of a marquee tent full of corpses and his reflection that, in Turkey, 'I thought of Suffolk and it seemed a happy place for the first time.'[3] The First World War becomes trauma and turning point for village England, with gains since in living standards and labour relations but losses in a diminished rural culture, old intimacies of work gone as efficiency succeeds. A grandfather who fought in the First World War is buried (Blythe plays the parson), and the service incorporates memories of the Suffolk Regiment at Gallipoli. The old Tom's voice speaks to a grandson who is himself determined to get away, not to the army but to Australia. A repeated story tells of grandfather Tom walking 40 miles to Newmarket to find a job in stables, only to walk back again, never (save for war) to leave. After fifty years on the farm a former vicar sends a condolence note saying Tom was 'the backbone of old England'. Young Tom, though, chooses Australia, leaving his fiancée and rejecting the offer of grandfather's old cottage. A 2004 film, *Akenfield Revisited*, showed

Shand at the site of the cottage, now demolished and replaced with a new-build, named Akenfield Cottage, Blythe's work shaping the modern village.[4] Hall's film concluded with young Tom getting a lift to the station with his young gravedigger friend, bound for London and beyond, and passing grandfather Tom walking back along the lane. The gravedigger, seeing Tom out of the village after making his grandfather's resting place, is the film's cheeriest figure.

A year after Hall's film, Paul Fussell's 1975 *The Great War and Modern Memory* presented an influential account of the literary to and fro between frontline and home, English pastoral placed on the battlefield in literary anthologies distributed to troops and deployed in ironic mode to comprehend the horrors of a mechanized war. The blasted landscape of the Western Front sits in counterpoint to an intact idealized home country, pastoral England reinforced by a counter-pastoral elsewhere. Fussell, himself a U.S. infantry officer in the Second World War, quoted Blythe's Thompson on Gallipoli, and cited *Akenfield* alongside Williams's *The Country and the City* in his discussion of English Arcadianism.[5] Fussell's book, and Hall's *Akenfield*, show First World War pastoral retaining its resonance sixty years on, and are far from unique in their poignant period play of cornfield and battlefield.

In 1969 Shirley and Dolly Collins recorded the LP *Anthems in Eden*, Shirley's folk song accompanied by Dolly's period instrumentation, with help from colleagues in the early music movement such as David Munrow. *Anthems in Eden* conveys a traumatic national story in national musical style, a meeting of general stories of paradise and fall with a specific history of a world broken by twentieth-century cataclysm.[6] The 'Eden' is the countryside before 1914, and the first side of *Anthems* comprises 'A Song-Story', a medley, conveying the breaking of life by the First World War. The medley ends with an optimistic 'A New Beginning: The Staines Morris', a maypole morris dance, as if to emphasize that things go in cycles rather than down a line of loss, and that life might be retuned to the seasons. Renewal, however, only comes after the 'Whitsun Dance', where widows remember fifty years hence, in other words, in 1968. Where the maypole once stood is a roll of honour, and the ladies, without the men, dance at Whitsun. Memorials usurp maypoles.

Anthems reminds us how relatively recent the First World War was in the late 1960s. The first rather than the second war is seen as the great historic divide, and here Collins and Collins echo *Akenfield* and other works of the time, such as Joseph Losey's 1971 film of L. P. Hartley's *The Go-Between* (discussed in Chapter Seven), and Philip Larkin's 1960 poem 'MCMIV', about 'the irreplaceable world that came to an end on 4 August 1914'.[7] Larkin's title is a memorial date, the poem's final line 'Never such innocence again.'[8] The early twentieth and late nineteenth centuries were hardly prelapsarian, as indeed the concurrent 1960s film adaptations of Thomas Hardy novels confirmed, but Collins and others evoke an order that had come down and held on, but was about to be shattered. The evocation is culturally conservative, but politically could be Tory or radical, depending on the late Victorian or Edwardian reference points.

Anthems in Eden underlines also that 1968 was not only a year of student unrest, racial controversy and an emergent environmentalism but also the fiftieth anniversary of the end of the First World War. Many people living could recall the Armistice, and remember relatives who would have been growing old had they not died young. Those who had made pension age recalled those who never saw such benefits. As a four-year-old in 1968, my grandparental stories included brothers lost in the Dardanelles, and occasionally a one-toothed great-uncle would appear who had served as a mechanic in the Royal Flying Corps. The wartime memories circulating in 1968 were not only of the Second World War. In *Anthems* the general late 1960s idealization of a balanced, more natural world lost met specific social histories, making sense to old as well as young.

Remembrance continues to be an arena for reflection about England. In an afterword in 2000 to a reissued *Great War and Modern Memory*, Fussell suggested that 'To sense the British obsession with the Great War, all that is necessary is to stand at the Cenotaph in London on any Remembrance Sunday and listen to the two minutes of silence.'[9] At the national memorial, and at local memorials across the country, on the Sunday nearest to Armistice Day, and/or on 11 November itself, the annual ritual proceeds, in dutiful, well-turned-out repetition, the silence accompanied by the weather, sound dampened or breezy. Memory is marked by restrained conduct, decorum maintained. Almost every place in the country marks local dead, save for those 54 'Thankful Villages' who lost no one in the First World War: the term was coined by Arthur Mee in the 1930s and marked in the twenty-first century by a 'Thankful Villages' song project from 2015 by Darren Hayman.[10] Over the century of remembrance, direct memory has been succeeded by memories of those who were there, or memories of their memories, albeit they may never have spoken of things.

The annual rituals sustain the official mode of commemoration established post-1918, and expressed in the restraint of most memorial designs, coping with trauma through dignity rather than demonstrative assertions of glory. When you come across different kinds of memorial they can surprise, even shock. Thus in east Yorkshire the Sledmere Wagoners' Memorial, built in 1919–20 and designed for his own Wagoners regiment by local landowner and MP Sir Mark Sykes (the Sykes of the 1916 Sykes–Picot Agreement which apportioned prospective British and French spheres of influence in a post-Ottoman Middle East), shows graphic conflict scenes of alleged German atrocities against Belgian civilians. On the neighbouring Eleanor Cross, soldiers are transfigured to noble crusaders, rendered in what Nikolaus Pevsner in his guide to the buildings of the East Riding of Yorkshire termed 'somewhat comical brasses'.[11] The memorials are now Grade I listed, so unusual in their rendering of atrocity, their clinging on to glory.

Departure from design convention may occasion surprise or amusement, but breaking the conventions of conduct can cause affront. In 1985 Patrick Wright discussed the furore, the 'clash between opposed modes of public remembrance', when Michael Foot attended the Cenotaph as Labour leader in 1981 in less formal clothing, wearing what was termed either a donkey jacket or duffel coat, green against November chill. Wright suggested that Foot 'stood there as bearer and manifestation of the history of the common people', as something distinct from Establishment remembrance.[12] Foot, pursued by the Conservative press for political ends, was a socialist politician proud of his patriotism, which would be deployed a year later around the Falklands conflict, as discussed below. In 1981 he became a man standing accused of disrespect, breaking a code at a moment where it was impossible for anything to count as trivial. For those seizing on the act to undermine Foot's reputation, it could never be only a duffel coat; or rather, the fact that some could see dress as incidental suggested their lack of regard for the untrivial dead.

The politics of respect on display around Remembrance Day 1981 has been renewed in the twenty-first century, and translated into practices of mourning for the new war dead. Simon Roberts's 2017

England Shaken

Simon Roberts, 'Repatriation of Deceased British Soldiers', Royal Wootton Bassett, Wiltshire, 9 April 2010, pigment print.

collection *Merrie Albion* includes a photograph taken on 9 April 2010 in Wootton Bassett, Wiltshire, where a civilian and ex-service crowd await the passing of repatriated military bodies.[13] People line to pay respect in a Wiltshire town which, happening to be nearest to RAF Lyneham, the air base to which the bodies of 345 British soldiers killed in Afghanistan were returned between 2007 and 2011, assumed a national responsibility. Medals are worn by those who won them, the grieving are consoled, the flag is at half mast, the traffic light is green. In 2011 the town was awarded the prefix 'Royal' for its gesture, but this began as impromptu, unofficial mourning. The Princess Royal presented the Letters Patent granting the 'Royal' prefix on 16 October 2011, and was presented with a specially baked Bassett Crown Bun, in a box designed by Laurence Llewelyn-Bowen. A council web page hosts the Royal Wootton Bassett Town Council Repatriation Archives, the term 'repatriation' here signalling a very different story of movement and belonging to that associated with the term in national debate fifty years earlier.[14] The browser can view the memorial books for individual soldiers, poetic tributes, emails of appreciation and Christmas cards sent to the town in thanks.

Wootton Bassett marks a twist in patriotism for the twenty-first century, signified also by the prolific public presence of the charity Help for Heroes, launched in 2007. The repatriation archive is in effect a repository of pride and anger, with respect for military sacrifice, at times approaching emotional conscription, accompanying scepticism or even hostility towards the political causes of conflict. Bodies from Afghanistan, and especially those from the Iraq war, receive respect for having been led astray, even betrayed, by government. The First World War can again inform the present, in a narrative inaugurated during the conflict by works such as Wilfred Owen's ironic 'Dulce et decorum est', on the 'old Lie' that in such a conflict it might be sweet and fitting to die for one's country. Such sentiment was restated most publicly in recent decades by the 1989 First World War television series *Blackadder Goes Forth*, where the knockabout laughs of earlier *Blackadder* series turned to mordant comedy. In the final episode, shown a week before Remembrance Day, even the characters' sardonic humour could not escape a final slow-motion mowing down. Judgements on the validity of war need not undermine respect for those lost; if the death may not have been fitting, that only makes the decorum of remembrance more appropriate, and so in 2010 Roberts photographed a respectful crowd.

From 2014 to 2018 the centenary of the First World War was marked by things beyond an annual parade. The UK's government art programme '14–18 NOW' set projects in resonant spaces around the country, as when on 11 November 2018 Danny Boyle's 'Pages of the Sea' presented sand portraits of service personnel on 32 UK and Ireland beaches, remembered before the tide washed their likeness.[15] The most prominent official spectacle of commemoration was the filling of the moat of the Tower of London between July and November 2014 with 888,246 ceramic red poppies, each representing a British military fatality. In Paul Cummins and Tom Piper's installation *Blood Swept Lands and Seas of Red*, the moat became a surrogate trench grave, with a roll of honour intoned each day at sunset, and the 'Last Post' played. The Tower recorded 5 million visitors, while the visual drama kept First World War memory in the media public eye. In November 2018 the Tower marked the war's centenary end with Tom Piper and sound artist Mira Calix's installation of thousands of flames in the moat, the poppy-dead succeeded by memorial light.[16]

The poppies and flames in the established space of the Tower contrast with the vernacular humility of another '14–18 NOW' project,

Jeremy Deller and Rufus Norris's *We're Here Because We're Here*. On 1 July 2016, 1,400 male volunteers aged between sixteen and 52 marked the centenary of the Battle of the Somme by standing in First World War uniform in locations around the UK, past presences in everyday modern settings. In railway stations and shopping centres, on beaches, high streets and car parks, groups stood and moved silently, occasionally breaking into the titular war song, and handing cards to the public giving the name and regiment of the soldier they represented, killed on the Somme's first day. The question of why they were here answered, the figures remained sartorially out of time, triggering thoughts of where they would have been off to. 'We're Here Because We're Here' twists the 1914 recruiting song by Paul Rubens, 'Your King and Country Want You': 'Oh! we don't want to lose you but we think you ought to go/ For your King and Country both need you so.' We wouldn't have wanted to lose you, and had we been there, would we have thought that you ought to go?

Twenty-first-century commemorations have increasingly acknowledged the First World War as a global war, fought across the world by people from across the world, an imperial war in the sense of both the powers in conflict and the people enlisted, willingly or otherwise. The power of *We're Here Because We're Here* indicates, however, the continuing emotional resonance in the UK of the well-trodden muddy path across the English Channel, the Western Front still a prime spot for modern memory. Blythe's *Akenfield* stories show, however, that even within a narrowly defined English memory of the First World War there is variety. Leonard Thompson's awful counterpoint to English landscape is not the Somme but the Dardanelles and Gallipoli. A site more prominently associated with Australian and New Zealander 'ANZAC' memory also chimes in England.

In 2010 P. J. Harvey released *Let England Shake*, from which the title of this chapter is derived. Harvey's songs convey battle horror, arms and legs blown into trees ('The Words That Maketh Murder'), orphaned children as the fruit of the land ('The Glorious Land') and men heading hellwards ('In the Dark Places'). References to No Man's Land might trigger Flanders associations, but mention of ANZAC trenches ('The Colour of the Earth'), dinars and belly-dancers ('Written on the Forehead') takes us to Turkey and Gallipoli, 'On Battleship Hill', and to 'Death's anchorage' off Bolton's Ridge ('All and Everyone'). Honour and glory are hollow here, as in Owen or

Blackadder, but Harvey's visceral music, attentive to bodily feeling since her first 1992 LP *Dry* (if earlier records stress the female, *Let England Shake* foregrounds the corporeal male), takes things beyond any ironic mode. And if the 'England' of the album title may be shaken, its emotional power remains, rendered in songs which do not dismiss the sentiments of the patria. The title track has the country's dancing days done, the silent dead weighing England down, its shake a death twitch, and Harvey's vocal adopts an American twang, the sentiments perhaps those of an American century for a fading power. In the song 'England', though, in Harvey's English voice, love for country remains. The accompanying video shows cows, faded Constable prints, Black men with red, white and blue scarves, Bobby Moore with the World Cup, a man reading a magazine as snow falls. England, through which the singer lives and dies, may leave bitterness and sadness, its life may stagnate, but nonetheless the song presents a love, undaunted and never-failing, for England.

The English South Atlantic

For three months in 1982, the UK daily news turned to the South Atlantic. On 2 April Argentina invaded the Falkland Islands, prompting British mobilization. A task force sailed from Portsmouth on 5 April, an action that received cross-party parliamentary support, including from Michael Foot as Labour leader. South Georgia was recaptured on 25 April, Margaret Thatcher exhorting television viewers to 'Rejoice' at that news. The Argentinian warship the *General Belgrano* was sunk on 2 May, HMS *Sheffield* was sunk on 4 May, British troops landed at San Carlos on 21 May, Goose Green was taken after battle on 28 May and on 14 June Argentinian forces surrendered in Port Stanley. The Falklands War was over, experienced and claimed as a national drama, and posing questions about the state and status of Britain and England in the 1980s.

In a speech at Cheltenham racecourse on 3 July the Prime Minister declared that 'the spirit of the South Atlantic' was 'the *real* spirit of Britain', countering 'those who believed that our decline was irreversible – that we could never again be what we were'. Thatcher asserted that 'Britain found herself again in the South Atlantic and will not look back from the victory she has won.'[17] Anthony Barnett's 1982 analytical riposte to the conflict, *Iron Britannia*, suggested, 'Perhaps the Falklands crisis will come to be seen as a final spasm to this process of *masked* decline,' Thatcher's wartime Churchillian mode a mask, albeit a popular one.[18] Barnett's book, written as the war proceeded, proposed that Argentina be given sovereignty of the islands but that the Falklanders and Britain should retain government under a form of leaseback. The Thatcher government, however, presented sovereignty and territory as non-negotiable.

As in the two world wars, the Falklands conflict saw Britishness and Englishness mobilized. The naval Task Force evoked a wave-ruling past, and its destination was styled as British, not only in jurisdiction but in character, notably in a rural way of life which somehow manifested Englishness in the south Atlantic. Barnett highlighted the 'pastoralism' of the Falklands campaign, English pastoral projected from island to islands across the ocean, redeploying a not uncommon trope of historic imperial settlement.[19] For Barnett there were even echoes of *The Archers*, the Falklands 'at once as remote and as mythologically intimate as Ambridge', and thereby a way of life worth defending.[20] The trope was also picked up as an anti-war absurdity, as in Crass's 1983 anarcho-punk single 'Sheep Farming in the Falklands', a follow-up to their August 1982 *Belgrano*/Thatcher-themed 'How Does It Feel to Be the Mother of a Thousand Dead?'

Island commonality across oceanic distance also framed Jonathan Raban's *Coasting*, published in 1986 but an account of sailing around Britain at the same time as the Task Force headed south: 'within twenty-four hours of my departure, England decided to go off on a voyage of her own.'[21] Britain and the Falklands lay at similar latitudes, off larger continents, with the Falklanders 'visibly, audibly, our kith and kin . . . The Falklands held up a mirror to our own islands, and it reflected, in brilliantly sharp focus, all our injured belittlement, our sense of being beleaguered, neglected and misunderstood.'[22] On the first weekend Raban watches arguments forming:

> The very bareness and monotony of the islands themselves, together with their tiny population, gave them the lucid purity of a symbol. Their blankness was their point: you could make them mean nothing or everything. And England had run out of symbols. Over this windy weekend, it was busy writing meaning into the Falklands, making that undulating, desolate land *signify*.[23]

Later Raban sees that Vera Lynn has recorded a Falklands song, 'I Love This Land', with lyrics by Leslie Bricusse, music by André Previn and funding by Peter de Savary (who in 1987 would buy Land's End, not for the nation but for commercial development). Lynn performed the song at Portsmouth Harbour, alongside her Second World War favourite 'We'll Meet Again', for the returning troops, for Raban a statement of 'a dotty kind of truth . . . the terms of the daydream in which England was living in 1982'.[24]

The popular patriotism of the Falklands War also prompted critical reflection on English identity on the political left. For Barnett, 'the left especially should not forget the powerful feelings of nostalgia and solidarity that the fighting engendered, sentiments that apparently engulfed a majority in all social classes.'[25] A subtly dialectical treatment of patriotism and class came in another song, which might have formed an antagonistic double A-side with Lynn's 'I Love This Land'. 'Shipbuilding', written by Elvis Costello during the war, was recorded as a single in August 1982 by Robert Wyatt, with sleeve designs featuring details of Stanley Spencer's Second World War paintings of shipbuilding on the Clyde. Wyatt's plaintive English voice (less harsh than Costello, who recorded the song on his August 1983 LP *Punch the Clock*) conveyed the dialectics of work and war. The song opens by asking if this is worth it. Conflict promises the reopening of shipyards in a time of recession, promises money for clothing and treats, sparks conflict between those objecting to war and those gaining war work, carries potential death for those enlisted. Telegrams will notify the next of kin. Piano, drums, organ and double bass carry the song, the opening question answered with a considered 'no'.

The Falklands War prompted left intellectual reflection on popular and populist nationalism, thoughts which would become newly topical in the twenty-first century, when many 1980s and '90s works were reissued, publishers sensing a renewed market. Patrick Wright's 1985 *On Living in an Old Country*, with its discussion of remembrance, Labour and patriotism, was reissued in 2009, and 2014 saw the return of the 1986 *Englishness: Politics and Culture, 1880–1920*, edited by Robert Colls and Philip Dodd. *Englishness* had been prompted by the Falklands: Dodd recalled in 2014 that in 1982 the unity of government and opposition over the Falklands War 'baffled' him, notably its easily understood appeal to ancestral memories.[26] Englishness, and its formative episodes in the late nineteenth and early twentieth centuries, hence required examination. A longer academic publishing time lag produced *Patriotism*, a 1989 three-volume set (itself reissued in 2018) on 'the making and unmaking of British national identity'. The editor, Raphael Samuel, presented the books as 'born out of anger at the Falklands War ... it seemed that the country had gone mad'. The project began with a History Workshop conference meeting on the issue, seeking to critique such sentiment, but Samuel suggested that 'What the Workshop signally failed to do – with the exception of an explosive section on the English countryside – was to come to terms with, or address, the patriotic sentiments in ourselves.' Landscape discussion had served to explode any easy separation of left and right in claims to national mythology, not least around 'spirit of place'.[27] The mode of enquiry inaugurated by Samuel, Wright and Colls and Dodd helped shape my own 1990s work in *Landscape and Englishness*, and *About England* revisits this connection of landscape and nation, its mode of enquiry itself part of the history under investigation.

Anthony Barnett's essay in *Patriotism*, 'After Nationalism', emphasized the 'heterogeneous existence' of the contemporary English, with their 'life of multiple overlapping sovereignties – in the regions, in terms of industry and with respect to Europe'.[28] Overlapping sovereignties, not least in Europe, would become an increasing preoccupation of Thatcher in the remainder of her premiership. The Falklands War, with its assertion of unoverlapping sovereignty, signals matters of political geography that would shape Conservatism for the next forty years. For the cheerleaders of war the Falklands marked a return to British greatness, to a solo sovereignty without overlap. From another perspective, though, it was a final gesture of global sovereign power. Since 1982 the UK has engaged in several wars, far from or close to home, but never alone against another sovereign state. The Falklands was the last such war, and the last governmental mobilization of martial patriotism; last at least for now.

England and the Bomb

In 1956 the Queen opened the world's first civil nuclear power station at Calder Hall in Cumberland, next door to the Windscale plant processing plutonium for the UK's nuclear weapons programme. The links between nuclear energy and nuclear weaponry would be controversial, whether the two could be seen as distinct elements in what Jonathan

Hogg terms 'British nuclear culture' or whether any such separation was meaningless.[29] The hundreds of yards between Calder Hall and Windscale could be a gesture of separation or an indicator of entanglement. The Queen outlived the power station. Operation ceased in 2003, and the cooling towers were demolished in 2007. Windscale continues as the UK's largest nuclear site, though it was renamed Sellafield after a catastrophic reactor fire in 1957.

The early years of nuclear power brought some landscape celebration, Sylvia Crowe's 1958 book *The Landscape of Power* setting out the design possibilities: 'Its scale is cosmic rather than terrestrial, and the idea which its appearance should express, is the harnessing of universal forces to the service of the earth.'[30] The UK never quite matched France, where, as Gabrielle Hecht shows, nuclear power became a badge of national identity, shaping a national 'mentality of the future', but Crowe's work indicates a narrative of nuclear power adding to rather than destroying English landscape.[31] Weaponry, though, was something else, and the anti-nuclear movement harnessed English landscape and English pastoral against the bomb. Even before the formation of the Campaign for Nuclear Disarmament (CND) in 1958, a sense of atomic out-of-placeness had informed landscape commentary. W. G. Hoskins's influential 1955 landscape history *The Making of the English Landscape* included in its dystopic vision of 'The Landscape Today' an image of East Anglian fields: 'Over them drones, day after day, the obscene shape of the atom-bomber, leaving a trail like a filthy slug upon Constable's and Gainsborough's sky.'[32] Meredith Veldman places CND as itself in a tradition of 'romantic protest', including in the twentieth century the fantasies of Tolkien and C. S. Lewis, and the politics of E. F. Schumacher and the Green movement.[33] CND's early modes of demonstration, notably the Easter Aldermaston marches, set pastoral pilgrimage against the bomb, the sleek, streamlined technocratic powers of the UK and U.S. military met by a ragtag duffel-coated springtime vernacular of banners and songs and guitars, setting a different example to the world. The 'march' was not a disciplined display but something of a different order, 'an annual call to repentance and renewal, both a physical penance and a spiritual revival'.[34] The first march in 1958 went from London to the Atomic Weapons Establishment at Aldermaston in Berkshire; later marches went from Aldermaston to London. The event remained a reference point when in 1989 Samuel presented the sparking of the *Patriotism* volumes by the

Falklands War as 'consternation at the apparent failure of the anti-War half of the nation (the half which had opposed the Suez adventure and supported the Aldermaston Marches) to assert itself'.³⁵

Veldman highlights the anti-nuclear mobilization of Englishness, as something whose pastoral qualities were vulnerable to militarism and the ultimate destructive powers of modernity, and as a scale at which, in a post-imperial age, a moral rather than imperial leadership could be exercised. Some in CND looked back to a wartime spirit of Britain standing alone against the odds, while the UK government's 1955 decision to make its own hydrogen bomb was presented as a moral failure, a desperate attempt to assert a global military standing the country no longer deserved, not least after the 1956 Suez campaign. From this perspective a unilaterally disarming Albion could be the spark for global redemption; Anthony Barnett traced Michael Foot's later support for the Falklands campaign back to this form of 'moral imperialism' found in early CND.³⁶ Veldman suggests that CND's early 'symbiotic relationship' with the post-Stalinist New Left also brought an English framing, not least through the work of E. P. Thompson, prominent in CND until his death in 1993.³⁷ Thompson's 'radical patriotism' spoke, as Michael Kenny argues, 'very deliberately to an English sensibility'.³⁸ Thompson's 1955 biography of William Morris had emphasized its subject's journey from 'romantic to revolutionary', and a Morrisite English socialism, as much green as red, informed Thompson's nuclear campaigning.³⁹ Thompson could also deploy Englishness in left-wing theoretical debate, as in his 1965 essay on 'The Peculiarities of the English'. Seeking an image to critique the New Left's growing preoccupation with structuralist theory, something rural and English came to mind, Thompson styling *New Left Review* editor Perry Anderson 'a veritable Dr Beeching of the socialist intelligentsia', closing the 'uneconomic branch-lines and socio-cultural sidings', as 'Old Left steam engines were swept off the tracks' and 'the lines electrified for the speedy traffic from the marxistentialist Left Bank'.⁴⁰ Thompson's imagery tapped a sensibility paralleling the 1953 Ealing comedy *The Titfield Thunderbolt*, on the rescue of the oldest branch line in the world, or Flanders and Swann's 1963 song 'Slow Train', with its litany of Beeching-closed stations and halts. Kenny suggests Thompson 'opened himself up to the accusation that he had fallen back upon the kind of parochial patriotism to which Englishness was invariably prone'; in peace campaigning, however, the parochial and the pastoral could carry a powerful political charge, and gain international reach.⁴¹

The very names of nuclear sites became a shorthand for monstrosity. Aldermaston, for example, became an English place name freighted with globally destructive power, as shown in the 1965 seventeen-minute film *Aldermaston Pottery*, produced via the BFI Experimental Film Fund and directed by Michael Darlow and Anthony Searle. *Aldermaston Pottery* sets the nuclear research establishment (not itself depicted) in counterpoint to the pottery, set up by Alan Caiger-Smith in 1955 in a disused smithy in his home village, and operating until 2006. Tanya Harrod notes Caiger-Smith's attempt to foster an idyllic co-operative spirit among fellow potters at Aldermaston, and the 1965 film evokes this in contrast to the power of the bomb.⁴² The film intercuts craft in an English village, where four potters, one female and three male, are at work, with scenes from the aftermath of Hiroshima and Nagasaki. The pottery stands for values of nurture against a nightmare nuclear modernity, and for a different scale and pace of energy, the rhythm of the potter's wheel against the destructive flash of nuclear weapons. A soothing mother's narrator voice emphasizes the nurture of a child alongside that of clay into pot, but the film's gentle tone and rhythm, with just a hint of anxiety in the squeak of the wheel, are intercut by horrific images of disfigurement. At its close the film comes to rest in the consolations of an English country garden. The more famous Aldermaston, the nuclear establishment, is never shown or mentioned, but remains near by, out of shot, overshadowing the village, even in its name. What a bargain we have made, the film seems to suggest, and all we can do is campaign, and strive to nurture something else, a something else symbolized by a potter's wheel, craft, a village and a mother's voice.

In the early 1980s, CND support was resurgent as discussions of a potential 'limited' nuclear conflict generated fear that the UK might be devastated in a 'tactical' superpower engagement, not least due to the presence of U.S. cruise missiles at USAF bases in England. The gendered critique of *Aldermaston Pottery* was extended through feminist anti-nuclear campaigns, most prominently the women's peace camp at the U.S. base at Greenham Common in Berkshire. In 1984, reflecting on the English countryside in environmental charity Common Ground's book *Second Nature*, Fay Weldon noted:

England Shaken

When required recently to pin a photograph on the Greenham wire, it was one of the English landscape I put there, and not as I would have expected of myself, a family group. I can, it seems, tolerate the death of people more easily than the death of landscape. So much of our past, of human aspiration, and struggle, and joy is invested in these hills and fields of ours, that the present pales beside it.[43]

Weldon set landscape prospects against the prospect of annihilation, the fear that, in contrast to the targeted trauma of wartime bombing, a future conflict would simply wipe out the country. In 1983 geographers Stan Openshaw and Philip Steadman mapped 'The geography of two hypothetical nuclear attacks on Britain', modelling scenarios from the postponed 1982 official governmental Home Defence 'Hard Rock' exercise (deemed an unrealistic public relations effort) and alternatives from their own work with Owen Greene on CND's 'Hard Luck' exercise, with its 'fairly optimistic' estimate of around 80 per cent dead within two weeks of an attack.[44] Analysis was extended for a public readership in Openshaw, Steadman and Greene's 1983 *Doomsday: Britain after Nuclear Attack*, which modelled a devastated land:

> even a moderate, realistic, level of attack would be likely to result in at least four-fifths of the country's population being killed and injured by the direct effects, 65 per cent of all buildings in the country being seriously damaged, set on fire or demolished, and 70 per cent of the inhabited land area of Britain being subjected to levels of radiation from fallout which would be fatal to any person (and most animals) in the open.[45]

The *Doomsday* cover showed a montage of a Central Office of Information mushroom cloud on a photograph of Little Torrington, Devon, by Janet and Colin Bord, authors of works on alternative earth mysteries.[46] The title played on an earlier survey, and an earlier conflict:

> It is almost exactly 900 years since William the Conqueror ordered a survey to be made of the land which he had conquered and of the people under his rule. Only much later did the survey come to be know as 'Domesday', that is the 'day of judgement'... If Britain were to be 'conquered' again, this

time with nuclear weapons, what would be the condition of its land and how many people might be left living?[47]

The response to such scenarios could, of course, be to argue for the maintenance of nuclear weapons as a deterrent against their realization, but Doomsday mapping tended to align with disarmament campaigns. Geographies of nuclear annihilation indeed reflected a wider geographical engagement with peace studies, a notable move for a discipline long connected with military knowledge. In 1987 the radical journal *Contemporary Issues in Geography and Education* (*CIGE*) produced a 'War and Peace' issue, edited by Ian Cook, including Brenda Spandler's use of *Doomsday* as the basis for a classroom exercise featuring maps, graphs, campaign material and simulations: 'There are great opportunities also for drama.'[48] The issue featured photomontage work by Peter Kennard, known to *CIGE* founder Dawn Gill through radical politics in Hackney, including for his 1983 CND montage *The Haywain, Constable (1821). Cruise Missiles, USA (1981)*.[49]

Kennard's montage plays on 25 years of anti-nuclear Englishness, making an incongruity of Hay Wain and missile. The operational mode of cruise missiles made this only partly absurd; indeed the wagon mount alludes to the mobility of such weaponry. One of the *Doomsday* scenarios was 'a specific pattern of attack intended to destroy ground-launched cruise missiles dispersed on their launch vehicles to a number of sites scattered through southern England':[50]

> in times of international tension, the U.S. plans to disperse them up to 100 miles from base to make them less vulnerable to attack. They may be sited anywhere from the Peak District to the New Forest or from Devon to Norwich ... The most likely dispersal sites are in areas of the countryside well away from other prime targets.[51]

'Constable Country', on the Suffolk–Essex border, received varying casualty estimates in CND's 'Hard Luck' model, Suffolk 40–59 per cent and Essex 80–100 per cent. East Anglia included several U.S. air force bases, likely targets of any Soviet tactical strike. Kennard, like Hoskins in 1955, harnessed Constable as an icon of vulnerable English landscape, cruise missiles taking the *Hay Wain* for support, an English symbol under U.S. hegemony.[52] A painting with a long association

Peter Kennard, *The Haywain, Constable (1821). Cruise Missiles, USA (1981)*, 1983, photomontage.

with conservation campaigns, hanging in the National Gallery and known via reproduction on everyday souvenir objects, is chosen as a recognizable image, and in doing so Kennard courts national values, continuing the associations of CND and the virtues of Albion.

CND espoused a different internationalism from that of NATO and the close UK–U.S. alliance, including in the 1980s a campaign for European Nuclear Disarmament (END), with Thompson prominent. Internationalism and neutralism did not, however, imply a turning from national value; indeed for Thompson support for END could be consistent with opposition to the UK's membership of the European Community. Without knowledge of Kennard's politics and CND's philosophy, the *Hay Wain* montage could be read not simply as national but as nationalist, a 'get off our land' retort to the U.S. military, an anti-American mobilization of the English cultural cavalry. Yet even with knowledge of Kennard and CND's distaste for nationalism, this is still an image which only works by being about England, through an English icon. Nuclear conflict would wipe all the *Hay Wain* stands for off the map, and the *Hay Wain* stands for England.

ABOUT ENGLAND

England under COVID

World Beating

The early Conference attendance,
Three figures or so,
Swells.

Lower league stadia
Fill to capacity.

The nation promoted,
Thousands are gathered.

And now,
At the highest table,
Old Wembley fills.

26 January 2021

About England was under way pre-COVID, the writing process grinding on through the pandemic, through lockdown and home schooling, and all the time tracking how what was happening was very new but kept on echoing old stories, the past being dragged up for inspiration, consolation or parallel. The UK occupied a particular place within the global epidemiological story, in its receipt of the virus, its response to it and its death toll. Whatever the future verdict, more lives were lost than would have been expected, and when the figure of 100,000 was reached within a year, on 26 January 2021, youthful memories of sporting numbers were triggered, reflected in the verse above, 100,000 appearing when the old Wembley hosted a cup final or a popular international game. The noughts and commas flashed an image of a full stadium, deceased. The tendency in recent years, not least by some in government, to wrap the country's future in supposed former glories, gave the old 'Empire Stadium' another resonance. The Prime Minister had proclaimed on 20 May 2020 the 'world-beating' qualities of the NHS's coming 'Track and Trace' system, but these never quite materialized, the UK statistically punching above its weight as the toll rose.

The pandemic was a global event, but as with other global events and processes, such as climate change, it was lived through different geographical scales: global, local, national. The 'national' in COVID was complicated by the devolved nature of powers over decision-making on health within the UK, indeed made those variations evident across the UK for the first time. The UK government's writ in effect ran only to England, and while the initial lockdown announcement applied to the whole UK, the relaxation of measures occurred at devolved national level, divergence evident. This devolved political geography, with England unusually and evidently alone within the UK, met long-standing cultural geographic tropes as the country lived through a strange time. This section examines England under COVID, in its attention to the natural world, its dramas of landscape and leisure, and its revisiting of the Second World War and post-war experience in NHS eulogies and evocations of wartime spirit.

Lockdown was announced on 23 March 2020, with an injunction to stay at home to save lives, with a daily walk permitted. The Prime Minister wrote to every household in a 'moment of national emergency': 'in just a few short weeks, everyday life in this country has changed dramatically.'[53] Stuck inside, people looked outside, walking to a park and back again, or round the lanes, and those with gardens finding solace in the domestic outdoors. Lockdown coincided with, across much of the country, weeks of settled, dry, fine weather, the closed down human lives meeting the ongoing spring, with reduced pollution clearing the air, traffic noise down and bird song audible. The human relationship to the natural world quickly became a focus for consolatory stories. From 25 May the BBC's *Springwatch* programme broadcast from various presenter homes, Chris Packham's New Forest home the anchor. Winner of the 2021 BAFTA 'Live Event' award for programmes in 2020, *Springwatch* gathered up popular nature stories, its running theme the ways in which nature could console and inspire. COVID produced a re-engagement with nature, part of a wider pondering of whether some aspects of lockdown – reduced car use as commuting paused, the stopping of passenger flights – might give environmental lessons for the future, pointers to the Anthropocene from an unplanned 'Anthropause'.[54]

From April 2020 for six pandemic months Melissa Harrison, whose work was discussed in Chapter Two, presented a weekly podcast on 'The Stubborn Light of Things', the title a line from Alison Brackenbury's poem 'Brockhampton'. Harrison took a field recorder on solo Suffolk walks, with poems and guest appearances, regular passages from eighteenth-century parson–naturalist Gilbert White, and no danger of invading anybody's social distance. Remote post-production by Peter Rogers added some music. Harrison thought of 'urban friends enduring Covid-19 lockdown in gardenless flats', hoping to spark joy rather than resentful envy.[55] The podcast title was shared with her 2020 book of *Times* nature columns, which reflects that, despite everything, the noticing of nature in lockdown could be the 'start of something wonderful', people reattentive to the non-human world, in wonder and responsibility.[56] The first podcast episode, 'Endurance', transmitted on 6 April, found Harrison in the iconic English setting of a country churchyard, nature lasting beyond human life. The walk encountered flood debris from a few weeks earlier, waters now receded, the flood plain doing its work, fertility renewed. The sound of farm machinery signalled ongoing essential outdoor labour. White's *Natural History of Selborne* offered a model for local attentiveness, his 6 April passages on returning swallows heard across the years, and his book noted as taken by soldiers to the trenches of the First World War; it had also been reprinted during the Second World War for inspiration in a time of conflict.[57] Pastoral amid trauma receives its latest twist.

Getting outdoors in the pandemic also reprised old stories of crowds. With the loosening of daily travel restrictions, just in time for summer warmth, beaches became crowded and tourist spots littered or worse. Government guidelines were amended on 28 May 2020 to allow people to drive any distance for outdoor recreation, and people went to the coast, with Dorset a focus for news reports on the anxieties of release. Crowded beaches prompted fears of a COVID spike. On 2 June the BBC reported from Durdle Door that 'Jurassic Coast beach crowds "showed shocking disregard for area"', with extensive litter, including 'human waste, sanitary items and disposable barbecues'. Volunteer wardens were abused, and three people were airlifted to hospital after tombstoning off Durdle Door's limestone arch. Jurassic Coast Trust chief executive Lucy Culkin stated: 'It was clear to see that some had all but forgotten the guidelines of social distancing or welfare for themselves and others, or indeed any respect for the natural environment they were visiting.'[58] Lockdown becomes a story of freed people not knowing how to conduct themselves, suffering injury from lack of local knowledge. The joys of freedom turn to anger as cultures of landscape clash. With a late June heatwave crowds returned to Bournemouth beach, thousands from as far away as Birmingham arriving, the council condemning 'irresponsible behaviour' and declaring a 'major incident' as social distancing became impossible.[59] Traffic gridlock ensued, and roads to Durdle Door were closed.

Concern over COVID crowds echoed older commentary on leisure challenges; indeed this was one of many areas where the pandemic was novel in some ways and very familiar in others:

> It cannot be said that the squalid crowding of Haytor Rocks and Becky Falls, with the legacy of filthy litter, is an improvement in the recreation of the people. The people who do these things should, in their own interests, be taught better, and when they have been taught they will derive more pleasure from their visits.[60]

That was Vaughan Cornish, speaking about Dartmoor in 1930 for the Council for the Preservation of Rural England (CPRE) in support of national parks as a means to encourage better conduct, while in 1935 E. P. Richards reported for the CPRE on recreational legacies near reservoirs: 'excretal matter, decaying organic matter from vegetables, fruit, food; and other waste matters etc lying about ... and fouling of places where in either small or large numbers one cannot be allowed to relieve nature.'[61] Interwar imagery was reprised at post-lockdown beaches and beauty spots, visitors venturing beyond usual haunts in their gladness to be out. With no opportunity to book accommodation at home or abroad, decent weather, a desire to get away after being cooped up and public toilets still closed, the delights of many became the horrors of others. 'When you've got to go, you've got to go' might have been the slogan for lockdown release.

In December 2020 the CPRE (now renamed the Campaign to Protect Rural England) released a report on *Litter in Lockdown*, the pandemic seeing litter reduced in urban areas but increased in parks and countryside, a sign of a 'throw-away culture' but with some novel items, the discarded mask 'a very visible emblem of these unprecedented times'. The Countryside Code's injunction to 'leave no trace of your visit and take all litter home' had buckled:

Sadly this did not always happen in 2020. Record numbers of people visited the countryside but rubbish, litter and abandoned camps followed close behind. The Lake District National Park Authority collected 300 bags of rubbish over a single weekend in June – it had never seen anything like this before.

The term 'fly camping' was coined for the discarding of camping gear after single use.[62] Cornish's Dartmoor commentary of ninety years before is phrased anew:

> It has been suggested that part of the reason for this litter deluge is that many visitors were from different demographics who had less awareness of, or consideration for, nature and the countryside and had not learnt how to engage with it. However, it is important that this suggestion is not used to stereotype against groups of people or as a reason for not enabling greater access to the countryside for all. Indeed, one significant upside is that many people have had a new and positive experience of the countryside.[63]

COVID prompted the new navigation of old questions.

The dramatic novelty of the pandemic prompted frequent appeals to the past, for historic parallels, for inspiration or consolation, and for a sense of a collective identity to sustain an uncommonly difficult shared experience. While the influenza pandemic after the 1914–18 war was the clearest epidemiological precedent, the Second World War and its aftermath quickly became a 2020 reference point, as a formative traumatic memory for a generation still living but also for the foundation of the NHS in 1948 by the Labour government elected in 1945. The tendency in recent years for politicians to prefix mention of the NHS with the word 'our', seeking thereby to claim the issue, however genuinely or cynically, for their party, reflected and signalled a mix of collectivism and sentimentality accentuated under COVID.

On 26 March 2020 the first 'Clap for Our Carers' occurred, a dose of applause for those on the frontline of an epidemiological conflict. Following European example, the gesture was proposed by Annemarie Plas, a Dutch woman living in London. An individual thought became a national ritual, as every Thursday at 8 p.m. until 28 May people emerged from homes to clap on doorsteps and balconies.

The gesture rearticulated community for those who happened to be in residential proximity, at a time when domestic friendly or familial visits were prohibited and all were potentially vulnerable. Neighbourhood community met the national collective in the prominence of the NHS within the 'carers' category, home-made rainbow banners proclaiming window support. The collectivism of wartime effort, a 'Blitz spirit' in adversity, the values of the post-war settlement and the dancing nurses of the 2012 Olympic ceremony found an echo. And on 6 April 2020 Tom Moore, aged 99, started to walk up and down his garden, hoping to raise £1,000 from sponsorship by his 100th birthday on 30 April. An old man walking up and down his garden for charity is an admirable news story, but what gave Moore extra national charge was the wartime resonance. A veteran of Second World War campaigns in India and Burma mobilized himself, with considerable effort, for those combatting COVID. Moore was seen to exemplify a generation to live up to, and by his birthday had raised £30 million. After RAF flypasts, a gold Blue Peter badge and appointment as Honorary Colonel, Moore was knighted by the Queen at Windsor Castle on 17 July 2020.

The Queen had already invoked the war when, on 5 April 2020, she broadcast to the nation, giving stoic reassurance to the isolated that 'we will meet again', a deliberate echo of Vera Lynn's wartime song 'We'll Meet Again,' press and public picking up on a message of getting through. The wartime mood was also reprised when, on 18 June 2020, Vera Lynn died, at the age of 103, reports saluting her best-known songs, 'We'll Meet Again', 'There'll Always Be an England' and 'There'll Be Bluebirds over the White Cliffs of Dover' (though not the 1982 Falklands tune 'I Love This Land'). Labour leader Keir Starmer commented: 'Her songs still speak to the nation in 2020 just as they did in 1940.'[64] In 2004 Paul Gilroy had noted how the 'potency' of the Second World War was 'undiminished', and how this could be connected to senses of 'endangered whiteness' and a wider melancholy: 'I think that there is something neurotic about Britain's continued citation of the anti-Nazi war' as 'a place or moment before the country lost its moral or cultural bearings'.[65] The Second World War rode again in 2020, but attention to race under COVID predominantly concerned the disproportionate impact of the virus on Black and minority ethnic groups, a consequence in part of employment patterns in high-risk occupations. In general, the tone of all being in it together was careful not to exclude anyone from the 'all'. The pandemic certainly, though, confirmed the continuing potency of wartime memory, the 'cultural bearings' signified by earlier conflict able to be invoked in both support and critique of government actions, and personified by Tom Moore, whose Asian war service locations also indicated the complex imperial nature of the 1939–45 conflict.

A particular tribute gesture conjoined the NHS and the Second World War when, in the summer of 2020, the Aircraft Restoration Company, owned by John Romain and based at Duxford airfield in Cambridgeshire (also the site of the Imperial War Museum's Air Museum), flew a 'THANK U NHS' Mark II Spitfire over 255 hospitals and medical institutions across the UK. The plane used had been built in 1944 for photographic rather than combat service, Romain suggesting that flying for the NHS during COVID in a combat aircraft would not have been appropriate. Beginning in May with a local flight over villages to coincide with Clap for Our Carers, after a few weeks the message was painted on the underside, THANK on one wing, NHS on the other and U on the fuselage. A JustGiving page enabled people to nominate names to be engraved on the plane, monies going to the NHS Trusts Together charity; 6,400 were there as the plane toured hospitals in the summer of 2020, first over Addenbrooke's Hospital in Cambridge on 28 May, and then nationwide after discussion with the NHS.[66] While this particular Spitfire had never been a fighting plane, that nuance might have passed many spectators by. Flypasts saw the NHS's battle against COVID meet the Battle of Britain, in popular memory a triumph against the odds through bravery in the air and organization on the ground. For the pilots read nurses and doctors, for the ground crew read hospital porters, managers, caterers, cleaners.

This chapter began with the popular memory of the First World War, and has come to present memories of the Second World War, having called at the Falklands and Armageddon on the way. Past conflicts shape responses to present trauma. When England is shaken in future, how will pandemic memories be summoned?

The Home Internationals

Uncertainty over the place of England within Britain, the United Kingdom and the British Isles has characterized the early twenty-first century. The English question also stirred in the 1970s, a time of debate over the devolution of power from Westminster, the transfer of power to Brussels and tension and conflict in Ireland. Present English questions are un-novel, but in the twenty-first century have reached a particular pitch.

From the early 1970s I recall bedroom wallpaper showing footballers, action scenes in strips red, white, blue and green, with national badges around for Wales, England, Scotland and Northern Ireland. The paper must have meant something to stick in my mind, and memory lingers of seeing if the span of small fingers could stretch from one badge to another, nodding off as light faded. The wallpaper showed the 'Home Internationals', the end-of-season tournament whereby all the 'home' nations of the United Kingdom played one another. England v. Scotland at Wembley or Hampden Park was the supposed showpiece fixture; Northern Ireland v. Wales at Windsor Park, Belfast, or in Cardiff, Swansea or Wrexham, received less attention from the London press. In 1973 England v. Scotland at Wembley (1–0) attracted 100,000; Northern Ireland v. Wales (1–0), shifted from Belfast to Goodison Park in Liverpool for security reasons, drew 4,946.[67] The wallpaper marked a friendly competition, an 'international' tournament within a country, the internal geopolitics of the UK in play, with joy beyond England if England's dominance was undermined. Between 1947 and 1973 England were winners or joint winners on all but five occasions. International fixture congestion and hooliganism, notably around the England v. Scotland fixture, led to the 'British Home Championship' being killed off in its centenary year of 1983–4.

As wallpaper, and as a football tournament, the 'Home Internationals' appear anachronistic. The phrase, though, captures something of the UK's strange arrangement, as a state encompassing not only regions but nations, with one much larger than the others, with claims to global significance (not least in football history) and with plenty of local difficulties. In the 1970s, as today, powerful political movements in Scotland, Wales and Northern Ireland would suggest that any 'Home International' games should really just be internationals. A few years after my wallpaper was printed, and in the year when Scottish fans celebrated the tournament-winning 2–1 defeat of England at Wembley with a spectacular pitch invasion, an influential book by Tom Nairn predicted, and sought to hasten, *The Break-Up of Britain*. Nairn's 1977 context was a nationalist political revival in Scotland; a public vote on a devolved assembly in March 1979 brought a 51.6 per cent yes vote, but with insufficient numbers to meet the threshold laid down in the

1978 Scotland Act to enact the legislation. Momentum for devolution would, however, revive as successive Thatcher governments received steadily less Scottish support, with the trialling of the Poll Tax in Scotland in 1989 fuelling anger. The election of Labour in 1997 led to a further referendum on a proposed Scottish Parliament, with a 74 per cent yes vote and the parliament operating from 1999.

Devolution within the UK raises questions about England, and Nairn, in foreseeing a socialist Scottish state, attended to English identity. Nairn's chapter on 'English Nationalism: The Case of Enoch Powell' drew attention to Powell's pastoral racialized Englishness, with Powell in 'certain respects ... the most original of Britain's bourgeois politicians', his work illustrating the complexities of conservatism, and the challenges of cohabiting an island with England.[68] For Nairn any transformation of the UK begged English questions, shaping the kind of neighbour an independent Scotland would have. In this at least Nairn echoed Powell, who in a Commons debate on 4 February 1974 on possible devolution to Scotland and Wales had stated that underlying the issue was 'the problem of England'.[69] Nairn argued that 'the English need to rediscover who and what they are, to re-invent an identity of some sort better than the battered cliché-ridden hulk which the retreating tide of imperialism has left them.'[70] Analysing 'The English Enigma', Nairn found hope in elements of the New Left and especially History Workshop, as representing a form of 'left-nationalist popular culture'. This, however, was 'a cultural nationalism which has not yet come to consciousness of its own nature and purpose. Hence it has remained closer to ideas of a rather undefined socialism, politically, rather than to ideas of England. But this may not be for long.' Nairn foresaw 'the attempt to find strength for a better, more democratic future by re-examining (on occasion re-inventing) a mythic past ... To those who care for England and strive to see her free of the old harness, this hope is critical.' Nairn concluded:

> The English revolution is the most important element in the general upheaval of British affairs . . . It is also the hardest to foresee, and will take longest to achieve. Upon its character – conservative-nationalist reaction or socialist advance – will depend the future political re-arrangement of the British Isles, as federation, confederation, or modernized multi-national state.[71]

Nairn's 1977 questions remain open.

The year before the publication of *The Break-Up of Britain*, and from a part of the British Isles rent by tensions of Britishness, Seamus Heaney reflected on 'Englands of the Mind'. Insights on England again proceeded from elsewhere, indeed from two places elsewhere, Heaney lecturing to the University of California, Berkeley, on how things appeared from nationalist Ulster. Heaney considered Ted Hughes, Geoffrey Hill and Philip Larkin as poets treating 'their region as England', using the 'cultural depth-charges' of language to indicate an emergent English predicament. Finding England in times of trouble, the three exhibited 'that defensive love of their territory which was once shared only by those poets whom we might call colonial – Yeats, MacDiarmid, Carlos Williams'.[72] Heaney reflected on Larkin's 1972 environmental poem 'Going, Going', with its catalogue of worry and melancholy, and Larkin's phrase: 'And that will be England gone':

> I think that sense of an ending has driven all three of these writers into a kind of piety towards their local origins, has made them look in, rather than up, to England. The loss of imperial power, the failure of economic nerve, the diminished influence of Britain inside Europe, all this has led to a new sense of the shires, a new valuing of the native English experience.[73]

The UK had entered the European Economic Community in 1973, and voted in a 1975 referendum to maintain its membership, so Heaney's Europe comment could here be taken two ways, indicating either Britain's diminishing influence within Europe or, more likely, the diminished global influence of a Britain now firmly within a European community.

Heaney also highlighted Donald Davie's 1974 collection *The Shires*, written from California and with a poem for each English county at a time when local government reorganization under the 1972 Local Government Act meant that some of Davie's subjects (Westmorland, Cumberland, Rutland) would be abolished.[74] The internal political geography of England also shapes the country's identity. County by county Davie mixed private and public history, and geographies of varying scale. William Davies suggests Davie presents 'an Englishness of its own unique history, comprised of its own unique patchwork of regions, which is nevertheless European and, beyond that, global'.[75]

Moving through *The Shires*, the reader encounters plenty of the unrustic, and points of interconnection within and beyond England, with references to Marshal Pétain in Bedfordshire, A-roads being quiet now that motorways run (Buckinghamshire), industrial ruin in Cheshire, Perspex flotsam off Cornwall, memories of Italian prisoners of war (Huntingdonshire) and in Shropshire 'the troublesome chores of Empire'. In Nottinghamshire, 'Rosebay willow herb pushing/ through patches of old slag/ in the curtains of driving rain/ obscured the Major Oak.' In Dorset, though, Davie still finds 'Pastoral England's longest summer day', the backdrop illustration to his Dorset poem also the book's cover.[76] For Heaney *The Shires* explored 'not just the matter of England, but [of] what is the matter with England'.[77]

Heaney's 'what is the matter with England' gained renewed prominence in the early twenty-first century, the devolutionary moment of the late 1990s one spark for a range of enquiries on English culture and politics.[78] Power had been devolved, but Tam Dalyell's famous Westminster parliamentary 'West Lothian question' was unanswered, as Scottish MPs continued to vote on matters for which Westminster's writ no longer ran in Scotland. At a time of continuing Labour dominance in Scotland, it was not implausible to foresee scenarios where laws relating to England might be carried by Scottish votes. Parliamentary arithmetic tallied with wider cultural reflection on where England stood within a less united kingdom. As noted above, the COVID pandemic brought such questions into sharp focus, sharper still for the Scottish political dominance of the Scottish National Party (SNP). From 2007 the SNP was the largest party in the Scottish Parliament, and dominated Scotland's Westminster representation from 2015, winning 56 out of 59 seats. In the 2014 independence referendum only 44.7 per cent of voters backed independence, but the reaction of the British government after the 'No' vote, David Cameron announcing on 19 September 2014 that is was now time to hear 'the millions of voices of England' and examine 'English votes for English laws', boosted SNP support, with Brexit later giving this a further twist, as discussed below.[79] Writing in 2014 in *The Politics of English Nationhood*, Michael Kenny warned against overstating devolution as a factor reshaping Englishness, rightly pointing to a range of other forces; this was, however, pre-independence referendum and pre-Brexit.[80] The combined aftermath of 2014 and 2016 has made a further independence referendum more likely, and the cultural and political momentum again appears behind a 'Yes' campaign (though this was also the case in 2014). If, in Nairn's terms, the devolution settlement forestalled any English 'revolution', its increasing unsettlement again raises the matter of what England would be in a future non-UK.

Scottish disunion rather than devolution would leave England the largest entity in a lingering UK of England, Wales and Northern Ireland. The position of Northern Ireland post-Brexit may become further entangled with the Republic of Ireland, and the UK Parliament even more an English entity, with the West Lothian question potentially mutating into a Ceredigion question. One possibility is increasing Welsh political as well as cultural distinction, and a de facto English parliament. If present trends are projected, the politics of that parliament would appear to be Conservative, but the departure of Scotland would have effects on the English polity that cannot be foreseen. Claire Westall and Michael Gardiner comment: 'there is no way of anticipating what form England might take as a nation distinct from British imperial ideology and state dominance.'[81] The long-standing variety in political claims to Englishness, manifest in the twenty-first century in conservative efforts such as Roger Scruton's 2000 *England: An Elegy* or the socialist *Looking for a New England* ambitions of Labour's 2015 'Red Shift' group ('Understanding England as it is – Inspiring England as it could be'), would resurface, their mixed ingredients restewed.[82] The change would be significant, the outcome not predictable.

Tom Nairn's 1977 chapter on 'The English Enigma' began with the opening of G. K. Chesterton's 1908 poem 'The Secret People'.[83] A year before, Melvyn Bragg had used the same Chesterton quote to open his *Speak for England*, an 'Essay on England' in the twentieth century, based on interviews with residents of his home town of Wigton, Cumbria.[84] Chesterton's poem has been a common reference point for those searching for definitions of the English, and especially, with its theme of reticence, for those identifying a lack of explicit definition as part of the story. Patrick Wright notes the poem as being regularly cited from 2016, an Edwardian phrasing somehow anticipating the sentiments driving Brexit.[85] Chesterton's poem begins:

> Smile at us, pay us, pass us; but do not quite forget;
> For we are the people of England, that never have
>   spoken yet.

'The Secret People' is a poem of stoic grievance, presenting a voice unheard by the governing class since Norman times. It is also a poem of evasion, avoiding any blame for war and empire, invoking a people who did what they were asked to, but whose concerns were never listened to; instead they were patronizingly smiled at, paid in work and war and then passed over. Chesterton suggests that others speak 'for us of new laws strong and sweet,/ Yet there is no man speaketh as we speak in the street.' When Chesterton gives a hint of the popular language, it is not idealist or ideological; when in the civil war the King's head falls, the people look to another King's Head: 'And a few men talked of freedom, while England talked of ale.' The grievance of 'The Secret People' also targets the alien, the 'new unhappy lords' shuffling papers with 'bright dead alien eyes'. Earlier 'the squire' is 'stricken' as 'he clutched a cringing Jew'. And so 'a new people takes the land: and still it is not we.'

Ale, anxiety, grievance against aliens, an unheard voice, all tropes which would be mobilized in the early twenty-first century, though none of which exhausts England and Englishness. The next section examines the ways in which England was manifest in arguments over Europe, building to the 2016 referendum and its aftermath. Future Scottish independence would, however, give another occasion for the voicing of Englishness, the consequent institutional shifts allowing a no longer so secret people a variety of voices, and surprise might follow. Perhaps the Home Internationals might make a comeback, the 'home' a geographic space independently shared. And if Chesterton's 'we', in all its present variety, did turn out to 'take the land', and could speak in an English parliament, what might they say?

England, off Europe
Dreams of Leaving

In 2010, on *Let England Shake*, P. J. Harvey's First-World-War-set song 'The Last Living Rose' begins by damning Europeans, and asking to be taken back to beautiful England. There may be grim alleys by the Thames, but there is beauty by the moonlit river and delight in the patina of old dirt, the shaking of hedgerows and the quivering of the last living rose. The video for the song takes in sea views, beaches, fields, people, houses, churches, ducks and swans; the message is of upbeat vulnerability, the shake and quiver denoting a mood less desperate than the rest of the war-graven LP. The last living rose is still moving. England remains, off Europe.

The sense of England not simply lying off but going off Europe has been a significant early twenty-first-century cultural and political theme, for some a key element in the outcome of the 2016 referendum on European Union membership. Even ten years before, that possibility seemed remote. Thus in 2006 Peter Mandler, in his study of ideas of English national character, considered a possible move beyond national to universal values, with Europe their possible home: 'After national character, after nation – humanity, just as the Enlightenment imagined things before national character? Maybe so. Yet history is full of surprises.'[86] The year 2006 now seems politically and culturally far away, other surprises having intervened, the distance signalled too when Mandler identifies the author of a 1997 quote criticizing the national mourning for Diana as 'the Tory journalist Boris Johnson'.[87]

The terms of cultural and political trade between the UK and Europe have since shifted, with Englishness an element in that shift. Fintan O'Toole terms Brexit a 'crisis of English identity', marked by a sense of 'heroic failure', and with 'the colonizer imagining itself as the colonized', anxious over loss of status.[88] Amid worries over the post-imperial role and character of the UK, the Brexit narrative of a 'Global Britain' released from EU shackles offered one answer. For some Brexit is as an English/British end-of-empire story, Robert Saunders noting post-imperial patterns of thought on both sides of the 2016 argument, whether informing debate on migration or on Britain's global role and leadership.[89] Danny Dorling and Sally Tomlinson suggest that the 'catalyst' for Brexit was 'that a small number of people in Britain have a dangerous, imperialist misconception of our standing in the world'.[90] 'Leave' visions of 'Global Britain' tended to emphasize the global rather than imperial, a small island punching above its weight rather than an empire punching down on the subjugated, although global history and the UK's status as almost major power could not help but call empire to mind.

O'Toole notes how the 2016 referendum occurred after two decades where English identity had already 'resurfaced', not least in relation to Scottish devolutionary debates, laying the ground for its mobilization around Brexit.[91] While critics of the EU have come from across the political spectrum, the political push for Brexit came from the right, from organized forces such as UKIP and elements within the Conservative Party tapping into an existing cultural formation connecting affection for country with scepticism over the EU. *This England*, discussed in Chapter Three for its projection of English pastoral, chipped in. Thus Roy Faiers's autumn 1993 editorial mixed its welcome for the restitution of ancient county boundaries after their 1974 redrawing under Edward Heath ('Mr Heath is a bachelor so he won't understand the pain felt by parents who have suffered the indignity of seeing "Humberside" stamped on their children's birth certificates'), and its celebration of loyalty ('largely based on where you were born') and roots ('We don't want our roots pulling up'), with a Euro-warning: 'the bureaucratic nightmare of a "United Europe"... Twelve countries, all with different languages, cultures, history and outlook, being ethnically blended into a single super-state against the overall wishes of the people?'[92] Faiers predicted collapse.

In May 1990 *The Field*, a magazine promoting country sports, presented the symposium 'Fanfare on Being British', where 'seven Britons' spoke out.[93] The Maastricht Treaty was on the 1992 horizon, and the 'British' emphasis here was English. One of the Conservative voices, Michael Heseltine, was sympathetic to EU possibilities, noting that 'environmentally at least, we live in one Europe', though he compensated with some pastoral nationalism: 'There is a tiny church. Eight centuries of England lie buried about it. It allows a glimpse of an England that has not changed.'[94] Other contributors, however, hymned England contra the EU, including judge Lord Denning, historian A. L. Rowse and Conservative politician Norman Tebbit, his words accompanied by the white cliffs of Dover photographed from the sea. Tebbit was 'thankful for our insularity', and the part of the island he cared for was England: 'Our nationalism is of a different kind to much of that on the Continent, although it has to be said that Scottish and Welsh nationalism (not to mention that in the island of Ireland) have more in common with the Continental variety.'[95] The final voice in the symposium was that of Enoch Powell, reminding readers of his opposition to 1973 entry, and outlining failures in the Common Agricultural Policy: 'Never did so ill-matched a pair approach the altar as the UK and the European Six in 1972.' Divorce would benefit a trading Britain: 'The great truth is that for a nation ... there is no substitute for independence.'[96] On 24 January 1972, speaking in Brussels against the UK's entry into the EEC, Powell had argued of Europe that 'the English have never belonged, and they have always known that they did not belong to it.'[97]

Through the debates over the 1992 Maastricht Treaty such sentiments acquired the label 'Eurosceptic', and drove a new political party, the UK Independence Party (UKIP). Robert Ford and Matthew Goodwin's *Revolt on the Right* traces the rise of UKIP, putting a 'value divide' on the political agenda with its appeals to the 'left behind', its connection of Euroscepticism with concern over immigration and national identity, and its wariness of the global and cosmopolitan.[98] UKIP saw an uneasy merger of UK unionism and English nationalism, styled as an English concern through the charismatic leadership of Nigel Farage, an MEP for South-East England from 1999 until the UK's departure from the EU. A City commodities trader, Farage had been a Conservative Party member from 1978 to 1992, but left at the signing of the Maastricht Treaty under John Major. Farage's political persona traded on Englishness, regularly pictured at iconic English sites, not least the pub, holding or pulling a pint, a jovial bitter man. Farage is not the only politician to have commandeered the white cliffs of Dover, but the site regularly served to project the UKIP message across the Channel, and to emphasize an island distinction from the Continent; indeed terms such as 'island' and 'continent' gain their extra charge from this perspective.[99] Farage as bumptious pint-holder carried populist argument, speaking a cutting-through language and making a significant difference to British political life.

UKIP had been founded in 1993, growing out of the Anti-Federalist League founded in 1991 by Alan Sked, a former Liberal parliamentary candidate who taught European Studies at the London School of Economics, and becoming a political force under Farage, leader from 2006 to 2009 and 2010 to 2016. Ford and Goodwin note how this revolt of the right kept a public distance from the far right, as when in 2008 Farage rejected attempts at an electoral pact with the British National Party (BNP); UKIP member and former British tennis star Buster Mottram had acted as the go-between for the faction in favour.[100] UKIP won 7 per cent of the vote and three MEPs at the 1999 European elections, and 16 per cent of the vote and twelve MEPs in 2004, their 2004 campaign shaped by former Clinton adviser Dick Morris, with former Labour MP and television presenter Robert Kilroy-Silk a candidate, and celebrity endorsements from Joan Collins, Edward Fox, Patrick Moore and Stirling Moss. By 2009 the vote was

17 per cent, with a wider geographic base, London and Scotland the exceptions, and thirteen MEPs. At the same election the BNP won 1 million votes and two MEPs, meaning 3.5 million people voted for radical or far right parties, the parliamentary expenses scandal boosting anti-establishment support. On the political right something was stirring; the BNP collapsed through infighting, but in 2014 UKIP took 27.5 per cent of the vote, with 24 MEPs. An increased emphasis on grassroots campaigning achieved 12.6 per cent of the general election vote in 2015, UKIP's strength generating sufficient tension within the Conservative Party for David Cameron to pledge a referendum on EU membership if he won the 2015 general election. An unexpected absolute majority meant that Cameron had a promise to keep, and in this case he kept it, and the referendum took place on 23 June 2016.

Farage is one of the more influential figures in British politics never to have won election to the British Parliament, but without Farage UKIP would stutter and fracture, just as earlier radical right forces had lost momentum once the figurehead departed or was deposed. Farage, however, played a significant role in the Leave campaign, and in November 2018 founded the Brexit Party, with 26 MEPs paradoxically elected in May 2019. In 2014 Ford and Goodwin noted the place of specifically English imagery in UKIP material, campaigns often featuring 'rural villages and country pubs, symbols of an idealised traditional England', and the Leave campaign too played on Englishness.[101] Leave.EU posters promoted 23 June as 'Independence Day' by showing a Union Jack balloon sailing into the sunlight over a rolling English landscape, away from thunderstorms framed by the EU stars.

Brexit was a question of emotional geography, wrapping place and fear, place and hope, belonging and alienation, and affections and ambitions of settlement and movement. The Leave campaign was adept on this terrain, in contrast to the risk-averse economic focus of Remain. Michael Gardiner takes Brexit, like the Scottish independence movement, as a 'revolt of place', and suggests that 'serious responses to the vote might rather go with the grain of its collective and localist thinking than react against it.'[102] In 2017 David Goodhart's *The Road to Somewhere* gave one reading of this geography, of a 'populist revolt' reflecting distinctions between 'anywheres' and 'somewheres', denoting the degree to which people value rooted connection to a specific place or embrace mobility and cosmopolitanism as virtues.

For Goodhart such a distinction echoed Leave/Remain, and there is an echo of Theresa May's October 2016 Conservative Party conference speech with its provocative assertion that 'If you believe you are a citizen of the world, you are a citizen of nowhere.' Goodhart notes, however, that 'few of us belong completely to either group', and crude mobilization of an anywhere/somewhere distinction ignores the strong affections for place and home held by many for whom education brings a financially beneficial mobility, whose new somewhere may not quite be the old somewhere.[103] Conversely mobility and broadened horizons also follow less privileged labour movement, and the geographies of 'Somewhere' lives are far from narrow.

The referendum unlocked electoral geography, with votes not tied to a locality, as in a general election, but counting only towards a national total. This electoral geography was much less controllable for political campaigners, with the targeting of marginal seats meaningless. In a less manageable campaign other questions came to the fore, with migration achieving prominence, the free movement of labour within the EU meeting longer standing arguments over immigration and identity, back to 1968 and before. In the early 1990s annual net migration to the UK was around zero, but by the mid-2000s net migration was over 200,000, with gross immigration at 550,000 a year, and the EU a newly prominent source. In 2004 the Labour government gave unrestricted access to the UK labour market for migrants from ten EU accession countries in Central and Eastern Europe, differential wage rates prompting movement. In 2014 restrictions on migration from Bulgaria and Romania would be lifted under EU rules. Migration debate thus received a new twist, ostensibly outside a postcolonial frame, with the focus now on white European migrants.

As Wendy Webster shows, in the immediate post-Second World War period the 'European Volunteer Worker' refugees, over 400,000 by 1950 and mainly from Eastern Europe, had generated relatively little anxiety.[104] In Bedfordshire, with significant Italian migration into the local brick industry, road signs were made bilingual as Middle England happily accommodated continental Europe. The twenty-first-century reception took a different turn, UKIP leading campaigns against EU freedom of movement. Farage described this in 2013 as 'a rebirth of identity politics' in England, paralleling (though rather different from) that in Scotland, but one which politically 'no one had noticed'.[105] From 2010 UKIP blended opposition to EU migration with older strands of argument against supposed alien culture, with Islam placed on the other side of its value divide. The controversial Leave campaign poster suggesting a 'Breaking Point' had been reached, and showing a queue of mostly non-white migrants and refugees as illustrative of EU failure, gathered all the strands of anti-migrant sentiment a week before the referendum. Farage has since maintained his profile through post-Brexit anxieties over Channel-crossing migrants, the EU still retaining villain status, here presented as permitting non-Europeans to cross the Continent and embark for England. In July 2021 Farage would criticize the Royal National Lifeboat Institution for rescuing migrants, putting himself on the wrong side of an emblematically good English/British charity.

Composite Emotions

While Leave won, and Brexit happened, the history of the UK within the EU remains resonant for the future. Nothing can be taken for granted in the future political and cultural geographies of England, the UK and Europe, and an excursion through earlier European arguments, especially through attempts to nurture a positive outlook on Europe, may help frame future scenarios, returning us to the emotional geographies of Europe in England.

In 1963, in her Penguin Special *The General Says No*, prompted by the French president General de Gaulle's veto on the UK's application to join the EEC, Nora Beloff began with a passage redolent of 2016 and its aftermath:

> What hit us? For almost two years the British people have been re-examining their national identity. Are we still a great power? Is there any reality left in the old notions of national sovereignty, patriotism, Commonwealth leadership, and military independence? If not, should the British surrender a large slab of public business to a Community in which they would be minority partners only? Are there other more appropriate international groupings, or should Britain accept irrevocable links with Western Europe, that small exposed peninsula, with its tremendous human resources and peculiar capacity for self-destruction, at the tip of the Eurasian landmass?

Party-political outlooks, however, showed the opposite of 2016:

To answer these questions has proved agonizingly difficult. When the Conservative Party came round to saying 'yes' to the European Community, Labour leaders charged them with turning their backs on a thousand years of history: the Conservatives retaliated by claiming that the future was on their side – at which the reviving Liberal party protested that they had been for joining Europe all the time. And then, while the country was still locked in argument and passions were red hot, General de Gaulle said 'No', and Britain's own views on her national destiny suddenly appeared absurdly irrelevant.[106]

By 2016 things were different. The Liberal Democrats were hardly reviving, indeed in parliamentary terms were barely a rump. The Conservatives had been split for decades, the heart of the party saying Leave. Labour were officially for Remain, though with some divergence at the grassroots, and, since Corbyn had become party leader, ambivalence at the top. Euro-division, though, had always cut across party lines. In 1973 the Conservative government under Edward Heath took the UK in, though only with the support of some rebel Labour MPs. In 1975 Labour under Harold Wilson called a referendum on continued membership, supporting a 'Yes' vote. The 'No' campaign, with its slogan 'Out of Europe and into the World', was led by prominent Labour figures such as Tony Benn and Michael Foot, but also by Enoch Powell, by then estranged from the Conservative Party and sitting as Ulster Unionist MP for South Down.[107] Benn presented the 1975 referendum as a chance for 'Britain's independence day', the UK acting in anti-colonial fashion.[108] In Scotland the SNP led the Scottish 'No' campaign, seizing on Labour disunity to present European withdrawal as a step towards breaking up Britain. The 1975 results, with an overall 67 per cent vote to remain, showed a reverse political geography to 2016, with Scotland least enthusiastic for continued membership (with a 41.6 per cent leave vote), and England registering the strongest vote in favour. In 2016 Scotland voted 38 per cent Leave (not much less than 1975), but England 53.4 per cent Leave, with London the only region in England with a Remain majority. The voting shift between 1975 and 2016 was therefore primarily an English one.

The 1975 'Yes', like the 1973 entry, denoted pragmatism more than emotional commitment. Attempts to present the country as culturally Europhile were often half-hearted, in the 1970s as in 2016, when the

Remain campaign in effect conceded the emotional ground to Leave, concentrating instead on the economic risk of departure.[109] Back in 1973, however, a week of 'Fanfare for Europe' events sought to celebrate entry and spark popular enthusiasm, and on Wednesday, 3 January 1973, Wembley staged The Three v. The Six, a 'Common Market Football Match'. The new members (Great Britain, Republic of Ireland and Denmark) met the rest (Belgium, France, Italy, Luxembourg, Netherlands and West Germany). Players from each country (and each of the four 'home' nations) appeared, an all-star event with Franz Beckenbauer, Dino Zoff and Günter Netzer on one side, Bobby Moore, Pat Jennings, Steve Heighway and Bobby Charlton on the other. The Three won 2–0, with goals from Henning Jensen (Denmark) and Colin Stein (Coventry and Scotland). A four-language programme note from Edward Heath hailed 'a major landmark in the history of European football'.[110] Both teams were in effect representing the

Front cover of Common Market Football Match official programme, 1973.

Common Market, the programme's cover showing a reconfigured EEC map, yellow for the three, red for the six. While the Irish Sea is still open, the Channel disappears, as if geopolitical tectonic plates have shifted. With all the fanfare, the Empire Stadium was only just over a third full, the crowd 36,500 on a January night, the game one for the connoisseur of football styles. The national sentiment that drew crowds near to Wembley's 100,000 capacity for competitive matches was absent. Even on my first and only visit to Wembley, for the 1973 League Cup final exactly three months later (Norwich v. Spurs, 0–1, eight-year-old sadness), there were 100,000.

The 1975 referendum 'Yes' campaign emphasized the economic benefits of membership at a time of economic crisis, and enlisted celebrities to popularize the cause.[111] 'Voting Yes' posters showed Arthur Lowe, Katie Boyle, Richard Briers and Henry Moore as 'People for Europe', while sportsmen urged voters not to 'knock' (boxer Henry Cooper), 'hit' (cricketer Colin Cowdrey) or 'drive' (racing driver Jackie Stewart) Britain out. Neither in 1975 nor in 2016, though, was a case made for Britishness or Englishness as a European identity. In advance of the 2016 vote Ailsa Henderson and others noted from public attitude surveys that '"Europe" appears to have developed as Englishness's "other" in a way that does not currently seem to be the case for Scottishness, Welshness or, in England at least, Britishness', and concluded: '"Remain" campaigners in England appear to struggle to articulate a cultural case for EU membership, which may in turn allow the "Leave" campaign to dominate the "cultural" dimension of the debate.'[112]

Emotional imagery for the Remain cause was striking for its rarity. On 3 June 2016 the *Times Literary Supplement* presented its particular readership with a commentary section on 'Culture and the EU', presenting 31 views from the UK and beyond of the UK–EU relationship in cultural life.[113] The heading, 'Please Don't Leave Us Alone', indicated the tenor of the contributions, asserting the EU relationship as part of a common European cultural identity, though even here few asserted a European Englishness. Poet Sean O'Brien was an exception: 'I love England; I also love elsewhere: why lose either, when you can have both?'[114] Only four out of 31 refrained from hostility towards Brexit: Robert Tombs presented global connections as more significant than the European; Jan Morris was ambivalent; D. J. Taylor and Simon Jenkins thought leaving might make little difference. The

ABOUT ENGLAND

Cartoon by Axel Scheffler, published on the front cover of the *Times Literary Supplement*, 3 June 2016.

cover of the issue showed an image by illustrator Axel Scheffler, born in Hamburg and who had lived in the UK since 1982. Scheffler's commentary reflected on his work with children's author Julia Donaldson, most famously *The Gruffalo* (1999), translated into almost all European languages and whose 2009 animated film was for Scheffler 'a truly European collaboration facilitated by British membership in the EU'. *The Gruffalo*, a story of fear and cunning, and of made-up monsters which turn out to be real ('Oh help! Oh no! It's a Gruffalo!'), becomes 'a symbol of unity as well as diversity in Europe'.[115] Scheffler could perhaps have forced a visual Euro-allegory out of *The Gruffalo*, but chose for his cover image the white cliffs of southern England, some litter washed up on the shore below. The national symbols of lion and unicorn converse as Britannia considers taking a sword to the EU cord, its stars stretching to distant French chalk: 'She is not going to do it, is she?' And three weeks later she did. Oh Help! Oh no!

Post-Brexit, photographer Simon Roberts would return to southern white cliffs to question England's future. The final photograph in his *Merrie Albion* collection, 'Beachy Head, Seven Sisters Country Park, East Sussex, 24 March 2017', was taken in the week Theresa

England Shaken

May signed Article 50, triggering the transition period to prepare for departure.[116] In 2018 Roberts restyled the image as a poster, 'Between the Acts', named after Virginia Woolf's novel, for display on billboards and bus shelters. People peer gingerly over the Seven Sisters cliffs in Sussex, with a Woolf quote below: 'They looked at the view; they looked at what they knew, to see if what they knew might perhaps be different today. Most days it was the same.'[117] Is the view an abyss? Is there something fascinating on the shore if only we could find a way to get down? Are we too near the edge? The titles of subsequent 'Between the Acts' works by Roberts, 'The Brexit Lexicon' and 'Folly Marches on', along with a 2020 zine 'The Brexshit Times', indicate Roberts's view, but the view from Seven Sisters is an open one. The shape of post-Brexit England remains an open question, determined in part by things far beyond the edges of England: the global economy, geopolitical conflict, climate change, the future EU. And, as

Simon Roberts, 'Between the Acts – Part 1, 2018', Artist poster on blue-back paper, various sizes.

noted above, there are also those things just beyond English edges, concerning the future of the UK. So a photograph looking out from the opposite edge of England, the Solway Firth in Cumbria, might in future look over the water to Scottish hills moving to become part of another state, and possibly rejoining the EU. The English orientation to Europe might be north as well as south, and the white cliffs iconography might suffer some erosion. Two thousand years ago Solway was the edge of Roman Europe, its series of Hadrianic fortlets facing supposed barbarianism beyond. The near future could see a strange reversal of view. May barbarism begin at home?

In the pre-referendum 2016 *Times Literary Supplement* Declan Kiberd brought a perspective on Irish identity to the English question:

> It's a long time since Bernard Shaw described England as the last, most fully penetrated of the British colonies – which could be why its people feel such ambivalence about the more recent transnational scheme. It's probably easier – as the Irish discovered – to accede enthusiastically to the European project when your people have had a chance to explore in an unfettered way over some decades the cultural values of their own nation.[118]

Fintan O'Toole similarly suggests that 'it is perfectly possible to see the re-emergence of England as the final stage in the dismantling of Empire,' with Brexit, despite being sometimes fuelled by suppositions of imperial glory, an episode in the conclusion of that story.[119] Perhaps the question of England and Europe should be revisited around 2040, by which time the world and Europe will be quite different, and the UK may be no more. *About England* may in retrospect offer one kind of starting point for reflection.

Save for the stars of the EU emblem on signs marking projects that received EU funding, there are few English monuments celebrating the period of UK membership. The celebrities of the 1975 referendum have passed, the Empire Stadium which once held 36,500 for the Common Market fanfare match has gone, and while there *is* such a thing as a Gruffalo, Scheffler's hopes for Britannic restraint were not realized. A few modest English EU sites remain, though, and it would be instructive to compile a guidebook to places in England celebrating membership in the years between 1973 and 2016.[120]

England Shaken

Tree circle for Europe, planted 1993, Dovecote Park, Beeston, Nottinghamshire.

Plaque on bandstand commemorating planting of tree circle for Europe, 1993, Dovecote Park, Beeston, Nottinghamshire.

To conclude this chapter, a first entry, a park in Beeston, a town on the edge of Nottingham, described earlier in this book. In Dovecote Park, on Dovecote Lane, a ring of trees circles the bandstand, product of a 1993 'Tree Circles for Europe' project.[121] Twelve trees represent the then twelve countries, before the major expansion. Twenty years after the Three joined the Six, there were the Twelve, and the council got its spades out: 'The trees (*Acer platanoides*) forming this circle, representing each of the twelve EC member countries, were planted in January 1993 by members of Broxtowe Borough Council's Technical and Leisure Services Committee.' One needed replanting and remains shorter, but eleven have topped the bandstand's height. What now for the Beeston tree circle? After nearly thirty years of decent growth, should one be reduced to a symbolic stump? Or uprooted and replanted near the playground, to see if it still flourishes? Or perhaps twelve tree preservation orders are needed to commemorate another time and allow a composite memory to grow.

PART II: ENGLISH PLACES

5
English and Suburban

Perec, Perrin

The BBC television situation comedy *The Fall and Rise of Reginald Perrin*, first broadcast in 1976, presented the anxieties of a middle-aged sales executive in suburban London played by Leonard Rossiter. Sunshine Desserts, Reggie's employer, had decided on a new line of 'Exotic Ices', and David Nobbs's script, and the novel preceding the series, evoke an absurdity of exoticism, of attempts, through novelty desserts, to at once domesticate the exotic and spice up the banal, with test flavours including pineapple, mango and lime. Market research indicated that '73 per cent of housewives in East Lancashire and 81 per cent in Hertfordshire had expressed interest in the concept of exotic ice creams.'[1] Exotic ices become part of a suburban story, which Perrin rejects, of which more later in this chapter. The comedy here is one of absurdity, diagnosing a consumer society as ludicrous, its self-belief preposterous.

In his 1973 essay 'Approaches to What?', Georges Perec asked:

> How should we take account of, question, describe what happens every day and recurs every day: the banal, the quotidian, the obvious, the common, the ordinary, the infra-ordinary, the background noise, the habitual? ...
> What's needed perhaps is finally to found our own anthropology, one that will speak about us, will look in ourselves for what so long we've been pillaging from others. Not the exotic any more, but the endotic.[2]

In Sunshine Desserts' ices project, the exotic becomes endotic. In 1976, the same year as *Perrin* broadcast, Perec published an 'Attempt at an

118

Inventory of the Liquid and Solid Foodstuffs Ingurgitated by Me in the Course of the Year Nineteen Hundred and Seventy-Four', including 'Three ice-creams, one green lemon sorbet, two guava sorbets, two pear sorbets'.[3] Perec's drily comic inventory of exotic foodstuffs formed part of his attention to the French 'infra-ordinary', and this chapter pursues, with *Perrin* and others, the English infra-ordinary through a location often deemed characteristically English, the suburb.

Endotic suburbia had become the demographically dominant English settlement type in the twentieth century, for some a place of monotonous sameness, for others one of subtle variations, eccentricities and even exoticism. The suburban infra-ordinary has become the sign of a 'middle England', its sociology stretching from upper working class to upper middle class, a middling place which in the late twentieth century became vital and marginal political ground, with the main parties staking claim to its virtues. 'Suburbia' and, indeed, 'middle class' are often held to be narrow, even restrictive terms, but both turn out capacious. To those occupying both categories, internal variations may be crucial to geographical and social identities. There is the suburb of the genteel upper middle class, dominated by substantial detached property, of the semi-detached-with-garden housing the lower middle class and of the semi-detached upper-working-class public housing. All are beyond the centre of town, and make for varied suburban social geographies. Distinctions are cut across in turn by architectural ages, signalled by housing design, garden size and shape, the patina of walls, the provision of parking. While those castigating the suburb have tended to project uniformity and conformism, those finding virtue there tend to assert variety, even individualism, regular patterns of living allowing expressions of personality. Suburbia has been an object of hostile or affectionate critique, and of loving documentary attention, whether through architecture, painting, comedy, politics, film, photography, planning or music, and this chapter moves across such source material.[4] As with pastoral, commentary and analysis shape the cultures of suburban landscape, suburban studies becoming suburban stories. Commentary becomes part of the very landscape it addresses, notably when broadcast (as in Perrin) via the television set. The new twentieth-century domestic focal point displayed images not just of a wider world but of its own surroundings, the endotic domestically endemic.

In *Forever England*, her study of femininity, literature and conservatism between the wars, Alison Light identified suburbia as a key locus for an interwar 'conservative modernity', nurturing and sheltering 'an Englishness at once less imperial and more inward-looking, more domestic and more private'. Light found a coping identity, dealing with and incorporating change, and with an excited caution concerning novelty, the new welcomed as long as the old wasn't shaken too much. The television set in the corner of the sitting room was the later twentieth-century extension of this conservative modernity, a new family hearth. For Light suburbia helped Englishness step back from expansive imperial masculinity, denoting 'a contradictory and determining tension in English social life . . . Janus-faced, it could simultaneously look backwards and forwards; it could accommodate the past in the new forms of the present.'[5] This 'new kind of Englishness' could "feminise" the idea of the nation as a whole, giving us a private and retiring people, pipe-smoking "little men" with their quietly competent partners, a nation of gardeners and housewives'.[6] Negotiations of the modern and conservative, shaped by preoccupations of gender and class, also characterize the later twentieth- and early twenty-first-century strains of suburban Englishness covered in this chapter. These cultural 'strains' denote a form of Englishness often marked by anxiety, seeking settlement and security and in consequence straining to work out its worries. Stereotypes of reticence and repression come out to play, with comfort sheltering violence and anger on a simmer. Sometimes things boil, as conveyed in the 1978 Siouxsie and the Banshees song 'Suburban Relapse', describing the chores of a suburban woman, where emotions held in check erupt and a string snaps, suburbia relapsing into something less controlled.

This chapter examines critiques and appreciations of suburbia in the 1960s and '70s, considers the properties of suburbia claimed across political parties, and analyses commentary on suburbia in art and photography, comedy and painting. The conjunctions of class and gender emphasized here are those of suburban masculinity, complementing the analysis of Light and others of earlier gendered conservative modernity, and examining the ways in which English men have been presented as, or have presented themselves as, shaped by suburban living. In her 2019 memoir *Another Planet*, on a Buckinghamshire suburban childhood, prompted by 'my realisation that the kind of suburbia I grew up in is endlessly fascinating to me', Tracey Thorn describes her earlier home: 'Brookmans Park was a village but not a village. Rural but not rural. A stop on the line, a space between the two landscapes that are both more highly rated – the city, and the countryside. A contingent, liminal, border territory. In-betweenland.'[7] This chapter pursues the ways in which, however in-between, suburbia has been configured as English settlement. Thorn emphasizes the female experience of growing up suburban in the 1960s and '70s, and the stress in this chapter on suburban masculinity may reflect my own experience a few years after Thorn, a couple of social notches down, on the edge of a provincial city with farming country nearby. There is also a parallel of generational moves from urban working class to suburban middle class to next-generation first in the family to tertiary education. The resultant intergenerational geographies will be returned to in conclusion.

Suburban Anatomy

In the late 1960s and early 1970s suburbia became one focus for stories about England, with books, films and sociological analysis anatomizing the suburb as a typical English present. In *Dunroamin: The Suburban Semi and Its Enemies*, Paul Oliver, Ian Davis and Ian Bentley note how from the interwar period the sunrise became a frequent motif in suburban exterior and interior design: 'The sun of the suburbs was essentially a *rising* one, signifying a sunny future, the dawn of a new day.'[8]

In 1972 the design varieties of suburban sun were captured in Brian Rice and Tony Evans's *The English Sunrise*. The book showed 76 photographs documenting sunshine in suburbia, one per page in isolation, and with a caption list at the end. Evans was the photographer, known for his commercial still-life work, and Rice was a printmaker whose abstract work in the late 1960s included Art Deco sunrise patterns. Issued in paperback at 95p in the new money, here was a relatively cheap, high-quality tracing of an image. The optimism of the sunrise is suspended in still-life, made curious, in such varied objects as chairs, radios, car doors, tea cosies and wafers. While the domestic objects featured might be in any home from town house to cottage, the outdoor scenes, and elements of the domestic setting, make this a suburban work, predominantly in the southern half of England. Ordinary spots lift beyond the humdrum through a decorative sunrise: two driveway gates with a black-and-white sunrise each, a blue-painted sunrise on a gable above a bay window, a stained-glass sunrise in the upper parts of front windows in Nantwich and Waltham Cross. Near Ventnor,

Gate at Ventnor, Isle of Wight, from Brian Rice and Tony Evans, *The English Sunrise* (1972), photograph by Tony Evans.

Isle of Wight, a gate to a garden path has a green sunrise in its upper section, with the house name above: 'The Bungalow'.[9] As a collection, *The English Sunrise* suggests that, as you go around England, you might look out for such patterns, English life marked by a designed domestication of the elements. The infra-ordinary is enchanted, and enchantment brought home.

Rice and Evans's new suburban observations went alongside other early 1970s analytical works. Alan Jackson's 1973 account of suburban development in *Semi-Detached London, 1900–1939* gave an almanac of house types, train, tram and bus routes and specimen districts: 'Southern Electric Stoneleigh', 'Edgware, the Underground Suburb'. While Jackson's book was framed with laments for the lack of 'positive planning' and the 'shallowness of local allegiance' in 'the outer suburban belt', the degree of documentary detail makes *Semi-Detached London* a work of appreciation rather than condemnation.[10] Analysis also came from suburban commentators of longer standing. J. M.

Richards's 1946 *The Castles on the Ground*, subtitled 'The Anatomy of Suburbia', was reissued with a new introduction in 1973, and revised illustrations by John Piper. Richards and Piper, as established architectural and visual commentators on English landscape, urban and rural, extended what in 1946 had been a relatively generous view of suburban design in a story of suburbia as an environment of 'participation': 'An environment only matures when the people inhabiting it have visibly influenced it by the way they have used it.'[11] Suburbia becomes a site whose character is less planned in advance than accidental, 'an accumulation of happy accidents'. The suburb is thus 'neither the town spread thin nor the country built close, but a quite different type of development with its own inimitable characteristics', with the 'essence of suburbia' a 'closed-in, self-contained style'. Post-war change had only heightened the importance of suburbia, which 'as a consequence of greater mobility, is increasingly becoming the way of life of the typical Englishman'. For Richards the key change since the 1946 edition was expanded car ownership, 'a new and disruptive element' in the distinctive suburban environment, though not 'wholly alien to the suburban ethos', given its basis in mobility: 'The suburb may still have to adjust itself to the car-owning habit, but the motor-car has already been captured and tamed by it.'[12] The car had become the focus of the suburban weekend, as a means of excursion and as an object for washing and maintenance. Car-based suburbia had, however, become 'less spontaneous' and more of 'a planned process', developing under planning controls where architecturally 'the conscious aim is now unity instead of variety.'[13] Richards criticized new suburbs on the urban periphery as not yet having acquired 'form or identity', with a 'brittle' housing design and 'wasteful' use of space: 'But we must not be deceived; time and the growth of vegetation will work wonders.'[14]

Piper's illustrations reflected Richards's hopes and anxieties over car suburbia. Best known as a painter of houses grand and minor, stained glass and church towers, Piper found himself picturing the modern suburban street. Of the eight lithographs of 1946, only three remained in the eight illustrations of 1973, all in a lighter key, the enigmatic shadows of earlier images giving way to a starker 1970s modernity.[15] The five new illustrations recognized new suburban forms: cars parked and passing, newly built semis and detacheds. In one image, a pollarded older tree and a newer tree coming into leaf foreground a row of new builds. A hanging basket silhouetted on

Untitled illustration by John Piper for J. M. Richards, *The Castles on the Ground* (1973), facing p. 24.

a plain porch completes the foliage, and a car exits left.[16] It is as if Piper had found himself lurking on the verge across from Bob's new house in the sitcom *Whatever Happened to the Likely Lads?*, aired in 1973–4, where childhood friends Bob and Terry, introduced to a mass audience in *The Likely Lads* (1964–6), follow divergent social trajectories, though they never escape their mutual affection. Terry (played by James Bolam) is stuck in old ways, while Bob (Rodney Bewes) is married and suburban, a new-build man on the Elm Lodge housing estate. If the joke there is on Bob's upward mobility, *The Castles on the Ground* sees Piper on a downward social excursion, stretching his style to make sense of a new world.

Richards and Piper projected sensibilities from earlier decades on to 1970s suburban England, and in that sense echoed another significant and popular suburban commentator, John Betjeman. Fondness for suburbia had not always characterized Betjeman, especially for less well-appointed places, his semi-jocular 1937 poem 'Slough' envisaging 'friendly bombs' falling on consumer-oriented lower-middle-class development.[17] Betjeman's 1952 essay 'Love Is Dead' had similarly lamented commonplace uniformity: 'The suburbs which once seemed to me so lovely with their freckled tennis girls and their youths in club blazers have spread so far in the wake of the motor car that there is little but suburb left. We are told that we live in the age of the common man. He would be better described as the suburban man.'[18] By the 1970s, however, Betjeman's prevalent tone and public persona had softened. A popular poet, especially after the publication of his *Collected Poems* in 1958, and from 1972 Poet Laureate, Betjeman also became a popular broadcaster and architectural campaigner, who was fond of, campaigned for and personified idiosyncracy, as discussed further in Chapter Seven. From 1974 Betjeman also recorded a series of LPS for the Charisma label, his poems, often far from light-hearted, set to music by Jim Parker in settings ranging from tea dance to jazz and ragtime. 'The Licorice Fields at Pontefract', on the 1974 *Late Flowering Love* album, sees Betjeman with backing akin to the Velvet Underground. That Betjeman's voice might sell records reflected his broadcasting fame.

In 1973 Betjeman presented a televisual homage to London suburbia, *Metro-land*. The film journeyed along the Metropolitan railway outwards from Baker Street, attending to the underground and overground's historic role in urban expansion. Andy Medhurst describes *Metro-land*, filmed in 1972 and first screened on 26 February 1973 at 10.10 p.m. on BBC 2, as 'an exercise in enthralled camp', Betjeman achieving an 'amused toleration'.[19] *Metro-land* calls at St John's Wood, Neasden, Wembley, Harrow-on-the-Hill, Pinner, Moor Park, Croxley, Chorleywood and Amersham, and heads beyond the current terminus to Quainton Road and the rural halt of Verney Junction, where at the end of the programme Betjeman expresses relief that the houses never got that far: 'Grass triumphs. And I must say I'm rather glad.'[20] Skylark and sheep track the closing credits, but en route viewers are offered joys of suburbia: club gatherings, summer fairs, leisure pursuits and a variegated landscape of commonality and exclusivity. Serious architectural history is there, Betjeman pausing over Norman Shaw and Charles Voysey designing prototypical suburban dwellings, but the amused side of Betjeman's comic-serious persona dominates. *Metro-land* displays suburban difference through Betjeman's anthropological eye, showing another country in which viewers might just happen to live. The film also highlights differences within the suburb, notably of class. Thus the security guard at the private estate of Moor Park is shown exercising a pompous right to turn back any drivers lacking legitimate reason to visit; Bevis Hillier notes that the young woman turned away was a film assistant instructed by Betjeman and director Eddie Mirzoeff, the guard blithely unaware of the set-up.[21]

Elsewhere the suburb is inclusive, a site of community as well as privacy, Betjeman alighting on fairs and fêtes, and the invention of suburban tradition registered at 'The Croxley Green Revels – A tradition that stretches back to 1952'. A Revels queen is crowned with some comedy, a ceremony presented as at once humorous and profound for those taking part, with Royal Courts, parchment and speeches. The teenage queen announces, 'In this very lovely corner of England, of which we are so proud', and giggles.[22] The inclusivity of Pinner fair, where people mill high street stalls on 'the Feast Day of the Parish Saint, a medieval fair in Metro-land', also shows the single break in the exclusive whiteness of the film, as one Black face is shown in close-up, almost pointedly as an exceptional presence, a boy walking alone in the crowd.[23] If some differences are yet to be wholly accommodated, eccentricities are easily welcomed. Betjeman delights in the ladies' Byron Luncheon Club meeting at Grim's Dyke, the former Harrow house of W. S. Gilbert, and admires the Croxley Green bagpipe band, fully kilted. Carnival floats pass by with sombreroed ladies, all this in London's ordinary fringe. In Chorleywood, Len Rawle has installed the Wurlitzer organ from the Empire Cinema, Leicester Square, and downstairs in his modest brick detached house gives Betjeman a demo, ending with mock-steam-train puffs: 'O happy indoor life in Chorleywood where strangest dreams of all are realised.'[24]

If the film's narrative is tube-train-driven, with speeded-up sequences along the rails between the stops, a new car-based suburban normality also appears, most notably in a sequence from which Betjeman is absent on film and was absent for the filming. In retrospect this perhaps most precisely marks the suburban England of 1972, as Betjeman's narrative voice states: 'Along the serried avenues of Harrow's garden villages, households rise and shine and settle down to the Sunday morning rhythm.' A one-minute sequence, filmed on 25 June 1972, shows lawn-mowing and car-washing, and over the images comes a radio soundtrack from the day of filming, the Sunday lunchtime *Family Favourites* programme, whose remit was in part to connect, via requests, families across the former white British empire, notably in Australia and New Zealand. English culture, 1972, is captured as, over pictures of a postcolonial suburban Sunday, requests read by Australian ABC co-host Rod McNeil connect English families at home and those migrated down under, to the tune of The Osmonds' 'Down by the Lazy River'.[25] U.S. pop plays as a young woman washes the car, water streaming the windscreen and suds applied. Suburban English life proceeds in its new-old global ways.

At Chorleywood, as the film shows a train passing and horse riders galloping from under the bridge across a common, Betjeman states: 'This is, I think, essential Metro-land. Much trouble has been taken to preserve the country quality here.'[26] It is instructive to set Metro-land alongside academic commentary of the time, with Betjeman here echoing the title of an influential piece of social geography, Ray Pahl's 1965 *Urbs in rure: The Metropolitan Fringe in Hertfordshire*.[27] On London's fringe, as in Betjeman's Metro-land, new forms of living are found, in Pahl's case mostly to the northeast of Metro-land's track, though with some overlap south of Watford; Chorleywood is on the southwest edge of Hertfordshire. *Urbs in rure* gives a social analysis of how Hertfordshire villages as well as suburban towns were becoming part of a metropolitan system in a mobile society. Pahl described postwar 'centrifugal movements', with migration to the 'Inner Country Ring' and 'Outer Country Ring'.[28] A new kind of rural as well as urban and suburban England was emerging, its 'structure held together by the motor car'.[29] Pahl studied three parishes in detail, Hexton (still a paternalist estate village) and Tewin and Watton, with significant private and public housing development respectively post-war. Pahl pursued 'the social reality of what might be a new type of social environment', household interviews conveying a new suburban country, with social and spatial segregation between established populations and mobile middle-class commuters.[30] New private developments attracted the latter; in Tewin Wood, 'at the time of the survey, the woods echoed to the sound of Tudor beaming being hammered into place.'[31] Pahl had described Tewin under the pseudonym 'Dormersdell' in *New Society* in February 1964, with dormitory village commuting marking a change from a hierarchical settlement to a 'two class village'. Dormersdell was a place 90 per cent middle-class, with 60 per cent of those in 'the Wood', a woodland area beyond the village centre: 'The community was not only polarized spatially but also socially.' A thirty-year-old mechanical engineer outlined the new normality in the Wood, with women fashioning new community through club activities: 'It's a self-contained community; the wives form their own coffee groups, wine-making groups and so on. It's only 35 minutes from town yet it's quite secluded. We have the best of all worlds.' Pahl concludes: 'National class divisions come into sharper focus in the local setting of such metropolitan villages as Dormersdell.'[32]

If the sociological originality of Pahl's thesis lay especially in its village work, *Urbs in rure* also produced urban statistics for Metroland. Chorleywood, Betjeman's 'essential Metro-land', fell into that group of Hertfordshire towns whose population had grown between 1951 and 1961 by 1,000–2,999 people, with 87.9 per cent of the increase in Chorleywood due to migration.[33] The Chorleywood urban district had, in terms of rateable value, 'a remarkable proportion of its domestic properties assessed at the top of the scale'.[34] New forms of mobility, combined with the new planning system, including the Green Belt, were making a distinct form of metropolitan fringe: 'The distinctiveness of the British fringe may be attributed to the effects of Town and Country Planning Development Control – a fundamental cultural variable!'[35] Pahl suggested 'considering the fringe in terms of itself and not solely in relation to the central city', with the development of 'what might be described as a "fringe city"' since 1950.[36] If Betjeman's radial narrative befitted a programme geared around Metro-land's historic development (as indeed Pahl's second chapter discussed Hertfordshire's rail-shaped past), *Urbs in rure* presented a new cross-cutting metropolis, twenty years before the M25 would provide a connecting braid for London suburbia.[37]

Political Properties

In the same year as *Metro-land*, Nicholas Taylor's *The Village in the City* (1973) presented suburbia as typical modern living, in contrast to architectural Brutalism and the high-rise: 'most of us in the industrially developed countries live in suburbs, and enjoy it; and for Englishmen in particular there is nothing new in this.'[38] Taylor projected the Englishness of suburbia back, with Brutalism's ancestor the formal lines of Roman planning and suburbia carrying a Saxon heritage of functional vernacular settlement, a 'gently accommodating humanism'.

The 'basic Saxon dwelling', comfortable, adaptable and extendable, was the ancestor of the cottage and the semi-detached. Taylor suggested that, while contemporary planning authorities might overlook this, advertisers spotted the appeal:

> The ability to alter and adapt one's own home to one's own desires is a fundamental freedom for Englishmen and woe betide the council committee who ignore it . . . to the Englishman, in his colder climate, the cosy pitched roof is a sacrament of family love – and the Abbey National Building Society's admen knew what they were doing when they drew that young couple holding a pitched roof over their heads as an umbrella.[39]

Taylor, a Labour councillor in the London borough of Lewisham, called for social attention less to inner-urban communities or outer-urban estates than to 'typically mixed and multifarious . . . suburban villages', and the '"sense of identity" rather than the higher emotional and moral intensity of the word "community"' found therein.[40] The urban villages Taylor looked to were not well-known 'glamorous villages' (Hampstead, Dulwich) but 'ordinary mundane suburbs'. A corresponding shift was required from the 'preservation of the special to conservation of the pleasant'.[41]

Taylor noted his experience of political canvassing as raising his awareness of the individuality of the suburban dwelling, but such sentiments could pull across the political spectrum. Suburbia, and its relationship to local authority planning, would become a key political battleground in the 1970s and '80s, and the political variance of settlement planning, suburban or otherwise, is illustrated by *New Society*'s March 1969 special feature 'Non-Plan: An Experiment in Freedom'. *New Society* editor Paul Barker, who would commission Taylor's *Village in the City* and who in 2009 produced his own book hymning *The Freedoms of Suburbia*, brought together authors wary of over-regulatory planning. Peter Hall, planner, geographer and author of the 1963 *London 2000*, and architectural writers Cedric Price and Reyner Banham were invited 'to take the plunge into heterogeneity'.[42] Each took a part of the English countryside and suggested what non-planning might produce. Hall considered 'Lawrence Country', Banham 'Constable Country' and Price 'Montagu Country', though in each case the areas covered – respectively the eastern edge of the Peak

District, north Essex and Hertfordshire around Stansted and Royston, and the hinterland of the Solent – stretched the cultural references. Hall envisaged a car-based future region of mobile 'life in far-flung suburbs, close to open countryside', the M1 as a regional connection. Prospective developments included 'New Dukeries Fringe Villages' (pit closures were not anticipated), a state Countryside Commission operating country parks, a 'Forest Fun Park' (Center Parcs would eventually come to Sherwood), and 'Motorway Fun Centres' (yet to materialize).[43] 'Non-Plan' deliberately posed awkward questions of environment and class, Banham suggesting: 'taking the planning lid off would produce a situation traumatic enough among the amenity lobbies to make their real motivations visible; to show how much is genuine concern for environmental and cultural values, how much merely class panic.'[44]

'Non-Plan' brought *New Society*, as a journal read by the professional class, lively correspondence, and future political fault lines came into view. Planners unsurprisingly wrote to criticize 'Non-Plan', highlighting that freedom from planning would simply defer to the power of money. Peter Davies commented: 'If all are to display choice, each must command roughly equal resources.'[45] For Jennifer Grist, 'In a society without curbs, the strongest and richest will always get what they want', while Duncan Macintosh of the Bartlett School of Architecture at University College London suggested: 'Non-planning would merely transfer power from the planners to the builder.'[46] Defences of planning were countered, however, by a figure who would be influential in the development of Thatcherism, and for whom 'Non-Plan' might signal a positively marketized landscape. Alfred Sherman, writing from the Urban Research Bureau, supported 'Non-Plan', presenting Macintosh's letter as defending 'what claims to be town planning but is in fact the attempt to impose socialistic values on a society which rejects them'. Sherman presented a 'socialist fallacy':

> if free choice is fettered by income inequalities, therefore planners must substitute their choices for that of the market. But the real corollary of the first assumption is that income inequality should be dealt with. Planners' intervention has the contrary effect of further reducing choice by the less affluent as well as the average and more affluent.[47]

Suburbia was a powerfully symbolic political constituency, with parties claiming Middle England as vote territory and suburban areas key electoral battlegrounds. Particular constituencies were upheld as indicative and emblematic of political trends: Basildon from 1979, when David Amess took the New Town seat, which he held in 1992 to signal John Major's unexpected victory; Worcester in 1997, when Labour under Tony Blair went in search of 'Middle England' voters (a mythic 'Worcester Woman') and won Worcester for the first time. Suburban home ownership and its private unplanned freedoms have been most prominently associated with Conservatism, and shaped key political campaigns under both Thatcher and Major. Both leaders were happy to be associated with suburban values in an attempt to shift the Tory image away from landed and City wealth, and to present modest capital as a starting point for individual security.[48] Thatcher's flagship 'Right to Buy' policy, which allowed council tenants to purchase their houses from local authorities, tapped into a range of political emotions, in the process shifting English electoral geography.

The term 'property-owning democracy' was promoted by Thatcher from her first leader's speech to the Conservative Party conference in 1975, setting herself as following 'in the footsteps of Anthony Eden, who set us the goal of a property-owning democracy – a goal we still pursue today'. Home ownership was a site of aspiration, freedom and enfranchisement, the mortgage a badge of identity. In 1979, 54 per cent of UK dwellings were owner-occupied, but in 1990 it was 67 per cent, with half the increase a result of right-to-buy schemes. Matthew Francis notes that more than 2.5 million homes eventually passed from public to private tenure, the Conservative Party 1983 manifesto claiming 'Right to Buy' as 'the biggest single step towards a home-owning democracy ever taken'.[49] To celebrate the policy, Thatcher was pictured visiting a purchased house at Harold Hill, near Romford, in August 1980, handing over the deeds to the family. Privately purchased council houses were presented as becoming homes rather than housing, and the differences in interior and exterior decoration which followed ownership were seen as signs, for Thatcher and her allies, of pioneering action breaking up local authority territory. Thatcher herself promoted, and in her early period as party leader sought to personify, the virtues of good housekeeping, and extended the language of domestic order to national economic management.

As part of the English Conservative culture of property, it is instructive to set 'Right to Buy' in counterpoint to the National Trust's Country Houses Scheme, in operation from the 1930s. There a charity took over a house from private owners but allowed them to remain living in part of the property, although their home was no longer their house. Right to Buy conversely made tenants owners, confirmed their existing home as their house, asserting property values lower down the social scale. The two schemes signal two strands of Toryism, respectively in decline and ascent in the mid-twentieth century, with the Thatcher governments from 1979 shifting the emphasis from the landed to the suburban. Right to Buy, and Conservative policy in the 1980s, were not, however, without paradox. The scheme, with its sense of both entitlement and responsibility, tapped into a distinction between the responsible property owner and the less well-rooted renter, whether in public or private property. A later Thatcher policy would, however, twist the distinction, the community charge (or poll tax) demanding that everyone should contribute to council funding, with property-owning ratepayers not the only ones 'paying their way'. The poll tax would thus effectively abolish one of Conservatism's most iconic figures, the ratepayer, with all its respectable associations.

Suburban Toryism, and Tory suburbanism, helped John Major succeed Thatcher as prime minister, Major positioning his suburban background as connecting to party members and prospective voters in a manner different from his more patrician rivals Douglas Hurd and Michael Heseltine. In his 1999 autobiography Major described the suburban culture of his south London childhood in Worcester Park, the family home a bungalow with garden, his father a maker of garden ornaments including gnomes.[50] Ordinariness became a political asset in the 1992 general election campaign, where Major's speaking from a soapbox contrasted with increasingly slick Labour campaigns. A passion for cricket, including Surrey county cricket, cemented Major's English persona, as did a preoccupation with the frustrations of motoring, Major establishing a 'Cones Hotline' whereby motorists could report traffic cones not promptly cleared. Mockery could follow, notably on the satirical puppet show *Spitting Image*, where Major was shown at home enjoying garden peas for dinner, a Mr Pooter accidentally become premier. Long-standing putdowns of suburbia as ordinary, petty and overly modest were wheeled out, but the putdowns were perhaps too easy, and appeared smug in their own right.

One of Major's most notable evocations of suburban England itself turns out to have a cultural and political complexity. In a speech to the Conservative Group for Europe on 22 April 1993, in the context of bitter argument within the party over the Maastricht Treaty, Major argued that Britain would remain 'distinctive and unique' within Europe:

> Fifty years from now Britain will still be the country of long shadows on county grounds, warm beer, invincible green suburbs, dog lovers and pools fillers and – as George Orwell said – 'old maids bicycling to Holy Communion through the morning mist' and, if we get our way, Shakespeare still read even in school. Britain will survive unamendable in all essentials.[51]

This was a very English Britain, but also, as Major acknowledged in his citation, not solely a Conservative one. Major's words were presented by critics as a sign of Tory fantasy, of dwelling in a world past, but the components alluded to – cricket, beer, pools fillers (football rather than swimming) – were demotic and hardly arcane. The old maids presented a peculiar image, but were taken almost verbatim from 'England Your England', part 1 of George Orwell's 1941 essay 'The Lion and the Unicorn: Socialism and the English Genius', which evoked 'the old maids biking to Holy Communion through the mists of the autumn mornings'.[52] Orwell sought an Englishness to bolster a socialism which for him was overlooking, and looking down on, national culture. 'The Lion and the Unicorn' did not mention dogs, football pools or county grounds, but Orwell did note that 'the beer is bitterer' in England and anticipated Major in evoking 'the *privateness* of English life', geared around hobbies such as darts, crosswords and stamp-collecting: 'All the culture that is most truly native centres round things which even when they are communal are not official.'[53] Orwell's old maids also, however, cycled amid images of industry and poverty:

> The clatter of clogs in the Lancashire mill towns, the to-and-fro of lorries on the Great North Road, the queues outside the Labour Exchanges, the rattle of pin-tables in the Soho pubs, the old maids biking to Holy Communion through the mists of the autumn mornings – all these are not only fragments,

but *characteristic* fragments, of the English scene. How can one make a pattern out of this muddle?[54]

Orwell's 'The Lion and the Unicorn' also noted a sensibility that Right to Buy would tap into:

The modern council house, with its bathroom and electric light, is smaller than the stockbroker's villa, but it is recognisably the same kind of house, which the farm labourer's cottage is not. A person who has grown up in a council housing estate is likely to be – indeed, visibly is – more middle-class in outlook than a person who has grown up in a slum.[55]

For Major, as for Thatcher, suburbia denoted an England escaping or secure from the inner-urban or the Labour Exchange. The suburb was a stepping stone to material advancement. The calculation of late twentieth- and early twenty-first-century political parties, Conservative and Labour, was that suburbia was a stepping stone to power.

A Reggie and Two Martins

Analytical accounts, political campaigns and social commentary respond alike to debates on English society from the 1970s: a questioning of those nuclear family structures seen to be personified and sustained by suburbia, the impact of mass car ownership on modern selves and environments, critiques of modern architecture and planning, and a revaluing of the suburban house. Suburbia is variously critiqued, admired, mocked, re-evaluated. Later in this section photographic commentary is considered in a discussion of the particular suburban urbanism nurtured in Milton Keynes, but the starting point is comedy. Some of the most significant suburban reflections have come, as with *Metro-land*, via the very medium deemed to dominate suburban living, the television.[56] A period of mass television ownership and record viewing figures coincided with the projection of satires of suburbia into the suburban home. Watch this and be amused at your condition, or at least the condition of those you might know. Two situation comedies convey the mainstream of suburban amusements in the 1970s and '80s.

The exotic ices project mentioned at the start of this chapter was a minor plotline in *The Fall and Rise of Reginald Perrin*, aired in three series on BBC 1 between 1976 and 1979. At a time of three television channels, ratings could exceed 10 million, with viewers from adolescent upward. David Nobbs's book *The Death of Reginald Perrin* (1975) had preceded the programme, and was reprinted and retitled after its TV success, probably the first grown-up book I ever bought, at the age of twelve. Leonard Rossiter, playing Perrin, was familiar to mainstream television comedy audiences from the ITV sitcom *Rising Damp* (1974–8) as the frustrated landlord Rigsby. In Perrin, Rossiter's talent for anxiety moved up the social scale. The programme dramatized an attempted male escape from suburban constraint, tension within an executive existence, a fake suicide and a return to a different life with the same associates. In the second series Perrin achieves absurd commercial success as the founder of a 'Grot' retail chain selling goods which he is proud are useless, and later founds an altruistic commune. The cast remains broadly the same throughout, but the first series is the most common retrospective reference point. There the comedy is sharpest, most pointed, the situation of the comedy constraint and tension, not subversion and liberation. As the joys of Perrin's life increase, the comic returns diminish.

Reggie's fake suicide involves clothes left on a Dorset beach, the title sequence showing him swimming out to sea at West Bay, only to turn and regain land. Catchphrases make memorable gags from the repetitive nature of office life, the repeat gestures of the commute, the train always eleven minutes late. Each episode commences with Reggie leaving home, saying goodbye to his wife, Elizabeth, and walking the quiet 'Poets' Estate' to the station. The route is described on the opening page of David Nobbs's original novel, and the corresponding television sequence was filmed in Ealing:

> Swifts were chasing each other high up in the blue June sky. Rover 2000s were sliding smoothly down the drives of mock Tudor and mock Georgian houses, and there were white gates across the roads on all the entrances to the estate.
>
> Reggie walked down Coleridge Close, turned right into Tennyson Avenue, then left into Wordsworth Drive, and down the snicket into Station Road.[57]

Here is closely observed suburbia; the natural world pursuing its routine freedoms up above, cars of reliable distinction and with architecture newish yet traditional, though the 'mock' indicates an identity less sure of itself than it might appear. Gates mark the territory, though these are not present in the television version, signs of exclusivity excluded from an everyman story. Romantic poets lend their names to sites of routine and conformity, but the figure walking from the Close is in his own way a romantic rebel, making a poetry of the absurd from projections of flan sales. Andy Medhurst comments: 'Perrin causes chaos by shaking the certainties on which suburbia depends. He becomes unpredictable, capricious, selfish, irresponsible, pleasure-seeking, truth-telling – each of which inverts a cardinal suburban virtue.'[58]

Invert Medhurst's list (with the exception of the last) and you have Martin Bryce, lead character of the BBC sitcom *Ever Decreasing Circles* (1984–9), or at least Martin's sense of himself: predictable, reliable, community-oriented, enjoying life (but only if things are just right) and honest. *Ever Decreasing Circles* was written by John Esmonde and Bob Larbey, also responsible for *The Good Life* (1975–8); Richard Briers starred in both.[59] The series is set in Surrey, with Bryce working in stock control for Mole Valley Valves, the Mole Valley a district around Dorking and Leatherhead. This is generic southern Home Counties suburbia, though the genre's internal social differentiation is evident. If *Perrin* and indeed *The Good Life* were set in substantial detached properties of early twentieth-century suburbia, *Ever Decreasing Circles* is middle-middle-class new build, a cul-de-sac known only as The Close. The term is fondly enunciated by Martin in the same proud manner as that in which the snobbish Margot in *The Good Life* defends an exclusive 'Avenue', though here the pride is more modest and more desperate. When in the final episode the prospect of moving to Oswestry following work relocation horrifies Martin, he invites Ann to look out of the window. Her comment that in effect there are similar closes everywhere, Oswestry included, prompts Martin to assert The Close's uniqueness in the genre, unique from the many activities he has overseen there. The Close is 'a bit of England', a normality of distinction, an exemplar which others might follow. Heightened English normality is for Martin both refuge and aspiration. In the same concluding episode Martin comments to the neighbour Howard, apropos of trivial work disputes: 'our Close is where England lives.' Martin's occasional resort across the series to an English frame of reference indicates that, for him, the story he inhabits is indeed about England.

In the final episode Martin also takes Howard to the cricket ground in a diversion from their final walk home together from the station, a gesture of emotional bonding, though Howard is keener to get home for his tea. Episode 2 of series 2 involved a cricket match, filmed at Wisborough Green, West Sussex. Martin is team captain, a source of fulfilment and frustration, and the cricket ground is hallowed space. Before the game, Martin and Howard converse on the square:

Martin: You see, that could only happen in England.
Howard: Good old England.
Martin: Yes, good old England, Howard.

In isolation this might appear crude cricket patriotism, a variant of Henry Newbolt's 1892 poem of imperial manliness 'Vitai Lampada' ('Play up, play up and play the game') for the 1980s, but it is prompted by Howard's memory of the day he proposed to his wife, Hilda, on the first day of a season. Howard had got into double figures, a rare eleven, and emboldened, proposed. Hilda burst into tears and hid in the ice cream van, but she did say yes, as the shock of surfaced emotion eased. This was Howard's good old England, not quite Newbolt.

For Andy Medhurst, writing in 1997, *Ever Decreasing Circles* was 'the most sustained attack British sitcom has yet made on traditional suburban values', with the suburbs shown as 'the site of petty status-seeking, unimaginative repetition and a ferocious hostility to difference'.[60] This may be so, yet the viewer is shown endearing qualities in all the characters, and even Martin becomes one of those comic monsters whose appeal resides from elements of sympathy, even empathy. Martin is married to Ann (played by Penelope Wilton), without children, although one is due at the end of the fourth (and final) series. Both are intelligent in their ways, with neuroses evident in Martin and hinted at in Ann. At various points the question is begged as to what keeps them together, the presumed answer being love, but their peculiar settlement is disturbed by new neighbour Paul Ryman, played by Peter Egan. Paul is divorced, suave, with a hair salon in the town, who accomplishes whatever he needs to do with ease, without any need for the systems and plans that structure Martin's slightest initiative. The cricket match episode involves Paul being brilliant and saving the day, only for Martin to be accused by his opposing captain of fielding a ringer, against the spirit of the game. Paul has won the game, but Martin still cannot win. The mutual attraction of Ann and Paul helps drive a sitcom which at times becomes darkly comic drama. The other regular characters are neighbours Howard and Hilda Hughes, comically dressing in matching outfits, kindly set in their ways, but whose conformism is happily tolerant of Paul's difference. Howard and Hilda nuance any presumed opposition of outgoing openness and introvert intolerance.

As with Rossiter as Perrin, the casting of Briers was key to the show's quality and popularity. A popular television sitcom performer since the early 1960s, Briers came to fame through *The Good Life*, such that viewers of *Ever Decreasing Circles* could connect but also contrast the two shows, placing Martin Bryce within an inter-series casting of the suburban male. In 1976 Briers had also starred in a television adaptation of Stephen Potter's comic *One-Upmanship* books, satires on middle-class mores and spoof guides to getting ahead in work and leisure life.[61] As Potter in *One-Upmanship*, Briers in effect anatomized the lives he played elsewhere. Like Rossiter, Briers brought a fast, nervous acting style to the roles of Good and Bryce, the antithesis of the barely-appearing-to-act-at-all style of, say, Terry Scott in *Terry and June* (1979–87). Actorly pace marks out Martin from Ann, Paul, Howard and Hilda, signals his tics.

Carefully chosen suburban nomenclature can say a lot. Within The Close, Martin names the house 'Brooksmead', the name hanging over the front door, an allusion to a pre-development land of fields and streams. The present is, however, certainly suburban; when in the final episode Paul turns up at the door in historic farmhand gear to take them to the 'village fête' Martin retorts: 'This is not a village.' *Ever Decreasing Circles* is a comedy of the home rather than the office, but Martin's company's name, Mole Valley Valves, is also emblematically chosen. Mole Valley indicates a topography of suburbia, that however new-build and town-edge, there is a land holding the houses up. Martin carries a certain mole-like quality, like Mole in *The Wind in the Willows* proud of his domestic space, and more attentive to it, in however petty a fashion, than many male sitcom characters. Hunkered in his home office, Martin organizes community clubs and associations, printing off agendas from his hand-cranked bander. That the life depicted in the series depends on a salary from Mole Valley Valves nicely indicates a hydraulic theme, Martin a test case in the hydraulics of emotion. Blockage, release, flow and eruption mark the comedy. Martin tries to make middle England run smooth, but anxiety flows from rigid adherence to the norms he upholds.

For a mid-1980s mainstream programme, *Ever Decreasing Circles* curiously lacks a comedy of consumption. At a time when consumer goods and their acquisition and display were a central theme of cultural commentary, Martin and Ann, while comfortable, give little attention to dress and decor, gadgetry and display, and Paul may simply not need to show off. Elsewhere, though, the emphasis on middle-class identity as defined by modes of consumption became prominent in the 1980s, notably in the work of another Surrey Martin, the photographer Martin Parr, whose 1989 collection *The Cost of Living* pictured the English middle class at leisure.[62] Parr grew up in middle-class suburban Surrey, his watching habits shaped by an ornithologist father and a trainspotting habit, and by visits to a photographer grandfather in Yorkshire, before studying photography at Manchester Polytechnic. Parr's earlier work, on working-class life, included documentary studies of leisure with *The Last Resort* (1986) showing New Brighton on the Wirral. *The Cost of Living*, like *The Last Resort*, was notable for being in colour, and Parr's later work, including the 2000 *Think of England* collection, would extend this in often garish form.[63] *The Cost of Living*, shot following Parr's 1987 move to Clifton, a genteel area of Bristol, offers a photographic equivalent of Pierre Bourdieu's contemporaneous sociological analysis of consumption as a site of cultural capital and a marker of class distinction. Bourdieu's 1979 book *Distinction: A Social Critique of the Judgement of Taste* appeared in English translation in 1984, and informed cultural commentary on new forms of middle-class identity.[64] Colour photography of the middle class became Parr's own mark of distinction.

Parr described *The Cost of Living* as concerned with 'the comfortable classes', but it covered diverse middle-class terrain.[65] Some photographs show the upper middle class, distinctly posh sites and occasions, including public schools and horse trials, where Parr conveys an intergenerational sense of superior entitlement. There is political Conservatism at Tory balls, fêtes and parties, and the superior gestures of hair tossed or lips pursed. Elsewhere, though, Parr shows more middling suburban sites of leisure and consumption, some long-standing, such as craft shows, but others novel to the times: the chains of Ikea and Majestic Wine, artificial ski slopes, aerobics classes, barbecues, the National Childbirth Trust. A new England takes shape, though one which is happy to take in old English places and practices. A dozen images in effect form a landscape and heritage sequence, with ordinary people shown at leisure: at Stonehenge and Longleat, in the Peak District, at the National Trust village of Lacock. Parr indicates stresses and barriers, with Lacock crowded, Peak District stepping stones congested and Stonehenge cordoned. The backs of two older ladies' heads look down Gold Hill in Shaftesbury, permed and waved hairstyles framing iconic England. This is their, and perhaps our, viewpoint. One critical reading of Parr's images is that they poke fun, look down on their subjects, but there is more complexity in *The Cost of Living*. If caricature is anywhere, it is in those images which take a literal position of looking up at the well off, Parr's low viewpoints spotting superior airs. The more middling images point out ironies, yet in complex fashion. A morris dance outside McDonald's is no less distinctively and truly a folk dance for its location; indeed the image could be read as one of easy cohabitation, new and old Englands rubbing along.

Temporal and spatial complexities appear too as Parr reaches suburban Milton Keynes. Two photographs, both titled 'Milton Keynes', show new-build thatched and beamed houses, detached and well-appointed cottage homes on a building site. In the 1970s Milton Keynes had mixed the architecturally modernist and traditional, but from 1981 the Development Corporation had instructed architects to build in neo-traditional styles, and Parr's pictures capture such building.[66] One shows a house in isolation, the other foregrounds stacks of bricks from the Redland brick company, their 'Olde English Range', with the end of a cottage home and a distant medieval church tower in trees. Raphael Samuel would note how conservation culture had entailed a 'return to brick', with housebuilders capitalizing via antique ranges and reclaimed stock.[67] Parr makes an ironic observation of the building site contrivance of old England. If cultural analysis in this period promoted the idea of identity as a social construction, here is the literal brick and thatch equivalent. Overlay this with the words 'Milton Keynes' and a layer of new town critique is added, a place name often evoked as somewhere lacking substance and authenticity, here the butt of what could be taken as a photographic joke.

There are, however, complexities here, linked to the particular form of suburban urbanism shaping Milton Keynes, a development whose

Photographs by Martin Parr, both entitled 'Milton Keynes', from *The Cost of Living* (1989).

plan was characterized by the authors of 'Non-Plan' as trying 'to shy away completely from planning'.[68] Guy Ortolano notes that one of the Thatcher government's first privatization initiatives, fifteen days after the 1979 election, was to allow the sale of housing held by New Town Development Corporations to their tenants, a year ahead of the introduction of 'Right to Buy' under the 1980 Housing Act. Government could act in the new towns without parliamentary legislation; Ortolano argues that sites such as Milton Keynes, while products of social democracy, became 'stages for policies foundational to Thatcher's Britain'.[69] On a visit to Milton Keynes on 25 September 1979, during which she opened Europe's largest shopping centre, Thatcher was photographed presenting the house keys to a family who had chosen to buy their home, former renters now part of a property-owning democracy, Milton Keynes showing a Conservative future.

Milton Keynes also, however, set up a dialogue of future and past, the houses photographed by Parr an authentic part of a place trading on the old within the new. One of the later generation of new towns, built from 1967 with car ownership in mind, the city was structured around community neighbourhoods bypassed by traffic arteries, with historic villages and towns as foci for new living. Milton Keynes thereby claimed pastoral and village qualities in its newness, and an identity grounded and lively. The same year that Parr published *The Cost of Living*, Ruth Finnegan's *The Hidden Musicians* described Milton Keynes as a place of grassroots cultural life, strong in its local identity, with prolific amateur music-making – classical, pop, country, jazz and folk – embedded in pre-existing towns and villages within the Development Corporation area.[70] Orchestras played, amateurs theatricalled and performers took Milton Keynes's most famous work of public art, Liz Leyh's 1978 sculpture of grazing *Concrete Cows*, for inspiration, with bands including Urban Cows and Concrete Cows, and folk singers singing at the Concrete Cow Folk Club. The new central boulevards were named after the ancient Wiltshire sites of Avebury and Silbury, with one called Midsummer for its alignment to the midsummer sunrise. Milton Keynes was no simply new city, and a dialogue with the past was built into its layout and nomenclature. Parr's home of new-build thatch and beam appears quite in keeping here.

If for some Milton Keynes was, as Steen Eiler Rasmussen put it in a preface to Derek Walker's 1982 book on its architecture and

English and Suburban

Image from Google Earth showing Shenley Church End, Milton Keynes, accessed 19 October 2018.

planning, 'utterly English', its Englishness (like all Englishnesses) was geographically and temporally complex.[71] Viewing Parr's new-build photographs thirty years on, the question arises: does the cottage home of 1980s England stand? Curious as to where Parr's cottage home was, whether it was still there and what the building site had turned into, a search proceeded, in twenty-first-century desk-based fashion. The distinctive tower of the background church in Parr's photograph is identifiable as Shenley Church End, and roaming via Google Earth, taking orientation from the church, leads the viewer to Thirlby Lane, not far from the A5, here with its Roman name of Watling Street. Here in this new-town comfortable suburbia, just off the main road, 1980s thatch is visible, although the house Parr pictured is only evident if you lift off, the street view obscured by tree and shrubbery growth of thirty years. A leafy, well-grown, gardened patch of England occupies the building land, Parr shown to have photographed an incipient pastoral for the comfortable classes.

The new town of Milton Keynes was named after one of its constituent villages, and Parr's 'Milton Keynes' might be set alongside another photographic image of the place, from another book about England, from forty years before. W. G. Hoskins's *Midland England* (1949), celebrating the vernacular landscape and architecture of 'the

Photograph of Milton Keynes, Buckinghamshire, by F. L. Attenborough, from W. G. Hoskins, *Midland England* (1949).

Country between the Chilterns and the Trent', presented landscape as 'a manuscript written on again and again, a palimpsest with endless discoveries waiting to be made'.[72] Hoskins is discussed further in Chapter Six, but his prevailing tone was to assert historic local value against destructive modern development. Visual imagery played an important role in Hoskins's documentary salvage, and *Midland England* was illustrated with photographs by Hoskins's University College Leicester colleague F. L. Attenborough, the father of David and Richard. Milton Keynes was pictured within a chapter on 'The Old Midland Village', and zooming on Google Earth into Milton Keynes village, Attenborough's building remains. The junction is recognizable, and the Swan Inn still stands, in the Milton Keynes village overtaken by Milton Keynes city. Photograph echoes photograph as building mimics building, intentionally or otherwise, Parr showing an England overwritten in its own image.

Serious Midland

With the exception of the Tyneside setting of *Whatever Happened to the Likely Lads?*, and Peter Hall's non-planned 'Lawrence Country',

English and Suburban

Milton Keynes is about as far north as this chapter has gone so far, itself indicative of the prominence of the southeast in suburban commentary. This section moves from Milton Keynes's southern edge of Midland England north across the region, considering some determinedly serious examinations of suburbia made since the 1970s in paint, photograph and poem. The suburbia encountered here is a consciously ordinary one, lower middle or upper working class, in an England often overlooked by surveyors of national identity looking north or south. At times such regional overlook has prompted assertions of Midlandness. Patrick Wright notes the 1990s political 'Movement for Middle England', arguing for regional devolution, framing their appeal in terms of Chesterton's English 'Secret People' that never have spoken yet and appealing to a pre-Conquest collectivism, a Mercia for the modern age.[73] Political campaigns for Midland regionalism are however rare, and the Middle England movement petered out, local politics more commonly mobilized around civic identities, whether Joseph Chamberlain's early twentieth-century Birmingham as second city of the country or Nottingham's interwar claim to be 'Queen of the Midlands'. Urban rather than regional assertions take the political stage, not least in twenty-first-century moves to establish powerful mayors, as in the West Midlands (covering Birmingham and Coventry) and Leicester, but in the wings sits a standard, suburban Midland, mulled over and brooding.

In 2018 the Yale Center for British Art showed a retrospective exhibition of paintings by George Shaw entitled *A Corner of a Foreign Field*. Shaw signalled Englishness in the title for a U.S. show, with the allusion to Rupert Brooke's First World War poem 'The Soldier', and the title was retained for the exhibition's move to Bath in 2019.[74] The focus of Shaw's painting is the post-war Tile Hill estate on the edge of Coventry. Shaw, who was born in 1966, grew up in Tile Hill, and his parental home remains there, still council-owned on a former council estate, many of whose other residents exercised a right to buy. Over twenty years Shaw has returned to childhood landscapes, evoking a generally settled domesticity. In a 2003 watercolour, 'Dad's Roses', one of a series of the well-tended front and back gardens of the family home, Tile Hill is still in bloom.[75] More commonly Shaw paints in Humbrol enamel, a medium itself associated with childhood pursuits of model painting. Unpeopled pictures of estate houses, garages, public houses, public buildings and surrounding woodland inscribe an ordinary suburbia. However far away the child may have moved in adulthood, via study and work in Sheffield, London and Nottingham, and now residence in Devon, Tile Hill remains the place for self-examination. Shaw's landscapes without figures are in effect self-portraiture.

In the year of Shaw's birth, the 'outer Coventry' section of Nikolaus Pevsner and Alexandra Wedgwood's *Warwickshire* volume in the 'Buildings of England' series described Tile Hill, begun in 1953, as 'probably the most successful of the earlier city estates . . ., with several patches of wood left untouched'.[76] Tile Hill is the edge of the city with country adjacent, resembling in that sense, though no other, Betjeman's 'essential Metro-land'. Shaw's often luminous realism elevates the ordinary as a place of valued life and memory, the everyday enamelled. Enigmatic titling also elevates the humdrum, some paintings in series labelled from a Catholic childhood: *Scenes from the Passion* or *Ash Wednesday*. The 2004–5 painting *Ash Wednesday: 7.00am* shows early spring light, roof frost fading in sun, mature trees standing bare, traffic-free neatness.[77] Figures are absent; sunlight stirs curtained sleepers. Elsewhere folkloric and mythic resonance is tapped, notably in the tree paintings of Shaw's 'My Back to Nature' National Gallery

George Shaw, *Ash Wednesday: 7.00am*, 2004–5 , Humbrol enamel on board.

George Shaw, *Portrait of an Old Midlander*, 2015–16, Humbrol enamel on canvas.

residency (2014–16), where Coventry's edge met sacred groves, holding its own.[78] *Portrait of an Old Midlander* (2015–16) turns to the woods, to something there before the estate, and which has witnessed its shifts, a tree figure knotty and persistent.[79] More self-portraiture; the Old Midlander a Tolkienesque, Entish equivalent to an ageing human observer. Shaw maps a variegated living space: the private house, the public house, the private in the public in the form of lock-up garages, the public becoming private in the dens of woodland. If memory is cherished, neither past nor present is idealized, and decay registers, the public realm especially scuffed. A Shaw painting of 2017, *The Buildings of England*, shows tatty garage doors in red, white and blue.[80]

Shaw's work is framed as about England in subject-matter, style and cultural reference. Shaw's self-presentation in speech and writing presents Coventry's past as a touchstone in the music of the Specials, the poetry of Larkin and the story of Lady Godiva and Peeping Tom. In a talk in Nottingham in November 2010 Shaw gave reference points of English masculinity from Thomas Hardy through Tony Hancock to *The Likely Lads* and Les Dawson, and added in Georges Perec.[81]

The Englishness of Shaw's English art could seem a comfortable backdrop, with childhood memories of sitting room television and bedroom listening, but recent commentary injects anxiety into the frame, paintings of Midland England overlain with political debate in an altering world. If Shaw's earlier work tended to imply structures and memory intact, in recent years the sense of decay increases, with structures fallen, institutions eroded and welcomes lessened. *A Corner of a Foreign Field* included 'The End of . . .' series, registering loss, personal and socio-economic, as industrial sites and working-class institutions go. *The End of Pleasure* showed a closed working men's club, though another image at the end of the 2018 show, *Sunrise over the Care Home*, gestured to possible hope, in the circumstances.[82] Shaw has expressed political anger at decay being a matter of design rather than entropy, yet at the same time political puzzlement at recent shifts. Aggressively racist national sentiments which Shaw hoped had been left in the 1970s, or at least had become crazily marginal, swim back up the mainstream.

Shaw's painted place could lend itself to easy Brexit comment on the left behind, the insularly provincial. Shaw comments that he is anti-nationalistic, and that recent paintings showing England flags displayed in windows (*The Man Who Would Be King*, 2017) or on poles are a recognition rather than endorsement of a newly visible mode of patriotism.[83] One 2018 picture of a flag flying behind spiked railings is pointedly titled *Someone Else's House*.[84] Shaw's is a first-generation Englishness, his parents Irish migrants to Coventry, and he claims a counter-jingoistic, less bombastic Englishness, where figures claimed by some for the monocultural happily share a symbolic realm with the multicultural, chiming with Shaw's devotion to Two-Tone. If this is England, it is more akin to Shane Meadows's 2006 film *This Is England* than to the England of *This England* magazine. In aggregate, Shaw's Tile Hill makes for an Englishness of atmosphere, a place of memory, gesture and ghosts which, recent isolated examples notwithstanding, needs no especial flag.

Another variant of Midland suburbia appears in John Myers's photography. Myers's early 1970s portrait series *Middle England*, taken in Stourbridge in the West Midlands, where Myers taught at the local art college, was first published in 1974, and exhibited and republished as part of a retrospective *Middle England* show in Birmingham in 2011.[85] The exhibition also took in Myers's photographs of domestic television

English and Suburban

John Myers, 'House and garden, Chawn Hill, Stourbridge', 1979, from *Middle England* (2011).

sets, substations, a furniture store and houses. A 'Boring Photos' category, with people deliberately absent, presented 'landscapes without incident'. Alongside lift doors and dual carriageways, Myers pictured a row of lock-up garages, echoing Shaw's Tile Hill subjects. The housing photographs, from 1979, include newer-build private, as in Chawn Hill, Stourbridge, where conifers and low brick edge the front lawn, dwarf for easy maintenance. The house is brick with some cladding, modest but detached. Wrought iron is over the porch, adding a touch of romance, though you would hardly climb up there. Near England's geographic middle, here is a not bad place, a steady suburbia.

Middle England mixes exterior and interior landscapes with portrait photography. In his portraits, most from 1972 to 1974, Myers presents a peopled photographic indoor equivalent to Shaw, though a social notch up, lower middle rather than working class. Photographs are full-figure, their subjects set in careful relationship to space, domestic or otherwise. The use of a tripod-mounted plate camera heightens the work's formality. Everyday spaces are shown, but these are no everyday snapshots. People pose with their surroundings, decor sparse but cherished: Mr Jackson and his cabinet of glassware, Nicola with her Donny Osmond posters, Mr and Mrs Seabourne and their sofa, Mrs Tate and her mantelpiece. Young 'David in knight's armour' stands by the bed, sword ready for anything that might lurk in the wardrobe. And Christmas comes to Stourbridge, Santa standing at Tescos in 1972 by cardboard boxes holding varieties of washing powder, and at Stringers in 1973, where a woolly-chinned man is enthroned before gifts for English children: a 'Block Puzzle', a 'TV Squeezy', accessories for the 'Psychedelic Look' and a guide to 'The True Story of the Old West'. Santa presides, a little worn but ready to smile. Whatever the Christmas 1973 circumstances, of oil crisis and industrial strife, someone has been good this year. Myers's pictures denote the effort in the ordinary, in photographer and photographed. Middle England pauses for a moment, but does not have it easy. The time for taking Myers's non-snapshots draws out reflection; look into Santa's eyes, and wish for something.

Scrutinizing the work of Myers and Shaw, and setting it alongside that of Betjeman and others, highlight the ambiguity and variety in the category 'suburban', and its relationship to different modes of the urban: the metropolis, the provincial city, the small town. If Betjeman documents the metropolitan suburb, Shaw paints a city edge, while Myers shoots town suburbia. The designation of suburban settlement geography is less than straightforward, its landscape of homes and gardens set in morphological variation. If all are suburban, no two are alike, with differences of class, ownership structure, architectural style, historical setting, settlement hierarchy and age. For all but a few years I have lived suburbanly, but within this is marked variation, with childhood spent in a suburb, formerly a village, on the edge of a city, and much of adulthood lived in a town which is a suburb of a city. Evocations of Middle England, whether geographical, social or political, navigate, exploit or trip over such suburban variations. What might flow from a West Midland meeting between Myers's Stourbridge Santa and Tony Blair's targeted Worcester Woman? Or between those haunting Tile Hill's woods or Chorleywood's Metroland commons? Attention to Middle England demands precision as to which middle is evoked, to the reasons for its definition and to the particular surroundings which make it middle.

A precise poetic attention to Midland settlement geography can end this section. In his 2014 collection *The Midlands*, Tony Williams's title poem evokes a region of 'suburb-like towns and town-like

John Myers, 'Santa Claus at Stringers', 1973, from *Middle England* (2011).

suburbs'.⁸⁶ Identity proceeds in part from such indistinctness, from settlement patterns not fitting typical models, disobeying geographical convention. The poem, which opens with 'The Midlands are crying', finds: 'Here is neither one thing nor the other.' Poetic precursors such as Geoffrey Hill and Roy Fisher join hands, as the poem's final lines set out the region's state, ordinary and in between. The prosaic new overlays the past, and law and wildlife trundle on, as plainness simmers, though it might not take much to bring it to a low boil:

> There is not even clarity and rage, but only
>   rain setting in on a plain between ridges,
>   the magistrates courts as busy as ever,
>   the chorus of starlings chattering trenchantly on
> in the skies, an unfound grave of a Mercian king
>   under wurzels, new housing. And out-of-town Asdas
>   that mop up the rheum of the foothills
>   that lean-to the North.

Driving Home for Christmas

In 1986, the year that George Shaw started at Sheffield Polytechnic and series 3 of *Ever Decreasing Circles* was broadcast, Carolyn Steedman published *Landscape for a Good Woman*, combining memoir with political and theoretical reflection. Steedman offered 'a story of two lives', her mother's working-class Conservative life in Burnley and London and her own social and psychological inheritance. A year later Margaret Thatcher would win a third term, and three years later Martin Parr would publish *The Cost of Living*. In retrospect, *Landscape for a Good Woman* makes sense, as do Parr's photographs, within a landscape shaped by dispute over rights to buy and the values of consumption. Steedman reflected on her mother's 'desire for the things of the earth' against forms of 'politics and cultural criticism' which might find such matters 'trivial'.[87] Her book does not tell a suburban story, but in its attention to place, and to the navigation of social and geographical stereotypes, *Landscape for a Good Woman* echoes much of the material covered in this chapter. Steedman draws out 'with what creativity people may use the stuff of cultural and social stereotype, so that it becomes not a series of labels applied from outside a situation, but a set of metaphors ready for transformation by those who are its subjects'.[88] Steedman's conclusion on the storying of landscape applies too across suburban Englands: 'I think now of all the stories, all the reading, all the dreams that help us to see ourselves in the landscape, and see ourselves watching as well.'[89]

In a 2019 discussion of 'the new suburbs', Danny Dorling set out a gloomy prognosis that England's suburbs are slowly 'dying', with a particular demographic geography:

> The mantra that there is no such thing as society, just families and their children, rings both true and hollow in the suburbs. The suburbs are becoming places in which the elderly who have not quite made it into the best-off echelons reside. Not rich enough to decamp to idyllic villages, to private health care and eventually an exclusive retirement complex, those who did well, but not exceptionally well, face an isolated suburban old age. Their grown-up children live in another suburb far away, or have not yet escaped the central city and renting – still waiting for the inheritance that is their ticket to suburbia.[90]

Dorling points to a specific geographic phenomenon, shaped in part by increased mobility and by the expansion of tertiary education, both factors breaking the geographical proximity which once characterized intergenerational family responsibilities. The gloomy prognosis risks overemphasizing suburban entrapment; an old age in relative isolation might appear an advance for those whose childhood had been spent in cramped inner urban housing, sleeping top-to-toe with siblings and lacking amenities taken for granted in the suburban home. There is a ring of truth, however, in Dorling's account, matching my own experience, which points to a shift in recent decades whereby English suburban geographies are increasingly marked by geographical displacement. The longer-term implications of such changes are unclear, not least because of their intergenerational qualities, but they will shape the emotional and financial properties of early twenty-first-century suburban England.

Martin Newell's 1993 song 'Christmas in Suburbia' catches something of this predicament, one not exclusive to England but refracted through its particular suburban cultures. Newell is a north Essex-based singer and poet concerned with place and landscape; his 2001 poetry collection *Late Autumn Sunlight* has an introduction by *Akenfield* author Ronald Blythe.[91] Newell also ponders what it is to be English, and 'Christmas in Suburbia' appears on the LP *The Greatest Living Englishman*, produced and co-performed by Andy Partridge of XTC. The album cover carried a passage from Orwell's *The Lion and the Unicorn* on the distinctiveness of England, on its 'different air ... Are there really such things as nations?', a passage immediately followed in the original by John Major's bicycling old maids. 'Christmas in Suburbia' hymns a 'shoe-string saturnalia', tiddly and a little awkward, of plastic and chrome and cotton-wool snow. The opening lines sing of going home for Christmas in suburbia, with street lamps shining in rain, and playing the song in the car became for some years a personal seasonal ritual, driving to the parental home before Christmas, less obvious than Chris Rea's hit 'Driving Home for Christmas' but with jangling poignancy. Population mobility in the later twentieth century made temporary seasonal migration from home to Home not uncommon, in Steedman's terms one of the stories helping people see themselves in the landscape.

Routines and duties, trifles and delights, comfort and entrapment, all played out in winter generation games. Orange streetlights would show if it was raining, but just occasionally there might be snow, and the test was to look, at an angle, just up the road, through the front-window blinds, to the lamp's flaking gold. If only for a few days, in a seasonal fall, things might settle.

6

English Particulars

From Trumptonshire to Royston Vasey

The local, the geographically particular, has been a focus of claims to cultural distinction and authenticity, with particular spots within England held to say something about the country. Sometimes this is a matter of typicality, sometimes one of eccentricity, somewhere held to be emblematically English in its peculiarity. This chapter concentrates largely on places beyond the city and suburb, examining how over six decades the local has served to concentrate (in both intellectual focus and heightened flavour) stories about England.

In the late 1960s the BBC's *Watch with Mother* slot, a lunchtime treat for the pre-schooler, took children, and whoever might be watching with them, to Trumptonshire. Gordon Murray Puppets produced *Camberwick Green* (1966), *Trumpton* (1967) and *Chigley* (1969), a televisual town and country projecting a particular England into the sitting room. Born in 1964, these programmes were made for me, and I watched with Mum, visiting a locality different from my own yet friendly and familiar. What kind of England was I shown?

Accounts of Trumptonshire tend, in looking back, to suggest the programmes are set in an old England, a place where the modern is kept out or suppressed. A 2016 obituary of Murray thus presumed a setting 'probably before the First World War'.[1] Southern Englishness is also assumed, but simply watching the programmes suggests an England far from simply traditional, indeed highly contemporary, and geographically indeterminate. The backdrops to journey scenes in *Camberwick Green* show substantial hills, and the landscape is of pastoral farming, Trumptonshire a composite region of upland and lowland. Rachel Moseley's analysis of Murray's 'orderly toytowns where everyone has their place' finds in Trumptonshire an English countryside 'on the cusp between past and present', though her comment on 'the perpetual triumph of the traditional over the modern' is perhaps overstated.[2] The modern and traditional both come in for gentle mockery when the plans of a landowner, a mayor or a factory owner go awry, but only after their traditional and modern qualities have been appreciated. Lord Belborough of Winkstead Hall in *Chigley* runs a restored steam railway, has a dutiful butler, opens his house to the public and receives general deference, but *Chigley* also houses the most modern biscuit factory, whose watchword (and theme song) is efficiency. The factory workers dance at the end of the day as Belborough cranks a Dutch organ. *Chigley* curiously blends the old and modern, in a manner entirely consistent with 1960s England, a programme of its time, about its time. Plotlines often turned on tensions between the modern and traditional, as with the friendly rivalry between *Camberwick Green*'s Farmer Bell and Windy Miller. Windy, with his wind-powered mill, is in tune with natural rhythms, drinks home-made cider, lets his hens roam – traditional tropes at one with an emerging 1960s counterculture. Jonathan Bell loves machinery, produces eggs in bulk and is a new farmer on a 'modern mechanical farm': 'in modern times use modern ways.'[3] Bell is in tune with another 1960s, and is sure the white heat of his new truck will trounce Windy's Penny Farthing in a race, though hubristic defeat follows as he runs out of petrol. Trumptonshire shows a cohabitation of old and new Englands, everyone ultimately getting along.

Trumptonshire's routines, with stock episode openings and closings and character songs, produced reassuring familiarity for the young viewer alongside playful curiosity. *Camberwick Green* began with a featured character emerging from a musical box; *Trumpton* opened with town clock figures chiming the morning hour. Moseley argues that the quality of movement in the stop-frame animation is commensurate with an aesthetic of child's play, offering an intimate compositional realism appropriate for the small television screen.[4] Trumptonshire is whimsical but not fantastic, the vehicles equivalent to children's toys, a miniature child's play England evidently resembling parts of the country, whether or not they are parts the viewer knows. Brian Cant as narrator (a voice familiar to children from BBC television's *Play School*) reported the speech of characters rather than lending them a voice, thus avoiding the exclusionary effect than any geographically located accent might have had for viewers. Trumptonshire becomes an

English national space in its composite backdrop, and in Cant's standard speech, which carries only faint trace of his Suffolk upbringing. Trumptonshire is rooted, but crucially not by voice, able therefore to be a local for everywhere.

Moseley's critical appreciation of stop-frame animation describes, in the first two-thirds of the following sentence, my own lived televisual childhood:

> Hegemonic notions of mothering and the hand-made, and the meanings attached to the concepts of comfort, safety, home and recognisability which might emerge almost instinctively from pastoral, past-set animated television for a child of white, English, lower middle-class origins might register very differently, or indeed not at all, for the working-class, immigrant or looked-after child.[5]

Whatever might register with different viewing individuals (and they might be loved by anyone), such BBC children's programmes could be viewed, as Jean Northam puts it, as 'rehearsals in citizenship'.[6] This was how a society might be modelled, presenting a good life where disputes were resolved and order sustained. Trumptonshire appears a place of character and distinction, whether or not you could imagine belonging there.

Grown-ups have watched other kinds of locale, drawn by other qualities. From 1999 to 2002 the BBC screened three series of *The League of Gentlemen*, created by Mark Gatiss, Reece Shearsmith, Steve Pemberton and Jeremy Dyson. Initially a stage and radio show, the television rendering of the League's setting, Royston Vasey, brought grotesque characters, and grotesque localism, into the home. The title sequence gave a prospect view of a small town, just up the hierarchy of settlement geography from Trumpton, zooming past the war memorial to the high street, taking the viewer into the place. Strangeness is registered in odd signs and shopfronts, and then the characters appear, most of whom, if they emerged from *Camberwick Green*'s musical box, would terrify the children.

Royston Vasey is introduced via a visitor coming to stay with relations, a normal young man who finds himself in another part of the country and a strange branch of the family. The country in general is thus related to Royston Vasey, which sits as a disturbing element, a warning as to what might be within us, a land whose characters variously stand for obsessive policing (the domestic rules of Uncle Hilary and Aunt Val), grim temptation (the special stuff sold under the counter of butcher Hilary Briss) and cruel authority (employment officer Pauline commanding her jobseekers). The ur-locals here are Edward and Tubbs, cohabiting the isolated hillside 'local shop', 'a local shop for local people', themselves seldom seen in town and indeed almost out of place when they do pop up there, as in the 2017 revival episodes. Edward and Tubbs's habitat is isolation, and anyone who enters their space must be subsumed, to keep local grotesquery pristine. Their question to straying visitors, 'Are you local?', is at once wary and threatening. The answer can only be no, and the outcome only horrible.

Is there a rehearsal of citizenship in Royston Vasey? Perhaps the capacity to parody citizenship, to find absurdity all around and to pause before shouting the geographical odds. Conventional plotlines of localism do, however, occasionally intrude, notably a first-series story of a proposed new road, improving Royston Vasey's connectivity. Tubbs and Edward are not keen, Edward declaring: 'We don't need new road. This is a community. We don't bother the outside world and we don't want it bothering us.'[7] For Edward and Tubbs 'new road' becomes the occasion for torturing surveyors in defence of locale. At one point a lost construction worker, John, enters the shop and shows Tubbs a map:

Tubbs: Lines and lines and lines! What do they mean?
John: They're the roads. They connect you to other places.
Tubbs: Local places?

The worker meets an unspecified fate, but Tubbs finds geographical temptation in the map and in 'new road': 'You lied to me, Edward! There is a Swansea.' There are, finds Tubbs, 'other places too'. Edward says he has concealed them, 'To keep you clean and pure and local', and tears up the map, Tubbs trying to pick up the pieces.[8] When Edward and Tubbs's improbable son returns, himself involved in the road project, they gather him back, gruesomely.

Royston Vasey is peculiar, and familiar, its characters part of an English family of grotesques and eccentrics, its geography at once just down the road and off the map. As Edward tears up the map to maintain local belonging, he strangely echoes Sylvia Townsend Warner's 1926 novel *Lolly Willowes*, where Laura Willowes moves to a small Chiltern village, embraces witchcraft and signifies her belonging by throwing her map and guidebook down a disused well: 'She scarcely knew what she had done, but she knew that she had done rightly, whether it was that she had sacrificed herself to the place, or had cast herself upon its mercies – content henceforth to know no more of it than did its own children.'[9] Warner and Willowes mediate the geographies of knowledge, of worldly experience and deep locale. The English local has its charms; it can be plainly charming, or cast strange spells. The remainder of this chapter explores the navigation of the local by historians, planners, campaigners, photographers, musicians, pub-goers, tourists and television viewers, all drawn by English particulars. What will emerge from the box? What special stuff might we find?

In the Vernacular

The League of Gentlemen was filmed in Hadfield, north Derbyshire, in the High Peak. Not far away, across the Lancashire county boundary, a few decades before, local character had been at issue in campaigns against the new national electricity Super Grid. Threats were less 'new road' than 'new wire' and 'new pylon'. Katrina Navickas shows how from the early 1950s new high-voltage power lines prompted the mobilization of local conservationist narrative in the Lancashire south Pennines.[10] Preservationists, residents and local authorities campaigned against projects of national planning by nationalized industries, in this case the British Electricity Authority. The local becomes a scale at which to configure amenity as a defence against development. *The League of Gentlemen* would amplify such sentiment to distortion, but its comedy made sense in part by inhabiting a country accustomed to upholding the local against change.

The local emerges as a distinctive terrain of value in the post-war decades, whether in amenity campaigns or the related field of local history. In 1955 came two publications which set the tone for valuing the local. Ian Nairn's special issue of the *Architectural Review*, 'Outrage', diagnosed a creeping uniformity in development and planning, journeying across England and finding his starting point of the edge of Southampton and his end point on the edge of Carlisle much the same.

Nairn took negative associations of suburbia to damn this England: 'Subtopia: Making an ideal of suburbia. Visually speaking, the universalization and idealization of our town fringes. Philosophically, the idealization of the Little Man who lives there (from suburb + Utopia).'[11] One response to such present pessimism was to look to the past, and 1955 also saw the publication of historian W. G. Hoskins's *The Making of the English Landscape*. Consideration of the work of Hoskins, noted for his *Midland England* in the previous chapter's discussion of Milton Keynes, and in Chapter Three for his commentary on nuclear bombers over English landscape, allows appreciation of the manner in which the local, and the related cultural and architectural theme of the vernacular, could become a reservoir of anti-modern value.[12] In its outlook on the modern, local history here appears less culturally complex than Trumptonshire, though less grotesque than Royston Vasey. A 'Yes' from landscape to the question 'Are you local?' would, however, have brought Hoskins's approval.

Hoskins's academic career at Leicester, Oxford and Exeter established local history as a discipline, and *The Making of the English Landscape* presented landscape as a historical document at risk of erasure by development and planning. The past became a refuge from the present, with vernacular rather than elite buildings and landscapes the focus, ordinariness joining hands across the years. Hoskins produced popular guides alongside academic works, notably on Leicestershire, Rutland and Devon, including Shell Guides to *Rutland* (1963) and *Leicestershire* (1970).[13] After a 1972 television documentary based on *The Making of the English Landscape*, in 1976 and 1978 he wrote and presented a BBC 2 series on *Landscapes of England*, the historian in the field speaking local truth to camera.

For Hoskins the local signposted a scale of enquiry and a meaningful geography, somewhere to retreat from and stage resistance to modernity. The cover of the *Rutland* Shell Guide included a county boundary sign stating 'Rutland Fights to Keep Local Government Local', and Hoskins's text played on contemporary ecological language to suggest the county, the smallest in England, as 'England's first Human Conservancy'.[14] In 1959, in *Local History in England*, Hoskins suggested people were feeling 'an unquenchable desire to know all there is to be known about the past' of their 'small piece of England':

we are not born internationalists and there comes a time when the complexity and size of modern problems leaves us cold. We belong to a particular place and the bigger and more incomprehensible the world grows the more people will turn to study something of which they can grasp the scale and in which they can find a personal and individual meaning.[15]

The local appears a scale of detail and depth, with 'the local historian's basic tool . . . the microscope'.[16] Local history was thus 'a science of Human Ecology', Hoskins taking inspiration from U.S. urbanist Lewis Mumford to suggest: 'Men are attached to places as they are attached to families and friends. When loyalties come together, one has the most tenacious cement possible for human society.' Stable settlement made for 'cultural humus'.[17] Particularity was cultural fertility, and Hoskins quoted William Blake's generalization: 'To Generalise is to be an Idiot. To Particularise is the Alone Distinction of Merit.'[18]

Reflecting on the emergence of local history, Raphael Samuel commented: 'Local historians, conjuring villages out of suburbs, rediscover the fields beneath the streets.'[19] Did such rediscovery redeem the present or put it to shame? For Hoskins history might console, but it rarely redeemed. In 1957 Hoskins published *The Midland Peasant*, a study of Wigston Magna, near Leicester, excavating the settlement's history and ending with it becoming an urban district. Today's place had a population fifteen times that of the early fourteenth century: 'But a whole culture, a qualitative civilisation, had perished to bring about this quantitative boom.'[20] Hoskins's *Leicestershire* Shell Guide gazetteer entry was dismissive:

> **Wigston Magna** has been engulfed in Leicester within the last 20 years and lost nearly all its village character . . . There used to be some decent brick vernacular building near the parish church – perhaps still there, though one always fears the worst near a developing city like Leicester. Turn one's back for a month and something good disappears in rubble and dust in the path of what is laughingly called Progress.[21]

In Hoskins's England, twentieth-century building erodes local character. Others in the 1970s, however, sought new build *in* local character. In his essay on 'The Return to Brick' Samuel notes a rediscovery

'Segregated footpath at Melbourne Cedars, Chelmsford', from Essex County Council, *A Design Guide for Residential Areas* (1973), p. 38.

of vernacular architecture by the 1970s, notably through the work of Ronald Brunskill, which included the assertion of brick as characterful English building material.[22] The Olde English bricks photographed by Martin Parr in 1980s Milton Keynes reflect this rediscovery. For Brunskill vernacular architecture was 'regional personality as expressed in buildings', and some planning authorities sought to promote a new vernacular in their areas.[23]

In 1973 Essex County Council produced *A Design Guide for Residential Areas*, with a foreword by Conservative environment secretary Geoffrey Rippon. The influential 'Essex Design Guide', as it became known, shaped by Melville Dunbar of the council's planning department, sought to improve development through variety, imagination and local character. G.C.S. Curtis, chairman of the planning committee, stated: 'Few Essex people are happy at the form which post-war housing development in the County has taken. It has a dreary suburban uniformity and lacks any specific Essex characteristics.'[24] 'Suburban' here denotes standardization, and the Guide instead sought

'Regional Character': 'To perpetuate the unique building character of the county and to re-establish local identity, development shall generally employ external materials which are sympathetic in colour and texture to the vernacular range of Essex materials.'[25]

Photographic imagery of the happy living fostered by guided design showed children moving safely, toddlers pedalling and girls in pedestrian space at Melbourne Cedars in Chelmsford. New design was in contrast to the 'typical suburban scheme' dominated by road space, the latter indicative of 'subtopian' development 'devoid of identity or sense of place'.[26] The Guide proposed principles of enclosure; in higher-density development buildings were to enclose space, while in lower-density sites landscape was to contain buildings in 'formal Arcadia' or 'informal Arcadia'.[27] The Guide listed plant species for verge, avenue and hedge, 'A Guide to Planting for Arcadia', with beech and plane, oak and lime, yew and hazel.[28] Colour drawings showed the planting and paving of informal Arcadia.[29] The Arcadian theme echoed Ian Nairn's 1956 'Counter-Attack' against the 'Outrage' of subtopia, where he offered a 'Casebook' for the five 'categories of landscape – metropolis, town, arcadia, country and wild'.[30] Arcadian, not subtopian, suburbia sat between town and country.

'Informal Arcadia', from Essex County Council, *A Design Guide for Residential Areas* (1973), p. 82.

The foreword to the 1983 reprint of the Design Guide hailed the 'excellent schemes' at 'the County Council's new town at South Woodham Ferrers'.[31] This small 1970s new 'country town', planned for 18,000 people on the north side of the River Crouch, north of Southend and south of Chelmsford, was built by the council in partnership with private developers in neo-vernacular style. A 1978 Asda store in Essex tithe barn style was a key development hub, and the Queen formally opened the new town square in May 1981. Street names in the southwest part of South Woodham Ferrers were taken from Tolkien: Hobbiton Hill, Arwen Grove, Gandalf's Ride, Elrond's Rest, magical names for a new English vernacular. Essex County Council's 1981 promotional film 'A Riverside Country Town' showed a place generating new life and new business, the old retained within a consumer lifestyle, where people and houses were to be individual. Commentary stressed that there were 'no high-rise blocks, and no conventional estates': 'England has many old country towns, some very picturesque, and all with a distinct identity. Something of these qualities, that have evolved over many centuries, are [sic] being designed into this new town, where nothing is as old as it seems.'[32] Local band 'Right Hand Man' won a contest to write a soundtrack song, hymning the family lifestyle of 'a whole new place to be', with the natural surroundings of a river by the sea. Upbeat female vocals and mild synthesizer backing suggest a strange blend of Depeche Mode (from nearby new town Basildon, whose first 1981 hit also reflected on 'New Life') and the conventional family-oriented pop of the then popular, now forgotten, Dooleys.

In his 1982 book *The English Vision* David Watkin praised South Woodham Ferrers, with an image of the clock tower and pedestrian town centre captioned: 'One of the most thoroughgoing of the many recent attempts to produce a kind of picturesque folk-architecture in reaction to the lack of historical resonance in modern architecture ... an example of the continuing English preoccupation with the charms of the village.'[33] For heritage commentator Dan Cruickshank, however, South Woodham Ferrers failed, an 'illusion ... badly created', with 'clumsy detailing' and 'pretend old buildings', where 'all pretence at tradition is left on the doorstep.'[34]

The exteriors of South Woodham Ferrers asserted the vernacular, though a community with Asda as a keystone was hardly removed from the modern world, and for some this duality was a selling point.

In January 1978 the trade paper *Building Design* carried two articles by David Pearce, 'Making Places' and 'Return to Metroland', praising the Essex Design Guide's 'new-old style' as 'quite simply *nicer* than almost all other recent housing in the UK':

> in the case of the town centre hypermarket at South Woodham Ferrers the Ovaltine farm image has run riot. A vast corrugated-roofed 'shed for selling in' has wrap-round vernacular architecture and pitched roofs (360,000 hand-made Swallow clay tiles), a timber boarded and weather vaned clock tower.[35]

For Pearce this happily left modernism behind: 'the last thing the form is going to do is follow function!' Pearce asked: 'Can one really set out to build a "place", like the country towns of England which have evolved over a millennium? Can one do it overnight? Essex will soon provide the answer.'[36]

Architectural commentary was elsewhere more sceptical, although when in February 1980 the Royal Institute of British Architects' journal convened a feature on 'Vernacular – The English Disease?', Melville Dunbar (by then of Chelmsford-based Ruffle Dunbar Partnership) spoke up for 'Forever Ambridge', suggesting an enduring 'need for community, quaintness and the picturesque'.[37] In a 1980 *Architectural Review* article Adrian Forty and Henry Moss gave a critical account of 'pseudo-vernacular', including its 'rural and suburban' variant in Essex, as an owner-occupied 'housing style for troubled consumers'. Vernacular sought to accommodate, but could never quite defuse, conflict: 'while conveying an illusion of harmony, pseudo-vernacular succeeds in incorporating a set of thoroughly discordant and disconnected social beliefs.' Forty and Moss concluded:

> Security in the all-too-obviously changing present is achieved by a simultaneous view of very selective versions of the past and the future, to convey the impression that it is possible to enjoy the benefits of progress without having to endure the discomforts of change. Pseudo-vernacular provides just such a moment of double-vision.

Essex design fostered 'a static scenery for mobile people', a village style for commuting life. If the rendered and weather-boarded frontages conveyed a village 'sense of order', the backs and interiors were 'the scenery of progress', though the skill of it was acknowledged: 'The collision of images, between old and new ... is done with considerable panache and unselfconsciousness.'[38] The resultant regulated eclecticism matched a social and political mood valuing both community and individualism, stability and opportunity – what Charles Holland terms the 'spatial corollary' of a 'particular combination of social conservatism and economic liberalism', in Essex terms 'the antithesis of the new town modernism of Harlow and Basildon'.[39] South Woodham Ferrers was a place perfect for the emergent 1980s England. In a critical reflection in 2018, Gillian Darley presented South Woodham Ferrers as 'just the beginning of a state of mind, and a reality, from which we are about to take our leave'.[40]

In 2004 Ronald Brunskill reflected that, while vernacular revivals were far removed from historic rural vernacular buildings, 'the Vernacular Revival, considerably modified, is the popular or vernacular architecture of our time'.[41] Samuel commented that the return to brick pointed at once to the future and the past, to conservation and capital, to the local and beyond: 'Neo-vernacular brickwork has some claim to being the international style of our times, even though it taps sentiments which are regional and claim to be indigenous.'[42] For Samuel's 'even though' one could, however, read 'precisely because', the claims of place heightened rather than diminished in a globalizing world. The geographies of late twentieth- and early twenty-first-century English vernacular indeed indicate the more-than-local, as in 2001 Essex County Council sold the freehold of most of South Woodham Ferrers to Asda, which in 1999 had been acquired by the U.S. retail giant Walmart, who would own the chain until 2021. Complex geographies shape English particulars.

On Common Ground

In 1983, the same year that the Essex Design Guide praised South Woodham Ferrers, Common Ground was established, an environmental charity for whom English places have been a preoccupation. In Common Ground's 2006 compendium *England in Particular*, the old English counties are praised ('the historic counties tell us about deep identity'), and Essex's pantiles, weatherboarding and fingerposts feature, but neither South Woodham Ferrers nor the Essex Design Guide is mentioned.[43] Common Ground has taken the particular for other purposes, in part a Hoskinsian assertion of the local, common and vernacular. Through a notable range of campaigns, Common Ground has sought to reshape English cultures of place.

Common Ground was set up in 1983 by founder directors Sue Clifford, Angela King and Roger Deakin. All three had been involved in Friends of the Earth, and the name was borrowed from *The Common Ground*, a 1980 book by naturalist Richard Mabey, a key supporter and the editor of Common Ground's first major publication, the 1984 collection *Second Nature*.[44] The aim was to promote the common, local and everyday cultural heritage, and to link conservation and the arts. Common Ground argued that the common was being overlooked by an environmentalism valuing the rare or exotic, and that conservation's proper desire for scientific legitimacy risked ignoring the very cultural values which drove everyday concerns. The local was the scale at which such ideas were best pursued, with the arts a key vehicle. Common Ground was based in central London, initially near Covent Garden in the London Ecology Centre, before relocating in 2001 to Shaftesbury in Dorset. Clifford and King were the key figures, and when they stepped down the directorship passed in 2013 to Dorset-based Adrian Cooper, also owner of Little Toller Books, which specializes in commissioning new and reprinting old nature- and country-writing.[45]

In *Holding Your Ground*, their 1985 'action guide to local conservation', Clifford and King wrote that while fifty years ago there were 'real regional and local differences in the landscape and in villages and towns', now 'regional and local distinctiveness are disappearing so fast.'[46] Particularity was under threat, and the 1990 'Local Distinctiveness' campaign lamented an 'erosion of difference and bleaching of identity'. There was a need 'to recognise the difference and the detail that enrich our places', and the campaign leaflet blended land and personal identity as geology turned to a fingerprint, particularity to be mined for the cultural good. Difference and detail could be self-consciously ordinary as well as unique or eccentric. Common Ground proposed 'an alphabet of local distinctiveness', with an 'exploratory' example running from Ayrshires and ammonites to Yorkshire Pudding and Zennor, by way of barns, cooling towers, gasometers and level crossings.[47] Places might claim quirkiness, but could also be proudly and profoundly prosaic. While 'experts' might value 'the special

Cover of 'Local Distinctiveness' campaign leaflet by Common Ground (1990).

things', ordinary people could appreciate the vernacular.[48] Locals carried special knowledge: 'Be positively parochial. Never forget that YOU are an expert in your place. No one knows what you think or feel unless YOU say so.'[49] For Common Ground one way to prompt local reflection was through the arts, as in the New Milestones project, launched in 1985 in Dorset. Initial commissions by Simon Thomas, Peter Randall-Page and Andy Goldsworthy generated 'small-scale imaginative works which complement and conspire with the place'.⁵⁰ Thomas's wooden *Grains of Wheat* evoked Bronze Age crops on what had since been pasture; Randall-Page's *Wayside Carvings* of shells invoked chalk formation. No plaques explained; rather, the works were to acquire local meaning and a local name.

In *Second Nature* Fraser Harrison, a leading Common Ground supporter and trustee, wrote on 'England, Home and Beauty': 'the ordinary places and objects that make up our everyday landscape, our personal countryside, stand as living monuments to our continuing survival and feeling response to the world. Without such monuments, and they are not necessarily a rural monopoly, our sense of identity begins to crumble and warp.'⁵¹ There is a complexity here, though, as the monumental turns out not necessarily to be certain or stable. In his 1986 book *The Living Landscape* Harrison, describing the 'visible world' as 'restlessly evanescent', extended qualities of 'ceaseless mutation' to land itself:

> At first sight, it seems that land is the solid sand over which the mirage of landscape plays, yet it turns out that land too has its own evanescence. A closely observed, familiar and lived-in topography adds up to a very complex compound of signs and meanings, all of them in a state of perpetual change. Place – if *place* is the word to describe the unity of one's own land and landscape – is a restlessly changeable phenomenon.⁵²

Common Ground's work in general is marked by a reflexivity concerning what might seem obvious terminology. Whether the local patch or the national England, place is put into question as it is valued, and pastoral too is subject to scrutiny. The *Second Nature* anthology was introduced by Mabey as 'in the broadest sense . . . a radical one', a quality indicated by the inclusion of those critics of pastoral discussed in Chapter Three above: John Berger on 'Animal World', John Barrell on 'The Golden Age of Labour' and Raymond Williams on 'Between Country and City'.⁵³ *Second Nature* evoked pastoral while at the same time putting its appeal in question, seeking critical reflexivity in its readership, Mabey presenting the collection as both part of and divergent from a tradition of rural writing.⁵⁴

Common Ground also sought critical reflection on a basic practice of place-orientation, mapping. From 1986 the Parish Maps project encouraged people to map their valued place through an extended cartographic language, complementing conventional maps with annotations and illustrations, or producing maps in alternative media, including textile, sculpture and ceramics.[55] Jonathan Raban, commenting in 1986 on the retreat of the village ideal and the Anglican church in national life, had suggested: 'By 1970, no one, not even the vicar, could persist in seeing the parish as the small, self-contained microcosm of England.'[56] Common Ground, however, took the parish as a term to mobilize place affection, with its combination of buildings and land, the civil and the ecclesiastical, the secular and spiritual. Mabey again provided a prompt, having introduced his 1977 edition of Gilbert White's *Natural History of Selborne* by claiming 'parish' as 'the indefinable territory to which we feel we belong, which we have the measure of'.[57] Clifford and King took 'parish' to denote a scale of intimate knowledge, England at small scale.

Common Ground launched the Parish Maps project with a London display of commissioned artists' maps in 1987, *Knowing Your Place*. Art variously defined as political, feminist, multicultural and environmentalist framed the project, with mappers including Helen Chadwick, David Nash, Balraj Khanna, Pat Johns, Conrad Atkinson, Stephen Willats and Simon Lewty. The aim was to inspire and provoke imaginative cartography, and from the artists listed above a visiting community group could have taken, respectively: mapping as an articulation of place, gender and the body; mapping as working with the substance of land; mapping as meditation on urban global ethnic belonging; mapping as finding enchantment in nature; mapping as revealing place poisoned by power; mapping as conveying alienation in the everyday; and mapping as placed personal story.[58] Community parish maps tended more to the celebratory than the critical in content, though were not without their critical use. Maps registering value in place could be mobilized as evidence in battles over proposed development. Within ten years over 1,500 community maps had been made, with in 1996 a celebratory London Barbican display of 'people's parish maps', and regional and local shows around the country.

The production of a map could both reflect and shape community politics, with the registering of divergent voices alongside one another, the assertion of one voice over another or the accommodation of difference in a composite sense of place. Common Ground released the Parish Map model, but took no charge of its diffusion.

English Particulars

Common Ground's 1988 newsletter, *The Parish Mapper*, included a map by county of projects completed and in progress at December 1987, the distribution reflecting local initiative, with the largest circles for South Yorkshire (between 51 and 100) and Humberside (21–50), with the next category (11–20) spanning Hereford and Worcester, London, Somerset, Norfolk, Devon, Suffolk and Buckinghamshire.[59] If, for some, 'parish' invoked a southern English rurality, the distribution of maps indicated a wider purchase for the term. I recall a launch event in the Nottinghamshire village of Calverton, a mining village not far from Nottingham, in early 1986, which I covered as a media worker for Nottinghamshire Rural Community Council, looking for stories for the weekly 'Monday-at-9.05' rural slot on BBC Radio Nottingham. A crowded evening village hall was addressed by Common Ground's national parish maps co-ordinator, Tom Greeves, invited after interest was kindled by a local artist. Greeves opened up the possibilities, and local voices had their say, jockeying for committee positions, wondering what form things might take, what content might be. Listeners heard the uncertainties. *The Parish Mapper* listed Calverton as done: 'painting (completed) and display panels on purpose-built structure'.[60] In a review of the Parish Maps project thirty years on, two Calverton participants noted disappointment at how the map's valuing of a green space was ignored in development plans.[61]

In 2006 Common Ground published *England in Particular: A Celebration of the Commonplace, the Local, the Vernacular and the Distinctive*. Clifford and King's major published work, crafted with typical illustrative and typographical care, presented England as particular and made out of local particulars, the national a composite of places within. Their introductory essay lauds detail, patina, authenticity and identity, and an alphabet of 'Common Ground Rules for Local Distinctiveness' follows. A prescribed English sensibility emerges, a careful mix of insider virtues and openness to difference, including:

Remember the depth of people's attachment to places.
   Know your place. Facts and surveys are not the same as knowledge and wisdom. Itinerant expertise needs to meet with aboriginal, place-based knowledge so that we can make the best of both worlds.
   Exile xenophobia, which fossilises places and peoples.
   Let the character of the people and place express itself.[62]

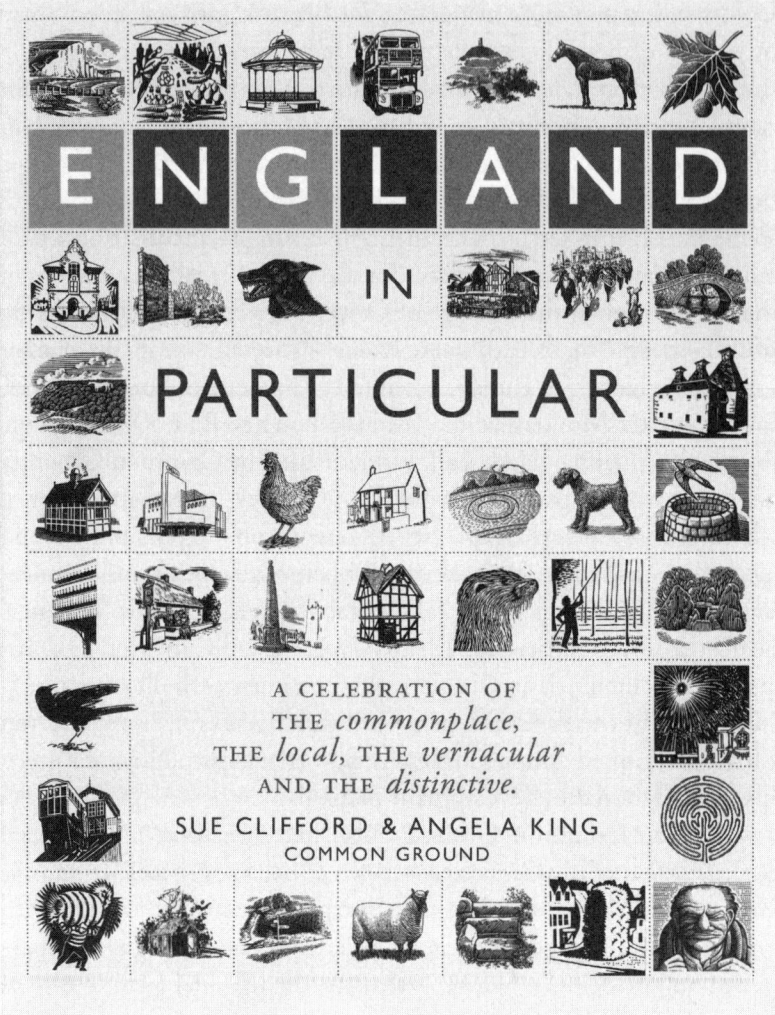

Cover of Sue Clifford and Angela King, *England in Particular* (first published 2006; 2013 edition).

England in Particular in effect inflates the 1990 *Local Distinctiveness* leaflet to 512 pages of alphabetical gazetteer on 'aspects of locality', with a short reflective essay on each entry. The Englishness of things is rarely asserted; rather, national character emerges through local accumulation. Being alphabetical, the book 'shuffles and juxtaposes in ways that surprise'.[63] Airfields and Albion: perhaps a Battle of Britain link? Tors and tower blocks: prospects or vertigo? Cottages and council houses sit together, the character conventionally ascribed to one evident too in the other. Corn dollies follow cooling towers. Eccles cakes precede edible dormouse. Varied tastes are catered for, though the unparticular is put down: 'A Somerset hedge laid in a Midland pattern, a Bakewell pudding made with almond essence, *Tess of the D'Urbervilles* filmed in France: these things fall short. We are deprived by the ersatz, the kitsch, the substitute.'[64] *England in Particular* locates places in their historic counties, 'the bounds laid down a thousand years ago or more ... our heart is in the geographical use of historic meaning.'[65] Avon no more, Cleveland no more and Yorkshire once again a trinity of Ridings.

Alongside the Parish Maps project, one of Common Ground's more successful initiatives has been 'Apple Day', launched in 1990 at Covent Garden, near to their headquarters, as an annual 21 October celebration of tastes and varieties. By 1999 over six hundred events were held nationally, and the day gained its own *England in Particular* entry: 'Traditions have to begin somewhere.'[66] In 2014 Virginia Astley produced 'A Poem for Apple Day. 21st October 2014', published by the nature-attentive cultural journal *Caught by the River*, with an apple tree a sign of sustaining life, as an old man looks on a 'half-fallen tree' as old as he.[67] In October 2018, driving back to Nottingham from a Peak District excursion, a stop at Cromford in Derbyshire found an Apple Day celebration. People brought pickings and windfalls to be pressed for juice, and there were a variety of stalls and folk performance, Apple Day an occasion for co-operative vernacular culture. An organizer, David Mitchell of the nearby Scarthin Books (billed as 'a bookshop for the majority of minorities'), thanked people for coming and sang, unaccompanied, Vaughan Williams's 1901 setting of William Barnes's poem 'Linden Lea', where an apple tree leans down in Dorset, a classic of the first English folk song revival.[68] A Victorian Dorset poem set for Edwardian national music, its dialect edges smoothed, sung as appropriate in twenty-first-century Derbyshire. Cromford is part of the Derwent Valley Mills World Heritage Site, discussed further in Chapter Seven; one English heritage folds into another, English particulars wrapped in association on Apple Day.

The establishment of Apple Day had followed Common Ground's 1988 'Save Our Orchards' campaign, supported by a 1989 photographic exhibition by James Ravilious on West Country orchards. Ravilious had an affinity with Common Ground's celebration of the particular and ordinary, and had contributed three sheep images to *Second*

Nature. Ravilious moved to north Devon in 1972 with his wife, Robin, whose family had owned a small estate there since the 1680s, and his photographic work there archived the locality.[69] The nearby Beaford Arts Centre had been set up by the Dartington Hall Trust in 1966, and director John Lane commissioned Ravilious to photograph the region in a 10-mile radius, wanting a photographic equivalent to the kind of cultural documentation pursued by writer H. J. Massingham in the 1930s.[70] The resultant Beaford Archive, made between 1972 and 1990, comprised 80,000 images taken by Ravilious. Ravilious also gathered 10,000 historic images, including prints from local people, further embedding his photographic practice as local chronicler. Ravilious effectively undertook a photographic residency, in the colloquial rather than artistic sense. Black-and-white images record a peopled landscape of farms, hamlets and villages, with community events, individual portraits, valley and moor, interior and field. Ravilious died in 1999, and has himself since been celebrated as an example of England in particular. In Common Ground's dream England, in every hamlet a particularist.

Ravilious's work attracted the English label, and he was happy with this. The Royal Photographic Society's 1997 exhibition of Ravilious's work in Bath, and the subsequent book by curator Peter Hamilton (with a foreword by Alan Bennett) was entitled *An English Eye*. Bennett set Ravilious in 'a very English tradition of photography', documentary images of everyday life presenting things and people which seem 'old-fashioned' yet have a 'dignity and reticence' in 'an England one had thought long gone'. Englishness is here a quality of survival despite modernity, and English places persist despite a world changed, Ravilious offering not 'nostalgia' but 'compassionate witness'.[71] For Hamilton, when Ravilious photographed beyond England, his 'English eye' was still more evident.[72] Ravilious had entitled a 1995 collection *A Corner of England: North Devon Landscapes and People*, the county meaningful as part of a country.[73]

In the photography magazine *Ten:8*'s 1983 issue on 'Rural Myths', noted in Chapter Three above, Paul Lewis criticized Ravilious for attending to older patterns and ignoring new technology, presenting 'a gentle, even idyllic, country community. This perpetuated the myth which Ronald Blythe had demolished in East Anglia.'[74] Ravilious persisted despite, and almost to spite, such critique. Blythe, who could critique pastoral myth yet also have regard for the old and traditional, provided a foreword for Ravilious's 1980 collection *The Heart of the Country*.[75] Ravilious set his work as observing the authentic and workaday, a lived world which any visitor passing through or staying for a weekend might never discern. These were images of residents by a resident, and if in Devon some things were threatened by change, that did not mean the camera should shy away from the present. In *Down the Deep Lanes* (2000), collaborator Peter Beacham emphasized Ravilious's attention to 'the stuff of everyday existence' which shapes 'regional identity': 'It would please us if the day dawns when corrugated iron is as sought after as thatch, protesters march to demand the reopening of the local quarry, and guide books tell us how often it rains.'[76] *Down the Deep Lanes* took its title from the last line of a 1975 Ted Hughes poem, 'Last Load', published in *Moortown Diary* (1979), about securing hay bales in the barn before rain.[77] Ravilious had contributed photographs for Beacham's 1990 book *Devon Building*, a study of vernacular architecture, dedicated by Beacham to W. G. Hoskins in recognition of his service to Devon County Council as Historic Buildings Consultant between 1968 and 1978.[78] Ravilious pictured the Devon vernacular of farmyard and barn in one of Hoskins's cherished counties, but his photographs could also show things which could only be from the late twentieth century. If his photographs are not viewed through a presumption of nostalgia and loss (a narrative which tends to frame, for example, the selection in the collection *The Recent Past*, issued in 2017), many things contemporary (if not necessarily modern) are evident.[79] Thus an image of 'Kitchen Implements, Bridge Reeve, Devon, *c.* 1990' shows utensils hanging from hooks on a wall, the manner resembling an antique collection or a Dutch interior, but the content clearly showing the potato mashers, ladles and scissors of today.[80]

Adjacent pages on *An English Eye* show the customary mixing of old and contemporary, complicating old country assumptions with present reference.[81] 'Huntsman Cutting Off Fox's Tail, Hatherleigh, Devon, 1975' shows a dead fox, a huntsman standing to de-tail, mounted riders and onlookers behind and several boys coming to watch. The hunt costumes of older men and the dead fox appear alongside 1970s boyswear. A Devon scene, not eternal but 1975. Two years later Ravilious pictured 'Wombles and Cavaliers, Gymkhana, Cross, Torrington, 1977'. An older, suited man plays guitar under a tree; children in everyday clothes sit and listen; three men are dressed as

'Huntsman Cutting Off Fox's Tail, Hatherleigh, Devon, 1975',
photograph by James Ravilious.

cavaliers in some kind of historic re-enactment; and three adults are in Womble costumes: Uncle Bulgaria, Madame Cholet and an unusually slim Orinoco. A current popular cultural craze, *The Wombles* achieving TV and pop musical fame from 1973 in adaptation from Elisabeth Beresford's books, appears at a local event. The gymkhana, and the photograph, could only be of the 1970s, an England particular to time and locale – 1970s Devon, Wombles and Cavaliers, all perfectly civil, on common ground.

Arcadian Plots

Common Ground's 1984 *Second Nature* included an essay by Colin Ward on plotlands, particular types of 'makeshift landscape' celebrated in the same year by Ward and Denis Hardy in their book *Arcadia for All*.[82] There is Arcadia and then there is Arcadia: the Arcadia of the Essex Design Guide, with safety in new build, and *Arcadia for All*, a very different kind of place. There was no entry on plotlands in *England in Particular*, though they were noted briefly under 'bungalows'.[83] Hardy and Ward documented the surviving and lost plotlands of southeast England, interwar private developments with individual plots bought from landowners, with often improvised dwellings for

'Wombles and Cavaliers, Gymkhana, Cross, Torrington, 1977',
photograph by James Ravilious.

residence or holiday. This was an Arcadia of freedom from care and escape from the city. Hardy and Ward told a complex story of property and freedom, sometimes bohemian, sometimes anarchic, and in conflict with emerging planning and preservation movements who promoted a rather different Arcadia of ordered pastoral Englishness.[84] From Hardy and Ward's work plotlands would become a late twentieth- and early twenty-first-century reference point for an alternative pastoral, an English particular of dissident value.

Arcadia for All had a strong Essex component, and South Woodham Ferrers gave the plotland story a further twist. The new town development entailed the removal via compulsory purchase of plotlands laid out between the 1890s and 1930s on farmland and riverside. Hardy and Ward, writing as the plans were enacted, noted the hardship suffered by often elderly residents in the clearance: 'by the utilitarian test of catering for the greatest happiness of the greatest number, the County Council's intervention can be readily justified. As always, the private visions of the relatively poor were sacrificed for those of the relatively affluent.'[85] In his *Building Design* articles on South Woodham Ferrers, David Pearce had described the pre-rebuild site as 'a strange, remote, dishevelled and haphazard place, or rather non-place – a sort of unplanned shanty arcadia in 1972'.[86] For Pearce the development was an improvement, but his piece prompted the future *Robinson* filmmaker Patrick Keiller of London NW3 to write in complaint. Keiller recalled a 1974 visit to South Woodham Ferrers:

> one of the best surviving examples of the owner built communities of Essex ... examples of a vernacular far more important than anything in the county's dolls house *Design Guide* ... surely such a rare example of user control in planning deserves a more constructive response than to be drowned out by the sort of Hitler Youth-inspired historicist dross that your article purveys.[87]

Longer-term South Woodham Ferrers resident Terry Philpot also wrote to uphold the existing plotland buildings over the council's 'mock-rustic environment'.[88]

Hardy and Ward's investigation was in line with Keiller rather than Pearce, presenting plotlands as sites of popular invention, reflecting Ward's anarchist philosophy and politics. Here was a makeshift landscape, improvised building, community beyond authority, place as experiment. The politics of the unauthorized could move in different ways, from unorthodox collectivism to happy tolerance to wary defensiveness to aggressively contrarian. Jaywick, for Hardy and Ward the 'largest and most spectacular plotland settlement on the Essex coast',[89] would in the twenty-first century become a common journalistic reference point for east coast deprivation (named in 2015 as the most deprived ward in England) and for political support for UKIP and Brexit. The area was represented for a time by UKIP's sole Westminster MP, Douglas Carswell (following his defection from the Conservatives), and in February 2016 the *New Statesman* reported from Jaywick as 'a dispatch from Ukipland'.[90]

Recent plotland narratives have tended, however, to cultural positivity. The 2004 reissue of *Arcadia for All* fed off and generated cultural interest in surviving plotlands as an alternative, dissident, unconservative English landscape. Singer Robert Wyatt, mentioned in Chapter Four for his recording of 'Shipbuilding', and a resident of Louth in Lincolnshire since 1988 with his wife, Alfreda Benge, commented in 2001 on owning a summer shack chalet at Humberston Fitties on the north Lincolnshire coast near Cleethorpes: 'it might be a way forward. It's like something from a different era – the word freedom comes to mind.'[91] In the sleeve notes for his 1997 LP *Shleep*, Wyatt wrote of Benge's lyrics:

> Alfie's words arrived in and around our old wooden dacha at Humberston Fitties. The Fitties are on the Humber estuary opposite Spurn Point, a vital resting place for migrant birds and home to many others. 'September the Ninth', for example, was an unusually early day on which many hundreds of swallows gathered around our dacha and rested awhile before disappearing into the blue yonder. It was a moment of pure awe for us.

Plotlands here nurture nature, freedom, improvisation. Benge had researched the history of the site, declared a conservation area in 1996, though in 2017 the council, in austerity mode, would sell the lease to a holiday park company. Plotlands became musical too on Saint Etienne's 2017 album *Home Counties*, on the penultimate track, 'Sweet Arcadia'. Saint Etienne (singer Sarah Cracknell and musicians Bob Stanley and Pete Wiggs) had made records since the early 1990s, often evoking London places, and were happy with an English label. Simon Reynolds's sleeve notes for their 2000 LP *Sound of Water* termed them 'the group that took imported exotica ... and paradoxically created something quintessentially English'. On *Home Counties* Saint Etienne looked to the Green Belt and beyond, and on 'Sweet Arcadia' sang a pop *Arcadia for All*. The track journeys out of London to makeshift towns, tumbledown shacks, a handmade people's land, a sweet Albion with a plotland place-name litany of Laindon, Dunton, Pitsea and Benfleet, Box Hill, Dungeness, Seasalter and Peacehaven.

If *Arcadia for All* was a southeastern study, plotlands across the country drew those with an eye for different English particulars. Jonathan Meades's 1990 BBC television series *Abroad in Britain* included the film 'Severn Heaven', visiting the shack settlement near Bewdley in Worcestershire, finding a 'folk architecture' and 'a parody of a picturesque suburb'. Meades's companion 1990 essay 'First Shack' recorded a shack curiosity since childhood, with Bewdley 'the greatest extant shack colony in Britain', 'a place uncontaminated by planner's wisdom'. The plotland is a site of recycling and improvisation, of a rare unselfconscious nonconformity:

What we find beside the Severn is folk architecture, a demotic idiom which is the built equivalent of slang: it has that vitality, that urgency, that humour.

An environment which is self-determined to this degree is unusual in Britain.

This slang place is Common Ground with knobs on. Bewdley's shacks carried a particular sense of character and distinction: 'Local pride can be an ugly thing, but here it's born of an intimate knowledge of the sheer struggle it took to create the place.'[92] Meades's film interviewed residents in a manner showing a demographic variety to match the buildings, in intergenerational meaning, ecological consciousness, residential style, peculiar taste. If this was a community, it sheltered private lives, Meades finding a marked sense of boundedness around dwellings, a community far from communal. Aerial shots showed the pattern of living, the shacks in clear rows and grassed space between. As the end titles roll, the camera flies over, with the closing soundtrack the melancholy 1968 single by Birmingham band The Move, 'Goodbye Blackberry Way'. Roy Wood's song becomes an ode to West Midland Arcadia.

Plotlands have gained fascination in part through vulnerability, as settlements not especially solid. *Arcadia for All* is part memorial to clearance, to a makeshiftness unable to hold out against commerce and the local state, South Woodham Ferrers one example. Vulnerability also comes from geographical marginality, plotlands often developed on coastal locations at risk of erosion, limited futures cutting land values. The 1953 east coast floods demolished sites in Essex and elsewhere. Jaywick was hit severely on the night of 31 January/1 February, with 35 dead, 5 per cent of the resident population, the casualties mostly elderly. Hilda Grieve's 1959 account of the Essex floods, *The Great Tide*, recounted that water rose 'so fast that people died in their beds without moving': 'The clocks in the Jaywick bungalows, on mantelpieces, tables and walls, were stopped at two o'clock.'[93] Where destruction did not occur, local pride in resilience could follow, in survival against environmental and governmental odds. On the northeast coast of Norfolk is Eccles, one of those sites where an older village disappeared into the North Sea (the church tower remained on the beach until 1895), but a plotland settlement succeeded. The interwar Bush Estate has survived 1953, and later storm surges, though with touch-and-go

English Particulars

The Bush Estate, Eccles, Norfolk, 27 July 2016.

moments behind the coastal dunes. The historic name of Eccles-next-the-Sea conveys not only spatial proximity but possible temporal fate, with anxieties and occasional evacuations on a coast where 'managed realignment' has become official policy.[94] The estate hangs on, and a visit in July 2016 found original bungalows well set and replacement builds well fenced. Under green corrugated metal, a modest veranda faced south for the sun. Across the road, a high wooden fence lent privacy to a house named from the nearby sea, 'Juxta-Mare', as a St George's flag flew, just visible to the passer-by. English Arcadia hangs on next-the-sea.

Down the Local

An England of the particular, from Trumpton through Royston Vasey to various arcadias and common grounds, finds value in the local. Concerns for local and regional identity have also highlighted a particular kind of 'local', the pub, where geographical scale and colloquial terminology meet. From the 1960s, campaigns to preserve the local, and the products available there, made beer the focus of debate over English cultural authenticity. Going down the local, you could down the local, if the local was still there and still serving.

Beer as English drink, and the pub as English environment, nurtured a distinctive consumer campaign. Christopher Hutt's 1973 *The Death of the English Pub*, its cover showing a funereal wreath around hand pumps, was prefaced by a quotation from Hilaire Belloc: 'When you have lost your Inns, drown your empty selves, for you will have lost the last of England.' Belloc's 1912 essay 'On Inns', written in a southern English inn, had diagnosed an institution 'in peril': 'From the towns all Inns have been driven: from the villages most.' Belloc concluded his essay: 'Change your hearts or you will lose your Inns and you will deserve to have lost them. But when you have lost your Inns drown your empty selves, for you will have lost the last of England.'[95]

Belloc's diagnosis of the inn as locus of English identity, of beer as English self-sustenance, was taken by Hutt to capture something about 1970s England, of cultural dilution by corporate interests. Hutt critiqued the dominance of the 'Big Six' brewers, their takeovers and closures of other companies and their promotion of keg beer, whereby the application of carbon dioxide pressure to dispense beer went alongside standardization and diminished flavour. The Big Six accounted for over 70 per cent of beer output in 1972, and controlled 56 per cent of pubs, up from 24 per cent in 1960. From 1963 the Surrey-based Society for the Preservation of Beers from the Wood had promoted beer served from wooden barrels, their chief target keg beer, with metal barrels tolerated if traditional beer was served. The society did not seek a campaigning role, but in 1971 four Manchester men set up the Campaign for the Revitalisation of Ale, with Michael Hardman their first chairman, to counter the supposed devitalizing sterility of keg. In 1973 the group was renamed the Campaign for Real Ale (CAMRA), the term 'real ale' coined in early issues of their monthly newsletter *What's Brewing?* CAMRA sought publicity and membership, leading what sympathetic journalist Richard Boston, who from 1973 wrote a *Guardian* beer column (collected in his 1976 book *Beer and Skittles*), termed a 'consumer revolt', showing that 'you *can* stand in the way of progress.'[96] Hutt encountered CAMRA while researching *The Death of the English Pub*, and by the time of publication was its chairman. CAMRA had 5,000 members by November 1973, seventy branches by the end of 1974, 30,000 members by May 1975 and 150,000 by 2012.

CAMRA tapped an enthusiasm for beer and an anger at its state, asserting the cultural authenticity of traditional beer against inauthentic keg. Lincoln Allison, writing in *New Society* in 1978, saw CAMRA as part of 'the English cultural movement'.[97] A geographical narrative drove the campaign for a national beer culture grounded in regional variation in production and consumed in local pubs. The national scale of the Big Six, and their national standardization of product, ran counter to an internally diverse national culture. Ian Nairn, architectural critic and CAMRA member, wrote a *Sunday Times* piece, 'The Best Beers of Our Lives', in June 1974 which boosted the campaign, warning against 'the arbitrary extinction of local flavours in favour of a "national brew"'.[98] For Boston the task was to defend 'fine English beer' and 'fine English pubs'.[99] Englishness was a matter not only of location but of style, and something which deserved to be more than the archaic irrelevance envisaged by the Big Six: 'If traditional beer was to survive it would be here and there in small pockets as a quaint reminder of Merrie England.'[100]

If English national style was regional variety, with the pub a site for the local experience of regional difference, hope lay with what Hutt termed the 'Independent Brewers'. Two-thirds of brewing companies operating in 1960 had been wiped out, but ninety independents continued, often long-standing family firms embedded in their regions via pub holdings. Hutt highlighted Young's of Wandsworth, Theakston of Masham and Adnams of Southwold as exemplary. The surviving English pub and brewery was therefore urban as well as rural, CAMRA deploying both as images of authenticity, whether in Hutt's lament for 'The Dry Villages' or in Iain Macmillan's evocative photography of urban pub interiors within Hutt's book.[101] Meaningful English everyday life, urban and rural, was under threat.

The Englishness of the English pub was conveyed in *The English Pub* (1976), the first book by Michael Jackson, who would be a key figure in defining drink cultures, notably around beer and whisky. Richly illustrated, *The English Pub* traded on the renewed interest in English beer, the book beginning: 'The pub is an institution unique to England, and there is nothing more English.'[102] For Jackson pub Englishness was a matter of history and naming, and of the geography of beer. Reflecting on pub signage, Jackson suggested: 'An endless pub-crawl would afford the best lesson in England's heritage and history . . . England's every square mile is a vast, open-air museum, detailing its own geography, topography, military history, heraldry; its personalities, birds and beasts, occupations and sports.'[103] Beer was 'the drink for the pub-goer . . . drawn from a cask and served by the pint': 'English beer is different. Unique. There are two kinds of beer in the world: the English kind, and the kind everyone else drinks. They are quite separate brews.'[104] Jackson's was not an insular viewpoint, and a year later he would publish *The World Guide to Beer*, but Jackson asserted England's particularity in global beer culture.[105] The corporate shift to keg had threatened this particular value: 'During the mass-marketing deluge, the geography of English beer shifted to a seismic degree.'[106] The expansion of London-based conglomerates had, however, prompted a heartening rediscovery of small independent brewers, in part through the actions of CAMRA, 'one of Europe's most successful consumer campaigns', within 'a widespread grass-roots revival which flourished to a degree no one had expected. A new level of awareness, and a militancy, emerged among English beer-drinkers.'[107]

The geography of CAMRA's revitalized country was mapped in the brewery gazetteers of Richard Boston's book, in Frank Baillie's 1973 *The Beer Drinker's Companion* and in the pubs included on members' recommendation in the annual CAMRA *Good Beer Guide*, published from 1974.[108] The *Guide* deployed environmental language, with the Big Six to blame for 'beer deserts', as in 1978: 'many areas of Norfolk are virtually a beer desert created by Watneys (Norwich Brewery).'[109] This was the setting for my own early explorations, first venturing to pubs in Norwich around 1981. Despite the city's rumoured pub for every day of the year, only half a dozen seemed adequate, the few free houses opened in the 1970s in a city dominated by Watneys' Norwich Brewery, with its Norwich Bitter and Castle Bitter. The Plasterers' Arms, the Ten Bells, the White Lion and the Golden Star held beer variety, whether East Anglian or from further afield. Norwich Brewery was itself, of course, local in manufacture and in branding, indicating that 1970s beer culture was less about geographical proximity than geographical authenticity manifest in taste. In retrospect, a visit to the Golden Star in 1981 appears a form of cultural induction, with beer from the Star Brewery out the back, no piped music, a piano and a mixed Golden Star morris team, a non-mainstream non-desert.[110]

CAMRA connected beer and pubs to a broader cultural movement for authentic value, Hutt commenting: 'Flavour and variety have died not only in the English pub. The flavour has gone from many foods, from bread to frozen vegetables, on through sweating cheeses to sawdust sausages. The word "variety" that used to have a special meaning in the world of entertainment, doesn't carry that meaning any more.'[111]

Entertainment could also play its part, as when in 1977 the National Youth Jazz Orchestra issued their *In CAMRA* LP, with sleeve notes by orchestra director Bill Ashton:

> The link between jazz and Real Ale is a very strong one ... both are utterly dependent on the atmosphere, the conditions and the skill of their creators. The parallel between pop music and keg bitter is just as exact. Both are fizzy, bland and utterly predictable.

The authentic plays off the inauthentic, revitalization here appearing defensively dismissive of the popular. Punning tune titles submitted by CAMRA members included 'That "Old Peculier" Feeling', 'Young's Makes Me Feel You So' and 'Samuel Smith and His Amazing Dancing Beer'. The cover showed orchestra members at Young's brewery, with logos of other approved brewers around, and cartoons by CAMRA supporter Bill Tidy on the rear cover.

The local and its beer were also a matter of environment. Hutt suggested there was an environmentalist 'blind spot' on pubs, but saw the 'happy spirited pub' as 'just as much an environmental issue as the future of Covent Garden, or what we do about pollution in the River Trent'.[112] Boston's *Beer and Skittles* noted E. F. Schumacher's 1973 Green manifesto *Small Is Beautiful* on the 'disease' of 'giantism', and suggested an efficiency of smaller units, not least for transportation:

> in the coming years it will make less sense rather than more to have enormous breweries in the middle of England and to carry very large quantities of water (which is what beer mostly consists of) about the country in vehicles running on expensive and irreplaceable fossil fuels.[113]

In 1977 Boston established the environmentalist journal *Vole*, with funding from Monty Python star Terry Jones and contributors including Richard Mabey. Beer and the pub sit alongside concern for place, crafts and tradition, with one 1978 issue of *Vole* devoted to the value of slowness.[114]

Beer and pubs have continued to inform a broad cultural-environmental sensibility, with the twenty-first-century proliferation of microbreweries and the emergence of the contentious category of 'craft beer', which for CAMRA, in its production and distribution process, awkwardly blurs the boundaries of 'real ale' authenticity. In 2015 *An Antidote to Indifference*, the 'tributary' publication of the journal *Caught by the River*, issued a beer special, including pieces on seasonality, on Ian Nairn and on Edward Ardizzone's 1939 book *The Local*, which had been reissued by affiliated publisher Little Toller, whose owner Adrian Cooper by then also ran Common Ground.[115] Belloc's 'empty selves/last of England' phrase has also achieved a second afterlife beyond its 1970s outing, generally as a term invoking virtuous identity and cultural warmth. The hard edges of Belloc's conservatism, shared with his contemporary Chesterton, tend to be bypassed in such citations. Belloc's Catholic Distributist political vision of resistance to the 'servile state', and of threats to England by things not appreciative of its particularity, shaded at times into antisemitism.[116] Belloc's 'On Inns' commented:

> If any foolish man pretend in your presence that the brotherhood of men should make a decent man cosmopolitan, reprove his error by the example of an Inn.
> If any one is so vile as to maintain in your presence that one's country should not be loved and loyally defended, confound so horrid a fool by the very vigorous picture of an Inn. And if he impudently says that some damned Babylon or other is better than an Inn, look up his ancestry.[117]

A strand of twenty-first-century Bellocry has nonetheless entwined beer and belonging to ostensibly benign ends. Thus the band British Sea Power, on 'Blackout', from their 2003 LP *The Decline of British Sea Power*, barely paraphrased Belloc in singing that when you had drunk all your beer you could drown your empty selves, having lost the last of this island.[118] The second chapter of Paul Kingsnorth's 2008 *Real England: The Battle against the Bland*, on pubs and beer, was entitled 'Drown Your Empty Selves', Belloc's phrase conveying threatened identity. Kingsnorth's first chapter, 'Citizens of Nowhere' (a decade ahead of Theresa May's parallel terminology), argued for a sense of place and belonging. Kingsnorth asserted that 'England matters to me', and sought 'a new type of patriotism, benign and positive, based on place not race, geography not biology'.[119] Beer and pubs were one ingredient: 'Among all the guff about Empire, cricket and the playing fields of Eton, Belloc thought he had pinned down where the heart of his adopted nation lay: in the ordinary, unglamorous, communal institution of the common people.'[120] For Kingsnorth, 'a good local pub, serving good local beer, is the ultimate antidote to placeless globalisation.'[121] The Old Crown in Hesket Newmarket, Cumbria, community-owned and with a microbrewery, is Kingsnorth's exemplar. The *Antidote to Indifference* beer special likewise cited Belloc, Paul Moody's 'The Last of England' beginning with the empty selves passage, and imagining the closure of the last pub in England in 2039. Belloc's harder 'look up his ancestry' edges of belonging are hinted at here, with a future social historian envisaged as explaining that 'in multi-media, multi-faith Britain, there really is no longer a need for pubs anyway.' Moody offers his 2039 fantasy as a warning, noting that 'more than half the villages of England are now "dry" for the first time since the Norman Conquest', such closures 'a bizarre process of cultural self-immolation'. Hope arrives with former Beautiful South and Housemartins singer Paul Heaton cycling around Cheshire performing in pubs to help landlords boost custom: 'something we love and believe in is being taken away from us.'[122]

Which English selves are emptying? Last orders for whom? Everyone cited in this beer story so far has been male, and, notwithstanding the presence of female voices in contemporary beer-writing, and attempts to diversify CAMRA membership and to highlight the historic and contemporary role of female 'brewsters', the tone of arguments in the works noted is one of anxious English masculinity. In that sense Heaton is an apt and eloquent reference point for Moody. Macmillan's photographs in *The Death of the English Pub* show older female drinkers, but Hutt's text is wary of brewers' emphasis on the female and youth market, with the removal of the public bar in pub redesign a threat to 'the working man'.[123] A male-dominated drinking space was at risk of merger with the female-friendly lounge. Jackson's *The English Pub* recognized the pub as 'still primarily a male domain' and, while happy that pub 'machismo' had 'mercifully subsided', was at best ambivalent about the undermining of masculine space.[124] Women featured in *The English Pub* primarily as barmaids and not as English beer drinkers: 'The popular understanding is that "lager" beers have a certain novelty value, and are suitable for women and hot days.'[125] The 1970s beer movement was in effect a fable of the English man, with gender, class, taste and cultural distinction framing English drinking.

If one vision of a twenty-first-century authentic English pub is community ownership, with the pub free to manage its environment and to source its beer as locally as it likes, another variant has chained the English high street. J. D. Wetherspoon was founded in London in 1979 by Tim Martin as part of a wider movement to make real ale the focus of new pubs. While other contemporaries such as the 'Firkin' chain of home-brewing pubs did not last, Wetherspoon's expanded to become a national brand in the 1990s, via a mixture of real ale from independent brewers, discounted pricing and distinctive design. The chain commonly took over redundant non-pub premises such as banks, theatres or post offices, retaining some of their features to lend distinction, often naming the pub with reference to its former use. A Wetherspoon's template of open-plan layout has all customers occupying the same space, without distinction and exclusivity, and no one sitting at or propping up the bar. Food is served but does not dominate, so this can remain a drinking space. Groups might mark their own territory via regular tables, but as in many late twentieth-century pub redesigns, distinctions of public bar and lounge disappear, the whole a common ground.[126] Wetherspoon's targeted female customers from the 1980s onwards, including via the admission of children. On a quiet afternoon here you could find a steady, know-what-you-are-getting place with somewhere to sit, relative security in the open plan and no need to wonder whether you should be there. Ordinariness accommodates.

By 2017 Wetherspoon's had 950 outlets in the UK and Ireland. CAMRA have provided members with vouchers redeemable in the chain; Wetherspoon's corporate success does not for CAMRA mark the death of the English pub. The chain itself plays on pub fantasy, its early pubs named with reference to Orwell's 1946 essay on the ideal pub, 'The Moon under Water', and in 1995 The Moon under Water opened in Manchester, a 10,000-square-foot largest pub in the world. Is this the authentic pub? Is this the real life? The company projects a non-corporatist style, overseen by a contrarian owner, Martin projecting a dishevelled counterpoint to standard executives, and happy to project his owns views within his pubs, as when issuing beermats against the EU during the 2016 referendum. In 2019, as Leave prospects faltered, Martin toured Wetherspoon's pubs to promote the virtues of a clean break with the EU. Martin appears a down-to-earth, defiantly non-progressive equivalent to the genially ruthless Richard Branson, and, as with Branson, critics have pointed to possible contradictions in image and policy, with labour precarity, the price undercutting of nearby pubs and the generation of wealth from the common touch. As a distinctive and contradictory part of millennial England styled as ordinary, Wetherspoon's has become a high street fixture trading on particulars, offering routine satisfaction in English towns. Future historians of the local might mimic the early twenty-first-century pub crawler, and start there.

English Fixtures

Three more long-standing English cultural fixtures conclude this chapter, all presenting places of character and distinction, and showing how English particulars become associated with the eccentric, the typically strange. All are culturally mainstream Englands, set in rural and small town life, and all have been labelled as distinctly English, as model specimens. The durability of each – one a television crime drama, one a television comedy, one a visitor attraction – indicates a popularity derived in part from saying something about England. At any time in the past six decades, one or more of the three could have served as English shorthand, whether in affection or despair.

The Murder County

Since 1997 the detective series *Midsomer Murders* has been a staple of prime-time television, its Chiltern-shot vision of English crime exported around the world as a characterization of the country. *Midsomer Murders* puts death in Arcadia, where in pastoral it has always belonged. Impeccably normal detectives investigate county goings-on, tapping conventions of southern rural Englishness to popular effect, with the infra-ordinary and extra-ordinary enfolded. Of the many crime dramas set in England, *Midsomer Murders* perhaps most attracts, indeed trades on, the English label, more so than Oxford's *Inspector Morse/Lewis/Endeavour*, where the city becomes the national and international selling point, and more than regionally based programmes set outside southern England, such as *Vera*, set and filmed in Northumberland. Two imaginary episodes will give a flavour of Midsomer; resemblance to fictional characters living or dead is intentional.

The Family Feudal: Three siblings quarrel over inheritance after the mysterious death of both parents in a cycling accident, when their tandem develops a lethal electrical charge. The family business, supplying bespoke leather goods, occupies a potential prime retail site, with a planning application submitted by a developer recently returned to Midsomer after two decades overseas. The developer attended school with one of the siblings, and is himself found dead at the level crossing on a steam railway. A pantomime performance of *Jack and the Beanstalk* by the Causton Players provides the denouement, faulty wiring in the lighting rig giving the detectives (one of whom plays the front end of a pantomime cow) a vital clue to the tandem tragedy. Costumed figures are pursued through the streets, scattering carol singers. The motive is revealed as relating to illegitimacy and a centuries-old curse.

The Kingfisher Killings: A Midsomer folk tale holds that, should a kingfisher cross the Parva Brook at sunrise on Lammas Day, misfortune will come to any who see the bird that day. A priest is found dead beneath a humpback bridge, suspicion falling on a recently appointed female curate. Theological arguments are enfolded with personal jealousies, as children attending a local summer camp prepare kingfisher costumes for Lammas celebrations. The seemingly unconnected death of an angler named King, found below a weir after being reported missing from his employment in the Causton Building Society, leads the detectives to an unlikely web of connections. Divers explore the Parva Brook, and an antique ring is found. An ornithologist preparing a manuscript on the kingfisher legend is arrested, and tragedy at the summer camp averted. The motive is revealed to relate to an obsessive interest in darting movement.

Neither of these episodes was ever made, as such, but neither would be out of place. Nothing is implausible in Midsomer. As drama, *Midsomer Murders* plays as an English archetype through setting, characterization, cast and plotline. Taking each in turn will offer the familiar or unfamiliar reader a guide to the Murder County.

The 'Midsomer' of *Midsomer Murders* is a county, with much of the filming in the towns and villages of the Chilterns, with excursions to sites such as Dorchester-on-Thames. Despite plotlines occasionally featuring villainous London connections, this is presented as a world beyond Metroland, still significantly rural. The landscape of Midsomer is effectively an amalgam of Buckinghamshire and Oxfordshire, producing a rolling countryside with woodland, pasture and arable. This is not a place of monocultural farming; indeed landscape variety serves plot variety, a murder ecology of shooting, hunting, harvest and equestrianism. Causton appears as the county town, with many villages having Midsomer as their first word; Midsomer Parva, Mallow, Worthy, Barrow and so on. Imaginative mapping is invited; indeed tourism in Buckinghamshire and Oxfordshire trades on connections, with walking tours and trails. The global popularity of the programme, which is reportedly shown in over two hundred countries, feeds on the clichéd England of the setting. Drama here inhabits cliché rather than resisting it, and in the process amplifies its nature.

The television Midsomer was derived from the Inspector Barnaby mysteries by Caroline Graham, first published in 1987 with *The Killings at Badger's Drift* (also the first TV adaptation). Graham's novels, like the TV series, have a keen eye for the stereotype. In *The Killings at Badger's Drift*, Graham describes Barnaby and assistant Troy, approaching an elderly victim's 'neatly and imaginatively thatched' Beehive Cottage: 'It was perfection. The sort of home that turns up on This England calendars and tourist posters.'[127] Inspector Barnaby (Tom for the first thirteen series of the programme, before being replaced by his cousin John) is a middle-aged man with a middle-aged wife, Joyce, and an actor daughter, Cully, who has left their solid detached home. Joyce does not work, but her range of hobbies and interests is often caught up in the plot, sometimes dangerously. Tom is set in his ways, though with occasional hints of a racier youth. Sidekicks come and go, younger officers learning from Barnaby. Pathologists diagnose death causes. The movement of the detectives across the county and the long local service of Barnaby allow the viewer to read the landscape through their eyes, although those eyes are far from all-seeing. The two-hour episode length demands that Barnaby does not work things out especially quickly, and the landscapes of Midsomer thereby acquire appealing puzzles for the viewer. Midsomer appears as if an idealized English country jigsaw to ponder on a wet winter evening, the cottages in sun, the trees in leaf and a corpse bottom right.

That Barnaby is mainstream makes him unusual as a television detective. Barnaby's lack of typical idiosyncrasies sets up a contrast between his normality of character and home and the strange motivations of those investigated, crucial to making stories of death somehow reassuring. The casting of the main character played a key role in the series success. From 1997 to the end of series thirteen, with eight episodes per series, Tom Barnaby was played by John Nettles. While having a significant stage career, Nettles was known to television audiences as Jim Bergerac of the Jersey police. *Bergerac* ran on BBC television from 1981 to 1991, Nettles already familiar as a detective embedded in place; Nettles indeed authored a book on *Bergerac's Jersey*, and also became known as a presenter of documentaries on his native West Country.[128] After a hiatus, Nettles returned as Barnaby, a detective a little older, less glamorous, more domesticated and, as the series extended its run, less adept at sprint pursuits. Nettles's own career helped embed *Midsomer Murders* in a familiar televisual landscape, at home in the home, Bergerac in the Home Counties.

Midsomer Murders dramatizes Englishness not only through its setting but through plotlines deploying familiar cultural tropes, social anxieties and environmental concerns. *Midsomer Murders* is aware of its own clichés: in one episode a brass band at a fête plays the series theme tune. The series music, with its eerie theremin signalling something sinister, is by Jim Parker, collaborator in the 1970s on John Betjeman's LPs, noted in Chapter Five. The series itself became a subject for debate in 2011, when comment was made on its cast fulfilling another English cliché in being almost entirely white, reproducing exclusive associations of rural Englishness and white identity. Series producer Brian True-May suggested to the *Radio Times* that this reflected it being a 'last bastion of Englishness', and was a reflection of Home Counties rural demography.[129] The series, however, moved to shuffle off what might have become a stigma. True-May ceased producing the series later that year, and BAME actors featured as regular cast members and in guest lead roles in subsequent series.

Plotlines of class and nature set *Midsomer Murders* within traditions of commentary on rural English particularity. Tropes of rural sociology structure stories: land disputes, inheritance disputes, old and new money, locals and incomers and their different outlooks on place, history and amenity. Celebrations of locality become occasions for strife. Clergy are tormented, bell-ringers die. House prices and land values inform relationships, with erotic attraction across class divides and across or within families. Sociology assumes clichéd form but retains plausibility, a sense that some people in rural England might well be like this. Cultures of landscape too become an occasion for dispute or worse: contemporary and historic landscape paintings, literary treatments of Midsomer and musical renditions. Thus Barnaby studies the historic holdings of Causton Library to deduce forgeries of a historical Midsomer painter, while a musical 'Midsomer Rhapsody' prompts murder, Jim Parker orchestrating pastiche pastoral. The particularity of place is celebrated, is enough to kill for.

Midsomer also carries mystical qualities. If nature mysticism has in recent decades been associated with countercultural values, here it is on prime-time ITV. Owls have strange powers, there are ghostly voices in the woods, and priests spontaneously combust at the altar. In Midsomer, at midsummer, in 'The Fisher King' (series 7, episode 3), a man seeks to greet the rising sun (and rekindle his marriage) by standing atop the Midsummer Barrow burial mound after an all-night festival reviving ancient pagan custom. As he fires an arrow to the sun, another lands in his back. Worldly arguments here, as in other episodes, turn out to trump the supernatural (the motivation is familial and professional), but the series regularly taps what John Lowerson terms the 'mystical geography of the English', and is happy to leave it hanging.[130] Barnaby works out that the ghostly voices in the woods come from speakers in the branches triggered by movement, yet when the device is dismantled the episode ends with Nettles still disturbed by uncanny sound. Voices continue and Barnaby twitches, Home Counties life haunted by something beyond itself. The theremin plays, and Barnaby goes home to Joyce and another case.

A Marathon of Whimsy

Between 1973 and 2010 the comedy series *Last of the Summer Wine* played on northern non-city Englishness, with its setting around the Yorkshire town of Holmfirth itself becoming a tourist destination, the series the main visitor pull. As in Midsomer, identifiable settings and outlandish plots attracted many, its northern small town eccentricity an unsinister Royston Vasey. Visit the Chilterns to imagine something nasty in the woods; visit Holmfirth to imagine the farcical pursuits of ageing men. The series became the longest-running situation comedy in the world, a marathon of whimsy on prime-time BBC, with 295 episodes and export to twenty countries. Whether loved, tolerated or loathed, *Last of the Summer Wine*, like *Midsomer Murders*, became a reference point in a common culture.

Last of the Summer Wine was written by Roy Clarke, who also authored book spin-off *Summer Wine Chronicles*. The proclaimed gentleness of the comedy proceeds from conversation between the players, with three male lead characters, all elderly and unmarried or widowed, and a range of supporting men and women with various foibles and tics. Most are socially middling working class, some with pretensions and others less reputable. One relatively young couple stand out for having a new house and a mortgage. There are no child characters, the three male leads childlike enough for one programme. The ragged Compo, played by Bill Owen, and the cautious Clegg, played by Peter Sallis, featured throughout until Owen's death in 1999. The third male lead varied, played by actors often familiar from other television comedies, such as Brian Wilde (1976–85 and 1990–97, known for Mr Barraclough in prison comedy *Porridge*) and Frank Thornton (1997–2010, Captain Peacock in *Are You Being Served?*). As the series carried on, *Last of the Summer Wine* gathered its own company, often carrying associations with programmes beyond. Owen himself brought extensive cinematic and theatrical experience to the series, while Sallis's stage career would be supplemented by his becoming the voice of Wallace in the *Wallace and Gromit* animations, his *Summer Wine* tones suited to further whimsical narration. Roy Clarke provided a foreword for Sallis's autobiography, and suggested of his 'magic' that 'With Peter it's a quintessential Englishness.'[131]

Last of the Summer Wine episodes are self-contained, 30-minute stories, with conversational rumination interspersed with unlikely action, viewers seeing the join as stunt men hurtle over drystone walls. Stereotypes of northern masculinity and femininity shape plots, women tending to dominate men variously pompous or timid. Sexual attraction tends to the absurd, though affections are genuine. Beginning in 1973, *Last of the Summer Wine* worked northern stereotypes in counterpoint to the then prevailing conventions of social realism in a period of industrial unrest and urban renewal. Stories set in a small town surrounded by hilly countryside, around which three men ambled, took viewers pointedly away from all that. As a country appeared more divided, *Last of the Summer Wine* found a space of reassurance where whimsy survived. Filmed around Holmfirth, only 6 miles from an industrial Huddersfield whose proximity would never be guessed, the programme generated its own tourist economy. A town centre café was a regular film setting and became a visitor attraction, with souvenirs available: mugs, tea towels, badges with a smiling Sallis. The programme's soundtrack also made for a northern pastoral, with theme tune and incidental music by Ronnie Hazlehurst framing each episode with relaxed strings and harmonica.

Last of the Summer Wine continued in the same vein across four decades, with cast members changing, some dying, as the ensemble played on. Across 295 episodes originality of plot ran thin, with ups or downs from the actors appearing at any time, long-term viewers enrolled in part through their own judgements as to better or worse performers. As series turned, *Last of the Summer Wine* became its own time capsule, the setting itself a lead character, Holmfirth stuck with the association. *Last of the Summer Wine* offered an English particularity, strange but entirely unthreatening. Clarke dedicated his 1986 *Chronicle*, titled *Gala Week*, with its plotline of a summer fair and a peacock, 'To gentle spirits and peaceful places'.[132]

Model Englands

Charm, whimsy, settlement and strangeness meet too in a visitor attraction, itself presented as distinctly English, the model village, a miniature architectural phenomenon whose heyday was the mid- to late twentieth century. Gordon Murray's modelled miniature televisual England of Trumptonshire echoed built mini-structures around the country. Located in the countryside or seaside resorts, model villages evoked not only rural but urban and suburban settings, offered England in microcosm.

Model villages were novelty attractions, their components often given punning business names; the jokes were part of the craft by which skilled model-makers drew the public. Model villages were serious labours, demonstrations of modelling art, paying attractions displaying specific or generic bits of England. Interwar sites such as Bekonscot, near Beaconsfield (created from 1928, incorporating a miniature railway, and opened to the public in 1931 by wealthy accountant Roland Callingham), the Cotswold stone Bourton-on-the-Water (1937) and Pendon in Oxfordshire (1930s, again with railway) were forerunners of a series of model villages constructed after 1945, notably in seaside resorts such as Skegness, Southsea, Babbacombe and Southport. Post-war villages, again often including model railways to animate the scene, appeared less as the unusual creations of private individuals than as commercial ventures deploying a template in variation. Southsea and Skegness indeed featured buildings cast from the same moulds. Individual entrepreneurs constructed sets of villages: Stan Deboo at Ramsgate, Hastings and Weston-super-Mare ('Little Britain'), the Dobbins brothers at Southport, Great Yarmouth and Torquay. From Tim Dunn's survey the late 1950s and '60s appear the 'Golden Years', miniature landscapes acting in cultural counterpoint to those models of future settlement informing planning policy at the time.[133] If photographs of the time promoting development featured planners and councillors pointing to models of the future, postcards of model villages showed children in unlikely commanding stature. Models permit command over place.

From the 1970s falling visitor numbers, vandalism and redevelopment saw model villages decline, though from the 1990s a revival in cultural interest accompanied commercial resurgence, the model village an English curio, its novelty from its survival rather than its newness. The model village became a site for imaginative play, with Bekonscot, in part for its handiness from London, featuring in literature, photography, film and television, cultural offshoots indicating the possibilities of the miniature. The painter George Shaw has commented on his delight in model villages and model railway landscapes, their attentive scaling echoed in his depiction of everyday structures.[134] Colin Falck's 2004 poem 'Model Village' tapped the ironies of historical recreation, presenting a village ('more like a country town') caught in 'a June afternoon in 1938', a quiet England with occasional hints of a disturbed wider world: 'It looks like peace in our time.'[135] Will Self's 1993 story 'Scale' featured an opiate-addicted scholar living in a bungalow next to Bekonscot, mental disintegration signified by a descent through a series of model villages within model villages.[136] Liam Bailey's 2006 photographic collection *Forever England* presented the figures in Bekonscot in social documentary style, frozen everyday actions in bright colour, residents forever posed.[137] Enchantment turns to tension, and nostalgia queasiness. The model village as a site for strange anxieties structured a 2009 *Midsomer Murders* episode, 'Small Mercies', with a man killed and tied down in Little Worthy's model village, like Gulliver in Lilliput. The perpetrator of this and other murders is revealed as Bernice, played by Olivia Colman, defending the model village from desecration, seeking obsessive security, tending the small figures and lashing out at change. Vulnerability turns to violence in model middle England.[138]

The sense of model villages as sites of idyllic or anxious escape from the present is, however, belied by their design history. Dunn's account of model villages includes a postcard of 'Little Britain' at Weston-super-Mare depicting 'The Contempory [sic] House', a striking modernist domestic design. At Ramsgate there was a modern airport with a Comet jet airliner, while 'Cornwall in Miniature' at St Agnes includes a replica of the modern County Hall.[139] The model village could display the glamour of modernity, scaled-down novelty domesticating and normalizing newness. Dunn notes the irony that in the 1990s at Bekonscot, the models of mid-twentieth-century modernity

Cover of guide to Merrivale model village, Great Yarmouth, 1972.

Postcard of 'Town Centre Shops, Model Village, Great Yarmouth', c. late 1970s.

were replaced with replicas of older structures to accentuate an atmosphere of heritage tourism. Biplanes replaced Concorde, oil tankers made way for sailing vessels. A miniature modernist Luton Town Hall faded from memory as a 1930s village was remade.[140]

The modern, the comic, the archaic and the clichéd are all on display at Merrivale on the seafront at Great Yarmouth. Merrivale, opened in 1961 and still standing, is the end of the line for this chapter. A 1972 guidebook to Merrivale, and assorted postcards, give a sense of how twentieth-century Englands were made miniature; the village was significantly rebuilt under new ownership after 2004, now appearing more historic than it once was.[141] In August 2021 Merrivale was chosen by Banksy as the site for one of a series of Norfolk and Suffolk coastal art interventions, his name and other words and phrases scrawled on a miniature stable. A replica was made, and the village owners auctioned the original and its additions in January 2022 for just over £1 million, securing Merrivale's future.[142]

Merrivale 1972 offered a model village Englishness amid the seaside Englishness of Yarmouth, visitors leaving the beach or amusements for a while to enter 'a typical section of the English countryside in miniature', with a population of 'nearly one thousand'. As in Trumptonshire, this was not a purely rural scene. Farms, villages, castle and 'the stately home of Lord Merrivale' sat alongside factories, a sports stadium, a zoo with penguin pool, a diesel main line and the market town of

Merritown: 'All in all, nothing has been omitted from this Lilliputian land of make-believe; it is the most authentic and realistic of models that delights young and old alike.' The simultaneous claim to authentic realism and make-believe indicates something evidently contrived yet claiming a cultural truth about an England of today. Laid out in the middle of the modern seaside, Merrivale had its own modern elements: 'Merritown offers first-class shopping facilities for its inhabitants.'[143]

Postcards, acting as souvenir mementoes or enticements to enter, showed Merrivale life. Cricket plays on the village green before the church. Modern bungalows line a street. Children play at the village school. Merrivale stadium hosts athletics. Lorries work the slate quarry. The town centre shows a bank, cinema and supermarket. A boy and woman crouch to view the high street, with an AA van outside the Eastern Electricity showroom and an orange sports car passing. A Yarmouth Corporation bus with distinctive and accurate blue livery carries on its side an advertisement for the model village. On the guidebook cover a boy stands before mock-Tudor houses, while another kneels on the high street, Woolworths behind him, and a blue bus. Public utilities, municipal transport and private enterprise share the twentieth-century English town, shape this English particularity. In the twenty-first century the mock-Tudor remains familiar, but Woolworths, the public utility company and the blue bus appear as from another age.

PART III: ENGLISH TIMES

7
English Heritage

On English Safari

On 13 May 1975, aged ten, I visited Longleat House in Wiltshire on a junior school coach party, children on their first field trip away from Norfolk. Staying at the youth hostel in Salisbury, we visited Old Sarum, Stonehenge, Lulworth Cove, Bovington Tank Museum and a Roman villa, sites to open history, archaeology and geography to junior minds. Longleat House showed us country house heritage, but its parkland had been turned over to safari. Here were wild animals, spectacular zoology, carefully noted in my write-up:

> When we arrived at Longleat, Derek stopped the coach and we got out and bought some postcards and presents. Then we got back into the coach and went into the Safari Park.
> The first section of the Safari park was the East African Game Park. In this section there were zebras, ankole cattle, giraffes, ostriches and camels.
> The second section was the monkey jungle. The monkeys there were baboons. The monkeys kept climbing over cars and one got on top of the coach.

After rhinos, antelopes and cheetahs: 'In the last reserve were some lions. We then drove through the grounds to Longleat House.' In the house we found an exhibition about Churchill, including 'stamps, things that Churchill used, and figures of Churchill', and displays on the BBC television historical drama *The Pallisers*, a 1974 adaptation of Trollope's novels. There was also 'a tablecloth over 100 years old'. The 'child' ticket for the visit shows an aerial view of the house and lake; my purchased postcards showed lions, with a modest car on

Ticket for visit to Longleat House, Wiltshire, May 1975.

Postcard of 'The Lions of Longleat', photograph by E. Ludwig, published by John Hinde, purchased May 1975.

Souvenir lion purchased at Longleat House, Wiltshire, May 1975.

safari behind. A poll of 44 children for 'favourite trips' showed one vote for Longleat House but seventeen for the Safari Park; for 'The Place People Disliked Most' the safari got two votes, the house nine. I bought a small model lion as a parental present, for ornament rather than cuddling, and took it home, where it remains. If Longleat's old tablecloth gave a sense of the past, the safari brought excitement. Here was, in the title of a popular BBC series on the natural world, 'The World about Us', only this was in Wiltshire. This was an evidently untypical site, but in its combination of artefacts and beasts Longleat made for a particular form of English heritage.

Longleat Safari Park, opened in 1966, presented the animal exotic in the English countryside through a slow-speed vehicle-based visitor experience, drivers and passengers present within but protected from their surroundings. Longleat had been open to the public from 1949, but, advised by circus proprietor Jimmy Chipperfield, the Marquess of Bath opened a safari park in 1966, around fifty lions arriving that spring, many acquired direct from east African habitats. Almost a thousand cars a day visited in August 1966; the entry queue for Easter Monday 1967 took five hours. Here was a compelling attraction. Day trippers could go, as a guide put it, 'To Africa and back in a day'.[1] The presence of lions in a landscape park laid out by Capability Brown two centuries earlier made for a postcolonial heritage experience. To Africa and back, patrolled by rangers in colonial-style dress on horseback or in Land Rovers, who might have stepped from an episode of *Daktari*, the popular American series that ran from 1966 to 1969. Images of African game might also be familiar from the activities of the World Wildlife Fund, established in 1961, which had reworked long-standing themes of imperial natural history into modern conservationist form. Visitors might, indeed some must, have hummed the famous theme song to the lion-themed *Born Free*, the film of Joy Adamson's 1960 book released in 1966.

Longleat offered a domesticated and democratized African safari. The lions may not have been free, but they roamed more than a zoo would allow, and driving through the park was the closest visitors without the wherewithal to holiday in Africa would ever get to beasts not evidently caged. At a time when the end of empire and immigration from former British colonies was becoming an acute political issue, Enoch Powell's incendiary speech only two years ahead, Longleat brought another African presence into symbolic English landscape. Imperial landscape was re-enacted in Wiltshire at a moment when empire, if politically diminished, was far from cultural closure. When David Nobbs needed an excursion to demonstrate Reginald Perrin's anxieties, a safari park was the perfect setting. A pleasant English day out in an African simulacrum turned out not so pleasant. On a hot, sweaty, anxiety-ridden family trip to the 'Hartcliffe Game Reserve' in Surrey ('If in trouble, blow your horn and wait for the white hunter'), Reggie abandons his malfunctioning car in 'lion country' and walks towards two lions, convinced they are 'doped'. Only a dart from a ranger's gun prevents a mauling. Safari sees an English breakdown.[2]

Complex geographies, histories and memories characterize the versions of English heritage considered in this chapter. Stories of movement within the nation, local ownership and/or devotion and global exchanges through empire and its aftermath shape the classification and narration of English heritage. Children and adults venture cross-country to view things labelled as theirs, finding lions in their own national garden. Heritage trades on inheritance, affinity, value, a cultural looking after of things worth caring for, but judgements over its content and form may provoke argument and hostility, England put into question just as it is valued. The geographies of heritage enfold national stories with the international and the global. The effect of the 1975 European Architectural Heritage Year on English heritage debate is discussed below, but global valuation is most apparent in bids for English sites to be granted World Heritage status under UNESCO's 1972 'Convention Concerning the Protection of the World Cultural and Natural Heritage'. The UK ratified the convention in 1984, and the first sites soon followed, including Stonehenge and Avebury (1986), Ironbridge Gorge (1986), Durham Castle and Cathedral (1986), Blenheim Palace (1987), Bath (1987), the Palace of Westminster and Westminster Abbey (1987). These early English sites indicate how claims for global significance follow established conventions of heritage value concerning historic and prehistoric sites, but Ironbridge denotes the emergence of industrial heritage, and further sites would also reflect the extended definitions of heritage considered in this chapter. In 2019 the designation of the iconic post-war structure of Jodrell Bank would signal the shift of English and world heritage to encompass the historic modern, discussed further in Chapter Eight. The Lake District's award of World Heritage status in 2017 would indicate too the ways in which the history of English heritage is itself deemed globally significant. The Lake District was recognized not for its natural beauty but as a cultural landscape, in part for its continuity of upland farming but also as the site where modern forms of landscape appreciation and conservation emerged in the nineteenth century. Wordsworth and the National Trust, as much as Grasmere and Skiddaw, make the Lakes a world place.[3]

This chapter explores varieties of English heritage, and shifts in valuation since the 1960s, proceeding through the country house, the historic town and the heritage of industry. The following chapter will address the emergence of modernism as a heritage style. From 1984 English heritage was not only, however, an idea but an organization, English Heritage. State responsibility for the historic shifted from former ministerial structures, such as the Ministry of Works, to a designated governmental body. The official nature of English Heritage could itself provoke response, including in general critiques of the term from the mid-1980s, discussed below. The official claim to definition could also bring ironic redeployments of the heritage label, as when in 1993, in the context of increasing tension over leisure in the countryside, specifically open-air raves, building to the passing of the 1994 Criminal Justice and Public Order Act, Canterbury electronic duo Ultramarine's LP *United Kingdoms* included a track titled 'English

Heritage'.[4] Ultramarine's gentle sardonic electronica played around official custodianship in a land anything but united. 'English Heritage' offered 8 minutes and 53 seconds of shuffling rhythm, noodling keyboard, occasional pauses, no words. Only the title indicates any intended meaning; indeed the album is mostly instrumental. The tracks 'Kingdom' and 'Happy Land', however, feature Robert Wyatt, the voice of a late 1960s Canterbury scene and later of 'Shipbuilding' and plotlands, singing of a happy land where to be poor is a crime. Wyatt marks dissident English pastoral, and internationalism with an English timbre.

Ultramarine's 'English Heritage' offers no audio guide to a cathedral, to Blenheim Palace or to Ironbridge, though it might suit Stonehenge on the solstice if there were a chill-out stone. That 'English Heritage' as a title and phrase made electronic sense indicates, though, the contested nature of the term, and its capacity to spark reflection. This chapter navigates six decades of care and dispute, considering debates over urban heritage in the 1960s and '70s, the ways in which heritage as an idea became the focus for intense cultural debate in the '80s and the emergence of industrial heritage as an object of national cultural value. Having begun at Longleat, the next section, however, gives further attention to the country house. Chapter Three considered recent debate around heritage, race and the country house, but here the focus is on why, in the post-war decades, such places welcomed visitors, and the effect this had on the country house as an English icon.

Country House England

In *The Fall and Rise of the Stately Home*, Peter Mandler shows how immediately after the Second World War country houses were often seen as a burden rather than an asset.[5] Donation of the house to the National Trust's Country Houses Scheme, set up in the 1930s by James Lees-Milne, or to the government in payment of death duties, appeared attractive options. The post-war Labour government, with its National Land Fund, was itself enthusiastic for the historic preservation of the country house as an item of national heritage, not least if that implied its social system had been consigned to the past. In the 1950s, however, the country house as a socio-economic and cultural entity revived. The Gowers Report of 1950 recommended public support for maintaining country house life as well as architecture, a

Conservative government was elected in 1951, publicity campaigns were raised against country house demolition, the Historic Buildings Council for England was established in 1953, and economic recovery by the mid-'50s included increasing land prices and agricultural prosperity. The sense of burden lessened, and in a more affluent society the country house gained tourist potential. As Mandler shows, country houses had long welcomed paying visitors, but a stately home business was now established, with around three hundred houses regularly open by 1960. Particular houses became iconic as spectacles for a leisure society, often with associated attractions as at Woburn (opened commercially by the Duke of Bedford in 1955, with a safari park added in 1970), Beaulieu (where Lord Montagu opened a motor museum in 1952) and Longleat.

From being symbols of a disappearing past, country houses offered glamorous days out in the present, escapism within rather than at odds with the modern world. The aristocratic public image, and self-image, modernized. The Historic Houses Association was formed in 1973, emerging from the Historic Houses Committee of the British Travel Association, set up in 1965, whereby owners opened houses on a more humdrum basis than Longleat or Woburn. The National Trust continued as a focus for country-house visiting culture, though in the 1960s saw internal arguments as to whether their emphasis should be on the upper-class family home rather than more demotic open leisure spaces.[6] Robin Fedden's 1968 summary of the National Trust's work, *The Continuing Purpose*, nonetheless restated the Trust's aim of having their houses lived in: 'They need the breath of life. Built for a family and the life a family creates, they know no better use.'[7] The presence of family, whether owners or National Trust tenants, helped suggest that, as Mandler suggests, 'a visit to a stately home was obviously something *more* than just another day in the country; it has a special kind of human interest that is not easy to analyse.'[8] Owners traded on such human interest. I recall visiting Woburn on what must have been a day coach trip from Norwich in the mid-'70s, but my only specific memory of the house is of seeing the remnants of the family breakfast on a table left for public view. Ordinary to the family, such debris marked a space at once splendid and lived in, and I can recall the breakfast cereal packet, 'Force', a then popular brand, though not one I ate. That this detail still sticks says something about an encounter between ordinary publics and elevated lives.

Despite such modern enterprise, the narrative of the country house as under threat and requiring salvage, established powerfully by Lees-Milne at the National Trust from the 1930s, remained available and potent. Such a sensibility moved from being what Mandler terms in the 1950s and 1960s a 'neo-romanticism . . . still a reaction against the main currents in the culture rather than a directing force', to become central to debate in the 1970s.[9] The popular traction of this outlook is evident even in critical presentations such as Joseph Losey's 1971 film of L. P. Hartley's 1953 novel *The Go-Between*, with screenplay by Harold Pinter. Mark Broughton terms *The Go-Between* 'a new kind of country-estate cinema', shot on location in Norfolk at Melton Constable Hall and its surrounding area, deliberately grounded in local geography rather than studio fantasy, and with 'the film's landscape shots . . . integral to its social commentary'.[10] Losey was an émigré, politically on the left, and *The Go-Between* presents the country house as a site of class ritual and formal entrapment, with twelve-year-old Leo the go-between for a clandestine affair between the daughter of the house and a local farmer. The country house sits in cinematic golden hue, yet in a scarred past. Hartley's protagonist, decades on, cannot shake off the memory, and the scars cannot but linger. The novel's celebrated and sometimes glibly cited opening line, 'The past is a foreign country: they do things differently there,' becomes a warning, and a forlorn hope that something might be put to one side.[11]

The Go-Between spatializes memory, the country house another place, apart from the contemporary. If for Losey, as for Hartley, there was ambivalence about this other country, for others the sense of the country house as a realm apart would become central to a very contemporary battle in its defence, indeed would allow its political mobilization. Mandler notes how in 1974 the country house was mobilized as a 'national symbol', something 'standing for England', in an argument about taxation.[12] That year saw a general economic crisis, and proposals from the recently elected Labour government for new higher levels of capital taxation, including a 'Wealth Tax', which would affect the contents of a house. Parliamentary opposition was mobilized by the Conservative MP for South West Staffordshire Patrick Cormack (elected in 1970 and serving until 2010), who in the summer of 1974 had formed Heritage in Danger, an 'All Party Committee for the Heritage'.[13] Cormack's deployment of national heritage for politically partisan ends was part of a wider 1970s mobilization of country house sentiment. John Cornforth's October 1974 report, *Country Houses in Britain: Can They Survive?*, prepared from 1972 for the Historic Houses Association, argued for the country house estate as a valued way of life. Cornforth stressed links between house and land: 'Country houses are part of the deep-seated British preference for a country life, with its feeling for landscape, its belief in the satisfactions and responsibilities of landowning and its enthusiasm for gardening and forestry.'[14] From October to December 1974 the Victoria and Albert Museum (V&A) showed *The Destruction of the Country House, 1875–1975*, organized by John Harris, Marcus Binney and Peter Thornton. A 'Hall of Lost Houses' pictured those gone, with a recording intoning a roll call; the accompanying book gave county lists for England, Scotland and Wales, photographs including a date of demolition, recorded as a death: 'Rollesby Hall, Norfolk. Tudor, d. 1949'.[15] Houses become English and British creatures, at risk of extinction, Binney warning of the consequences of 'a sharp, sudden and irreversible fiscal attack'.[16] Seven owners wrote on their houses: Woburn, Warwick Castle, Knebworth, Ragley, Castle Howard, Goodwood, Longford. The Duke of Bedford wrote: 'I feel that sometimes the government is not entirely in touch with the millions of people who are deeply appreciative of our great houses and their traditions and do not wish to see them dispersed in the ostensible interests of socialism.'[17] In their greatness, such places served the public, Harris noting that the country house was now 'the servant of recreation', and hence warranted public support.[18]

V&A director Roy Strong's introduction to *The Destruction of the Country House* navigated public and private rights and responsibilities. Strong imagined a passing motorist catching a 'fleeting glimpse of some noble pile' beyond park gates: 'The ravished eyes stir the heart to emotion, for in a sense the historic houses of this country belong to everybody, or at least everybody who cares about this country and its traditions.'[19] Care for country and care for tradition align, and the national everybody is divided between carers and don't-carers. Emotional ownership implies a collective duty to private property, and the fact that there are modern people – politicians, members of the public – with unstirred hearts underwrites a campaigning urgency, bolsters campaigners' self-image as gallant underdogs. Strong saw the optimism of the 1950s and '60s dissipating, with rising costs and the inability of the National Trust to take on more properties meaning that state help, rather than wealth taxation, was required: 'The country house as a work of art in its unity of building, contents, garden and landscape, can only survive with incentives to the owner from government.' The language of buildings and contents implies a form of state insurance for private owners ('those who actually struggle to live in a great house') who could thereby act as public custodians while remaining private owners.[20] Cultural sleight of hand and class politics entwine:

> The great houses of England and their occupants represent a continuity within our society... Country house owners are the hereditary custodians of what was one of the most vital forces of cultural creation in our history. They deserve consideration and justice as much as any other group within our society as they struggle to preserve and share with us the creative richness of our heritage.[21]

From theirs to ours, from they to us, Strong tangles England in hereditary knots; our heritage is their inheritance.

Marcus Binney made the V&A show a basis for a nationwide campaign, enrolling local newspapers and amenity groups. In 1975 Binney, along with David Pearce, noted in the previous chapter for his commentary on South Woodham Ferrers, established the pressure group SAVE Britain's Heritage, connecting the country house to wider amenity and environmental campaigns. Binney would also co-organize the 1977 V&A show *Change and Decay: The Future of Our Churches*.[22] Such campaigns, and the parliamentary efforts co-ordinated by Patrick Cormack, had political effect, helping persuade Labour Chancellor Denis Healey to grant exemption from Capital Transfer Tax for important artworks, houses and land, and in late 1976 the Wealth Tax plan was dropped, reflecting also wider fears of capital flight.[23] Exemptions were extended in return for, as Mandler puts it, 'a nominally greater public stake'.[24]

The successful attempt to align the landowner not only with national heritage but with the public interest was an extraordinary cultural achievement at a time of industrial unrest and economic crisis. The Historic Houses Association submitted a 1-million-signature petition to Parliament in autumn 1975, having circulated it in houses open to visitors. The Earl of March stripped a Goodwood room of its contents, asking visitors to sign a petition if they disapproved of such a potential effect of a Wealth Tax. Cormack's 1976 book *Heritage in Danger*, which suggested that 'It is perhaps in our country houses and churches that one comes closest to the spirit of England', included a photograph captioned 'The Earl of March sits in an empty room, demonstrating the devastating effect taxation could have at Goodwood'.[25] The image is credited to the Earl of March, suggesting either use of a self-timer or an unnamed servant behind the lens. In a time of severe economic hardship, public sympathy is elicited for the aristocracy via oxymoronic portraits of genteel poverty. The soundtrack could be the Kinks' 1966 song 'Sunny Afternoon', where the taxman takes the narrator's dough and leaves him in his stately home, lazing the sunny afternoon away.

Cormack's book was adapted into a television series by the Birmingham-based commercial television company ATV, and the 1978 edition of *Heritage in Danger* carried a foreword by Roy Strong: 'It is in times of danger, either from without or from within, that we become deeply conscious of our heritage.' Heritage was 'a deeply stabilizing and unifying element within our society', a one-nation object:

> In the 1940s we felt all this deeply because of the danger from without. In the 1970s we sense it because of the dangers from within. We are all aware of problems and troubles, of changes within the structure of society, of the dissolution of old values and standards. For the lucky few this may be exhilarating, even exciting, but for the majority it is confusing, threatening and dispiriting. The heritage represents some form of security, a point of reference, a refuge perhaps, something visible and tangible which, within a topsy and turvy world, seems stable and unchanged.[26]

Cormack's own introduction made a seamless shift from Wealth Tax politics to ineffable value. National heritage provided a general, seemingly unopposable flag under which to enact a politics as partisan as that which it opposed:

> When the Labour Government in the summer of 1974 published its Green Paper on the Wealth Tax it became apparent that the heritage . . . was not to be exempt . . . I was one of those involved in setting up a Committee called Heritage in Danger . . . to point out the danger that a Wealth Tax would

impose on the national heritage. When I am asked to define our heritage I do not think in dictionary terms, but instead reflect on certain sights and sounds ... of a celebration of the Eucharist in a quiet Norfolk church with the medieval glass filtering the colours, and the early noise of harvesting coming through the open door; or of standing at any time before the Wilton Diptych. Each scene recalls aspects of an indivisible heritage and is part of the fabric and expression of our civilisation.[27]

Cormack conveyed his sense of the absurdity of opposing such a view in his commentary on threats to private collections: 'With the exception of a few Marxist art historians, everyone giving evidence to the Select Committee on the Wealth Tax agreed that the future of the private collection and the private patron is gravely in doubt.' He singled out 'a certain Marxist art historian called Peter Fuller ... a political nonentity, and one can only hope and indeed trust that his view of the heritage will never prevail'.[28] The select committee had reported in December 1975, failing to agree on any recommendation and issuing five conflicting reports. The committee proceedings, with witnesses called and memoranda received, allowed space for voices opposed to the tax to mobilize, and as Howard Glennerster notes, oppositional voices dominated.[29] The space of the select committee also, however, allowed other visions of the country house to be articulated. Cormack's dismissive comment on art historians referred to one of the 'letters and memoranda from individuals' submitted to the committee. John Berger, Peter Fuller, William Feaver, Richard Cork and others argued for the application of the Wealth Tax to works of art, with partial conditional exemption used to encourage the public exhibition of works in private collections, including country houses, or their sale to public collections. Such a scheme could 'democratise access', with a consequent desirable 'weakening of the excessively strong relationship between art and private wealth' and the 'transference of works of art from the obscurity of private ownership in the country'. Berger and colleagues countered 'emotive and misleading campaigns' concerning 'Danger to "The National Heritage"', which put 'undue emphasis on possession, rather than on perception'.[30]

A counterpoint to Berger and Fuller's critical art analysis, and another vision for the country house, came in a memorandum on architecture from seventeen individuals from various cultural and academic backgrounds. The authors included John Schofield, Lords Esher and Kennet, architectural historian Mark Girouard, urban heritage campaigner Colin Amery, future CPRE director Robin Grove-White, artist Patrick Heron, playwright Arnold Wesker and historian of suburbia Paul Oliver. The Wealth Tax was here seen to contradict existing government heritage responsibilities, especially with its possible effects on the 'less rich' rather than the 'very rich':

> We are concerned for the immediate protection of such highly vulnerable and complex entities as country houses – and for a long-term philosophy to govern their use in the interest of society as a whole ... the fact that their original social purpose is obsolete does not diminish their continuing cultural value.

The country house, made by 'designers, craftsmen and gardeners', showed 'an unparalleled example of co-ordination of the arts and crafts. Our purpose is not to prop up the way of life which demanded them, but rather to protect these splendid expressions of our national creativity.' Country houses, contents and landscapes should 'be listed as entities', with the tax system used to support their preservation:

> We see the country houses as cultural monuments belonging to the British people, now and in the future, to live with, to visit, to study, perhaps to work in. What these essentially peaceful and contemplative places have to offer is something it is now, under the insistent stress of urban and industrial life, government's business to provide – or to protect: opportunities for regeneration and re-creation, sensually, spiritually and intellectually, for aspiration or inspiration through the experience of harmony between Man's own works and the forces and beauty of Nature. Here are examples and standards by which to judge our own co-operative achievements.[31]

Private holdings might be replaced by a new public harmony.

Art-historical and architectural memoranda did not win the political argument but indicated alternative futures, albeit ones which still rarely surface in country house debate. For Cormack the future was instead one of private–public balance, with private owners retaining the keys to national heritage. Cormack's was not a Conservatism opposed to state action; indeed he hailed the history of government protection and called for stronger institutional action and fiscal support, proposing a Minister for the Heritage and the Arts: 'if the siege of the country house is to be lifted, Government must lift it.'[32] Without 'positive action' on country houses by government, 'there will be almost none in private hands by the turn of the century.'[33] When the Earl of Rosebery proposed to sell the buildings and contents of Mentmore Towers in Buckinghamshire in 1977, forceful lobbying and outcry followed. Images of Mentmore illustrated the 1978 printing of *Heritage in Danger*, the country house 'under siege', the Mentmore Sotheby's auction making 'the contents of a treasure house disappear'.[34] The government was shown in effect to have missed a bargain in not accepting Mentmore in lieu of death duties, and the house was bought as a transcendental meditation centre by the Maharishi Mahesh Yogi, one-time adviser to the Beatles and future sponsor of the Natural Law Party, whose bemusing 1990s party political broadcasts encouraged democratic transformation via yogic flying.

Political transformation did, however, proceed from Mentmore's loss, as in 1980 the Conservative government's National Heritage Act, passed with all-party support, established a new National Heritage Memorial Fund. In 1984, after the 1983 National Heritage Act, English Heritage was set up under Lord Montagu of Beaulieu, landed conservatism and Thatcherite entrepreneurialism joining hands, one of several examples where 1980s Conservatism was able to entangle languages of nationhood and enterprise. Mandler comments: 'the effect was to make "national heritage" the centrepiece of public arts policy in the 1980s.'[35] Patrick Wright presents the National Heritage Memorial Fund as the Thatcher government's first attempt to 'revive the spirit of the Second World War' against the post-war settlement, part of a wider 'revivalist fable' calling for an entrepreneurial challenge to national decline.[36] Strong's 1978 commentary above on external and internal 'dangers' prefigures this. Wright also notes the wider 1980s dissemination of the country house aesthetic, with the vogue for country house interiors offering 'undesigned enchantment' to set against planning modernity.[37] Calke Abbey in south Derbyshire was acquired in 1983 for the National Trust (by then with over a million members) via the National Heritage Memorial Fund, its magic accruing from its interior, cluttered and unaltered. Calke's ordinary (in country house terms) and unremarkable nature made it a kind of upper-class everyhouse, a private interior whose privacy and interiority made it nationally symbolic.[38] Private gentility becomes public symbol under National Trust care.

The private country house itself was, however, far from moribund, the language of threat not entirely matching proprietorial experience. John Martin Robinson's 1984 book *The Latest Country Houses* showed the rich managing to cope:

> so much that has been written on the subject, including the reviews and publicity surrounding the 'Destruction of the Country House' Exhibition in 1974, seems to me so wrongheaded that I have felt impelled to produce an antidote and to show that the country house tradition in Britain is far from dead.[39]

Political Conservatism had a presence here, Robinson noting Quinlan Terry's classical 1982 summer house for Michael Heseltine at Thenford Hall, Northamptonshire, old country house style for an Environment Minister then charged with revitalizing derelict industrial cities via garden festivals.[40] Mandler estimates half of Robinson's nearly two hundred predominantly neo-Georgian new houses were built to replace demolished former houses; indeed Robinson noted that many houses in the 1974 V&A gazetteer of loss had been replaced.[41]

The country house at the turn of the 1970s and '80s could appear both threatened and lively, its cultural status enhanced rather than diminished by political debate, and two television events of the early 1980s reflected and fostered its iconic stature. One was on the BBC and set in the present, the other on ITV and set in the past. Whatever the social complexities in their narratives, the effect was, at a time of considerable social division, to present the country house as an ideal worth respecting.

The situation comedy *To the Manor Born*, written by Peter Spence, ran on BBC 1 from September 1979 to November 1981, a star vehicle for Penelope Keith following her success in *The Good Life* (1975–8). While Keith's *Good Life* character, Margo Leadbetter, had been laughed at for her suburban snobbery, *To the Manor Born*'s Audrey fforbes-Hamilton was a conveyor of cosy humour, someone the viewer was invited to admire, in her sense of taste and social responsibility. The plot had Audrey moving from her country house, Grantleigh Manor, to an estate cottage after the death of her husband, with new self-made supermarket entrepreneur Richard DeVere, played by Peter Bowles, becoming the new owner and the butt of jokes. The comedy of old and new money became romantic, with 24 million watching Audrey and Richard marry in the final episode. Deferential servants and eccentric friends add conventional humour, while Richard's Polish mother (he turns out to have been born in Poland himself) acts as both comic figure and sign of a traumatic migrant past, a story never more than a back reference signalling DeVere's enterprising achievements. At the opening of a new political era, *To the Manor Born* projected the country house as a site of social reassurance, of an elite class happily incorporating new members, of a resilient country England. The opening credits showed the manor at Cricket St Thomas in Somerset, home of Peter Spence's in-laws, who also ran a wildlife park in the grounds. The site had a televisual afterlife, as from 1994 to 1998 the location for Noel Edmonds's Mr Blobby theme park 'Crinkley Bottom', with its Blobby-themed suburban house, 'Dunblobbin'.

The dramas of the English country house are varied, but a 1981 television drama which itself became iconic in the medium conveyed and revelled in an aesthetic of lavish country life. The 1981 ITV adaptation by John Mortimer of Evelyn Waugh's 1945 novel *Brideshead Revisited* made stars of Jeremy Irons as Charles Ryder and Anthony Andrews as Sebastian Flyte, with an eminent supporting cast including Laurence Olivier and Claire Bloom. Through eleven hour-long episodes from October to December, Waugh's novel of memory became something of the present, a television event. The screen aesthetic of country house life (Castle Howard played Brideshead), baroque architecture and Oxford's decadence and languid sexuality, set against Geoffrey Burgon's wistfully stately musical backdrop, and all recalled in narrative voiceover by Irons's Ryder from the fallen novelistic present of a Brideshead occupied by troops during the Second World War, offered an enchanted contrast to a divided 1980s Britain. Looking back beyond a time of country house doom, the story chimed with political denigration of the post-war period as one of decline and landscape destruction, and gained popular cultural resonance. Emerging styles of new romantic culture found echoes in Brideshead, of the ways aesthetics might matter, of the delights and agonies of style, of the play of history. *Brideshead Revisited* offered a strange dressing-up box for a particular variant of 1980s popular culture, at once transgressive and deferential, sweaters over shoulders, flopping hair flicked. *Brideshead Revisited* (ITV, Tuesday, 9–10 p.m.) and *To the Manor Born* (BBC 1, Sunday, 7.15–7.45 p.m.) shared 1981 peak televisual space, offering variations in the English upper-class aesthetic, of sexuality, of family ffunction and dysfunction. Whether at Brideshead or Grantleigh Manor, the assumption was that here was a space of cultural worth, held in high regard, to be admired from below or aspired to.

The cultural value of the English country house should not be taken for granted. Mandler indeed notes that for much of the past two hundred years attitudes to the English country house have been ambivalent and sometimes hostile.[42] Ideals of continuity and tradition were made and mobilized in the mid- to late twentieth century, deployed by lobby groups with some success, to the degree that it might seem implausible, even sacrilegious, to suggest that someone might have come across the 1974 Victoria and Albert Museum catalogue in a public library and intoned the demolition roll with joy. Good riddance to a bombastic architecture of privilege! In the late twentieth century, such sentiments were made inadmissible, and a positive, or at least non-negative, narrative of the post-war takeover of the private country house by public institutions remains to be written. A starting reference point might be Henry Green's 1948 novel *Concluding*, where a scientist, Mr Rock, lives in retirement in the grounds of a country house converted to a training institute for female state servants. The women running the institute refer to the estate as the 'great Place', an idealized entity taken over from a private owner ten years before, a capital 'P' signifying claimed specialness. The novel covers one day, of the 'Founder's Day' dance, with rituals set to shape institutional identity: 'The decorations for Founder's Day were already traditional, although the Institute had only been open ten years.'[43] Miss Edge, one of the institute's two Principals, notes: 'One of the things we should provide here is memories, which is why I strive for the repetitive.'[44] After a day of excitements and unnervings, Mr Rock gets back to his cottage after the dance: 'On the whole he was well satisfied with his day. He fell asleep almost at once in the yellow woollen nightshirt.'[45] The indeterminate outcome of *Concluding*, with a missing girl not yet found and future relationships of property and affection unresolved, denotes the country house as a Place awaiting a settled conclusion. For now, a new world still made its way: 'Everyone was frozen in the high summer of the State.'[46]

If no one could seriously suggest pulling country houses down, they could still be sent up. Vivian Stanshall's 1978 LP *Sir Henry at Rawlinson End* offered country house absurdism, a preposterously landed Englishness askew. Stanshall, the former singer with the Bonzo Dog Doo-Dah Band, whose voice was also known for the narration on Mike Oldfield's 1973 album *Tubular Bells*, was often labelled as very English in his eccentricity.[47] Rawlinson episodes were recorded for Radio 1's John Peel show from 1975 to 1979 (and again in 1988 and 1991), and the 1978 LP gathered Rawlinson stories into one strange whole set to music variously pastoral and tea dance. Along with the bibulous Sir Henry were his wife, Florrie, effete brother Hubert ('in his mid-forties and still unusual') and servants Old Scrotum ('the wrinkled retainer') and sock-darning housekeeper Mrs E.[48] The opening words set the place:

> English as tuppence, changing yet changeless as canal water, nestling in green nowhere, armoured and effete, bold flag-bearer, lotus-fed Miss Havishambling, oxymath and eremite, feudal still reactionary Rawlinson End, the story so far.

A sunken garden, with 207 gnomes 'in stone postures various', prompts a ditty: 'How nice to be in England, now that England's here, I stand upright in my wheelbarrow and pretend I'm Boadicea.' Stanshall proffers a pun-filled idyll, yet one haunted by war and empire, and revelling in unpleasantness, the colic in the bucolic.

The format of *Sir Henry at Rawlinson End* mixes variety theatre, radio sketch, performance art and end-of-the-pier show; Stanshall's 1985 'English comic opera' *Stinkfoot* (co-written with his partner Ki Longfellow-Stanshall) would be set under a pier.[49] In the England of the Rawlinsons, in old houses where nothing much changes, curious creatures camp. Stanshall places Rawlinson End close to 'nearby Concreton', giving a sense of modern threat, the absurd made vulnerable, and more endearing for it. There is affection, even tenderness, in the irreverence; Rawlinson End receives appreciation as well as satire, and via that appreciation the country house becomes preposterous. Comic surrealism can of course be predictable, and country house eccentricity is hardly unusual, but Stanshall's voice, in varied character and rich narration, takes the Rawlinson country house through an irrevocably stained looking glass to an England properly strange.

ABOUT ENGLAND

English Townscape

Living in an ordinary suburb, lacking means to travel abroad and with local caravan holidays becoming routine, where might holiday excitement lie for an eleven-year-old in 1976? Why not try Butlin's again, after a fun time with extended family in Clacton five years before? Brochures consulted, the camp was picked, Skegness on the Lincolnshire coast, handily not too far away. Holiday camps appeared as miniature towns, wire-fenced to keep non-payers out, with all you could need or want inside for eating, drinking, play and entertainment. Butlin's offered lively delight, a week in a dream town. And the clinching brochure delight in Skegness was the monorail. A whole week where intra-camp travel moved on rails, almost in the sky, circling over huts and play areas, hopping on and off. A holiday in the future. A new English townscape by the sea.

Monorail novelty lasted a few days. Watching Roger Moore as James Bond in *The Man with the Golden Gun* from fading velvet seats, the cinema projector illuminating cobwebs and dust, perhaps this wasn't the future after all. Gate sentries were puzzled when we asked to walk on the beach of an evening. Why leave the camp with all its delights? We got back in, but never returned.

Monorail excitement and monorail disappointment, aged eleven, catch something of the delight and dismay felt around English

'Butlin's Holiday Camp, Skegness, Lincolnshire – The Putting Green & Monorail', postcard published by John Hinde Studios.

English Heritage

townscape in the decade up to 1976. Dreams of newness met fears of loss, ideals bumped into habits, the new rose and the old fell, and then the old was saved as the new palled. Motives on all sides were various: radical desire for change, conservative love of tradition, conservative love for profit, radical defence of community. English towns and cities received inner ring roads, even had monorails proposed, but the ring roads sometimes stopped halfway, and monorails never made it beyond Butlin's. This section of the chapter explores aspects of English townscape in the 1960s and '70s, covering conservative campaigns against the modern, governmental attention to urban heritage, the complexities of urban modernism and the emergence of urban heritage as a site for cultural dissidence. Processes of planning, conservation, slum clearance and comprehensive development enacted different visions of what English townscape had been and might be, cities and towns staging stories about England.

The Conservative Townscape

In 1975 architectural historians Colin Amery and Dan Cruickshank published *The Rape of Britain*.[50] Both authors were campaigners for the conservation of Georgian Spitalfields in London, and would later act as advisers on architecture to the Prince of Wales; Cruickshank would also become well known as a television presenter on heritage. *The Rape of Britain* began by evoking war, arguing that 'Britain has not been invaded by an enemy power for more than nine hundred years' and that, notwithstanding wartime bombing, the 'colossal' damage since 1945 'has been done by ourselves'. As with the country house, townscape prompted narratives of a lost peace, with commerce and government culpable and the ordinary person betrayed: 'to the man in the street it has always looked as though the ravishing of our cities was being carried out largely for private profit but always with official blessing.'[51] The language of ravishing is ratcheted up in a map labelled 'Scenes of Rape', drawn by Wally Conquy, who had also produced visualizations of Covent Garden plans for a critical *Architectural Review* article in 1972 by Cruickshank, Amery and Mark Girouard.[52] The map showed towns and cities covered in the book, the label presenting a vulnerable, feminized heritage, with Amery, Cruickshank and colleagues appearing as knights offering chivalric defence, a gallant minority, tilting at power.

The imagery of *The Rape of Britain* consistently presented architectural modernism as an alien destroyer of national heritage, in aesthetic opposition to the old and at odds with the public:

> Since the 1950s architects trained in the disciplines and dogma of an alien 'Modern Movement' have imposed an architecture on small towns and historic city centres that simply does not fit. The public has realised for some time that there is something wrong with modern architecture.[53]

Any idea, not uncommon in earlier decades, that the modern and the traditional might complement one another, whether through design affinities or in dramatic contrast, is abandoned.[54] A wedge is driven between heritage and the modern, in part a geographical story of local variety in style and building materials being replaced by large-scale standardized concrete in 'the licensed vandalism of the years 1950–75'.[55] Thus in Bath, office and shopping development replaced small Georgian terraces: 'the whole setting of the Georgian city has been ransacked.'[56] In Cheltenham the 'out of scale' Eagle Star Insurance building loomed over a historic town, and 'has introduced a new vertical style into the Cheltenham streets – almost all of them'.[57]

Townscape was also marred by roadscape: the centre of Gravesend 'has literally become one gigantic car park', while Huddersfield 'epitomises the redeveloped town', its centre 'arbitrarily defined and throttled by a wide ring road'.[58] In Salisbury an elevated road was pictured, 'Salisbury's folly', leading to a proposed multi-storey car park, currently ending incomplete in thin air; the authors hoped for demolition rather than completion.[59] What hope there was flowed from economic crisis. Amery and Cruickshank present the end of cheap oil as a prompt for the maintenance of smaller communities and a scepticism towards new technology and utopian progress: 'The enforced slowing down in economic growth is in fact an opportunity to be seized.'[60] Diminished progress might reinstate time: 'To lose all sense of the sequences of time in our towns is an irreparable loss.'[61]

The Rape of Britain carried a foreword by John Betjeman, who in promoting parallel arguments over previous decades had become a popular voice for historic townscape. Betjeman imagined 'the smooth tones of the committee man' and 'the swish perspective tricked up by the architect's firm' persuading councillors to destroy in the name of redevelopment: 'Places cease to have names, they become areas with a number. Houses become housing, human scale is abandoned.'[62] A sense of change eroding place and meaning had characterized Betjeman's poetry, as in the 1966 'Inexpensive Progress': 'Let no provincial High Street/ Which might be your or my street/ Look as it used to do.'[63] Betjeman also presented television films critical of development, effectively an alternative to official films hailing the achievements of town planning.[64] In a 1962 film on Bath, one of a series of twelve on West Country towns made with director Jonathan Stedall for independent television company Television Wales and the West, Betjeman set his own narration of historic buildings against the assumed voice of a London-based developer. Betjeman adopted a Cockney accent in counterpoint to his own received-pronunciation tone, presenting greed and architectural ignorance coming from London to destroy Bath. Modern architecture is the aesthetic villain, Betjeman lambasting any sense that the Georgian and the modern might have an affinity, and satirizing modernist functionalism. A lecture theatre extension from a modern block at Bath Technical College designed by Frederick Gibberd, best known for Harlow new town and Liverpool's Roman Catholic cathedral, is described in Betjeman's mock-developer commentary as the 'vital buttocks' of the building. Against supposed modernist disregard for place, and against the professional capacities of architect, planner and developer, Betjeman set his own amateur eye, offering himself as an educated everyman. Betjeman's narration encouraged the viewer to observe and notice everyday design features (the curve of a crescent, the sash windows of a semi), setting ordinary observation against expert vision. Betjeman's televisual techniques and rhetorics of persuasion set a tone for heritage campaigns over subsequent decades, through *The Rape of Britain* and, as discussed below, the 1980s interventions of the Prince of Wales.

Betjeman might have been in Ray Davies's mind when penning lines from the Kinks' 1968 'The Village Green Preservation Society', hymning the small, the quirky, the fragile, the intact, lines whose irony prefigured the outrage of *The Rape of Britain*. Davies invented societies against the office block and skyscraper, in defence of Tudor houses, and lined up other cherished or quirky English objects in a preservationist sensibility: little shops, billiards, china cups, antique tables. As if anticipating Amery and Cruickshank's ratcheting up of a gendered threat, virginity also makes an appearance, to be defended against a rapacious modern. Davies's song, and the LP it opens, *The Kinks Are the Village Green Preservation Society*, gather a gamut of emerging conservationist concerns, including village greens and the preservation of draught beer, into a wider sensibility anxious at change. Other pertinent or absurd things – custard pies, strawberry jam, Desperate Dan, Sherlock Holmes – are thrown in for good measure, Davies fearful that the modern world might iron out a country's quirks.[65]

The Conservation State

The Rape of Britain was published in 1975 as a warning shot in European Architectural Heritage Year. For Amery and Cruickshank government recognition for architectural conservation remained inadequate, lacking power in the face of development. The book set local and national public authorities alongside developers and architects as culprits, and thus formed part of a wider critique of state action. It is nevertheless important to register the governmental promotion of heritage and conservation in the 1960s and '70s. Just as historians have identified a 'nature state' constructed in the post-war decades, so a conservation state also emerges, albeit with governmental conservation bodies in tension with other state actors, and different departments of state at odds.[66]

In 1967 the Civic Amenities Act, introduced by Labour junior minister Lord Kennet, established the principle of Conservation Areas, whereby local planning authorities could designate 'areas of special architectural or historic interest'.[67] Former Conservative minister Duncan Sandys was a strong supporter; in 1957 Sandys had helped set up, and became president of, the Civic Trust. In 1967 the Ministry of Housing and Local Government (MHLG) issued *Historic Towns: Preservation and Change*, seeking to balance conservation and development via planning, while the 1968 Town and Country Planning Act introduced the principles of listed building and conservation area consent. Works affecting a listed building or conservation area would require local planning authority permission, with, as MHLG Circular 61/68 put it in December 1968, a 'presumption in favour of preservation'.[68]

Governmental favour for development restraint in part reflected financial constraints from the mid-1960s, making for less visionary plans, what Otto Saumarez Smith terms a 'determinedly unvisionary' outlook.[69] Official reviews of inner-city policy in the 1970s also provided space for critics of modernist planning within government, Saumarez Smith arguing that 'the conception amongst political and planning elites that modernism had to some extent created the inner city crisis was a core reason for its rejection.'[70] The designation of 1975 as European Architectural Heritage Year provided an occasion for the state to style itself conservationist, with government now including a Department of the Environment, established in 1970 under the new Heath administration via a merger of the Ministries of Housing and Local Government, Transport and Building and Public Works. The Department of the Environment's 1975 publication *What Is Our Heritage? United Kingdom Achievements for European Architectural Heritage Year 1975* presented 'Photographs of Restorations and Improvements Done between 1972 and 1975', with text by the chair of the executive committee organizing the Heritage Year campaign, the Countess of Dartmouth. The committee brought together campaigners, academics and representatives of public bodies. *What Is Our Heritage?* was an establishment product, with an introduction by the Duke of Edinburgh lamenting 'the indiscriminate destruction of old buildings and their replacement by socially and aesthetically disastrous structures'.[71] A cartoon by Osbert Lancaster showed a country house besieged by roads and pylons, and cover and section header photographs were provided by Earl Spencer, also on the executive as chairman of the National Association of Boys Clubs. Government and establishment defined a capacious heritage under its wing:

> What is our heritage? Is it the mills of the North, the half-timbered houses of the Midlands, or the thatched cottages of the South? Is it the palace, the church, the railway station, the water tower, the manor or the village green? It is all of them, and the extraordinary variety stimulates the mind and the eye.[72]

An appendix detailed the visits made by Lady Dartmouth in the UK and Europe, with a separate section listing eight new towns, though Northern Ireland was missed: 'The visit was cancelled due to outbreak of hostilities.'[73]

Lady Dartmouth thanked 'Johnnie Spencer' (father of Princess Diana) for 'driving far afield with his camera at all hours', and would marry Spencer in 1976, having become close via their committee

Cover of Department of the Environment, *What Is Our Heritage? United Kingdom Achievements for European Architectural Heritage Year 1975* (1975), photograph of King's Lynn by the Earl Spencer.

work.[74] Spencer's cover photographs showed Priory Lane in King's Lynn; on the front cover the book title was framed by an old arch, with a toddler on a tricycle below, her hand making an enthusiastic gesture of some kind. Our heritage is old, but it nurtures youth, and Section Ten of the book reflected on 'Youth and the Future'. In 1975, with the UK a recent joiner of the EEC, the 'European Connexion' was stressed, the Duke of Edinburgh commenting on the Heritage Year's achievement in showing 'the short-comings of our generation as curators of the European architectural collection'.[75] Dartmouth noted government support for Conservation Areas helping shift the emphasis 'from destruction to rehabilitation', and emphasized the intertwining of British and European heritage: 'Today European countries need each other more than ever before. Perhaps Heritage Year can bring us closer together.'[76] Europeanness, however, carried a complex geographical and historical meaning, Dartmouth quoting Hugh Trevor-Roper on 'European techniques, European examples,

European ideas, which have shaken the non-European world out of its past'.[77] European heritage appears a rallying point in a time of geopolitical and postcolonial anxiety through a reassertion of Western standing. The inclusively European becomes potentially exclusive for those bearing other heritages historically shaken by Europe.

What Is Our Heritage? kept the role of planning in the background, notwithstanding the Duke of Edinburgh's comments on destructive modernity. Another Heritage Year volume, however, sought to reassert planning's virtues. *Britain's Planning Heritage*, edited by Ray Taylor, Margaret Cox and Ian Dickins, was published by the Royal Town Planning Institute 'as a contribution to European Architectural Heritage Year 1975'. Organized by region, the book offered a parallel, alternative gazetteer to *The Rape of Britain*, a 'Guide' to a planning vision as something beautiful and improving, embedded in and creative of place rather than imposed and destructive. Planning carried a deep history as part of the British landscape, and its own historic traces were worth conserving. The contemporary achievements of planning should also be celebrated: 'The latest examples in the Guide are indicative of the importance of the planning process of today in helping the development of the economy and the achievement of social aims.'[78] Thus *Britain's Planning Heritage* directed 'tourists' with photographs of Plymouth's post-war city centre ('monumental formality'), Basingstoke shopping centre ('450,000 square feet of pedestrianised shopping space'), Reading's inner ring road, Harlow's neighbourhood housing, Bacton Gas Terminal on the Norfolk coast ('sensitive design and landscaping and a single architectural style'), West Burton power station on the Trent ('the best grouping and colouring of cooling towers and chimneys'), Coventry's 'revolutionary shopping precinct', Preston bus station, the Fylingdales Early Warning Ballistic Missile Station ('a striking landmark'), the 'Lillyhall Strategic Industrial Estate' at Workington with its Leyland bus factory ('which makes a high proportion of the country's buses') and municipal housing at Hulme in Manchester ('modelled on the proportions of the Royal Crescent, Bath').[79] Unlikely tourists might soak up planning achievements. Within forty years, as discussed in Chapter Eight below, several of 1975's modern planning achievements would themselves be listed as heritage objects.

The Complexities of Urban Modernism

Amery and Cruickshank, Betjeman and Dartmouth and the proponents of planning heritage wrote against a background of dramatic urban change in the 1960s, with the introduction of comprehensive urban development, under local authority guidance, in architecturally modernist style. Around four hundred urban renewal schemes are estimated to have been underway in Britain by 1965; Gunn's study of Bradford shows how the city's centre was largely demolished and rebuilt between 1955 and 1965, with the past seen as a 'locus of environmental problems, not charming relics'.[80] Such development has been retrospectively labelled by some as a programme of the political left, as when in 2009 James Stevens Curl, author of the 1977 polemical study *The Erosion of Oxford*, pinned blame on 'Leftist ideologues'. Curl lamented 'the obliteration of the past, the making of the tabula rasa from which the Leftist dream of Modernism would arise, and the dreariness of the environment foisted on the nation'.[81]

Retrospective polemic belies a historical political complexity; indeed if a post-war political consensus could be said to have held in the 1960s, this included a commitment on the part of both Labour and Conservative authorities, national and local, to modernist planning. Otto Saumarez Smith notes how, in the late 1950s and early 1960s:

> ideas such as comprehensive redevelopment, the segregation of vehicular and pedestrian traffic, higher densities, virulently anti-suburban attitudes, and an almost unquestioned use of a modernist idiom were upheld as ideals...The difference in the rhetoric of left and right was in how far radical transformations were to be achieved through public or private means.[82]

Labour, out of central government since 1951, emphasized the public sector achievements of Labour local authorities, with leading figures such as Hugh Gaitskell and Anthony Crosland criticizing 'subtopian' suburbia. Conservatives could uphold modernist development as a vehicle for prosperity and affluence, and for profitable development, with modernist architecture 'central to the self-presentation of the Conservative party in this period, acting as a Janus-face with the attributes of the country house, the grouse moor, or the golf course'.[83]

There was then a political complexity in urban modernism, but there was also complexity in its attitude to the past, going beyond any assumption of a desired *tabula rasa* for future building. The aim of wartime and post-war planning schemes to build the future while preserving choice elements of the past, thereby balancing the traditional and modern, continued into the 1960s.[84] Some urban plans did indeed seek to write over history, as in a 1962 new city plan for Buckinghamshire, where Buckinghamshire County Council and chief architect Fred Pooley envisaged a monorail-driven 'North Bucks New City' for 250,000 residents in a coming age of increased leisure (although the monorails were also to include suicide nets).[85] The monorail city was overtaken by the very different central government plan for Milton Keynes. If, however, the North Bucks monorails projected an uncompromising modernity, blithe to history, the urban motorways characteristic of 1960s urban planning turn out to have carried a conservationist impulse.

Writing on historic towns in the 1964 Penguin Special publication of his influential November 1963 government report *Traffic in Towns*, civil servant Colin Buchanan stated:

There is a great deal at stake: it is not a question of retaining a few old buildings, but of conserving, in the face of the onslaught of motor traffic, a major part of the heritage of the English-speaking world, of which this country is the guardian.[86]

Traffic in Towns had extended Buchanan's 1958 work on the 'mixed blessing' of 'the motor in Britain', arguing for the maintenance of increased traffic flow through making new networks for the motor vehicle, yet presenting modernist urban renewal as a means of conservation.[87] Buchanan envisaged the separation of traffic and pedestrians, part of what Gunn terms a 'new conceptual vocabulary' for planning, including the language of 'environment'.[88] Saumarez Smith quotes Liverpool planner Graeme Shankland in 1965 seeing Buchanan's approach as 'putting the environment first . . . forcing us to make up our minds about the kind of place we want'.[89] *Traffic in Towns* presented four case studies giving detailed analyses of and plans for Newbury, Leeds, Norwich and central London. Townscape was central to the visual presentation, with colour drawings by Kenneth Browne, who also worked for the *Architectural Review*, where Gordon Cullen had promoted townscape as a key visual idea for urbanism. The urban motorway, which in the U.S. commentary of Jane Jacobs and later Marshall Berman would be the symbol of planning's destructive capacity, was styled here as a vehicle for conservation.[90] Buchanan had himself drawn on U.S. experience through a study tour there in the autumn of 1962, seeing the power of the car to transform urban environments but also finding lessons in what not to do, and feeling the Europeanness of the British experience more acutely.[91] *Traffic in Towns* in part sought to dampen Americanization, and Buchanan's framing of his work within a 'heritage of the English-speaking world, of which this country is the guardian', reflected American comparison. Buchanan set traffic planning as a pursuit of national identity, a way of demonstrating Britain's capacities on a global stage, part of a planning project that in Guy Ortolano's terms 'pursued renewed global stature by building on the nation's urban history'.[92] The urban planning of the 1960s and '70s, like country house heritage, saw the navigation of England's place in a post-imperial world.

Dissident Townscapes

The partial collapse of the Ronan Point tower block in London in May 1968 following a gas explosion, in which four people were killed, has become the most prominent retrospective motif of waning confidence in planned modernization.[93] Critique, however, had already gathered pace across the country. Discussing the rise and fall of urban modernism in Bradford, Gunn notes from the mid-1960s arguments against the demolition of Victorian architecture, a mistrust of planning following elements of design failure, and rumoured or proven corruption between officials and developers: 'a political and popular consensus around urban modernism that seemed firm in the early 1960s had disintegrated ten years later.'[94] Deindustrialization undermined progressive planning assumptions about the city, while in Bradford Victorian housing previously earmarked for demolition housed migrant communities from south Asia, the postponement of demolition presented as socially expedient.

In such contexts, conservative heritage critique was only one element of townscape debate; indeed *The Rape of Britain* itself pointed to dissident and radical voices within heritage campaigns. In their entry on Lincoln, Amery and Cruickshank noted that ring road and office development plans promoted by Tory and Labour councillors were only thwarted when 'Democratic Labour' won control of the council in 1974, although they added: 'Democratic Labour has only to be toppled and they will all be revived.'[95] Europe turns out to shape the Lincoln story, as 'Democratic Labour' emerged when the Lincoln Labour Party sought to deselect MP Dick Taverne over his support for continuing membership of the EEC, and for his role in enabling UK entry by rebelling against Labour Party instruction. In March 1973 Taverne fought and won a by-election as Democratic Labour with a 13,000 majority, and founded the Campaign for Social Democracy, envisaging a new social democratic party. Taverne went on to be a founder of the Social Democratic Party, and later a Liberal Democrat peer, having lost the seat to Labour in October 1974. Taverne's 1974 book *The Future of the Left*, while not discussing local development arguments, recounted the episode, suggesting that 'Britain's role in Europe may therefore still become an issue that creates new alignments in British politics.'[96]

Amery and Cruickshank highlight an affinity between heritage and the dissident centre, notably around non-party forms of community politics. Taverne, in his discussion of the 1970s Liberal Party, noted such issues as 'an obvious attraction for radicals'.[97] Amery and Cruickshank also cited Covent Garden:

> it has taken almost five years of active work by the community to convince the planners that the area should not be comprehensively developed. Only through public awareness was this centre of London saved from a monolithic, concrete redevelopment, surrounded by a ring of new wide roads. Other cities have had less luck.[98]

In his 1994 book *Theatres of Memory* Raphael Samuel noted the political braiding of heritage, with direct action and 'folk radicalism' marking conservation work: 'Notionally backward-looking and apparently reactionary, conservation has been for twenty years or more a magnet for cultural dissidents.'[99] Urban debate had fostered such dissidence across the country; indeed Sarah Mass notes how Samuel's own London focus missed a range of 'provincial town and city activism'.[100] Mass describes the 'democratic action' behind campaigns to save commercial marketplaces in Chesterfield (successful) and Bradford (unsuccessful) in the late 1960s and early '70s. Here a 'commercial heritage' of communal space, a market *place* as well as a market, was defended against development by 'civic amenity and heritage societies, ratepayer associations, chambers of trade and commerce and women's groups', with resultant 'intersectional – yet often factional – amenity and heritage activism'.[101] Campaigns could involve the political right and left, and draw in national heritage voices, as when Betjeman supported the Bradford campaign for its defence of local uniqueness. National heritage could also be invoked by local campaigners, Mass suggesting the Chesterfield campaign (which, as in Lincoln, set Labour supporters against the modernizing Labour council) 'leveraged the language of deep, ancient England connoted by open market commerce'.[102] Something ancient and popular was threatened by a modern alliance of government and capital, Mass presenting Chesterfield's successful campaign as 'an exercise in moderate, inter-sectional protection of public space'.[103] In a time of economic recession, action could present conservation as an economical mode of intervention.

Such political and cultural alliances were echoed in campaigns against urban motorways, discussed in Chapter Eight below, where the environmental and conservationist elements from Buchanan's work became more prominent.[104] Townscape shaped languages of protest and resistance, informed by nostalgia and despair at the trajectories of the modern. Nicholas Taylor's 1973 *The Village in the City*, alongside its re-evaluation of suburbia as a site of ordinary community discussed in Chapter Five above, questioned modernist planning authority, seeing good intentions becoming dogmatic and expertise authoritarian. Taylor had compiled an influential 'Housing and the Environment' November 1967 issue of the *Architectural Review*, critical of modernist public housing, and in 1973 presented modern architectural plans conjuring 'a secret world of illusion ... in defiance of the real world of people'.[105] Taylor lambasted a tower block 'hypocrisy of double standards ... those who design them would never be seen dead living in them'.[106] The high rise had become a site of social isolation rather than vertical community, with a 'kind of municipal fascism' regulating conduct, as when landscaped grass areas carried signs prohibiting walking or playing on the grass.[107] Ronan Point was 'an almost inevitable nemesis for years of technological conceit', and against this Taylor set the middling English vernacular of the 'urban village', respectful of the past and the popular: 'society in England is undergoing an experience of galloping *pluralism*.'[108] For Taylor such a dissident vernacular might nurture a 'socialism' whereby people are 'fully free to choose their own peculiar personal or family or community life-style'.[109]

In 1972 Pelican Books published a UK edition of *After the Planners* by U.S. academic Robert Goodman, with an introduction by planner, academic and community activist John Palmer. *After the Planners* castigated the urban–industrial complex, expert technocracy and 'an architecture for architects', with planning, as 'part of the consensus', complicit in alliance with industry and politicians.[110] Palmer warned that planners had become 'facilitators in a grossly manipulated system'.[111] For Goodman the route 'toward liberation' was via 'community socialism' and 'guerrilla architecture', with 'environment as cultural revolution'.[112] Palmer presented Goodman as showing 'clearly the need for a rejection of obsolete symbols and values, but there are, of course, problems in constructing an alternative road'.[113] The alternative road could also fork. Palmer, like Nicholas Taylor, looked beyond modernist planning to a socialist vernacular, but in other ways the urban critiques of the late 1960s and '70s helped clear the political ground for Thatcherism. As noted in Chapter Five, resistance to planning power could signal right as well as left. *After the Planners* was dedicated to 'all those brave people who won't put up with it', a slogan aligned by Goodman with social radicalism but which could easily, in its critique of the post-war decades, move right. In the late 1970s, in terms of parliamentary politics, the Labour Party would find themselves governing a crumbling edifice. In 1979, a key tranche of voters, not putting up with it, swung to a promised new Conservative home.

Scrutiny of Heritage

In *Coasting*, his 1986 account of a 1982 journey around the British coast, Jonathan Raban reflected on 'The Merrying of England'. Raban encountered a parade of Sussex bonfire societies on Brighton seafront making a spectacle for themselves and tourists, Brighton's theatrical townscape a perfect spot for 'their parade of make-believe'. Raban foresaw a summer season of such performance across southern England, of village jousts, battle re-enactments and morris dancing: 'Nowhere outside Africa, I thought, were the tribespeople so willing to dress up in "traditional" costumes and caper for the entertainment of their visitors . . . The thing had become a national industry. Year by year, England was being made more picturesquely merrie.'[114]

Raban represents a powerful strand of commentary in mid-1980s England, that the past was becoming a national obsession and that this was in some sense awkward: a cultural delusion, or a sign and symptom of decline. 'Heritage' would come to stand for such diagnoses, the word itself a touchstone for cultural debate. Robert Hewison commented in 1987: 'As the past begins to loom above the present and darken the paths to the future, one word in particular suggests an image around which other ideas of the past cluster: the heritage.'[115] The terms of heritage discussion move beyond disputes as to which objects might be classed as heritage to concerns over a sensibility. Key 1980s voices are considered in this section, to show how the past as heritage could variously become a sign of decline, a radical resource or a symbol of enterprise. One very public figure, however, helped bring heritage, especially architectural heritage, to national prominence, and himself became a polarizing touchstone for those asking what the built environment said about England.

On 30 May 1984 the Prince of Wales gave a speech at Hampton Court on the 150th anniversary of the Royal Institute of British Architects, in which he critiqued the practice of most of his audience, with a focus on plans for two sites in London: Mansion House Square, in the City, and Trafalgar Square.[116] The prince's description of the proposed modernist extension to the National Gallery included a phrase since echoed in many planning disputes: 'what is proposed is like a monstrous carbuncle on the face of a much-loved and elegant friend.'[117] Polemic followed from both sides. RIBA president Maxwell Hutchinson's 1989 *The Prince of Wales: Right or Wrong? An Architect Replies* retorted on behalf of a wronged profession, arguing against 'bowing and scraping our way backwards into the Carolean age with a neo-classicism which ignores new technology'.[118] Since 1984, if a national or regional news programme covers a development controversy, the word 'carbuncle' has never been far away. A comment about a major metropolitan public building could translate across the country, the prince's aesthetic confidence, expressed through a vernacular term with a slightly archaic quality, conveying a potentially demotic connoisseurship. The monstrosity of carbuncles also travels through the particular voice of the prince, British royal utterances taken to stand apart from, yet also connect to, the people. If his experience, and the setting of his life, might be at one remove, his feelings of attachment to and companionship with familiar structures could translate. Everyone might have a valued site, an old friend, and if it was threatened with change, carbuncles could be royally invoked.

The prince effectively reprised the heritage arguments put forward by Betjeman, Amery and Cruickshank in the 1970s, with modernism rendered unBritish, unEnglish; Amery and Cruickshank attended a meeting at Highgrove in September 1987 on whether architecture was too important to be left to architects. The prince's ideas were conveyed through *A Vision of Britain: A Personal View of Architecture*, a 1989 book, connected to a 1989 V&A exhibition, which followed a 75-minute BBC television programme in October 1988. The book's back cover quote states:

> My chief object has been to try and create discussion about the design of the built environment; to rekindle an alert awareness of our surroundings; inspire a desire to observe; but, most of all, to challenge the fashionable theories of a professional establishment which has made the layman feel he has no legitimate opinions.[119]

The prince presents architectural fashion as having 'spawned deformed monsters which have come to haunt our towns and cities, our villages and our countryside'.[120] The 'professional establishment' identified is the architectural one, who 'set the cultural agenda' which planners, developers and local authorities followed.[121] The prince notes his post-bag, with Chesterton's 'The Secret People' in support: 'G. K. Chesterton once wrote, "We are the people of England, that never have spoken yet." Well, the people of Britain *have* now begun to speak about what kind of architecture they want.'[122] The centrepiece of film and book was a trip along the Thames with Christopher Booker, author of the critical 1969 study *The Neophiliacs*, itself republished in 1992.[123] The prince compared the National Theatre to a nuclear power station, and found riverscape diminished, monuments obscured, the skyline dispiriting. The new Docklands showed 'the triumph of commercial expediency over civic values'.[124] Against commercial modernity and high-rise modernism the prince evoked an urban village vision of vernacular architecture and community identity; one of the prince's enthusiasms was for the 'community architecture' movement championed by Rod Hackney. A more formal community design would be enacted by the prince in Dorset at Dorchester with the building of the new suburb of Poundbury on

Duchy of Cornwall land to an overall master plan by classicist Leon Krier, 350 acres between the town and a new ring road.[125]

London sites were key in the prince's interventions: the National Gallery, the proposed replacement for the Victorian Mappin & Webb building next to Mansion House, and plans to replace the post-war Paternoster Square near St Paul's. The square, designed by William Holford, was praised by Nikolaus Pevsner in 1956 as a distinctly English mixing of the modern and the picturesque.[126] For the prince, Paternoster Square was 'the prototype for all the windswept urban squares dreamt up in the 50s and 60s'.[127] Paternoster Square, as an example of modernism built on a bomb site, exemplified for the prince the national triumph of war followed by a squandered peace. On 1 December 1987, speaking to the Corporation of London at the Mansion House, the prince commented on Paternoster Square: 'You have, Ladies and Gentlemen, to give this much to the Luftwaffe: when it knocked down our buildings, it didn't replace them with anything more offensive than rubble. We did that.'[128] *A Vision of Britain* states: 'Some time during this century something went wrong.' People were 'appalled by what we have done to so many of our towns and cities since the last war' in terms of commercial development (surviving market halls are cherished) and housing (tower blocks are the main target).[129] The prince is shown operating machinery: 'Lending a hand to the demolition process. I am told that crushed tower block, mixed with soil, makes a very good basis for growing roses.'[130]

Between *Coasting* and *A Vision of Britain*, Robert Hewison published *The Heritage Industry*. The title coined a phrase, and the book became a standard polemic reference point, whether for those wanting to damn heritage or for those who thought its critique signalled an elitism out of touch with ordinary pleasures. Hewison presented heritage as all-pervasive, inauthentic, indiscriminate, 'bogus history' with people paying for the privilege: 'because we have abandoned our critical faculty for understanding the past, and have turned history into heritage, we no longer know what to do with it, except obsessively preserve it.'[131] Heritage became both a symptom of and a contributor to, as the book's subtitle put it, 'Britain in a climate of decline'.

Chris Orr's cover drawing for *The Heritage Industry* restyles the map of Britain as 'Dodo Brittanicus'. For Hewison the statistic that every week a new museum opened signalled 'the imaginative death of this country', a country 'obsessed with its past, and unable to face its

Cover of Robert Hewison, *The Heritage Industry* (1987), drawing by Chris Orr.

future'.[132] Heritage signalled entropy, presenting 'a history that is over', with the 'heritage industry' a 'new cultural force': 'instead of manufacturing goods, we are manufacturing *heritage*.'[133] Hewison's analysis of 'the climate of decline' draws, like Prince Charles, on Amery and Cruickshank to indict post-war development, but where the Prince asserts tradition, Hewison sees a stifling of imagination, with Martin Wiener cited on how traditional Englishness constrains the entrepreneurial spirit.[134] Hewison also offers a critical account of the cult of the country house, its ironies and interests, highlighting another meeting point of traditionalist architecture and political Conservatism to put alongside Michael Heseltine's Quinlan Terry summer house. In 1975 Terry erected a classical column in the garden of West Green House in Hampshire, a National Trust property leased to construction magnate and Conservative Party treasurer Lord McAlpine. A Latin inscription around the base translates as: 'This monument was built with a large sum of money, which would otherwise have fallen, sooner or later, into the hands of the tax-gatherers.'[135] The visiting public could pay for the privilege of viewing where their money had gone.

As ever, heritage is about more than building conservation: for Terry and McAlpine, as also for Hewison. The significant impact of *The Heritage Industry* in public debate came, however, from the way its critique went far beyond elite targets. Museums were 'turning into theatres for the re-enactment of the past', with a focus increasingly on nostalgic memories of the recent past, industry and the everyday. This, more than country house visiting, made such sites 'symbols of national decline'.[136] Hewison concluded: 'Heritage, for all its seductive delights, is bogus history. It has enclosed the late twentieth century in a bell jar into which no ideas can enter, and, just as crucially, from which none can escape.'[137] The fact that entry to Hewison's bell jar entailed payment further sealed critique. Hewison here activates an argument for commerce diminishing critical engagement with the past derived in part from the subject of one of his earlier studies, John Ruskin.[138] Twentieth-century precursors also signalled the social terms of such judgement. The frontispiece cartoon of Cyril Joad's 1934 *A Charter for Ramblers*, for example, showed visitors paying to watch a woman spinning yarn outside a thatched cottage, the car park jammed beyond the fence, the profits raked within: 'The Last (Or Museum) Stage of the English Country'.[139] Joad anticipated Hewison's own cartoon frontispiece for *The Heritage Industry* showing a heritage railway, discussed below.

Hewison appealed to a 'critical' culture, a 'fierce spirit of renewal', as something beyond commerce.[140] For others, though, commerce, especially when framed as enterprise, could make heritage a field of imagination and progress. Political rhetorics of enterprise as antidote to decline could harness heritage and conservation as future strategy rather than past fantasy. Thus SAVE Britain's Heritage emphasized the ways in which conservation could embrace adaptation and bring economic benefit. As Marcus Binney and Max Hanna put it in the title of a 1978 study of tourism and historic buildings, *Preservation Pays*. Binney and Hanna offered a plural vision, with conventionally valued picturesque villages, historic towns and cathedral cities supplemented with new heritage. A postscript to *Preservation Pays* imagined a new northern tourist region from Liverpool to Hull, with a new international airport between Liverpool and Manchester bringing visitors to historic regional sites and new projected attractions: a Musée d'Orsay equivalent in Manchester Central station, a museum of historic ships in Hull and a restored Albert Dock in Liverpool, which might house a museum of pop and folk music.[141] Heritage is projected beyond the obvious. Binney's 1984 *Our Vanishing Heritage* covered country houses, gardens, public buildings, churches, terraced and town houses, and the industrial architecture of railways and mills, warehouses and factories.[142] Binney emphasized stories of inventive reuse to forestall loss, including in the country house, praising work by Kit Martin, who had saved Dingley Hall in Northamptonshire by converting it from an early 1970s wreck into ten self-contained houses; Martin then moved on to Gunton House in Norfolk. In 1982 Binney and Martin co-authored *The Country House: To Be or Not To Be* on the rescue of 'problem houses', presenting inventive remedies, including at Gunton and Dingley, which in most cases did not involve maintaining a traditional family presence.[143] Heritage merges with property development. For empty houses, Binney noted: 'we have visited the houses on at least one occasion and Kit Martin has made plans to show how they could be divided up into a number of separate units without damaging their essential character.'[144] The 'essential character' of heritage shifts from ancestral connection to profitable futures: 'There is no need for these houses to be perpetual pensioners of the State, enjoying continual bouts of subsidy in the form of tax relief or grant. Simply by adapting them so that they are lived in by a number of families rather than just one family, the majority can take on a new lease of life.'[145]

The alignment of heritage and enterprise was elaborated in May 1989 in a Royal Fine Art Commission exhibition at the Royal Academy on *Conservation Today*, with accompanying book by SAVE co-founder David Pearce.[146] The exhibition explored the conservation and reuse of old buildings since European Architectural Heritage Year in 1975, with conservation here a 'money-spinner' to be celebrated.[147] Hewison's critique was put down, conservation becoming an enterprising pursuit aided by personal and corporate tax cuts and breaks, and triumphing over public architectural modernism. Pearce celebrated 'the unabashed entrepreneurship abroad in the land again'.[148] Illustrations contrasted dull images of former ramshackle structures with sharp pictures of restoration, whether the country house (including Dingley and Gunton) or the terraced house. The final chapter, 'The Way Ahead', began with a model of 'Wimbledon Theatre, London, enlarged into entertainments/conference centre', an old building with a dramatically new extension. Here are no carbuncles; indeed the Prince of Wales goes unmentioned in *Conservation Today*. For the book cover Pearce chose the classical facade of Billingsgate Market, with Britannia on its central pediment, now the HQ of Citicorp International Banking, and with a blue-glass-clad office block behind. Here was 'a creative synthesis of new and old'.[149] Reflective glass is frequently praised in the book as enhancing the setting of conservation, newness blessing the old in its image. Heritage becomes triumphant rather than defensive, calculating rather than wistful, confident in its future.

Such shining futures were a long way from another landscape sensibility, which celebrated vernacular conservation, and whose fundraising was less corporate than a garden fete or a bucket passed round. Set, for example, the reflective glass hymned by Pearce against the hand-shined gleam of an engine nameplate, which you might see your face in, thanks to the devotions of an enthusiast. Railway preservation had by the 1980s become a cultural icon in its own right, whether celebrated or mocked. The opening page of *The Heritage Industry* hit on the steam railway, Chris Orr's frontispiece cartoon presenting heritage centres, museums and the 'Little Bumpstead Preservation Railway'.

Frontispiece cartoon of Robert Hewison, *The Heritage Industry* (1987), drawn by Chris Orr.

Men with hats follow their roles as driver or fireman, playing at trains while a press crew covers the action, the only woman in the scene tied to the track in re-enactment of a silent movie. For Orr and Hewison the preserved railway is the symbol of a diminished country, a heritage absurdity staged for a gullible public, Joad's 'Last (Or Museum) Stage of the Country' fifty years on. For others, however, such acts signalled a profound engagement with the past, dutiful, popular and, if eccentric, then harmlessly so, giving pleasure to participants and passengers alike. Thousands might ride historic rails of a weekend, and be none the worse for it.

David St John Thomas's 1976 book *The Country Railway* shows how the steam train was part of a wider English landscape vision. Thomas described his childhood wartime experience, his 'first meeting with a country train' at South Molton in Devon, with the steam, the coal, the signals, the oil lamps: 'It was the total railway in the countryside, serving it as part of it, the smell of steam and oil, the people arriving and departing.'[150] Jeoffry Spence's 1979 popular survey of *Surviving Steam Railways* noted fifty lines, and covered 23 – six Welsh, one Scottish and sixteen English – in detail, all 'now part of our heritage'.[151] The first preserved narrow gauge line was the Talyllyn in west Wales in 1951, the first standard gauge the Bluebell Line in Sussex in 1959: 'For people who like nostalgia – within reasonable limits – the Bluebell provides it with oil lamps on the station platform and that air of mustiness (the word is used advisedly and in the kindest sense) that pervades the scene.'[152] Just as townscape conservation could articulate popular anger, so Spence's mock dedication for his book indicates a dissidence: 'Dedicated to Ministers of the Crown, government officials, civil servants (top), and other non-railway charlatans, who plotted, or aided and abetted, the rundown of the railway system. May God forgive them; for there are many who never will.'[153]

Preserved railways were highlighted as examples of 'living history' and as the place where 'the preservation mania' first appeared, in socialist historian Raphael Samuel's 1994 *Theatres of Memory*.[154] As noted above, Samuel, a figure of the New Left and founder in 1966 of the History Workshop movement, emphasized the cultural dissidence of conservation, and *Theatres of Memory* presented heritage not as bogus history, or enterprise culture, but as a popular, democratic and potentially radical force.[155] Revived steam sits alongside examples of 'resurrectionism' and 'retrochic' from architecture, film, museums, television, design and more, an eclectic theatre, with enthusiasms for the past pedagogically innovative and valuable. Heritage denoted the healthy fascination of a country engaged rather than vacant. Samuel hailed the 'unofficial knowledge' thereby generated, with history 'a social form of knowledge' not dependent on the mediation of figures of authority from academia or the state, and challenging 'a very hierarchical view of the constitution of knowledge, and a very restricted one'.[156] This was a 'new version of the national past ... inconceivably more democratic than earlier ones, offering more points of contact to "ordinary people", and a wider form of belonging'.[157] The proliferation of heritage ('we live ... in an expanding historical culture'[158]) left 'any unified view of the national past – liberal, radical or Conservative – in tatters. Culturally it is pluralist. Everything is grist to its mill.'[159] For Samuel, UK = Unofficial Knowledge. The nation is restyled via, and as, a history workshop.

Politically this could pull all ways; indeed Samuel's own work appealed beyond his own politics, Wright noting the Prince of Wales's approval of Samuel's 1989 contribution to the Spitalfields Trust's *The Saving of Spitalfields*.[160] Samuel, however, challenged 'Conservative appropriations' of such pasts, arguing that 'heritage cannot be assigned to either Left or Right', and that 'Historically, preservationism owes at least as much to the Left as to the Right.'[161] Samuel's counter-history emphasized the radical, with a 'predilection for direct action', whether in William Morris founding the Society for the Protection of Ancient Buildings or Ruskinian radicals shaping the National Trust.[162] For Samuel the Trust's history showed a radical commitment to public open space as much as a deferential concern for the country house. By 1990 the National Trust, 'no more than a pressure group for the first seventy years of its existence', had become 'the largest mass-membership organization in Britain' with 2 million members.[163] By 2015 the figure was 4.24 million; in 1970 it had been 226,200, and in 1942 6,000. Samuel offered this mass membership a radical heritage, a theme the Trust would itself emphasize in the twenty-first century. In 2019 the National Trust's 'People's Landscapes' programme, promoted in the spring issue of the members' magazine, would explore 'the stories of passion and protest hidden just beneath the surface at Trust places', with the 1932 Kinder Scout mass trespass and the Tolpuddle Martyrs sycamore tree prominent.[164] Radical protest appears alongside the country house, both safe in the Trust's keeping, available for national memory.

For Samuel the 'heritage-baiters', notably Hewison, missed such cultural and political possibilities in a rush to judge vulgarity, this 'favourite sport of the metropolitan intelligentsia'; Wright made a similar critique in a 1989 essay, 'Sneering at the Theme Parks', challenging Hewison's declinism and his 'educated snobbery'.[165] Samuel presented a 1993 photographic collection by Paul Reas (known for colour photographic critiques of consumerism) with text by Stuart Cosgrove, *Flogging a Dead Horse: Heritage Culture and Its Role in Post-Industrial Britain*, as marking 'anti-heritage's coming-of-age', following 'a kind of anti-heritage trail' and cast by the authors as a critique 'of the very notions of Englishness'. For Samuel, Reas and Cosgrove offered 'a sustained essay in disgust', with ordinary people, especially northerners, as 'grotesques'.[166] The sneer was a geographical one, across a presumed metropolitan/provincial divide. The back cover blurb of Hewison's book had claimed heritage 'may be even more debilitating to our culture than the loss of empire'; Samuel might respond by asking why both could not be sites of invigoration.

Samuel was a pioneer of 'people's history', which he identified as varied in politics, concerned for past solidarities, expansive in topic and material, and in contemporary form preoccupied with the subjective and the local. People's history and Marxism might thereby find mutual 'nourishment – or dialectical tension'.[167] *Theatres of Memory* effectively gathered heritage as people's history, as a mode of popular engagement for today and as something which in the future might itself become part of a people's history. Twentieth-century steam enthusiasts might take their place in a future people's history alongside miners and handloom weavers, strikers and Luddites, the machine restorers of today alongside the machine breakers of old.

Industrial Heritage: England, Birthplace of the Anthropocene

Heritage, then, might be radical, entrepreneurial, bogus, the variety of readings in part prompted by an expansion of its coverage, notably by the development of industrial heritage. From the 1960s industry had become a focus for heritage enthusiasm, prompted in part by work in industrial archaeology. The range of outlooks on the English industrial past since the 1960s again shows English heritage subject to competing political claims and entwined with regional and global geographies. As the socio-economic dominance of manufacture and mining receded and a service economy became prominent, industrial history could offer telling stories about England.

Industrial heritage marks a particular relationship between the English and the British, with the latter important as an overall frame, yet within which a regionalized England gains prominence. Thus historic industrial England is part of a British industrial and imperial economic unit, and industrial archaeology, shaped by a strong regional imagination, takes its geography seriously. General surveys are gathered under a British label, with the manufacturing and mining areas of Wales, Scotland and England as key sites. The strong regional imagination of industrial archaeology, shaped in part by radical traditions of regional social history, sees England through a regional map, no less English for that but with cultural nationalism seldom to the fore. In this sense the mill and factory carry very different heritage geographies from the no less global country house.

The heritage controversies of the 1980s brought different takes on the industrial. SAVE Britain's Heritage staged celebratory exhibitions on industrial mills and railways, while Pearce's 1989 *Conservation Today* celebrated 'industrial monuments'. Their conservation was 'an idea far removed from traditional concepts', commemorating economic activities and ways of life only recently lost, the workers' terraced house 'a museum attraction only decades after it was the way of life for the majority of the population'. For Pearce the entrepreneurial engagement with such past resources, whether for tourism or 'adaptive reuse', was to be celebrated, whether in textile mills, docklands or railway architecture.[168] For Hewison, however, the industrial museum was the ultimate locus of decline: 'The paradox of the industrial museum movement is that it is ultimately anti-industrial.'[169] *The Heritage Industry* began and ended at Wigan Pier, presenting a heritage site effectively dancing on the grave of manufacturing and extractive industry, and thereby muting the critique of economic policies happy to permit such closures. Enthusiasm for former industrial structures did not enthuse Hewison: 'The rise of industrial archaeology is an ironic commentary on the decline of the industries it studies.'[170]

By the mid-1980s, industrial heritage had a nuanced thirty-year history. Samuel notes how early industrial archaeology tended to shy from factory structures, as in Rex Wailes's work on windmills or studies of canal heritage; many local societies were based in southern counties beyond main centres of manufacturing industry. The decline of manufacturing, however, shifted the geography of industrial heritage, with the north and Midlands achieving new prominence. Samuel commented: 'By 1971 it was possible to publish a coffee-table book with the expressive title *Our Grimy Heritage*, "a fully illustrated study of the factory chimney in Britain".'[171] The term 'industrial archaeology' was coined by Michael Rix in a 1955 article in the *Amateur Historian*.[172] In 1967 Rix produced a Historical Association handbook on *Industrial Archaeology* asking for aesthetic reflection, 'an unprejudiced look', to reassess items:

> automatically condemned as ugly ... everyone with any visual sense needs to rethink his whole canon of aesthetic standards in the light of the paintings of L. S. Lowry. Having been brought up to regard factory chimneys, canals, railway stations, coalmines and gas works as revolting symptoms of Blake's 'dark satanic mills', it is exciting to find oneself deriving pleasure from looking at all these things. When the architecture of the present-day world comes to be assessed, cooling towers will be regarded as among the most beautiful items this generation has produced.[173]

An institutional culture of industrial heritage developed, the Council for British Archaeology appointing an Industrial Archaeology Research Committee in 1958, with Rex Wailes conducting a 'Survey of Industrial Monuments' from 1963. The Association for Industrial Archaeology was founded in 1973, and specialist journals appeared: the *Transactions of the Newcomen Society* had been published since 1921, and was joined in 1964 by the *Journal of Industrial Archaeology* (later renamed *Industrial Archaeology*) and in 1976 by *Industrial Archaeology Review*. A BBC television series on the topic was overseen by the historian Jack Simmons in 1965; the Ironbridge Gorge Museum Trust was formed in 1968 in part as a means of generating historic identity for Telford New Town's Development Corporation; and in 1970 Beamish Open Air Museum opened near Newcastle. In 2000 Neil Cossons reflected on such extra-academic origins, industrial archaeology rooted in 'local history studies and adult education and among people who a generation earlier might have recognized "self-improvement" as part of their educational ethos'.[174] Cossons directed

Coal drop at Seaham, County Durham, from Neil Cossons and Kenneth Hudson, *Industrial Archaeologists' Guide, 1969–70* (1969).

Ironbridge from 1971 to 1983, and in 1969 he and Kenneth Hudson, founder of the *Journal of Industrial Archaeology* and author of the 1963 *Industrial Archaeology*, issued the *Industrial Archaeologists' Guide, 1969–70*. Existing and proposed scientific and technological museums were listed, alongside on-site preservation schemes, local journals and 48 local and national societies. The *Guide* gave 'some sites worth seeing', beginning in Coalbrookdale.[175] A photograph of the harbourside at Seaham, County Durham, captured preservation in process. A coal drop was shown, its block components numbered for reassembly (L1, L2, ... L52, L53), 'awaiting removal' as 'material for the Regional Open Air Museum for the North East'.[176]

In the 1958 'Buildings of England' guide to Shropshire, Nikolaus Pevsner found in contemporary Ironbridge a neglect of 'what made this part of England the centre of English industry in the C18': 'The area with the early furnace is (at the time of writing) shockingly sordid.

A little money could put it right and create a monument to early English industry.'[177] From the late 1960s things began to be 'put right', and in 1977 Cossons, with photographer Harry Sowden, produced a richly illustrated account of *Ironbridge: Landscape of Industry*. Sowden was an Australian architectural photographer, known for his modernist study *Towards an Australian Architecture* (1968) and for documentary work on *Australian Woolsheds* (1972). Working places join hands across the world, with Ironbridge (granted World Heritage status in 1986) a place of historic global significance. The patina of recent decay made for 'a special sort of dereliction', a 'suspended animation', captured in the book at the point of rescue.[178] Ironbridge presented a heritage challenge: 'The crude laws of conservation ... are all defied by a place which is so totally a function of its past, and its past is exceptional.'[179] Ironbridge stood as a place of iron in its origins and fabric, its manufactures and ornaments, Sowden picturing bridges and machinery, posts and postboxes, gates and grave-markers.

Laura Carter presents Ironbridge, Beamish and other industrial museums as effectively a second wave of folk museums, following those established from the 1920s as expressions of regional sentiment, 'modern, democratic institutions that fostered the relationship between local identities and citizenship'. Industrial museums, connected to 'regional social change and the new academic social history', were for Carter expressions of professional masculine practice rather than the feminine amateur conservative modernity of earlier folk museums.[180] Frank Atkinson, founder of Beamish, thus aligned with academia through a historian such as Jack Simmons, the category of social history superseding folk life as a framework for past engagement. Industrial museums were, however, only one element in a wider vernacular heritage culture. Angus Buchanan's 1972 survey of *Industrial Archaeology in Britain* set out a maturing yet still 'curiously unorganized' field: 'Industrial archaeology is still predominantly an amateur, spare-time, subject, with the minimum of formal organization, depending largely on the spontaneous enthusiasm of men and women of very varied interests.'[181] The remains of the industrial past gave evidence for the history of technology, but here was a heritage in danger: 'All over Britain ... traces of past phases of industrialization are being rapidly wiped out by the pressing forces of industrial modernization, urban renewal, and motorway construction.'[182] Industrial archaeology, 'concerned with that common heritage of the people of Britain, their shared past, and in particular with the outstanding achievement of the last two centuries', was a topic 'to which everybody can bring some expertise, whether it be the skill of the architect or engineer, the experience of the manual worker or the housewife'.[183] Buchanan, a historian at the University of Bath and, as Director of the Centre for the Study of the History of Technology, responsible for the card index of the Council for British Archaeology's National Survey of Industrial Monuments (which had 7,000 entries by 1970), sought to codify the subject, seeking to gather diverse 'regional, and even parochial' enthusiasm into 'a national organization'.[184] Buchanan ended *Industrial Archaeology in Britain* with a 'Regional Survey', his 'English Midlands' section including Ironbridge, 'the so-called "Stonehenge of the Industrial Revolution"', and Cromford on the Derwent south of Matlock in Derbyshire, both with 'a legitimate claim to be considered as one of the birthplaces of the Industrial Revolution'.[185]

Scrutiny of heritage in Cromford and the Derwent Valley before and since Buchanan's claim gives an indicative study of industrial memorialization, and can open up further geographies of English heritage to conclude this section. Academic research, popular publication and organizational enthusiasm have taken Cromford from industrial decay to world heritage in forty years. In 1961 the University of Nottingham magazine *Survey* carried a piece by recent research student David Smith, 'History of Factory in the East Midlands', a retrospective counterpoint to the magazine's editorial devoted to the need for more scientists in the Atomic Age. Smith surveyed from the eighteenth century to the interwar period, with a double-page photographic spread including framework knitters' workshops, Victorian lace mills at Beeston and the cotton mills at Milford south of Belper, on the banks of the Derwent.[186] Smith revisited the latter in a mournful 1964 note in Nottingham's regional journal, the *East Midland Geographer*:

> At mid-day on Saturday, 29th February, 1964, the clock on the small tower at the Milford cotton mills was stopped for the last time. Demolition of the mills had begun ... It seems unfortunate that while battles rage over proposals to pull down undistinguished Georgian houses to make way for essential urban renewal and new roads, so few voices have been raised in defence of the Milford Mills ... The mills were a living museum of the earliest phase of the Industrial Revolution.[187]

Anglo-Scotian Mills, Beeston, photograph by David Smith, from the original photograph held in University of Nottingham, Manuscripts and Special Collections, published in David Smith, *Industrial Archaeology of the East Midlands* (1965).

In 1965 Smith published *Industrial Archaeology of the East Midlands*, the first book-length study on the topic, with textile works and the hosiery industry providing the distinctive regional heritage: 'The region has seen the birth of the factory system in textile manufacturing and the beginning of the steam age in the cotton industry.'[188] A detailed industrial history was followed by a regional gazetteer. The Anglo-Scotian Mills at Beeston again featured, pictured from the playing field of Round Hill Primary School: 'This factory, with its castellated façade, is among the most interesting examples of Victorian industrial architecture in the East Midlands.'[189] Smith concluded, in a passage also quoted by Rix in his 1967 guide to the topic, that industrial archaeology was

> ultimately concerned with people rather than things: factories, workshops, houses and machines are of interest only as products of human ingenuity, enterprise, compassion or greed ... Those responsible for the birth of our modern industrial society erected their own monuments. It is for us to attempt to read and interpret the inscriptions.[190]

ABOUT ENGLAND

Arkwright's mills, Cromford, photograph by David Smith, from the original photograph held in University of Nottingham, Manuscripts and Special Collections, published in David Smith, *Industrial Archaeology of the East Midlands* (1965).

Smith's language finds something more than regional in the East Midlands, reference to the birth of industrial society prefiguring the area's later world heritage designation, discussed below. Smith's *Industrial Archaeology of the East Midlands* was the second volume in a series on 'The Industrial Archaeology of the British Isles', issued by Devon-based publisher David & Charles, itself a key player in the print culture of industrial heritage. The firm was founded in 1960 by David St John Thomas and Charles Hadfield; the former's *The Country Railway* was quoted earlier in this chapter. David & Charles's advertisement in Cossons and Hudson's *Industrial Archaeologists' Guide, 1969–70* listed 89 books of interest to the reader, including regional history series on canals (Hadfield's specialism) and railways (Thomas's particular interest).[191]

Smith illustrated his 1965 book with his own black-and-white photographs, including that of the Beeston mills. Smith's images are themselves now as historically evocative as the objects which they depicted; one showed a sports car (not Smith's own) parked outside 'Richard Arkwright's cotton mills at Cromford, 1771 and later'.[192] The gazetteer noted: 'Substantial buildings still survive, now used as a laundry and colour works.' The original mill had 'burnt out some

250

years ago', but Cromford in the early 1960s showed industrial reuse amid decay.[193] At Cromford, as elsewhere in the region, relics hung on, Smith's book offering rare appreciation. The sports car parks up, a modern machine intruding in a worn-out spectacle, a site celebrated in paintings by Joseph Wright of Derby in the late eighteenth century now rarely given a glance.

Smith's account, however, helped stir interest, and new enthusiasm came to occupy Arkwright's mills. In 1971 an Arkwright Festival was held at Cromford celebrating the bicentenary of the site, and promoted in part from the University of Nottingham's adult education centre in Matlock. The festival led to the establishment of the Arkwright Society, which began to restore a corn mill as a visitor centre, and in 1979 bought Arkwright's original cotton mill from the dyestuffs company.[194] A local story of adult education and heritage enthusiasm, with steady restoration through volunteer labour, turned global in 2001, when the Derwent Valley Mills, stretching from Derby to Matlock, with Cromford a core site, were given World Heritage status. The Derwent mills joined Ironbridge Gorge, designated in 1986, which in 1973 had hosted the First International Congress on the Conservation of Industrial Monuments. UNESCO's 'justification for inscription' for Derwent concerned mills as examples of industrial development in a hitherto rural landscape, and the birth of the factory system. The sports car turns out to have been parked before a site of global significance where new forms of technological, economic and social organization had emerged.

National heritage becomes global heritage, in part through claims to the global significance of the English past. Rix indeed ended his 1967 guide to *Industrial Archaeology* with species-level comment:

Finally it is worth recalling that in the material field the human race has only taken two major steps forward in a million years occupation of this planet. The first was when agriculture was pioneered in the Middle East about 10,000 years ago ... The second was what we call the Industrial Revolution which had its origins deep in the history of Western Europe, and especially in England, where it goes back to the time of Queen Anne and beyond. Virtually every aspect of it was developed in Britain. Future generations of industrial archaeologists will look back upon the mid-twentieth century as a period shamefully marked by the destruction and neglect of the monuments left by this momentous movement. It is for us, the first generation of industrial archaeologists, to pursue this new subject with all the energy that we can muster.[195]

The energy of industry needed to find an echo in the energy of archaeology. In 1975, in *The BP Book of Industrial Archaeology*, Cossons welcomed 'an active appreciation that the remains of industrialization in Britain are the tangible marks of the beginnings of a new civilization which a thousand years hence the archaeologist and historian will identify, categorise and possibly revere in the same way as we do the ancient cultures of the Mediterranean'.[196]

Another kind of globalism has since been registered at Cromford. A site global in its significance has also been global in its interconnections, and recent scholarship and activism have sought to embed the site in global histories less celebratory, in the process opening up its stories to audiences beyond those enthusiastic for industrial technology. The Global Cotton Connections project, itself connected, like the 1971 Arkwright Festival, to the University of Nottingham, in connection with BAME community groups in cities such as Nottingham and Sheffield, has pursued the origins of the cotton imported for spinning at Cromford and elsewhere in the Derwent Valley, notably by the Strutt family at Belper. The project highlights a complex economic and social geography, with the historic undercutting of a powerful Indian cotton industry and the derivation of products from slave labour in the Americas.[197] Since 2015 the visitor centre at Cromford has featured a global cotton workers' mural by Brian Gallagher showing the conditions of labour across the world, sharing a wall with reproductions of Wright's celebratory portraits of Arkwright and other mill owners. Regional initiative, global imagination and local history meet, and English heritage is renewed. Cromford thereby finds its place within another heritage trend, acknowledging and highlighting connections to slavery, as noted in Chapter Three above in terms of the country house. Plantation labour in the Caribbean entangles with child labour in the Peak District. And as the birthplace of the modern factory, Cromford denotes a system whereby wealth is generated from labour relations which in turn make labourers conscious of themselves as a class. The world reorganizes. A renewal of heritage produces an expanded English story.

If English heritage, industrial and architectural, national and regional, is presented as of global significance, that significance flashes up at particular moments. In the 2010s debates on the role of slavery in shaping the modern world, and its legacies within a multi-ethnic Britain, made for new forms of illumination, not without tension. In the 1960s and 1970s lack of care for industrial structures implied for some the neglect of a global story over which Britain could claim ownership as the birthplace of the Industrial Revolution. How could such things (in the 1960s, or the 2010s) be neglected or ignored? The things that made Britain and England great, in economic power, carry undoubted, though not uncontested, significance, and industrial heritage might take a further twist as the concept of the Anthropocene takes popular hold.

The Anthropocene as a proposed new geological epoch signals the marking of the future rock record by modern human industrial structures. In terms of a stratigraphic sedimentary 'golden spike', the Anthropocene is likely to be dated to the global traces of atmospheric nuclear testing after the Second World War, but the processes shaping the Anthropocene are commonly traced back to eighteenth- and nineteenth-century industrialism.[198] What follows from an acknowledgement that the Anthropocene, whatever its precise stratigraphic start date, was significantly shaped by what happened in Cromford? Arkwright's mills may have been water-powered, so perhaps a narrative of sustainable industry might be claimed, but Cromford set in train a form of production that could harness steam power, and the rest is geological history. England, birthplace of the Anthropocene! English heritage and its many gifts to the world.

8

The English Modern

Doubling Back on the Modern

A Waddington's 'Jig-Map' jigsaw, surviving from the early 1970s, shows 'British Isles' in pictorial pieces. Well used at the time, the box a little battered now, here are countries that can easily break up, but which with patience can be reassembled. Castles and cathedrals, foxhunts and oasthouses, suggest a traditional England within a traditional British Isles, where national costumes mark constituent parts. Nothing much from the modern intrudes, but in the centre of England appears a dish, pointing skyward, the radio telescope of Jodrell Bank. The Jig-Map signals the future, a piece of Midland England in the space age. In 2019 Jodrell Bank Observatory was added to the UK's list of World Heritage Sites. A place of radio astronomy since 1945, the 76-metre diameter Lovell telescope, named after Bernard Lovell, the first director of the observatory, was completed in 1957. Jodrell Bank was inscribed by UNESCO for its demonstration of 'human creative genius' and scientific and technical achievement of 'outstanding universal significance'.[1] Universal value sits on the Cheshire Plain.

Jodrell Bank stands also as a monument to the post-war, a time of progress after devastation, suggesting a renewal of enlightened outlooks. In 1958 landscape architect Sylvia Crowe's *The Landscape of Power* presented Jodrell Bank as an interstellar pastoral, one of the 'new shapes' of the space age, detached from the ground but beneath which 'human life and the human scale can continue':

> Cows grazing beneath the radar telescope on Jodrell Bank do not appear incongruous. They carry on their calm, earthy life beneath the fantastic tool which has evolved from the

Waddington's 'Jig-Map', early 1970s jigsaw.

Detail of Jodrell Bank from Waddington's 'Jig-Map'.

mathematician's brain, designed to harness cosmic forces in pursuit of interstellar knowledge.[2]

In the 1971 'Buildings of England' guide to Cheshire, Nikolaus Pevsner described the structures of Jodrell Bank as looking like 'a huge piece of science fiction... They also look like today's abstract sculpture.'[3] If there is nothing especially English in its designation as a world heritage site, UNESCO presenting Jodrell Bank as part of a radio-astronomical 'global collaborative network', the Lovell telescope has become one of many post-war sites valued in England as part of the country's heritage. The telescope was listed Grade I in 1978, part of a wider move to value the architectural modern. At the same time as contemporary architecture moved beyond modernism, the modern built environment began to appear historic, and sometimes under threat.

This chapter begins by exploring the doubling back on the modern in England since the 1970s, and the emergence of modernism as a field of heritage through procedures of listing and the cultural values reclaimed through attention to the post-war. Nikolaus Pevsner has been a focus for reflections on Englishness and the modern, and the styling of Pevsner in the twenty-first century opens up further questions of what modern things stand for when they turn artefactual. Nostalgia for old futures, political reclamations and generational memories have come together around the English modern. The chapter then doubles back further through a key site of twentieth-century modernity, the motorway, exploring its emergence as modern landscape and its appreciation as a setting of modern life. The motorway as object in a landscape also, however, attracted objections, becoming a focus for late twentieth-century environmental protest, the symbol of a set of national and indeed universal values which themselves needed to be made historic, the modern as something to resist, to move beyond. While for some the English modern was to be cherished and conserved, for others it was best left behind; the motorway as anti-environment signals to themes addressed in the companion volume to this book, *England's Green*. A reflection on power station cooling towers concludes the chapter. We begin, however, with laments for another symbol of the car age, a tyre factory.

The Modern Remembered
Listing for England

In August 1980 the Art Deco Firestone tyre factory on the Great West Road in west London was destroyed by a developer just before it was listed, to the fury of SAVE Britain's Heritage and the Thirties Society, which had been founded the previous year. Environment Secretary Michael Heseltine responded in October 1980 by listing fifty interwar buildings. SAVE founder Marcus Binney's 1984 book *Our Vanishing Heritage* noted the Firestone loss as marking an attitudinal shift. Binney's chapter on urban housing discussed the Quarry Hill flats in Leeds, a 1930s modernist complex demolished in the 1970s, with 'no champions' for its preservation.[4] Firestone, however, galvanized campaigns to save the modern, and champions emerged. By 1989 David Pearce's *Conservation Today* included a chapter on 'Looking after Modern Classics', such activity 'entirely consistent with conservation practice' and challenging the 'limited perspective' disdaining 'that most unfashionable style, the one of the day before yesterday'.[5]

Modern heritage emerged in part through official listing, governmental and related bodies deciding that twentieth-century structures, including modernist ones, deserved protection. The official listing of twentieth-century buildings was announced in 1970, but was prefigured by a 1967 list informally known as the 'Pevsner 50', interwar modernist buildings chosen by Pevsner for potential listing by the Historic Buildings Council.[6] Later listing followed broader stylistic criteria encompassing more traditional structures and other variants of the modern, notably Art Deco, but Pevsner's selection reflected the sense that what was distinctive about twentieth-century buildings was their claim to modernity. Twentieth-century listing effectively memorialized the modern, raising the question about whether modernism had been superseded, and what it might mean to make it heritage. In 1987 statuary protection was extended to buildings at least thirty years old, making post-war buildings potential heritage.[7] If initial listings were generally of popular landmarks such as Coventry Cathedral or the Royal Festival Hall, the thirty-year rule soon encompassed 1960s developments. Structures only recently viewed as destructive of heritage could themselves turn historic.

Alongside official action came the voluntary organization of enthusiasm. The Thirties Society was formed in 1979 as an offshoot of the Victorian Society. In 1992, as a renamed Twentieth Century Society, it extended its coverage to all buildings since 1914. The society, with a London headquarters and regional groups, became an influential lobby group mixing historical architectural expertise (manifest in the scholarly journal *Twentieth Century Architecture*) with wider cultural enthusiasm for post-war modernism. Public campaigns were mounted around sites such as Portsmouth's Tricorn Centre, demolished in 2004. The 'architectural enthusiasm' and 'collective passion' of the society were expressed through architectural tours, whereby members shared delight in civic centres, churches and car parks, in places famous or obscure.[8] In 2014 the society published *100 Buildings, 100 Years*, highlighting one building per year up to 2013, showing 'how fantastic and varied the architecture of the last 100 years has been'.[9] In June 2013 the society chose as their 'Building of the Month' Bath Technical College, by Frank Gibberd, also the architect of Harlow new town. The college had been satirized by Betjeman in his 1962 film on Bath for its protruding 'vital buttocks', as discussed in Chapter Seven. Modern structures are reclaimed from condescension; Historic England published a celebratory book on Gibberd in 2017.[10]

Voluntary and charitable bodies could also become modernist custodians, as when in 1993 the National Trust acquired the modernist 2 Willow Road, architect Erno Goldfinger's 1938 Hampstead home. The Trust sought to preserve the building and its domestic contents, a dwelling contemporary to the 1930s just as a Trust country house might be contemporary to the Georgian period. That the National Trust could own 2 Willow Road signalled not only that modernism could be regarded as a historical style but that it could be gathered into an explicitly national heritage story.[11] The Trust's acquisition thus disrupted traditionalist and internationalist narratives, suggesting that modernism was of heritage value, and might have national meaning, the distinctive creation of an international movement landing in England. National heritage is reconfigured.

Modernism becomes English heritage in part through the actions of English Heritage in its independent advisory role to government. Attention to the post-war helped English Heritage brand itself as a contemporary organization, and between 1991 and 2003 a Post War Steering Group of architects, engineers and historians informed decisions. By 2005 over four hundred post-war buildings were listed, nine at Grade I and 95 at Grade II* (the level between Grade I, for buildings of the highest significance, and Grade II). The heritage value of modernism had been asserted in 1992 in *A Change of Heart: English Architecture since the War; A Policy for Protection*, published by English Heritage and the Royal Commission on the Historical Monuments of England, with text by Andrew Saint and linked to a Royal College of Art exhibition.[12] At the time only 29 post-war buildings were listed, and Saint sought to shift the grounds of valuation. *A Change of Heart*'s cover showed Denys Lasdun's ziggurat halls of residence at the University of East Anglia, built between 1963 and 1968, the forward look of the 1960s gathered into heritage. Architectural history here echoes wider cultural practice, with the 1960s a time of evocative memory. Just as an emerging 1990s pop musical culture revisited the Beatles or the Kinks (as they in turn had revisited Edwardian and Victorian culture), so architectural history rediscovered the 1960s as an architectural culture of which we were no longer part, but which offered an imaginative resource.

A Change of Heart presented a plural approach to the architectural modern, Saint identifying modernisms of method, style and good manners, corresponding respectively to the Bauhaus (reflected especially in post-war school building), Brutalism and an Arts-and-Crafts- or Scandinavian-inspired accommodation with tradition. The modern goes beyond the modern movement, noted by Saint as 'obdurately unloved in England outside the building professions', in a post-war architecture of 'variety, richness and inventiveness'.[13] Modernism and Englishness are thereby brought into creative relationship rather than antagonism.[14] In 1995 Nigel Whiteley criticized Saint as retrospectively dampening modernism's radical spirit, taming it for heritage via good manners and with a rhetoric 'dangerously close to chronic jingoism'.[15] Subsequent listing policy would, however, embrace the most brutal variants of the modern, and Saint called for pride to be taken in all such things: 'They belong to our history, and we need to come to terms with them.'[16]

Saint's pluralism is echoed in Elain Harwood's 2003 *England: A Guide to Post-War Listed Buildings*, co-sponsored by English Heritage, and encompassing public housing, private housing, town centres, civic buildings, libraries, theatres, law courts, office blocks, factories, bus garages, railway stations, bridges, churches, schools and universities.[17] The selections paralleled those in the 1975 book *Britain's Planning Heritage*, produced for European Architectural Heritage Year and discussed in Chapter Seven, or in Trevor Dannatt's 1959 survey of *Modern Architecture in Britain*, which praised factories, power stations, offices, shops, schools, universities, churches and houses.[18] In 1975, or 1959, here were forward-looking sites of the contemporary; in 2003 they are cherished in retrospect. Harwood asserts a plural post-war, including examples showing a 'gentle synthesis of modernism and fine brick building', but many of the buildings of *England* are assertively, indeed brutally, modern, from Lasdun's ziggurat halls to Goldfinger's high-rise Trellick Tower in west London.[19] Trellick, listed Grade II* in 1998, was seen as a problem building in the 1980s, before a security and concierge system helped make it a desirable and iconic residence. Just as with the country house, modernist heritage is enfolded within stories of class and property. John Pendlebury and Aidan While note the ironies of modernist gentrification while social housing remains neglected: 'post-war listing is simultaneously protecting the legacies of welfare state modernism and is part of the erosion of this legacy.'[20] Trellick is listed, and valued, while just across the Westway stands the shell of Grenfell Tower.

What Modern Things Stand for

In the 1970s townscape had stood for an anti-modernist conservationist vernacular, with modernist planning the destructive villain. By the end of the twentieth century modernism had itself, for some, become a townscape to conserve. The listing of individual structures in part reflected the distinctive designs of notable architects, but arguments to conserve modernist town centres suggested a wider admiration for the post-war modern. New towns, now getting older, became something to value. Both *A Change of Heart* and Harwood's *England* highlighted the central square of Stevenage new town, with its clock tower and raised pool, and its Woolworths behind, built in 1957–9 as the first pedestrian-only town centre and listed Grade II in 1998.[21] Pevsner had praised Stevenage as 'picturesque principles applied to urban conditions', a photograph in the 1964 edition of his *The Englishness of English Art* showing people relaxing in the square, with the clock tower, trees and a Fine Fare supermarket.[22] Pevsner commented that Stevenage and other modern English planning sites cut 'against the stupid prejudice that such new-fangled ideas as would give England modern and worthy town and city centres must be outlandish. It has,

I hope, been demonstrated how thoroughly inlandish they are.'[23] By the twenty-first century, Pevsner's new inlandish modern Englishness had come full circle, a heritage to be conserved.

In the relative boom years of the late 1990s and early 2000s post-war town centres could be presented as threatened by new commerce, a new 'urban renaissance' disturbing older urban renewal.[24] In Plymouth and Coventry, both reconstructed after extensive wartime bomb damage, post-war architecture of various modern style – Coventry's Lower Precinct shopping centre, Plymouth's Beaux-Arts layout of modern buildings and formal vistas – became something to defend. Post-war planning as well as architecture was valued, the imprint of the planner – Patrick Abercrombie's Plymouth work, Thomas Sharp's Exeter reconstruction – a modern equivalent to the Georgian landscape design signatures of Capability Brown or Humphry Repton.[25] Stories played out according to local circumstance, with different histories and present pressures making for what While terms 'local circuits of heritagisation' affecting the survival of the English modern.[26] Sharp's chief built legacies in Exeter were lost to new shopping. Coventry's Lower Precinct, with vistas to the ruined cathedral spire, attracted English Heritage in the early 1990s, though only its central Rotunda café was listed Grade II, and redevelopment in 2002–3 added canopies and arcades. No longer could modernist enthusiasts wander a pure post-war retail landscape, though getting off the train at Coventry could still, until recent redevelopment, take you back.[27] Listed Grade II in 1995, Coventry station, built in 1961–2 just as the city's new cathedral was completed, displayed a past modernity from a time of clean-lined nationalized rail. Here was something that could not have been built at any time before or since. Return to progress (change at Coventry).

The English modern, like any version of heritage, carries social and political sentiment. Saint's *A Change of Heart* followed his 1987 book on school-building in post-war England, *Towards a Social Architecture*. Saint explored 'the concept of architecture as social service', at a time when 'With the dissipation of the organizational momentum started by the Second World War, we are in danger of being thrown back to an earlier era.'[28] In the 1980s, laissez-faire was in vogue again, with 'the withholding of social investment' as 'the systematic and conscious aim of public policy'.[29] Saint focused on work in Hertfordshire, a county of post-war urban expansion and planning experiment, led by Stirrat Johnson-Marshall, 'an English, a very English Gropius'.[30] Technical innovation accompanied visionary outlooks, social architecture marked by 'imaginative practicality'.[31] Saint discusses how, when Johnson-Marshall became chief architect at the Ministry of Education in 1948, Coventry became a site for prototype school-building, including primary and secondary schools on the Tile Hill estate, later painted by George Shaw, as discussed earlier, in Chapter Five.[32] Saint's title, *Towards a Social Architecture*, conveys both the social vision of architectural modernism and the ways in which such buildings became a normal part of social life: 'Good was done and opportunities were brought to the lives of the post-war generations of English teachers and children.'[33] This was 'the biggest and most radical adventure ever undertaken in the history of British architecture', and if its buildings were later 'ignorantly vilified as dreary stuff', the photographs in Saint's book offer redemption, showing classrooms and playgrounds, models and murals, furniture and fun.[34]

Social architecture nurtured modern life, and the retrospective English modern becomes part of a wider cultural story circulating beyond architectural history and building conservation. In 1999 photographer Martin Parr published *Boring Postcards*, derived from his own collection of post-war postcards, reprinted in colour without contextual information.[35] While for some these postcards were, in their origin and reproduction, something ridiculous, for others they showed the sadly lost, their original celebratory quality quite reasonable. *Boring Postcards* prefigures Harwood's modern English heritage collection, but showing instead images of an unlisted, for the most part never-to-be-listed, sometimes since-demolished England.[36] Holiday landscapes feature, caravan site rather than country house, and newly built chalets and flatlets, something a little advanced for a post-war summer break. Postcards show pride in new civic middles, including 'The Precinct, Coventry' and Stevenage town centre with Fine Fare and the clock. There are also the less heralded centres of Burnley, Stockport, Burton, Crawley, Scunthorpe, Basildon, Barnsley, Leyland. Bus stations offer municipal hubs: Ashton-under-Lyne, Exeter, Halifax, Hanley, Preston. Postcards treat all regions the same in their difference. Provincial England becomes ordinarily modern.

Modernist enthusiasm has undergone select proliferation since 1999, still delighting in being a niche specialism, where dedication brings unlikely knowledge, paralleling the spread of Victorian enthusiasm in the 1960s. Hannah Neate and Ruth Craggs's 2016 collection *Modern Futures* catalogues modern architectural projects of documentation, intervention and transformation by historical researchers, urban wanderers, artists in residence. Thus Richard Brook photographs the 'Mainstream Modern' in the northwest, Ian Waites records the Middlefield Lane estate in Gainsborough, Lincolnshire, where he grew up in the 1960s, and Verity-Jane Keefe tours 'The Mobile Museum' through Barking and Dagenham, displaying banners, soil samples and models of the modern past.[37] Sometimes past bright futures and ideals of cohesive civic and national community predominate, but elsewhere edgier memories of aggressive architectural modernity and nuclear tension intrude. The Festival Hall or the Hayward Gallery? Brutalism, prominent in *Modern Futures*, is upheld by some for its 'anti-romantic honesty'.[38] A Tayler and Green vernacular terrace of Norfolk rural housing or a nuclear bunker? Parr's *Boring Postcards* included nuclear power stations, Hinkley Point or Sizewell appearing as normal novelties, but retro-nuclear now tends to relish the secret or hazardous, with a 'bunkerology' tracking those sites where administrators might have survived below a devastated country.[39] Cold War memorials inject menace into the modern, the remembrance of fear rather than hope and opportunity.

Modernist English heritage also entwines with the English colonial. Owen Hatherley has noted the absence of empire in recent reclamations of twentieth-century modernism; thus praise for Frank Pick's reshaping of pre-war London Transport through modern architecture and design often bypasses his modern publicity work with the Empire Marketing Board, just as it also bypasses his role in the Council for the Preservation of Rural England.[40] The English modern is never simply modern, or simply English. As noted in the discussion of Milton Keynes in Chapter Five, the post-war new towns were shaped by late empire. Craggs and Neate demonstrate connections between the new town programme and the 'post-colonial careering' of colonial administrators returning home on independence.[41] Here was another kind of end of empire migration to post-war Britain, with ten of the 28 British new towns managed by figures such as Richard Phelps, General Manager in the Skelmersdale and Central Lancashire new towns between 1967 and 1986, who had returned from Nigeria in 1961 after independence. New towns, as colonies for a new English urbanism, were shaped by colonial development expertise.

As the twenty-first century proceeded, and the global economy stumbled, two ages of austerity met. Interest in the era of post-war austerity encountered the revitalization of austerity as a political discourse, notably by the 2010 Conservative–Liberal Democrat coalition government. Pendlebury and While note how post-war architecture and design can be 'fetishised' in 'austerity nostalgia' at a time 'when the underlying principles of the welfare state are under attack'.[42] For Hatherley, a prominent enthusiast for 'militant modernism' and critic of neoliberal urbanism as producing 'the new ruins of Great Britain', the prolific reproduction from 2009 of a never issued wartime poster urging people to 'Keep Calm and Carry On', after its initial reissue by Alnwick-based Barter Books, shows a nostalgia for public modernism becoming reconciled with austerity, the past deployed to mute present critique.[43]

What then does it mean to remember social democracy? What, for example, if the 'Keep Calm and Carry On' poster were completed with a film title from the series whose name it contains? Keep Calm and Carry On What? Camping? Loving? Screaming? Abroad? Mugs or T-shirts carrying the full range of Carry On slogans might indicate in their sales just what it is that makes the post-war decades so different, so appealing. Is it the doctors and nurses, the teachers and constables, the sergeants and matrons? There is a pertinent history of memory here. Forty years ago, the post-war settlement could be critiqued from both left and right as a time of stifling cultural and political conformity and an overarching state. For the left in the 1970s the spirit of 1945 could be damned as social democratic compromise, Attlee's government clinging to delusions of global power via nuclear weapons and a lingering empire. After Thatcherism, and indeed after Blair, post-war social democracy took on a different hue, with *The Spirit of '45*, in the title of Ken Loach's 2013 film, to be recaptured against a neoliberal present, signifying governmental care for the people. In *A New Kind of Bleak* (2012) Hatherley praised the town centre of post-war Plymouth as representing 'something unified, public and civic': 'It's about time that social democratic Britain was the subject of something more than giggling and ridicule.'[44] Hatherley elsewhere updated Priestley's three Englands from his 1934 *English Journey* (the rural–traditional, manufacturing–industrial and interwar commercial) to add a fourth country of the post-war settlement, and a fifth for post-1979.[45] The fourth is upheld in critique of the fifth: 'I have spent much time as a writer attempting to rehabilitate the built environment created by this moment of social democracy.'⁴⁶

The shifting iconography of the post-war, from dullness to charm, entrapment to freedom, registers too in popular music, notably in renditions of the urban. In 1966 Jackie Lee's 'The Town I Live in', written by Geoff Stephens, chorused 27 churches and avenues lined with silver birches in a sardonically upbeat new town pop, before concluding with boredom, and nothing much happening. Listeners heard of brand-new houses and primary schools, and Lee sang 'etcetera etcetera', giving up on a new England as the song faded out.⁴⁷ A sonically edgy equivalent to 'The Town I Live in' was XTC's 1978 'New Town Animal in a Furnished Cage', on someone trapped with nothing to do but watch poor television.⁴⁸ New-town Englands entrap.

The twenty-first century, however, brought other sentiment in song, away from cages and dullness, in musical equivalents of Hatherley's rehabilitation. Darren Hayman's 2009 'folk opera' *Pram Town* offered a critically affectionate narrative of Harlow, elegizing early new town dreams.⁴⁹ The work of July Skies rendered a gently

Cover of July Skies, *The Weather Clock* (2007), sleeve design by Martin Andersen.

experimental ambient version of England after war, an innocent, pastoral modern with its social architecture of school buildings, new towns, holiday time, trains. On the 2007 July Skies LP and EP *The Weather Clock*, occasional vocals and period recordings supplement the musical conjuring of a modern time gone: 'Branch Line Summers Fade', 'Distant Showers Sweep across Norfolk Schools', 'Broadcasts for Autumn Term', 'Holidays to Wales', 'Harlow'. The LP cover includes Tayler and Green's vernacular housing at Ditchingham in Norfolk, a black-and-white image of houses with cloudy sky taken from Thomas Sharp's essay on 'The English Village' in the Ministry of Housing and Local Government's 1953 *Design in Town and Village*, montaged over grass and pool.[50]

How can post-war England gain such an innocent patina? It would be easy to point out things about England far from innocent, whether the opposite of innocence is experience or guilt. Yet, for twenty-first-century people of various generations engaging with this past, the period appeals: for seeming social simplicity, for the intervention of government, for planning, for an architecture with serious purpose, for confidence in the future, for not being neoliberal, for childhood memories, for memories of parents or grandparents recalling their own childhoods. Nostalgia, whether for the remembered or the heard about, gives a critical take on the present. Heritage, as ever, is harnessed for today.

Pevsner Abroad

The July Skies *Weather Clock* EP includes 'See Britain by Train (Pevsner Version)'. There are no discernible traces of Pevsner on the track, no sudden recorded interjections, but the bracketed name alludes to a guide. Architectural history pops up, and a sensibility is cited, Pevsner a sign of things passed. In his *North-East Norfolk and Norwich* 'Buildings of England' guide, Pevsner had stated that Tayler and Green's housing 'could almost be called post-modern'.[51]

Twenty-first-century Pevsner, like the buildings he assessed, has become a contested heritage. The 'Buildings of England' series, completed in 1974, with many volumes subsequently revised and with publication moving from Penguin to Yale University Press in 2003, is a fixture of English architectural commentary. In 2000, however, Timothy Mowl sought to unfix things, setting Pevsner against

The English Modern

Betjeman in a retrospective 'stylistic cold war', and condemning Pevsner's influence: 'should a man with no English social background have been encouraged so quickly to a position where he could exert an unwise and, in a very real sense, an "alien" influence?'[52] For Mowl, Pevsner becomes a prime culprit in persuading the country to modernism: 'That is the responsibility which those early volumes of the *Buildings of England* have to bear.'[53] The Pevsner version of England becomes somehow un-English.

For others, however, Pevsner was, like many shapers of England who had come from elsewhere, none the worse for his background. The prevailing tone of twenty-first-century commentary echoes Colin MacInnes in his 1960 essay on 'The Englishness of Dr Pevsner', where Pevsner is 'a sociologist of the English scene', 'an English stylist of the highest order'. MacInnes presented Pevsner as an 'inside outsider' like himself, whose achievement gainsaid resentful parochial 'idiocy'.[54] On his visit to England for two months in 1930 to research art and architecture, Pevsner had noted that 'Englishness of course is the purpose of my journey,' and Pevsner's appreciation of the mutual enrichment of modernism and national identity has been prominent in recent commentary.[55] The fiftieth anniversary of the county guides in 2001 brought a celebration of Pevsner as a shaper of Englishness, with a book on *The Buildings of England: A Celebration* and a parallel conference at the Victoria and Albert Museum. The 2011 Pevsner biography by Susie Harries presented a figure of cultural significance, his own complex relationship to Englishness part of the English scene, to be appreciated alongside the buildings he documented.[56]

This Pevsner-for-today presents a meeting point of the national and international, the parochial and cosmopolitan. On 25 June 2016 BBC Radio 4's 'Archive Hour' broadcast 'Pevsner: Through Outsider's Eyes', Tom Dyckhoff and contributors including myself reflecting on Pevsner's understanding of Englishness. The broadcast was the day after the EU referendum result, though interviews were recorded weeks earlier. The programme ended with my reflections on Pevsner, Englishness and Europe, noting an occasion in Pevsner's work where Midland England met European culture. In 1945, as the 'Buildings of England' series was being formulated, Pevsner had published a small 'King Penguin' volume on *The Leaves of Southwell*, a study of medieval stone-carved leaves in the minster church of Southwell, a Nottinghamshire market town. The photographs were by F. L. Attenborough, principal of University College Leicester and father of David and Richard, whose photography for Hoskins was highlighted in Chapter Five. Any expectation that a study of nature carving in an English country town would convey a nostalgic, anti-modern version of England is confounded, as Pevsner makes Southwell's leaves at once medieval and modern, English and European: 'the leaves of Southwell assume a new significance as one of the purest symbols surviving in Britain of Western thought, our thought, in its loftiest mood.'[57] Pevsner found at Southwell a medieval naturalism, a truth to materials and natural form, a proto-scientific botanical eye. English Midland pastoral and the modern European meet. The movements across the North Sea and English Channel informing Pevsner's work in 1945 – his own move from Germany, the invasion launched from England – may have been very different from the European migrations to the fore in 2016, but the complexities of cultural geography in *The Leaves of Southwell* seemed worth a revisit as the referendum campaign closed. And by the time of broadcast, further complexities were set loose. Pevsner had found European heritage in an English Midland cathedral town, visiting Southwell and finding Europe. After the Leave vote, some votive leaves.[58]

On the English Motorway
Objects in a Landscape

The photographic section of Pevsner's 1961 guide to the buildings of Northamptonshire ended with a picture of a motorway, an aerial view of 'London–Birmingham Motorway near Kislingbury, 1959', the MI curving into the distance, punctuated by bridges, with barely a vehicle. Pevsner presented the MI as an improving addition to English landscape, 'the C20 version of Watling Street', its course 'predetermined by undated reasons of geography'. The MI was the most notable newness in Northamptonshire. There were qualms, such that for Pevsner 'the Motorway is MODERN ARCHITECTURE only with reservations', Sir Owen Williams's bridges missing an opportunity for elegance with their central reservation column supports, a 'cyclopean rudeness' aiming for a misguided impression of permanence, where lightness might have been preferable.[59] In general, though, the motorway was good and deserving of illustration, the MI image surviving in Bridget Cherry's revised 1973 guide, though now as the penultimate picture behind new

'M4 Viaduct 1965', stamp designed by Jeffrey Matthews, 1965.

low-rise housing in Corby.⁶⁰ In his 'Some Words on the Completion of the Buildings of England' in the 1974 Staffordshire guide, Pevsner reflected on motorways: 'One got used to them quickly, and it seems odd already now that only twelve years ago I sacrificed one of my one hundred illustrations to so rich a county as Northamptonshire for the purpose of showing the M1.'⁶¹

In his study of the building of the M1 in the late 1950s, Peter Merriman shows how the motorway was a generally uncontested addition to English landscape.⁶² There were minor local objections, and architectural and landscape architectural debates over design features, but the presence of the motorway per se was not at issue, indeed could be celebrated as improving the English scene. In 1968 the Royal Mail tapped a celebratory motorway spirit when issuing four stamps commemorating 'British Bridges' from the prehistoric to the present. The 1s. 9d. stamp, designed by Jeffrey Matthews, showed 'M4 Viaduct 1965'. A clean, new empty motorway sweeps through fields and woods to the distant city. The Queen's head appears alongside the road as a proto 'Angel of the South', stamping official approval on a new English landscape.⁶³

As with new town centres and modernist schools, motorways, and the wider products of twentieth-century car culture, have moved from novelty to artefact. In 1992, when English Heritage held their *A Change of Heart* show on post-war building, Jonathan Glancey covered the story for the *Independent Magazine*. Glancey's warily sympathetic account was headed 'A Bridge Too Far?', and one of Owen Williams's M1 bridges, between Watford and Luton, was pictured. Glancey interviewed Andrew Saint, who commented: 'I'm rather fond of those Expressionist bridges ... They are fine structures, but they also capture the spirit of the early motorway age; they are an important part of our national heritage.'[64] The M1 bridges were not listed, though English Heritage have since taken stock of other motoring heritage. The petrol station has been recognized as a modern, if not necessarily modernist, fixture, with the 1930 Clovelly Cross filling station in Devon listed in 1989, and a further tranche of pre- and post-war petrol stations following in 2012.[65] One example of petrol heritage shows, however, the complexities of valuing the modern and/or contemporary, then and now.

In 1994 a 1928 petrol station at Beckenham in the London borough of Bromley, built in the style of a Japanese pagoda, was listed Grade II. In 1930, in the design manual *The Face of the Land*, conservationists had criticized the Beckenham structure, finding it wanting in comparison with a functionally modern station in Dorchester, Dorset: 'fitness for purpose versus the picturesque'. Beckenham's style, 'falling between a pagoda and a half-timbered manor', detracted from its layout, was out of modern time.[66] The station made it into John Newman's 1969 'Buildings of England' volume on *West Kent and the Weald*, but only as 'light relief': 'the servant of suburban Beckenham, PARK LANGLEY GARAGE, in a rampant "Road to Mandalay" style of *c*.1925'.[67] By 1994, though, Park Langley had gone beyond a joke, and was listed 'as a remarkable survivor from the early days of popular motoring', albeit a product of twentieth-century motoring not matching the architectural values of the Twentieth Century Society.[68]

The motorway, however, remains something altogether more modern. Val Williams's study of Martin Parr includes an 'ephemera' section from Parr's collection, showing the box for a 750-piece jigsaw of Spaghetti Junction, the Gravelly Hill interchange near Birmingham.[69] In 1972 Reyner Banham praised the new junction, designed, like the M1 bridges, by Owen Williams: 'when you stand back and take a long view of the totality, then something like a big Brummagem artwork begins to emerge.' Banham gave suggested routes through the spaghetti 'for those who want to dig the kinaesthetic scene at Gravelly Hill'.[70] The mobile modern opens Parr's 1999 *Boring Postcards*, fifteen motorway images taking the viewer back to an older kinaesthetics.[71] Three black-and-white postcards showed well-spaced cars on the M6 at Newcastle-under-Lyme and the M1 at Knebworth, new generic English landscapes, but most of Parr's motorway cards show service areas, the motorway equivalent to the roadside garage, but in their design and function marking a modern experience. Service stations were within the countryside yet cut off from it, accessible only from the motorway, an island of development surrounded by fields which the traveller could look over but not explore. Thirty-eight were developed by 1978, whereby the motorist could pull off the motorway but not divert from it.

Parr's postcards, celebrating and potentially sold from these new English stations, indicate place names formerly obscure now put on the national map: Newport Pagnell, Charnock Richard. In 1971, in his essay 'The Car, the Future', J. G. Ballard reflected on 'the shared experience of moving together through an elaborately signalled landscape', and service areas, and the commentary upon them, were one aspect of this shared landscape.[72] Exit left for a shared private experience in an unmingling crowd. Design kept the traveller within the contemporary. Parr shows the Forton service area on the M6 near Lancaster, opened in 1965, pictured with a few cars parked, one with the bonnet raised for checking or repair, a covered footbridge connecting northbound and southbound, and the Pennine Tower restaurant, a striking raised hexagonal structure, listed Grade II in 2012.[73] Banham, in an otherwise downbeat 1968 assessment of 'Disservice areas', found Forton an exception, 'so much better than one dared to expect anywhere in the British motorway system', imaginative in its landscape setting, and with the tower restaurant a panoramic advertisement for the site.[74]

Parr's pre-millennial attention to past service areas paralleled the affectionate satire of Peter Kay's 1998 mock-documentary soap *The Services*. This was a pilot episode for *That Peter Kay Thing*, a six-part Channel 4 series, one part of which would spin off into *Phoenix Nights*, and thus open the way for Kay to become the kind of comedian described as a national treasure. The service station is here a setting for Lancashire working-class life, Kay offering 'Bolton West Services' on the M61 between Bolton and Chorley as something typically contemporary. The programme acknowledged 'the staff and management of First Services, Bolton'.[75] *The Services* showed 'just another working day', occasional team conversations interspersed between monologues from characters (many played by Kay) to camera. Viewers meet the irate manageress, the frustrated drama student reciting Sophocles atop a skip, the bitter ex-RAC man, the coach driver losing two French tourists. At the end of the car park, a Chorley FM DJ plays '80s records to no one. Excitement builds at news that former TV star Bob Carolgees, once famous for his 'Spit the Dog' puppet, might pass through, and a red carpet is cleaned, only for the minor celebrity to arrive and depart southbound rather than northbound. A rush across the connecting bridge is fruitless, as a car registered SPIT 1 drives away. *The Services* shows a shared space where people bring their backstories to work, a life ordinary in its eccentricities. Whatever transpires at the services is mostly endearing, Kay's affectionate parody sitting halfway between the edge of Alan Partridge and the sentiment of *Last of the Summer Wine*. *The Services* was written by Kay with Sian Foulkes, who played Alison, a cafeteria worker. Foulkes, by then Sian Gibson, would co-write and co-star in Kay's later hit series *Car Share* (2015–18), featuring two work colleagues whose car sharing for convenience grows into love. Driving, a typical facet of contemporary English life, bookends Kay's comic career so far.

David Lawrence's 1999 'glove compartment history' of motorway services gives the architectural and cultural story of a neglected space, 'much-maligned outposts once representative of Englishness at its most basic'.[76] Service areas make themselves landmarks, and become places of commercial enterprise, working community, social interaction and happy memory. Lawrence also highlights one site where, rather than the service area being tied to the motorway and cut off from its other surroundings, the language of place and locality has been embraced. Tebay services, a local joint venture between a farmer and a baker, operates on the M6 in Cumbria, the western northbound services open from 1972 and extended through the 1980s, the eastern southbound service opened in 1993, and winning a Civic Trust award. The operating company name, Westmorland, maintains a county label itself abolished (into Cumbria) in 1974. Tebay's architectural style is embedded within rather than standing out from its locality, with limestone-built vernacular, and a catering ethos similarly embedded in local produce. Westmorland opened a second service area in 2014–15, Gloucester services, distinctive on the M5, locally embedded with a Gloucester Old Spot pig as logo and its roof green-planted. Looking down from the nearby Cotswolds, the building roof, if not the car parks, merges with surrounding fields. Tebay and Gloucester twist the motorway into locale, offering gestures of sustainability to the passing traffic on which they depend.

If the age of major English motorway construction began with the M1, it ended with the M25. Conservative transport minister Ernest

Marples inaugurated the M1 in November 1959, ordering all junctions to be opened via police radio, signalling a dynamic sprint to the future.[77] Margaret Thatcher officially opened the complete M25 in October 1986, cutting a ribbon between junctions 22 and 23, her speech celebrating enterprising construction companies and modern mobility, and efforts made to blend motorway and landscape. The M25 was both city bypass and a key final part of the regional and national network. Thatcher's celebration of enterprise is the point of departure for Iain Sinclair's 2002 *London Orbital*, a walk around the course of the road, keeping within its 'acoustic footprints' but effectively exploring that which is adjacent but unconnected, 'dull fields that travellers never notice'.[78] Mundane and arcane stories are triggered at Sinclair's tread. *London Orbital* and a related 2002 film with Chris Petit (also director of 1979 British road movie *Radio On*), shot from a car driving the motorway, use the road as an occasion for exploring a concentric zone. Within this zone, however, the motorway is discrete, as the site for the film and the stepping-off point for the book. The orbital zone reveals a psychogeography of adjacent somethings rarely encountered by mere drivers.[79]

In the late twentieth century the motorway, as a banal element of modern life, no longer especially exciting or novel, becomes something to ponder within the English infra-ordinary. Works appear appreciative of the monotony of driving, the separateness of the carriageway. From 1993 artist Julian Opie produced pictorial and sculptural motorway works presenting the road in pure form. The 1993 *Imagine You Are Driving* series showed a kind of ideal monotony, carriageways emptied of cars, verged by plain green under cloudless blue, as if in a peculiarly minimalist video game.[80] Images of M40, headlights and rearlights and lamplights at night, presented steady movement through the motorway illuminations.[81] The 2002 work *I Dreamt I Was Driving My Car (Motorway)* looks across from the hard shoulder against the flow of non-traffic, the other carriageway signalling a junction ahead, potential departures.[82] The dream is of driving, though the car seems to have stopped, and no one is around, motorway life suspended in dreamtime. Imagine how calming the road might be if you had it all to yourself. Opie's motorway images anticipated his ongoing landscape portfolio of ideal types, as in the 2000–2001 *Roadscape* series, further driving works in 2002, the 2012 series *Summer* and 2017 works on roadscapes, valleys, hills, fields, coasts. Paintings place landscapes in suspension, as specimen settings for contemporary life.

Julian Opie, *I Dreamt I Was Driving My Car (Motorway)*, 2002.

Opie is also known for his LP cover art, including an airport runway image, *engines voices footsteps*, for Saint Etienne's 2000 LP *The Sound of Water*, and a village and church spire landscape, *insects car church bells*, for the accompanying single 'How We Used to Live'. Saint Etienne have also hymned the motorway, the song 'Like a Motorway' appearing on their 1994 LP *Tiger Bay*. On an album weaving folk elements into reflective dance pop, the song's melody is taken from the folk song 'Silver Dagger', while the rhythm propels a story of heartache. A girl's life was like a motorway – dull, grey and long – until romance came along, only to exit. An English motorway pop single might put 'Like a Motorway' on one side with, on the reverse, Black Box Recorder's 'The English Motorway System' from the 2000 LP *The Facts of Life*. Luke Haines and John Moore's song, and Sarah Nixey's spoken-sung received pronunciation vocal, make the motorway at once decorous and full of foreboding, polite and scary. 'The English Motorway System' offers three-lane romance metaphor on an album filled with uneasy affections: relationship etiquette in 'The Art of Driving', 'May Queen' with its awkward folk ceremonials, human remains dug up in Notting Hill ('Gift Horse'), the closing 'Goodnight Kiss' with its litany of coastal place names. The motorway again takes its place within an English landscape portfolio. Here is somewhere beautiful, strange, unchanging and which we cannot do without. Accidents await in black ice and freezing fog. Exit signs hint at break-ups, at systems not quite hermetic. The motorway is an English fixture, hypnotic and seemingly emotion-free, yet where emotion creeps back in as the miles clock up.

Objections in a Landscape

Two of Parr's boring road postcards were a little different, produced not by service area owners or motorway celebrants but by branches of the Women's Institute. One, with 'Photo. by Mrs. J. MacRae, Cassington W.I.', shows 'A40 Traffic'.[83] Cars, lorries and caravans crowd a single carriageway on the A40 just west of Oxford. MacRae's image suggests something other than the banal recording of modernity dominating Parr's collection. This appears instead a postcard of complaint, the WI a local organization concerned for the amenity and ecological impact of traffic on a nearby trunk road. For once in *Boring Postcards* another narrative creeps in, of an environmental critique of modernity, the road (here an A-road, but the same sentiment is directed at motorways) as landscape problem.

From the 1970s the road in general, and the motorway in particular, are recast by some as destroyers, their planning and construction a cause for protest rather than celebration. Consideration of this shift in sentiment points forward to environmental concerns over change

'A40 Traffic', postcard from photograph by Mrs J. MacRae, reproduced in Martin Parr, *Boring Postcards* (1999).

in English landscape, issues addressed in the companion volume to this book, *England's Green*. Objections to the road were both rural and urban. Comprehensive urban development plans prompted campaigns against urban roads from the late 1960s, while rural motorway and bypass plans drew increasing opposition from the early 1970s. Protests brought together different concerns articulated at various scales: local visual and sonic amenity, local pollution, national landscape heritage, national connections to land, global resource depletion, critiques of a car-based society as exemplifying private over public interests, critiques of an oil-based society as exemplifying planetary disregard. Innocent joys of motoring appear tainted, and motorways are condemned.[84]

In 1978 John Tyme published *Motorways versus Democracy*. Tyme, until 1976 a lecturer in environmental studies at Sheffield Polytechnic, had in 1973 joined the National Transportation Working Party of the Conservation Society, founded in 1966 with population growth as its main concern. Tyme was West Midlands co-ordinator, and offered free consultancy to local groups opposing road schemes. *Motorways versus Democracy* brought together Tyme's blend of vocal protest and legal challenge, the motorway symbolic of government, notably the Ministry of Transport based in Marsham Street, London, acting regardless of popular sentiment:

> In the face of the (corrupt) alliance between the road lobby and the highway mandarins in Marsham Street, civil disobedience was, I had become convinced, the only means of showing the extent and depth of feeling and opposition to the endless proliferation of motorways and roads and the destruction of town and valley, woodland and farmland and the ruin of this nation's future which was its inevitable concomitant.[85]

England was at stake. For Tyme the 'motorway/trunk road programme', with a combination of bureaucracy and technocracy, posed 'the greatest threat to the interests of this nation in all its history'.[86] Tyme's cases are urban and rural, cast as 'the battle of . . .', effectively marking the English map with contemporary battle sites equivalent to historic crossed swords: Epping Forest, Aire Valley, Winchester, Ipswich, Boston, Archway Road. Tyme gives a roll call of 21 enquiries attended from 1973 to 1977, ordinary people challenging government in the 'ancient and honourable tradition' of 'Dissent'.[87] A repertoire of disobedient gestures follows: interjecting at public enquiries, slow handclapping officials, refusing to leave, breaking back in. At Winchester in 1976, 'Solid and respected citizens shouted, booed, slow handclapped, cheered, sang anti-motorway songs.'[88] Dissent here becomes both theatrical and relentlessly procedural, serving to mock and undermine governmental process, acting against 'Bureaucratic Absolutism, the Technocratic Monopoly and the Divine Right of the Technological Imperative'.[89] A language of English nationhood is deployed, including via historic quotation of the 1649 Agreement of the Free People of England against arbitrary royal power, and of Latimer's words at the stake on lighting such a candle 'in England as, I trust, shall never be put out'.[90]

In 1976 *New Society* presented its own 'John Tyme Inquiry', Terry Coleman describing a 51-year-old lecturer, born in Sheffield, with wartime army service and serving as a teacher and school inspector in Sudan until 1968. As with the careers of new town officials, colonial and postcolonial experience shapes English environmental action. Tyme is described by Coleman as objecting to any further motorway building, as never wishing to visit the USA, as seeing foreign travel being degraded by package tourism and as viewing the motor car and aeroplane as a disaster: 'he appears simply to oppose getting around.' Motorway enquiries were themselves a major crime deserving disobedience. Tyme admired China's policies of rural redevelopment rather than urban expansion, living 'on human resources rather than the machine'.[91]

The theatre of protest developed by Tyme, and the sense of fundamentals at stake, were extended in the anti-roads protests of the 1990s. As Joe Moran comments, 'the battles were not just about particular stretches of tarmac but about how roads are thought about and felt, how they feed into our collective desires and fears.'[92] The Conservative government's 1989 white paper *Roads for Prosperity* signalled a £6 billion programme, trumpeted as the biggest since the Romans. State ambition mobilized opponents, whether established environmental and amenity bodies, local groups or mobile groups of direct activists. The latter transplanted the tactics of anti-nuclear peace camps to tunnels, camps and treehouses on proposed construction sites. Derek Wall notes the key role of Earth First!, a direct action 'ecotage' environmental group active in the USA from 1980 and organized in the UK from 1991, partly with funding from James Goldsmith.[93] From 1992 Earth First! focused on anti-road campaigns, setting up 'Reclaim the

Streets' from 1992 to stage urban actions, with from 1995 increasingly ambitious attempts at the temporary occupation of road space. The construction of the M11 link road in east London in 1993–4 saw protests around construction through Wanstead, Leyton and Leytonstone. The short-lived republic of 'Wanstonia', mimicking the 1949 Ealing comedy *Passport to Pimlico* in its performance of independent underdog resistance, was ultimately quashed.[94] Graeme Miller's 2003 public sound art installation *Linked* memorialized the displaced (including resident Miller), as walking the route with headphones tuned the listener into lives lived before the road and to the traumas of displacement. Miller saw *Linked* as working against a 'denial of history', as something to 'make those houses reappear', marking 'an ecology of human memory and landscape'.[95]

Opposition to new road building was mobilized on a major scale at Twyford Down, near Winchester. In 1976 Tyme had supported the M3 Joint Action Group at Winchester, who succeeded in preventing motorway extension across water meadows, and Winchester again became the site for the most prominent 1990s battle with the proposed extension of the M3 in a vast cutting.[96] The setting of Twyford, cutting into downland to expose white chalk, generated land narratives. The motorway revealed the bones of the place, exposed geology lending energy to protest, which could set its ritual performance against a stark chalk backdrop. Local opposition to the M3 plans had been voiced from 1985, but was supplemented in 1992 by direct action activists styled as the Dongas Tribe. Alliances were made with local middle-class residents, 'Jerusalem' was sung, and public sympathy grew after destructive security responses, notably the eviction of a camp on 9 December 1992. Neo-tribalist, pagan identities, articulating land myth and nature reverence, and a language of ancient pre-Christian indigenous Englishness shaped the Twyford protests through what George McKay terms a 'political paganism'.[97] Ancient history shaped the story, the chalk cutting of Twyford in effect a ghastly counterpoint to the carefully conserved chalk hill figures of southern English downland. Imperial history was there too, as McKay notes: 'Dongas being a Matebele name originally adopted in the nineteenth century by Winchester College teachers for the medieval pathways that crisscross the Downs'.[98] A word encountered through empire is pinned to medieval drove roads, old lines of unmotorized transport turned against new lines of commerce.

The Twyford Down road was completed in 1994, protests failing to prevent its opening but succeeding in generating a repertoire of actions deployed at subsequent sites, and making a sometimes uneasy coalition of ideas and organizations. The geographical frames of such activism connect local campaigns, national policy, international alliances and the global environment. In 1995 plans for a Newbury bypass were approved, diverting the A34 around the town, which had been one of the bottleneck studies in Buchanan's 1963 *Traffic in Towns*. Thirty protest camps were set up along the 9-mile route early in 1996, articulating an eco-paganism in a wooded setting with treehouses, rituals and mysticism deployed against the road. Merrick's 1996 account of the *Battle for the Trees* shows an annotated map of the bypass route with camp names from Mary Hare to Tot Hill via Camelot and Rizla Ridge, camps never meant to be joined up by a road, but to form a dot-to-dot of a bypass prevented.[99] Treehouses stood as improvised structures in counterpoint to the rigidities of road planning, charms against the bypass. Merrick recounts singer Julian Cope's participation in the Newbury protests: Cope played benefits for the campaign and even presented *Top of the Pops* on 8 February 1996 wearing an anti-bypass T-shirt, a fluorescent jacket and a hard hat.[100] In 1994 he had entitled an LP *Autogeddon* after Heathcote Williams's apocalyptic 1991 poem, and Cope's 1996 LP *Interpreter* included the song 'The Battle for the Trees', dedicated to 'the happy campers on the Newbury protest': 'from Mary Hare to Tathill [*sic*], Keep that line serpentine.'[101]

Englishness was enlisted at Newbury, the protests styled as the 'Third Battle of Newbury', after two battles 350 years earlier in the Civil War. A fly-poster addressed to the 'Good people of Newbury!' and signed 'The Road Protestors' alluded to King Arthur and Robin Hood, and stated: 'We may look different, our ways and lifestyle may seem strange, but we are all here because we love the countryside of merry England. We can not sit back and let our heritage be destroyed in a fit of political madness.'[102] Merrick records a singing of a variant of 'Jerusalem' as the last trees fell, words sung over Bill Drummond's 1991 Justified Ancients of Mu Mu instrumental 'Jerusalem on the Moors', ending: 'till we have saved this place from them/ this England, green and pleasant land'.[103]

Evictions from January to April 1996 cleared the road's way. Newbury had its bypass, and the A34 north–south trunk route had its bottleneck cleared. If, however, the roads protested against in the

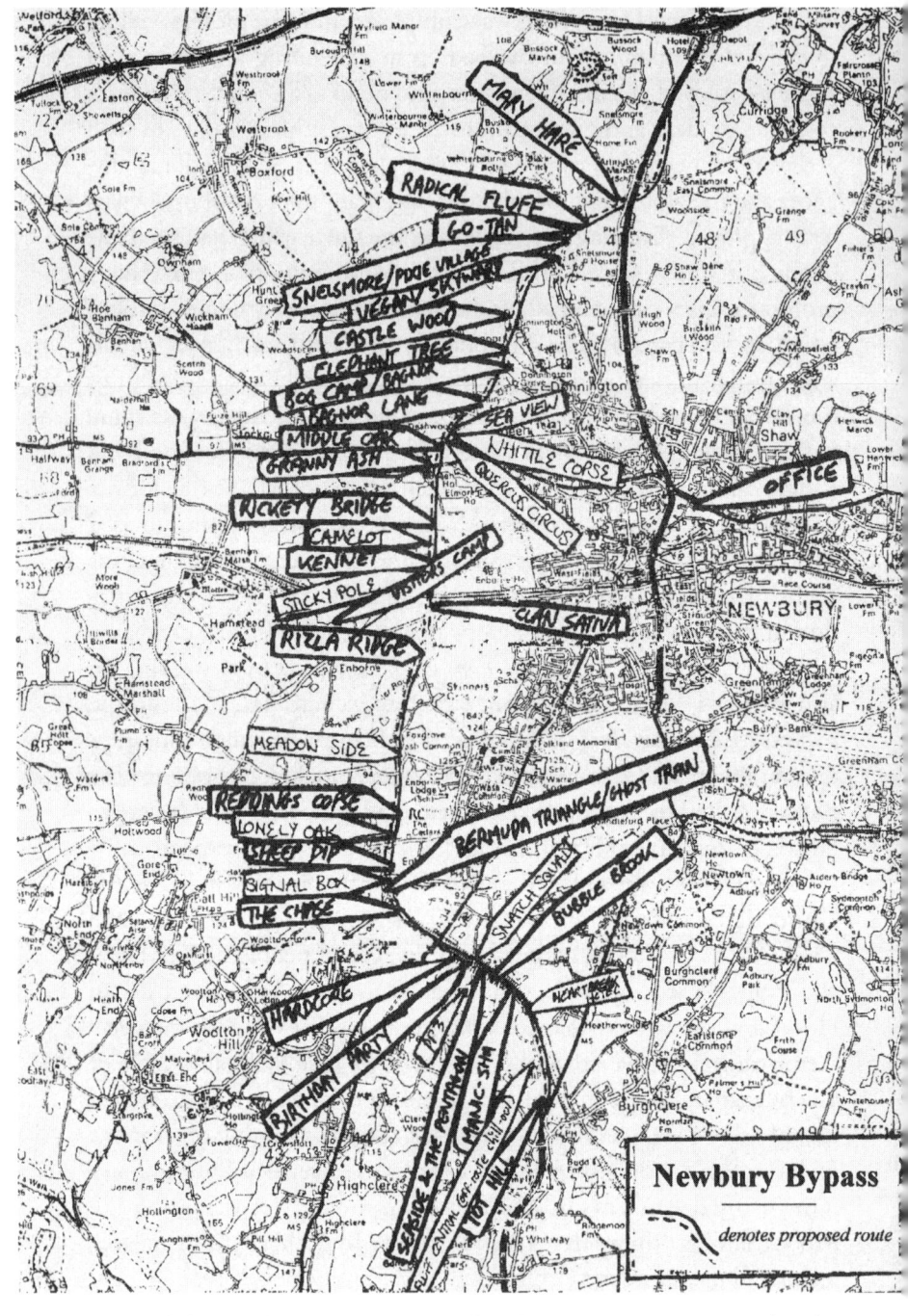

Map of Newbury Bypass protest camps, from Merrick, *Battle for the Trees* (1996).

1990s were built, the impact of the protests – financially on the costs of construction, politically on transport debates – helped redirect policy away from road-building, with changes of tone already apparent in the late years of the Major government confirmed by policy shifts under Labour from 1997. Objections shifted the ground, putting motorway futures on hold.

Fossils of the Anthropocene

In the 1988 Talking Heads song 'Nothing but Flowers' David Byrne presents an improbable future, improbable at least in the car-dominated late twentieth-century USA. The taken-for-granted landscapes of car culture are set aside as the country returns to an ecological agrarian lifestyle. Highways and cars are sacrificed for agriculture, the parking lot is a cornfield, the Pizza Hut is covered with daisies. Byrne's tone of bewilderment, akin to the 'How did I get here?' refrain in the 1980 hit 'Once in a Lifetime', conveys both the absurdity of a devotion to highways and parking lots and how strange would be their dereliction.

Ten years on, XTC's 1998 LP *Apple Venus* opened with the song 'River of Orchids', another meditation on the environmental and the automotive. In England, with the car less of a cultural cornerstone, Andy Partridge tapped a long-standing utopian green sensibility with a dream of nothing but flowers in an English landscape, a culture achieving closure on the road. 'River of Orchids' set flowers against the motorway, civilization against the car, a utopian dream of walking into London on your hands one day, orchids flowing where the road once ran. The song matches pagan themes elsewhere on *Apple Venus* in songs such as 'Easter Theatre' and 'Greenman'. Beginning with plucked strings, notes steadily dripping, 'River of Orchids' gathers pace to signal a renewing flow, the existing order overturned, the cars pushed from the road. Dandelions roar in Piccadilly Circus, seeds are scattered and grass appears greener as it bursts through concrete. As discussed in Chapter Two, XTC are from Swindon in Wiltshire, along the M4 from London, and 'River of Orchids' effectively inverts Jeffrey Matthews's 1968 M4 stamp, the highway to the city now carpeted with blooms, the world greened upside down, a motorway no more.

'River of Orchids' dreams of a car being reduced to a fossil. Since 1998 the car and the motorway have become symbols of the emerging Anthropocene, fossil fuel use shaping the climate change which signals the human capacity to amend the planet. The Anthropocene as proposed geological epoch will see the future rock record marked by a human presence. Might the fossil-fuelled itself be fossilized? What might be the relic fossil traces of the car age? How might old driving be memorialized?

Geological timescales might bring any eventuality, but in the closer future current technological projections envisage cars as non-fossil-fuelled, society still running but on different energy. The motorways would therefore stay, vehicles still needing something to travel on. Older modes of driving might, however, become nostalgic, just as vintage cars appeal to some today. In 1971, in his essay 'The Car, the Future', J. G. Ballard envisaged that in 2050, in a time of electronically guided vehicles, petrol cars would be driveable only as a heritage experience: 'At various points around the British Isles there will be so-called Motoring Parks, in which people will be able to drive the old cars in the old way.'[104] Aspects of the old motorway might thus be heritage-listed, asphalt in aspic. Relics may even be there already, if you know where to look. Joe Moran recommends the current M45, leading off the M1 and quiet since the completion of the M6, as a means 'to return to the early motorway era ... Britain's quietest motorway'.[105]

Or might a bigger change come, the regrassed road echoing those ex-railways crossing the English landscape, some recast as walkways and cycle trails? After the M3 had cut through Twyford Down, the 1930s Winchester Bypass was closed, recontoured with chalk and returfed. The road vanished back into ground, with only an incongruous railway bridge a clue to the loss and gain, and with turf cut from the lost Twyford Down relaid, not quite a river of orchids but a main road remade as a flower meadow.[106] Fifty years separated the peak of the rail network and the closure of significant parts, mainlines left but branches shut. If the completion of the M25 represented peak motorway, an analogous cycle would see debate in the 2040s on whether roads or motorways are worth keeping. The branch-line/main-line distinctions of the Beeching-era rail closures might, however, be inverted. Local roads are unlikely to be deemed obsolete, but the six- or eight-lane motorway? Grass could follow, and even orchids. And in the geological future, future palaeontologists of whatever species might dig down to fossil cars and hardened shoulders, to find the exhausts of the human.

The Cooling Warming Modern

In 1979 a new edition of Pevsner's 1951 guide to the buildings of Nottinghamshire was issued with revisions and additions by Elizabeth Williamson. The entry on the Trentside hamlet of West Burton was new, the site overlooked in 1951:

> Substantial earthen mounds and sunken roads mark where the village stood on the W bank of the Trent, until the early C19. The church was demolished in 1885, leaving the graveyard.
> Overshadowing it completely, the huge WEST BURTON POWER STATION, the eight towers and two chimneys grouped effectively, the surroundings well planted. Designed by the *Architects Design Group*, landscaped by *Derek Lovejoy & Associates*, it won a Civic Trust award in 1969.[107]

The power station adds something to the place, its prominence notable not only for its bulk, with its structures and landscape design granted Civic Trust approval. A series of power stations had been

THREE POWER STATIONS BESIDE THE RIVER TRENT

Roger Palmer, *Three Power Stations beside the Trent*, 1980, gelatin silver print, Letraset.

built in the Trent Valley north of Newark in the 1960s, the Central Electricity Generating Board taking river water for cooling and coal from the nearby Nottinghamshire and Yorkshire coalfield to power a transformed country. Williamson also noted the nearby stations at Cottam and High Marnham, intervisible along the wide valley. Roger Palmer's 1980 photographic work *Three Power Stations beside the Trent* gives a distant view from high ground near Oxton, west of the Trent Valley, the stations appearing equidistant, each sending up a south-tilted steam plume, signatures of power etched in the sky above a foreground hedge by a harvested field.[108] Trent power is gathered pictorially into English landscape.

West Burton's Civic Trust award reflected a wider landscape design interest in the landscapes such structures might make, especially given the distinct mass and shape of the cooling towers integral to coal-fired power. Sylvia Crowe's 1958 *The Landscape of Power* elevated these components of working industrial Britain to something elemental: 'The elemental shape of cooling towers is emotionally remote from the human spirit. Seen divorced from humanizing detail, it is as impersonal as a hill.'[109] Crowe, however, captioned a photograph of Stella South and Stella North power stations on Tyneside with a note of disappointment: 'The opportunity has not yet been taken to combine the shapes of towers, masts and slag-heaps into one fantastic composition.'[110] At Ironbridge B power station in Shropshire, constructed from 1963, the concrete of the four cooling towers had red pigment added to match the local soil. Neil Cossons noted in his 1977 collaboration with photographer Harry Sowden on Ironbridge's 'landscape of industry' that the River Severn's only contemporary industrial significance was as a source of cooling water for the towers of Ironbridge B: 'Specially tinted to make them more compatible with the surrounding earthcolour, they crowd and jostle into the view upstream from Ironbridge and Dale End, magnificent, cyclopean, organic and alive.'[111]

What though do cooling towers stand for in the twenty-first century? Simon Roberts's 2008 *We English* included a photograph taken at Ratcliffe-on-Soar power station, built between 1963 and 1968 west of Nottingham and alongside the main railway line to London, on the lower banks of the Soar just before it joins the Trent, its chimneys overlooking the Trent Valley. The photograph, entitled 'Ratcliffe-on-Soar Power Station, Nottinghamshire, 16th June 2008', shows three men, ex-employees at the station, enjoying their own company on

Simon Roberts, 'Ratcliffe-on-Soar Power Station, Nottinghamshire', 16 June 2008, pigment print.

the company golf course, evoking the power station as a site of stable employment in an era of state corporate responsibility:

> Ron Whitby, Derek Allen and Tom Burns play a round of golf in the grounds of the Ratcliffe-on-Soar coal-fired power station. The three men started work at the power station in 1966, during its construction, and were employed there until their retirement a few years ago. Despite no longer working at the plant, they still return to play on the employee golf course several times a week.[112]

If for Crowe cooling towers, 'divorced from humanizing detail', were elemental, Roberts marries them to golf, giant familiars accompanying work and play, the verticals of golfers and club swing meeting pylon and parabola. Ratcliffe's towers are visible for miles, their steam plumes distinctive in the western sky from my own walks around Beeston. The play of light on towers, the steam against the sky, make an English landscape picture. Viewed every day from the street or from a domestic window, the towers can accrue personal meaning, even personality.

High Marnham and Cottam were demolished in the 2010s, and Ratcliffe-on-Soar and West Burton are now the last two coal-fired stations in Britain. West Burton is due to close in 2023; a new gas-fired station began generation on an adjacent site in 2013. Ratcliffe is planned to close in 2024. And that will be that kind of England gone. As stations have been decommissioned, and towers demolished, some have protested, as when the towers of the Blackburn Meadows station at Tinsley in the Don Valley, by the M1 viaduct in South Yorkshire, were felled in 2008. A biomass plant was built on the cleared site. A 2013 campaign to list Didcot power station in Oxfordshire, designed by Frederick Gibberd, built between 1964 and 1968 and winner of a Civic Trust award, failed. The station ceased generation that year, with three cooling towers demolished in 2014 and the other three in 2019. Modern industry falls in pastoral southern England. For decades Didcot had been a feature of the view from Wittenham Clumps, the tree-topped hills well known from Paul Nash's earlier twentieth-century art, their sculptured forms echoing in some ways Nash's interest in the abstract and uncanny. From 2014, depending on the perspective taken, the view was restored or diminished.

Appreciation of striking industrial structure has, however, been overtaken, and undercut, by the prevalent twenty-first-century narrative of climate change. In the 2000s Greenpeace had staged direct actions at Didcot as power plants became symbols of planetary crisis. The steam clouds pluming from cooling towers may just be water, but the smoke emitted from neighbouring chimneys signals the burning of coal, and the towers become icons of a mode of power no longer aligned with progress. West Burton in 1969 signalled the new, coal powering industry and homes, but in the twenty-first century appears old and associated with a demonized energy. If anything in English landscape stands for climate change, it is a coal-fired power station, denoting the culpable modern. The caption for Roberts's Ratcliffe-on-Soar photograph shifts from 'Enjoying a Well-Earned Retirement' to 'Boys Keep Swinging While the Planet Burns'.

The Trent Valley power stations were constructed not long after the proposed geological 'golden spike' for the Anthropocene, the human imprint in future sediment from post-war atmospheric nuclear testing. Post-war power denotes not just technological modernity but a planetary epoch, with West Burton and Ratcliffe-on-Soar signs of the Anthropocene, caught in the twenty-first century's pervading narrative of climate change. What future for such award-winning English landscape? What might these towers stand for now? As stations wind down and generation ceases, perhaps the towers might remain, listed and conserved as a sign of the old twentieth-century modern. A monument to the Anthropocene, to the drivers of progress, to how humanity heated its home.

9
Concluding

Mr Rock rose with a groan. Crossing to the open bedroom window he shone his torch out on fog. His white head was grey, and white the reflected torch light on the thick spectacles he wore. He shone it up and down. – It will be a fine day, a fine day in the end, he decided.

Henry Green, *Concluding* (1948)[1]

Turning About

The opening lines of Henry Green's 1948 novel *Concluding* seem apt to begin *About England*'s end. Another day, another task. Looking into what has accumulated, spectacles thick from years of looking, illumination meeting indistinction, but something fine in the end, perhaps.

Back in Beeston and Attenborough, where the first chapter ended, things go on. Wars are remembered as new ones proceed, people live in old industrial buildings, bells ring over the cricket, St George's flag flies behind Ireton's old house, people work in listed factories and the symbolism of public art is mixed. The variegated local geography of a home patch set *About England* off, towards prospects and retrospects of English life, through English pastoral and all its tensions, to a country shaken by war and pandemic and political upheaval, through suburban amusement and anxiety, to England's particular locales and locals, visiting heritage rural, urban and industrial, and ending at the modern which turned out to be historic, and the sign of a new geological epoch. Under Trent Valley pavements, the gravel for construction. The companion volume to *About*

England, England's Green, will take up the story of England and the Anthropocene.

Along the way the various senses of 'about' in *About England* have been met. Commentaries about England have been seen to identify its qualities, claim to speak on its behalf, ponder contradictions and damn inequities. Going about England, sites concatenate English variants: the Olympic ceremonials, Virginia Astley's gardens, *Akenfield*, suburban London, Milton Keynes, *Trumpton*, South Woodham Ferrers, Merrivale, Longleat, Cromford, Bolton West services, Twyford Down, Ratcliffe-on-Soar. Sometimes estimates about England are very clear, as in the certain pastoral of *This England*; or clearly absurd, as at Rawlinson End; or all too clearly exclusive, access to some denied. And England goes about, changing course, tacking over six decades, buffeted within and without, by UK disunity, and on and off Europe.

Themes of space and time, geography and history, have run through *About England*, and offer ways of concluding, before a final local excursion.

England's Geography

The national is refracted through different sites and landscape types, and scales within and beyond the country: global and imperial, continental and international, regional and local. How do the consequent variation and complexity shape England's geography?

Across familiar differences and presumed divides of north and south, caught in Donald Horne and Martin Wiener's southern and northern metaphors, other takes on England east and west intrude, as when the 2016 referendum drew out an eastern coastal Leave line, or John Betjeman filmed West Country towns to combat modern urban trends. The rural refracts Englishness, but so does the urban, England in variation according to its setting, and different landscape types claimed for their modernity or otherwise, urban renewal building or destroying national quality. The late twentieth century sees a significant shift in the mapping of Englishness on to the rural, as agriculture is recast as environmental villain, the modernity of farming practice upsetting national cultural assumptions, a transformation to be addressed in *England's Green*. Meanwhile, suburban England watches suburban England, the television a late twentieth-century focus for domestic settlement, with some uneasy shifting in the armchair. Infra-ordinary

England – at leisure, in the suburb, down the local, on the motorway – becomes a topic for reflection. Geographical clichés of England's rural south are broadcast to the world, from the country house and Midsomer, while northern former industrial sites carry another global story, of England's shaping of a fossil-fuelled Anthropocene. England's geography undoubtedly carries global significance, and whether or not England's geography thereby becomes England's glory is a matter for dispute. Even in English pastoral, unsettlement and anger fuel affinities and affections, at the meeting point of Akenfield and the Dardanelles, or in Enoch Powell's postcolonial white pastoral. The global acts of the British state over several centuries cannot help but intrude, in contemporary acts of war, in the repatriation of the lost, in fears attendant on nuclear geopolitics. Empire and its legacies become stories about England, in governmental iconography, in defensive or expansive versions of pastoral, in the governance of new towns, in lions in the English garden.

England's geography thereby makes sense through scales other than the national, which enfold within the national, some from beyond the cartographic boundaries – international, continental, global, imperial – and some from within. The local and the regional can pull apart the national through contrary variation, or can be defined as a particularity whose varieties define a geographically heterogeneous whole. Such questions play out in the cultural work of a body such as Common Ground, where England is all over the place unique, in the disputes of culture and economy shaping the English 'local' of the pub since the 1970s, or in argument over England's internal political geography. If devolution has been a back-burner issue within England, with regional assembly initiatives frustrated by tentative politics and popular wariness, any formal disunion of the UK might flame the relationship between Westminster and the rest of England. Home internationals and home intra-nationals may be fixtures in a future English polity.

Internal heterogeneity and external connection account for England. Scales enfold, in pastoral and textile senses of that term. Stock fold into a pen, confined in contingent cohabitation, while the obverse of any smoothly folded national cloth shows a complex scalar geographical stitching, with some tugging at the seams.

Concluding

About Time

What is deemed national is configured by history and memory, and by the presumed connections or disconnections of past, present and future. Is the past a bedrock on which to build present and future, an escape route from today or a millstone dragging a country down?

Time may show vernacular custom and style, to be tapped and/or reimagined for continuity, in celebrating an Apple Day or building an Asda in Essex barn style, a new England made in line with something older, roots tended to nurture new growth. Heritage may offer something to look up to, the past a classy display underwriting present social structures or signalling a world moved on. Memories layer on memories, as *Brideshead Revisited* is revisited, a 1940s memory of the 1920s activated for a 1980s present. In other English parts, the past is valued for a working country now superseded, the relics of manufacture preserved and reanimated in a new service economy. For heritage industry critics, preserved millstones become a cultural burden, signs of a dodo England. For others millstones serve as foundations of regional pride, symbols of a working world wanting renewal. Histories anticipate futures. Elsewhere, the post-war world accrues value, modernism standing for a social democratic world. Just as Brideshead 1981 leaped over wartime and post-war change to find a dreamy England now lost, so new town or motorway enthusiasts vault Thatcherism to find other values manifest in built structures. Should the late twentieth-century loss of modernist buildings from model villages be a matter for regret?

Past stories carry the present, as when, in sporting London 2012, history defined an opening ceremony, showing a united country full of noises and, in Olympic celebratory fashion, full of itself. Accounts of the past imply and inform different futures, and particular moments keep returning over the decades. The First World War, a living memory after the Second World War, overhangs *Akenfield*, and Shirley and Dolly Collins's *Anthems in Eden*, a still resonant wartime shadow for the 1960s and '70s. In the twenty-first century, the First World War is regalvanized for its centenary, for an amended culture and politics of remembrance. And the pertinence of 1939–45 seems undiminished, with the passing of some prominent participants, and as still living memory for children of the 1930s now in late retirement. The domestic and global experience of the Second World War offers cultural and political shorthand for trauma and resilience, with its aftermath producing the social and political icon of the NHS. The COVID-19 pandemic was lived in part through wartime allusion. The England of the coming decades will be shaped in part by the intertwining of older and newer aftermaths, as memories of war, pandemic and referenda entwine.

An English May Day

To end *About England*, a return just down the road, for an English May Day. On the bank holiday created by a Labour government in 1978, the fair is in Beeston's Dovecote Park. Traditionally fun, not folklorically jolly. An annual takeover of football, walking, playing and dog space, by council permission, for daily entertainment. The public park denied for days, circled by the wagons. Returning after two years away, in 2022, normal interruptions are restored. A giant inflatable slide promises much. Jingles soundtrack squeals, spring delights on a school-off day.

Along the lane, at the memorial, a bugler blows a wrong note out of season. Squalls pass, and the day is bright. From Scottish-named streets, some venture out, passing judgements. Not bad after all for the grown-ups, not quite so exciting for the young. Middling to fair.

Funfair, Dovecote Park, Beeston, Nottinghamshire, 1 May 2022.

Concluding

The empty bandstand overlooks the fun. When rides pall, perhaps slalom-race the twelve European trees, circling the smaller one for luck. The winner mounts the steps and takes the stand, to shout whatever they choose.

A fine day in the end. The rides wind down, the fair is wound up again. Sun sinks behind the tree circle, the power station plume a picture. Steam is let off, for an English May Day.

REFERENCES

1 Six Decades in England

1 David Matless, *Landscape and Englishness* (London, 1998; rev. edn 2016).
2 Office for National Statistics, 'Ethnicity and National Identity in England and Wales: 2011', www.ons.gov.uk, 11 December 2012.
3 Ailsa Henderson and Richard Wyn Jones, *Englishness: The Political Force Transforming Britain* (Oxford, 2021), p. 2.
4 For an attempt to define a progressive Englishness see Billy Bragg, *The Progressive Patriot* (London, 2006). On the complex temporality and politics of progressive and conservative versions of Englishness see Emily Robinson, *History, Heritage and Tradition in Contemporary British Politics* (Manchester, 2012); and Emily Robinson, 'Radical Nostalgia, Progressive Patriotism and Labour's "English Problem"', *Political Studies Review*, XIV/3 (2016), pp. 378–87.
5 David Matless, 'The Predicament of Englishness', *Scottish Geographical Journal*, CXVI (2000), pp. 79–86.
6 Julia Bell and Jackie Gay, eds, *England Calling* (London, 2001), p. xi.
7 Ibid., p. x.
8 Jon Savage, *England's Dreaming: Sex Pistols and Punk Rock* (London, 1991).
9 Bell and Gay, eds, *England Calling*, p. xiii.
10 Ibid., pp. xi–xii.
11 Ibid., p. xii.
12 Ibid.
13 'Home Thoughts, from Abroad' is the 1845 poem by Robert Browning, written in Italy, with its oft-cited opening lines: 'Oh, to be in England/ Now that April's there'.
14 Peter Mandler, *The English National Character* (New Haven, CT, 2006). Mandler suggests that after the Second World War, and especially after the Suez crisis of 1956 with its concomitant narratives of British decline, English discussion tended to shift from national character to national identity, with character a matter either for nostalgic commentary from the political right, or for left critiques of stultifying preoccupations producing bad leadership.
15 'Armagideon Time', a cover of a reggae song by Willie Williams, was initially the B-side of The Clash's 1979 'London Calling' single. The 1980 10-inch compilation album *Black Market Clash* also included the track.

16 On a transparent flexidisc, 'The Guitar and Other Marketing Devices' (Fac 214), given away with the 1987 album, was printed news of Reilly's future 'collaboration with the Stephens – Morrissey and Street – live and on record in the New Year'. Stephen Street, producer of *The Guitar and Other Machines* and known for his production work with The Smiths, played bass on 'English Landscape Tradition', and Reilly would play guitar and keyboard on Smiths singer Morrissey's debut solo album, *Viva Hate*, in 1988, with Metcalfe playing viola and Street as producer. The makers of 'English Landscape Tradition' move into other English territory, via Morrissey songs such as 'Everyday Is Like Sunday', a meditation on the lassitude of the English seaside, though with more Armageddon lurking, the bomb never far away in the 1980s. Reilly embroiders the song's fabric, while Morrissey's words here and elsewhere on *Viva Hate* point to clichés and controversies of Englishness, as when 'Bengali in Platforms' attempts sartorial commentary on ethnicity and belonging. Morrissey's more or less subtle explorations of national identity in song would later be overtaken by expressions of support for far right groups. None of this necessarily flows from 'English Landscape Tradition' the track, or from anything deemed an English landscape tradition, although pastoral can, as Chapter Three of this book will examine, trigger hard-edged sentiment.

17 For an insightful local history see Frank E. Earp and Joseph Earp, *Secret Beeston* (Stroud, 2017).

18 Nikolaus Pevsner, *Nottinghamshire* (Harmondsworth, 1951), p. 143.

19 Nikolaus Pevsner and Elisabeth Williamson, *Nottinghamshire* (Harmondsworth, 1979), p. 69.

20 See the Beeston Civic Society website for images from the project: www.beestoncivicsociety.org.uk/beestonstreetart.

21 Ian J. Gentles, 'Ireton, Henry', *Oxford Dictionary of National Biography* (Oxford, 2004).

22 Robert Ramsey, *Henry Ireton* (London, 1949), p. 1.

2 England in Prospect and Retrospect

1 John Drinkwater, *Robinson of England* (London, 1937), p. 25.
2 Ibid., p. 31.
3 Simon Roberts, *We English* (London, 2008); Simon Roberts, *Motherland* (London, 2007); Simon Roberts, *Merrie Albion: Landscape Studies of a Small Island* (Stockport, 2017); see also Simon Roberts, *Pierdom* (Stockport, 2013), a photographic survey of British piers. Work from Roberts's project 'National Property: The Picturesque Imperfect' is included in Stephen Daniels, Ben Cowell and Lucy Veale, *Landscapes of the National Trust* (London, 2015). The range of Roberts's projects is shown on his website, www.simoncroberts.com.
4 Roberts, *We English*, 'Commentary' section.
5 David Matless, 'At Ease', in Roberts, *Merrie Albion*, pp. 149–50.
6 Roberts, *We English*, 'Commentary' section.
7 Ibid.
8 Ibid.

References

9 Ibid.
10 Roberts, *Merrie Albion*, p. 83.
11 Humphrey Jennings, *Pandaemonium, 1660–1886: The Coming of the Machine as Seen by Contemporary Observers* (London, 2012). *Pandaemonium* was compiled before Jennings's death in 1950 but first published in 1985, and reissued in 2012 with a foreword by Frank Cottrell-Boyce.
12 Bill Bryson, ed., *Icons of England* (London, 2010), p. 11.
13 G. K. Chesterton, *The Collected Poems of G. K. Chesterton* (London, 1933), p. 224.
14 Andy Partridge of XTC, quoted in XTC and Neville Farmer, *Song Stories* (London, 1998), p. 116.
15 The Ermin Street referred to crosses Wiltshire from Hampshire to Gloucester, a different Roman road from the London–York Ermine Street.
16 Ian Hislop, *This Union: The Ghost Kingdoms of England*, episodes detailed on the BBC website at http://bbc.co.uk, accessed 22 March 2022.
17 Michael Wood, 'Alfred's Cakes: Michael Wood on Historic Athelney', in *Icons of England*, ed. Bryson, pp. 341–3.
18 Michael Wood, *In Search of the Dark Ages* (London, 1981), p. 245.
19 Michael Wood, *In Search of England* (London, 1999), p. xi; H. V. Morton, *In Search of England* (London, 1927); Wood reflects on Morton in Chapter Ten of his book.
20 Wood, *In Search of England*, p. xi.
21 Ibid., p. 105.
22 Michael Wood, *The Story of England* (London, 2010), pp. xxiii–xxiv.
23 Ibid., p. 8.
24 Ibid., p. 47.
25 Ibid., p. 197.
26 Ibid., p. 401.
27 Geoffrey Hill, *Mercian Hymns* (London, 1971).
28 Seamus Heaney, 'Englands of the Mind', in *Finders Keepers: Selected Prose, 1971–2001* (London, 2002), pp. 77–95, at p. 87; William Wootten, 'Rhetoric and Violence in Geoffrey Hill's *Mercian Hymns* and the Speeches of Enoch Powell', *Cambridge Quarterly*, XXIX (2000), pp. 1–15.
29 Hill, *Mercian Hymns*, Acknowledgements.
30 The phrases are from *Mercian Hymns* I, III, I and XXI respectively.
31 Suburban dwellings and the battle names and dates are from Hill's 'Acknowledgments', The dwelling names also appear in Hymn XX, along with the phrase 'Coiled entrenched England'.
32 Hill, *Mercian Hymns*, Acknowledgements.
33 The BBC Genome archive listing *Radio Times* schedules shows that Hordern was a guest on that day, with presenter Robert Robinson, at 8 p.m.
34 Geoffrey Hill, 'An Apology for the Revival of Christian Architecture in England', in *Selected Poems* (London, 2006), pp. 109–10.
35 Heaney, 'Englands of the Mind', p. 87.
36 Hill, *Mercian Hymns*, Hymn I.

37 Geoffrey Hill, *The Orchards of Syon* (London, 2002), poem LXXI, p. 71; ibid., poem XXIV, p. 24.
38 Melissa Harrison, *All Among the Barley* (London, 2018).
39 Melissa Harrison, *The Stubborn Light of Things* (London, 2020), p. 157.
40 Ibid., p. 190.
41 Melissa Harrison, *Rain: Four Walks in English Weather* (London, 2016), p. xiv.
42 Harrison, *The Stubborn Light of Things*, p. 78.
43 Harrison, *All Among the Barley*, pp. 162–3.
44 Sylvia Townsend Warner, *Lolly Willowes* (London, [1926] 1993).
45 David Matless, *Landscape and Englishness* (London, 1998; rev. edn 2016), Chapters Three and Four. For an urban tale of an English fascist past haunting the English present see Jonathan Meades's 1984 story 'Filthy English', where a meeting with someone presumed lost leads to patricide (and prospective matricide) in Southampton. The story appears in Meades's collection, also entitled *Filthy English* (London, 1984).
46 Henry Williamson, *The Story of a Norfolk Farm* (London, 1942), p. 156.
47 Harrison, *All Among the Barley*, pp. 162–3, 209–10.
48 Ibid., pp. 201, 210.
49 Ibid., pp. 110–11, p. 201. Matless, *Landscape and Englishness*; Philip Coupland, *Farming, Fascism and Ecology: A Life of Jorian Jenks* (London, 2017).

3 English Pastoral

1 Martin Wiener, *English Culture and the Decline of the Industrial Spirit, 1850–1980* (Cambridge, 1981), p. 127.
2 Ibid., pp. 3, 5.
3 Donald Horne, *God Is an Englishman* (Harmondsworth, 1969), p. 22.
4 Wiener, *English Culture*, p. 79.
5 Ibid., p. 166.
6 Melissa Harrison, *All Among the Barley* (London, 2018).
7 Wiener, *English Culture*, p. 50.
8 Ronald Blythe, *Akenfield* (London, 1969).
9 David Matless, 'Doing the English Village', in Paul Cloke, Marcus Doel, David Matless, Martin Phillips and Nigel Thrift, *Writing the Rural* (London, 1994), pp. 7–88. See also the study of the Akenfield villages 35 years on, in Craig Taylor, *Return to Akenfield* (London, 2007). On Blythe's writing in general see Keith Snell, 'Ronald Blythe: "Just a Voice for His Time"', *Rural History*, XXXII (2021), pp. 3–22. On Akenfield and oral history see John Beck, *Landscape as Weapon* (London, 2020), pp. 13–16.
10 Blythe, *Akenfield*, p. 17.
11 Ibid.
12 Michael Bracewell, *England Is Mine: Pop Life in Albion from Wilde to Goldie* (London, 1997), p. 9. A comparable effect might be found in the paintings of the Brotherhood of Ruralists, founded in 1975 in Wellow, near Bath, by Peter Blake and others, artists who had left the city for the country to further an English painterly tradition: see the 1978 film by

John Read, 'Summer with the Brotherhood', broadcast on BBC 2 on 15 January 1978, available on YouTube.
13 Blythe, *Akenfield*, p. 17.
14 Virginia Astley, *The English River: A Journey down the Thames in Poems and Photographs* (Hexham, 2018), p. 39.
15 Ibid., p. 27.
16 See the Home Office's Identity and Passport Service document issued at the time, 'Introducing the New United Kingdom Passport', available at http://assets.publishing.service.gov.uk. Also Alan Travis, 'Country Houses and White Cliffs to Portray Britain in New Passport', *The Guardian* (26 March 2010), p. 6.
17 See the HM Passport Office document issued at the time, 'Introducing the New United Kingdom Passport.
18 For BBC reports on the Bibury story see 'Yellow Car Blamed for "Photobombing" Village of Bibery', www.bbc.co.uk, 29 January 2015; 'Notorious Yellow Car Vandalised in Bibery', www.bbc.co.uk, 4 February 2017.
19 H. J. Massingham, *Wold without End* (London, 1932), p. 16; David Matless, *Landscape and Englishness* (London, 1998; rev. edn 2016); Catherine Brace, 'Gardenesque Imagery in the Representation of Regional and National Identity: The Cotswold Garden of Stone', *Journal of Rural Studies*, xv (1999), pp. 365–76.
20 For a general account of pastoral see Terry Gifford, *Pastoral* (London, 1999).
21 John Berger and Jean Mohr, *A Fortunate Man: The Story of a Country Doctor* (London, 1967), p. 89.
22 Ibid., pp. 14–15.
23 John Berger, *Pig Earth* (London, 1979).
24 Berger and Mohr, *A Fortunate Man*, pp. 24–5. This image also forms the right half of a double-page frontispiece landscape image in the book, the left half showing adjacent fields and trees.
25 Raymond Williams, *The Country and the City* (London, 1973), p. 149.
26 Ibid., p. 150.
27 Terry Morden, 'The Pastoral and the Pictorial', *Ten:8*, XII (1983), pp. 18–25, at p. 19.
28 John Taylor, 'The Imaginary Landscape', *Ten:8*, XII (1983), pp. 2–13, at p. 3. See also the refinement of these ideas in John Taylor, *A Dream of England: Landscape, Photography and the Tourist's Imagination* (Manchester, 1995).
29 Peter Dormer, 'Fantasy Island', *Ten:8*, XII (1983), pp. 26–31.
30 Paul Lewis, 'Where the Wild Things Went', *Ten:8*, XII (1983), pp. 32–5, at p. 33.
31 Stephen Daniels, 'Marxism, Culture and the Duplicity of Landscape', in *New Models in Geography*, vol. II, ed. Richard Peet and Nigel Thrift (London, 1989), pp. 196–220, at pp. 197, 218.
32 John Barrell and John Bull, eds, *The Penguin Book of English Pastoral Verse* (Harmondsworth, 1974), p. 4.
33 Ibid., pp. 5–7.
34 Ibid., p. 381.

35 Ibid., pp. 432–3.
36 James Rebanks, *English Pastoral* (London, 2020); Rebanks's work is considered in the companion volume to this book, *England's Green*.
37 John Barrell, *The Idea of Landscape and the Sense of Place, 1730–1840: An Approach to the Poetry of John Clare* (Cambridge, 1972).
38 John Clare, 'The Village Minstrel', quoted in Williams, *The Country and the City*, p. 169.
39 Williams, *The Country and the City*, p. 166.
40 Barrell, *Idea of Landscape*, pp. 124, 161, 172.
41 Ibid., p. 120.
42 Ibid., p. 184.
43 John Betjeman, review in *Listener*, 19 March 1964, quoted in the back cover blurb of the 1971 Faber and Faber paperback edition of Philip Larkin, *The Whitsun Weddings* (London, 1971); Iain Sinclair, *Edge of the Orison* (London, 2005). See Simon Kovesi, *John Clare: Nature, Criticism and History* (London, 2017), on the claims made for Clare as a poet of place, an ecocentric writer and an authentic voice of the dispossessed, and of how these three may or may not be significantly aligned and how ecocriticism may deracinate class even as it values the local. On Clare see also John Lucas, *England and Englishness* (London, 1990), Chapter Seven.
44 Kovesi, *John Clare*, pp. 10, 11, 14.
45 Ibid., pp. 15, 41.
46 Ibid., p. 215.
47 Patrick Keiller, *Robinson in Space* (London, 1999), pp. 6, 20. The British Film Institute released DVDs of the two films, *London and Robinson in Space: Two Films by Patrick Keiller* (BFIVD649). See also Patrick Keiller, *The View from the Train: Cities and Other Landscapes* (London, 2013).
48 Patrick Keiller, *The Possibility of Life's Survival on the Planet* (London, 2012). The British Film Institute issued *Robinson in Ruins* on DVD in 2011 (BFIB1098); Mark Fisher's 'English Pastoral' essay first appeared in the November 2010 issue of *Sight and Sound*. On *Robinson in Ruins* see also Patrick Keiller, 'Landscape and Cinematography', *Cultural Geographies*, XVI (2009), pp. 409–14; Stephen Daniels, Patrick Keiller, Doreen Massey and Patrick Wright, 'To Dispel a Great Malady: *Robinson in Ruins*, the Future of Landscape and the Moving Image', *Tate Papers*, XVII (2012); Paul Dave, 'Robinson in Ruins: New Materialism and the Archaeological Imagination', *Radical Philosophy*, CLXIX (2011), pp. 19–35.
49 Keiller, *The Possibility of Life's Survival*, p. 63.
50 Ibid., p. 3.
51 Keiller, *View from the Train*, pp. 7–8.
52 Agriculture is the subject of a chapter in the companion volume to this book, *England's Green*.
53 See the account of Stephen Garnett, editor 2009–18, 'Farewell, This England', in the online *The Journal* (Autumn 2018), cioj.org/thejournal/farewell-this-england; accessed 24 March 2022.
54 Roy Faiers, Editorial, *This England*, VI (Summer 1973), p. 1.
55 Wyn Daniels, 'John Clare: Poet and Peasant', *This England*, VI (Summer 1973), pp. 50–51.

References

56 Patrick Wright, 'The Stain on St George's Flag', *The Guardian* (18 August 1993), p. 11.
57 Stuart Millson, 'Forever England', *This England*, XXVI (Autumn 1993), pp. 26–9.
58 Wright, 'Stain on St George's Flag'.
59 Geoffrey Hill, *Mercian Hymns* (London, 1971), Hymn XVIII.
60 Ibid., Hymn VIII.
61 Wootten, 'Rhetoric and Violence', p. 11.
62 For insightful analyses of Powell see Camilla Schofield, *Enoch Powell and the Making of Postcolonial Britain* (Cambridge, 2013); Bill Schwarz, *The White Man's World* (Oxford, 2011); Paul Foot, *The Rise of Enoch Powell* (Harmondsworth, 1969); Tom Nairn, *The Break-Up of Britain* (London, 1977), Chapter Six, 'English Nationalism: The Case of Enoch Powell'; Simon Heffer, *Like the Roman: The Life of Enoch Powell* (London, 1998).
63 Stuart Hall, 'The Great Moving Right Show', *Marxism Today* (January 1979), pp. 14–20, at pp. 19–20.
64 Stuart Hall, 'Preface', in Paul Gilroy, *Black Britain: A Photographic History* (London, 2007), pp. 5–10, at p. 7; see also Wendy Webster, *Englishness and Empire, 1939–1965* (Oxford, 2005).
65 Enoch Powell, *Freedom and Reality* (London, 1969), pp. 282, 286.
66 Ibid., p. 295.
67 Ibid., p. 298.
68 Enoch Powell, *Dancer's End and The Wedding Gift* (London, 1951); Powell had been a Professor of Greek in Sydney in the late 1930s.
69 Powell, *Dancer's End*, p. 39.
70 Powell, *Freedom and Reality*, p. 338; Powell was making a comparison with Athenians returning to their burned city to find a sacred olive tree still alive.
71 Ibid., pp. 338–9.
72 Ibid., p. 324. The phrase appears as the epigraph, misdated to 1946, in Wiener, *English Culture and the Decline of the Industrial Spirit*.
73 Quoted in Heffer, *Like the Roman*, p. 213.
74 Powell, *Freedom and Reality*, pp. 325, 335.
75 Ibid., p. 324.
76 Ibid., p. 313.
77 Ibid., p. 309.
78 Schofield, *Enoch Powell and the Making of Postcolonial Britain*.
79 Powell, *Freedom and Reality*, p. 289.
80 Ibid., p. 339.
81 Schwarz, *White Man's World*, pp. 37–40; also Amy Whipple, 'Revisiting the "Rivers of Blood" Controversy: Letters to Enoch Powell', *Journal of British Studies*, XLVIII (2009), pp. 717–35.
82 Schwarz, *White Man's World*, p. 12.
83 Ibid., p. 31.
84 Powell, *Freedom and Reality*, p. 282.
85 Ibid., p. 313.
86 Ann Dummett, *A Portrait of English Racism* (Harmondsworth, 1973), p. 48.
87 Ibid., pp. 48, 57.

88 Ibid., pp. 135, 152.
89 Ibid., pp. 14, 29.
90 Ibid., p. 50.
91 Ibid., p. 178.
92 Ibid., p. 293.
93 Ibid., p. 152.
94 Stuart Hall, 'Whose Heritage? Unsettling "The Heritage", Re-Imagining the Post-Nation', *Third Text*, XLIX (1999), pp. 3–13, at pp. 7, 10. Hall's essay is also included in *The Politics of Heritage: The Legacies of 'Race'*, ed. Jo Littler and Roshi Naidoo (Abingdon, 2005), pp. 23–35.
95 Hall, 'Whose Heritage?', p. 13.
96 Linton Kwesi Johnson, 'Inglan is a Bitch', in *Selected Poems* (London, 2006), pp. 39–41.
97 Michael Kenny, *The Politics of English Nationhood* (Oxford, 2014), pp. 103–5.
98 Simon Roberts, *We English* (London, 2009), Plate 44, 'Stanage Edge, Hathersage, Derbyshire, 3rd August 2008', and note 44 within 'Commentary' section.
99 Paul Gilroy, 'The Peculiarities of the Black English', in *Small Acts* (London, 1993), pp. 49–62; E. P. Thompson, 'The Peculiarities of the English', in *The Poverty of Theory* (London, 1978), pp. 35–91.
100 Paul Gilroy, *'There Ain't No Black in the Union Jack': The Cultural Politics of Race and Nation* (London, 2002), pp. xxvii–xxviii.
101 Paul Gilroy, *After Empire: Melancholia or Convivial Culture?* (London, 2004), p. x.
102 Gilroy, *'There Ain't No Black in the Union Jack'*, p. xiv.
103 James Garo Derounian, *Another Country: Real Life Beyond Rose Cottage* (London, 1993).
104 The phrase is the subtitle of *The Black Environment Network Report* (London, 1991), which noted its use of the term 'black' as 'symbolic', seeking to include minority communities who would not choose that label, including 'less visible white minorities', p. 3. On BEN see Phil Kinsman, 'Conflict and Co-Operation over Ethnic Minority Access to the Countryside: The Black Environment Network and the Countryside Commission', in *Rights of Way*, ed. Charles Watkins (London, 1996), pp. 162–78.
105 *The Black Environment Network Report*, p. 3. See also Julian Agyeman and Rachel Spooner, 'Ethnicity and the Rural Environment', in *Contested Countryside Cultures*, ed. Paul Cloke and Jo Little (London, 1997), pp. 197–217; Julian Agyeman, 'Black People in a White Landscape: Social and Environmental Justice', *Built Environment*, XVI (1990), pp. 232–6; Caroline Bressey, 'Cultural Archaeology and Historical Geographies of the Black Presence in Rural England', *Journal of Rural Studies*, XXV (2009), pp. 386–95; Divya Tolia-Kelly, *Landscape, Race and Memory: Material Ecologies of Citizenship* (London, 2010); Divya Tolia-Kelly, 'Fear in Paradise: The Affective Registers of the English Lake District Landscape Re-Visited', *Senses and Society*, II (2007), pp. 329–51.

References

106 Ingrid Pollard, 'Pastoral Interludes', *Third Text*, VII (1989), pp. 41–6; Ingrid Pollard, *Carbon Slowly Turning* (London, 2022); Phil Kinsman, 'Landscape, Race and National Identity: The Photography of Ingrid Pollard', *Area*, XXVII (1995), pp. 300–310; Taylor, *A Dream of England*.
107 Ingrid Pollard, 'Another View', *Feminist Review*, XLV (1993), pp. 46–50.
108 The image can be seen on Ingrid Pollard's website at www.ingridpollard.com.
109 Paul Gilroy, 'At the End of Black Boy Lane', in Pollard, *Carbon Slowly Turning*, pp. 10–19.
110 Corinne Fowler, *Green Unpleasant Land: Creative Responses to Rural England's Colonial Connections* (Leeds, 2020), p. 92.
111 V. S. Naipaul, *The Enigma of Arrival* (London, 1987); Fowler, *Green Unpleasant Land*, pp. 93–8; on post-imperial English rural literature including David Dabydeen's 1993 coast-set *Disappearance* see Dominic Head, *Modernity and the English Rural Novel* (Cambridge, 2017).
112 Dominic Head, *The Cambridge Introduction to Modern British Fiction, 1950–2000* (Cambridge, 2002), pp. 176–8.
113 Naipaul, *Enigma of Arrival*, p. 25.
114 Madge Dresser and Andrew Hann, eds, *Slavery and the British Country House* (London, 2013), p. xiii.
115 Horne, *God Is an Englishman*, p. 267.
116 Fowler, *Green Unpleasant Land*, p. 24; Sally-Anne Huxtable, Corinne Fowler, Christo Kefalas and Emma Slocombe, *Interim Report on the Connections between Colonialism and Properties Now in the Care of the National Trust, Including Links with Historic Slavery* (Swindon, 2020).
117 Nicholas Draper, 'Slave Ownership and the British Country House: The Records of the Slave Compensation Commission as Evidence', in *Slavery and the British Country House*, ed. Dresser and Hann, pp. 17–28, at p. 22.
118 Julian Agyeman, 'Alien Species', *Museums Journal* (December 1993), pp. 22–3.
119 Wood, *In Search of England*; Natalie Zacek, 'West Indian Echoes: Dodington House, the Codrington Family and the Caribbean Heritage', in *Slavery and the British Country House*, ed. Dresser and Hann, pp. 106–13.
120 Michael Wood, *In Search of England* (London, 1999), facing p. 209; in 1964 a BBC documentary, *The Colony*, had shown Caribbean immigrants in Birmingham touring a stately home; Webster, *Englishness and Empire*, pp. 163–4.
121 Wood, *In Search of England*, pp. 302–5.

4 England Shaken

1 Ronald Blythe, *Akenfield* (London, 1969), p. 40.
2 Peter Hall's 1974 film of *Akenfield* was released on DVD by the British Film Institute in 2016 (BFIB 1209). An accompanying booklet includes essays by Hall, 'Return of the Native', originally published in the *Observer* magazine on 26 January 1975, pp. 24–30, and Blythe, 'Filming Akenfield', originally published in the 1975 Aldeburgh Festival programme. The film is discussed in John Beck, *Landscape as Weapon* (London, 2020), pp. 18–21.

3 Blythe, *Akenfield*, p. 39.
4 *Akenfield Revisited* is included on the BFI DVD release of Hall's 1974 film.
5 Paul Fussell, *The Great War and Modern Memory* (Oxford, [1975] 2013), pp. 96, 252.
6 Shirley Collins's work is considered further in the companion volume to this book, *England's Green*.
7 Philip Larkin, 'The Living Poet', BBC Radio Third Programme talk, 3 July 1964, printed in *Further Requirements* (London, 2001), pp. 79–91, at p. 85.
8 Philip Larkin, 'MCMIV', in *The Whitsun Weddings* (London, 1964), p. 28.
9 Fussell, *Great War*, p. 364.
10 Darren Hayman, 'Thankful Villages: A Project about Rural Life', at www.thankful-villages.co.uk, accessed 29 March 2022. Hayman notes that 'the songs only rarely deal directly with The Great War.'
11 Nikolaus Pevsner, *Yorkshire: York and the East Riding* (Harmondsworth, 1972), p. 346.
12 Patrick Wright, *On Living in an Old Country* (London, 1985), pp. 136–7.
13 Simon Roberts, *Merrie Albion: Landscape Studies of a Small Island* (Stockport, 2017), p. 32.
14 See the Royal Wootton Bassett Repatriation Archives, www.royalwoottonbassett-repatriationarchives.uk.
15 The works associated with the 14–18 NOW programme are documented at www.1418now.org.uk.
16 This and other Tower of London projects are documented at 'Tower of London Remembers', www.hrp.org.uk, accessed 22 August 2022.
17 Anthony Barnett, *Iron Britannia* (London, 1982), pp. 150–53.
18 Ibid., p. 55; the book was in part published in advance in the August 1982 issue of *New Left Review*.
19 Barnett, *Iron Britannia*, p. 103; Klaus Dodds, 'Enframing the Falklands: Identity, Landscape, and the 1982 South Atlantic War', *Environment and Planning D: Society and Space*, XVI (1998), pp. 733–56; Klaus Dodds, *Pink Ice: Britain and the South Atlantic Empire* (London, 2002).
20 Barnett, *Iron Britannia*, p. 102.
21 Jonathan Raban, *Coasting* (London, 1986), p. 92.
22 Ibid., pp. 101–2.
23 Ibid., p. 113.
24 Ibid., p. 187.
25 Barnett, *Iron Britannia*, p. 143.
26 Robert Colls and Philip Dodd, *Englishness: Politics and Culture 1880–1920* (London, [1986] 2014), p. 1. See also Colls's and Dodd's later individual contributions to the debate on Englishness: Robert Colls, *Identity of England* (Oxford, 2002); Philip Dodd, *The Battle over Britain* (London, 1995).
27 Raphael Samuel, 'Preface', in Raphael Samuel, ed., *Patriotism: The Making and Unmaking of British National Identity*, vol. I: *History and Politics* (London, 1989), pp. x–xvii, at pp. x–xi; Raphael Samuel, ed., *Patriotism: The Making and Unmaking of British National Identity*, vol. II: *Minorities and Outsiders* (London, 1989); Raphael Samuel, ed., *Patriotism: The Making and Unmaking of British National Identity*, vol. III:

National Fictions (London, 1989). Samuel's work on heritage is discussed in Chapter Seven below. Volume III's 'Landscape' section included essays by Ken Worpole, Jill Franklin and Alex Potts, while Volume II's 'Childhood' section included a landscape and place-themed essay on 'I-Spy' books by Frank Cottrell-Boyce, then a research student at Oxford, later contributor of critical essays to *Living Marxism* and later still a writer for film, television, children's books and the 2012 Olympic ceremony.

28 Anthony Barnett. 'After Nationalism', in *Patriotism*, vol. 1: *History and Politics*, ed. Samuel, pp. 140–55, at p. 152.

29 Jonathan Hogg, *British Nuclear Culture* (London, 2016); see also the special issue of *British Journal for the History of Science*, XLV/4 (2012), on 'British Nuclear Culture', edited by Jonathan Hogg and Christoph Laucht, and the special issue of *Contemporary British History*, XXXIII/2 (2019), on 'Social and Cultural Histories of British Nuclear Mobilisation since 1945', edited by Jonathan Hogg and Kate Brown.

30 Sylvia Crowe, *The Landscape of Power* (London, 1958), p. 12.

31 Gabrielle Hecht, *The Radiance of France: Nuclear Power and National Identity after WWII* (Cambridge, MA, 1998), p. 43. See also Christine Wall, '"Nuclear Prospects": The Siting and Construction of Sizewell A Power Station, 1957–1966', *Contemporary British History*, XXXIII (2019), pp. 246–73.

32 W. G. Hoskins, *The Making of the English Landscape* (London, 1955), pp. 231–2.

33 Meredith Veldman, *Fantasy, the Bomb, and the Greening of Britain: Romantic Protest, 1945–1980* (Cambridge, 1994).

34 Ibid., p. 137.

35 Samuel, 'Preface', in *Patriotism*, vol. 1: *History and Politics*, ed. Samuel, p. x.

36 Barnett, *Iron Britannia*, p. 33.

37 Veldman, *Fantasy*, p. 185.

38 Michael Kenny, '"A Traditional English (Not British) Country Gentleman of the Radical Left": Understanding the Making and Unmaking of Edward Thompson's English Idiom', *Contemporary British History*, XXVIII (2014), pp. 494–516, at pp. 495, 498; Veldman, *Fantasy*, Chapter Nine.

39 E. P. Thompson, *William Morris: Romantic to Revolutionary* (London, 1955).

40 E. P. Thompson, 'The Peculiarities of the English', in *The Poverty of Theory* (London, 1978), p. 35.

41 Kenny, 'Traditional English Gentleman', p. 501.

42 Tanya Harrod, *The Crafts in Britain in the Twentieth Century* (London, 1999); Alan Caiger-Smith, *Pottery, People and Time* (Shepton Beauchamp, 1995).

43 Fay Weldon, 'Letter to Laura', in *Second Nature*, ed. Richard Mabey (London, 1984), pp. 67–73, at p. 72. On nuclear anxieties and environmentalist fiction see Daniel Cordle, 'Protect/Protest: British Nuclear Fiction of the 1980s', *British Journal for the History of Science*, XLV/4 (2012), pp. 653–9.

44 Stan Openshaw and Philip Steadman, 'The Geography of Two Hypothetical Nuclear Attacks on Britain', *Area*, XV (1983), pp. 193–201, at p. 197; Steadman and Greene were members of Scientists Against Nuclear Arms.
45 Stan Openshaw, Philip Steadman and Owen Greene, *Doomsday: Britain after Nuclear Attack* (Oxford, 1983), p. 5.
46 The Bords' alternative archaeology is discussed in the companion volume to this book, *England's Green*.
47 Openshaw, Steadman and Greene, *Doomsday*, p. 1.
48 *Contemporary Issues in Geography and Education*, II/3 (1987), 'War and Peace' special issue, end pages showing classroom exercise; on CIGE see Joanne Norcup, 'Geography Education, Grey Literature and the Geographical Canon', *Journal of Historical Geography*, XLIX (2015), pp. 61–74. Issues of CIGE are archived on the website of Geography Workshop at www.geographyworkshop.com.
49 CIGE, 'War and Peace', pp. 58–9; the montage was the main image in a selection advertising Kennard's educational poster exhibition 'Target London'. On London politics and the anti-nuclear movement see Hazel Atashroo, 'Weaponising Peace: The Greater London Council, Cultural Policy and "GLC Peace Year 1983"', *Contemporary British History*, XXXII/2 (2019), pp. 170–86. For Kennard's work see Peter Kennard, *Peter Kennard: Visual Dissent* (London, 2019), an anthology of his work for which the *Hay Wain* montage provides the front cover image.
50 Openshaw, Steadman and Greene, *Doomsday*, p. 2.
51 Ibid., pp. 95–6.
52 Kennard's image is discussed in Stephen Daniels, 'Marxism, Culture and the Duplicity of Landscape', in *New Models in Geography*, vol. II, ed. Richard Peet and Nigel Thrift (London, 1989), pp. 216–17; on Constable as English icon see Stephen Daniels, *Fields of Vision: Landscape Imagery and National Identity in England and the United States* (Cambridge, 1993).
53 The letter is archived on the UK government website at www.gov.uk.
54 Christian Rutz et al., 'COVID-19 Lockdown Allows Researchers to Quantify the Effects of Human Activity on Wildlife', *Nature Ecology and Evolution*, IV (2020), pp. 1156–9; Adam Searle, Jonathon Turnbull and Jamie Lorimer, 'After the Anthropause: Lockdown Lessons for More-than-Human Geographies', *Geographical Journal*, CLXXXVII (2021), pp. 69–77.
55 Melissa Harrison, *The Stubborn Light of Things* (London, 2020), p. 5; the podcasts are available on Harrison's website, at www.melissaharrison.co.uk.
56 Ibid., p. 206.
57 David Matless, *Landscape and Englishness* (London, 1998; rev. edn 2016).
58 The report is on the BBC website: 'Jurassic Coast Beach Crowds "Showed Shocking Disregard for Area"', at www.bbc.co.uk, 2 June 2020.
59 The report is on the BBC website: 'Bournemouth Beach: "Major Incident" as Thousands Flock to Coast', www.bbc.co.uk, 25 June 2020.
60 Vaughan Cornish, *National Parks, and the Heritage of Scenery* (London, 1930), p. 45; Matless, *Landscape and Englishness*, p. 104.

61 E. P. Richards, 'Report with Proposals on the Recreational Use of Gathering Grounds, Unpublished for CPRE (1935), p. 8; Matless, *Landscape and Englishness*, p. 104.
62 CPRE, *Litter in Lockdown: A Study in Littering in the Time of Coronavirus* (London, 2020), quotations pp. 8, 2, 4.
63 Ibid., p. 4.
64 Quoted in the BBC report of Lynn's death, at www.bbc.co.uk, 18 June 2020.
65 Paul Gilroy, *After Empire*, pp. 95, 97.
66 Details of the NHS Spitfire are on the Aircraft Restoration Company website at www.aircraftrestorationcompany.com/nhsspitfire; see also Elliott Marsh's article on 'The NHS Spitfire Summer', in the online Vintage Aviation Echo, www.vintageaviationecho.com/nhs-spitfire; I am grateful to Gruffydd Jones for alerting me to this story.
67 Information from the *News of the World Football Annual, 1973–74* (London, 1973).
68 Tom Nairn, *The Break-Up of Britain* (London, 1977), p. 256.
69 Simon Heffer, *Like the Roman: The Life of Enoch Powell* (London, 1998), p. 746.
70 Nairn, *Break-Up of Britain*, p. 259.
71 Ibid., pp. 304–5.
72 Seamus Heaney, 'Englands of the Mind', in *Finders Keepers: Selected Prose, 1971–2001* (London, 2002), p. 77.
73 Ibid., p. 95; Philip Larkin, 'Going, Going', in *High Windows* (London, 1974), pp. 21–2. Larkin's poem and its connection to environmentalism will be discussed in the companion volume to this book, *England's Green*.
74 Donald Davie, *The Shires* (London, 1974).
75 William Davies, 'Donald Davie and Englishness', *Review of English Studies*, LXX (2018), pp. 332–53, at p. 350.
76 Davie, *The Shires*, no pagination.
77 Heaney, 'Englands of the Mind', p. 95.
78 Arthur Aughey, *The Politics of Englishness* (Manchester, 2007); Arthur Aughey, '"England Is the Country and the Country Is England": But What of the Politics?', in *Literature of an Independent England*, ed. Claire Westall and Michael Gardiner (Basingstoke, 2013), pp. 46–59.
79 For Cameron's Downing Street post-referendum statement see the BBC report at 'In Full: David Cameron Statement on the UK's Future', www.bbc.co.uk, 19 September 2014.
80 Michael Kenny, *The Politics of English Nationhood* (Oxford, 2014).
81 Claire Westall and Michael Gardiner, 'Introduction', in *Literature of an Independent England*, ed. Westall and Gardiner, pp. 1–11, at p. 6.
82 Roger Scruton, *England: An Elegy* (London, 2000); Red Shift, *Looking for a New England* (2015), formerly online at www.redshiftlabour.co.uk, accessed 9 July 2019. The latter document took its title from a song by Billy Bragg, which had stated it was not looking for a new England, but just another girl.
83 Nairn, *Break-Up of Britain*, p. 291; G. K. Chesterton, 'The Secret People', in *The Collected Poems of G. K. Chesterton* (London, 1933), pp. 173–6.

84 Melvyn Bragg, *Speak for England* (London, 1976).
85 See Patrick Wright's February 2017 BBC Radio 4 programme within a series on *The English Fix*, 'The Secret People', details at www.bbc.co.uk.
86 Peter Mandler, *The English National Character* (New Haven, CT, 2006), p. 242.
87 Ibid., p. 237; the note is to a Johnson quote evoking the musical *Evita*: 'Where is this, Argentina?'
88 Fintan O'Toole, *Heroic Failure: Brexit and the Politics of Pain* (London, 2019), at pp. xxi, 76.
89 Robert Saunders, 'Brexit and Empire: "Global Britain" and the Myth of Imperial Nostalgia', *Journal of Imperial and Commonwealth History*, XLVIII (2020), pp. 1140–74.
90 Danny Dorling and Sally Tomlinson, *Rule Britannia: Brexit and the End of Empire* (London, 2019), pp. 2–3.
91 O'Toole, *Heroic Failure*, p. 214.
92 Roy Faiers, 'The Editor's Letter', *This England*, XXVI/3 (1993), p. 1.
93 *The Field*, 'Fanfare on Being British: Seven Britons Speak Out', *The Field*, May 1990, pp. 76–85.
94 Ibid., p. 78.
95 Ibid., pp. 76–7.
96 Ibid., p. 85.
97 Heffer, *Like the Roman*, p. 613; on Powell and sovereignty see Lindsay Aqui, Michael Kenny and Nick Pearce, '"The Empire of England": Enoch Powell, Sovereignty and the Constitution of the Nation', *Twentieth Century British History*, XXXII (2021), pp. 238–60.
98 Robert Ford and Matthew Goodwin, *Revolt on the Right* (London, 2014), pp. 10–11.
99 On the longer cultural history of the Dover cliffs see Paul Readman, *Storied Ground: Landscape and the Shaping of English National Identity* (Cambridge, 2018), Chapter One; Paul Readman, '"The Cliffs Are Not Cliffs": The Cliffs of Dover and National Identities in Britain, *c*. 1750– *c*. 1950', *History*, LCIX (2014), pp. 241–69. For a richly detailed study of Kent and the recent cultural politics of Englishness see Phil Hubbard, *Borderland: Identity and Belonging at the Edge of England* (Manchester, 2022).
100 Ford and Goodwin, *Revolt on the Right*, p. 75.
101 Ibid., p. 191.
102 Michael Gardiner, 'Brexit and the Aesthetics of Anachronism', in Robert Eaglestone, *Brexit and Literature* (London, 2018), pp. 105–17, at pp. 105, 116.
103 David Goodhart, *The Road to Somewhere* (London, 2017), p. 4.
104 Wendy Webster, *Englishness and Empire, 1939–1965* (Oxford, 2005), pp. 154–5.
105 Ford and Goodwin, *Revolt on the Right*, pp. 90–91.
106 Nora Beloff, *The General Says No: Britain's Exclusion from Europe* (Harmondsworth, 1963), p. 7.
107 Robert Saunders, *Yes to Europe! The 1975 Referendum and Seventies Britain* (Cambridge, 2018), p. 178.
108 Quoted in Saunders, 'Brexit and Empire', p. 1149.

References

109 Saunders, *Yes to Europe!*
110 Common Market Football Match, *Official Programme* (3 January 1973), p. 2.
111 Saunders, *Yes to Europe!*, pp. 106–8.
112 Ailsa Henderson, Charlie Jeffery, Robert Liniera, Roger Scully, Daniel Wincott and Richard Wyn Jones, 'England, Englishness and Brexit', *Political Quarterly*, LXXXVII (2016), pp. 187–99, at p. 198.
113 'Culture and the EU', *Times Literary Supplement* (3 June 2016), pp. 14–17.
114 Ibid., p. 16; see also Sean O'Brien, *Journeys to the Interior: Ideas of England in Contemporary Poetry* (Newcastle/Tarset, 2012).
115 'Culture and the EU', p. 16. Julia Donaldson and Axel Scheffler, *The Gruffalo* (London, 1999).
116 Roberts, *Merrie Albion*, p. 140.
117 See Simon Roberts's website at www.simoncroberts.com/work/between-the-acts; the same Woolf quote appears on the facing page to the photograph in Roberts's *Merrie Albion*, with an additional phrase at the start: 'When they were alone, they said nothing.'
118 'Culture and the EU', p. 15.
119 O'Toole, *Heroic Failure*, p. 232.
120 For initial historical reflections on the recent British and English cultural engagement with Europe see the 2021 special issue of *Contemporary British History*, and its summary introduction: Tobias Becker and Felix Fuhg, 'Writing Europe into British Cultural History: An Introduction', *Contemporary British History*, XXXV (2021), pp. 325–39. The potential complexities are indicated in Joanne Hollows, 'Enthusing about Green Peppers: The Europeanisation of British Food Culture in Post-War Britain, 1960–1975', *Contemporary British History*, XXXV (2021), pp. 392–416; Hollows shows, for example, how a cosmopolitan interest in European regional culinary authenticity included attention to neglected regional English and British food.
121 On the tree circle see Jo Norcup, 'Trees of Beeston', February 2019 article for local magazine *The Beestonian*, available online at www.beestonian.com.

5 English and Suburban

1 David Nobbs, *The Fall and Rise of Reginald Perrin* (Harmondsworth, 1976), p. 20.
2 Georges Perec, 'Approaches to What?', in *Species of Spaces and Other Pieces* (London, 1997), pp. 205–7, at p. 206.
3 Georges Perec, 'Attempt at an Inventory of the Liquid and Solid Foodstuffs Ingurgitated by Me in the Course of the Year Nineteen Hundred and Seventy-Four', in *Species of Spaces and Other Pieces*, pp. 240–45, at p. 244.
4 On suburban cultures see Roger Silverstone, ed., *Visions of Suburbia* (London, 1997); Paul Oliver, Ian Davis and Ian Bentley, *Dunroamin: The Suburban Semi and Its Enemies* (London, 1981); Rupa Huq, *Making Sense of Suburbia through Popular Culture* (London, 2013); Rupa Huq, 'Postcards from the Edge? Setting the Suburban Scene', *Political Quarterly*, XC (2019), pp. 6–14.

5 Alison Light, *Forever England: Femininity, Literature and Conservatism between the Wars* (London, 1991), pp. 8–10.
6 Ibid., p. 211.
7 Tracey Thorn, *Another Planet: A Teenager in Suburbia* (Edinburgh, 2019), at pp. 7, 3.
8 Oliver, Davis and Bentley, *Dunroamin*, p. 186.
9 Brian Rice and Tony Evans, *The English Sunrise* (London, 1972), p. 26. On Rice's work as painter and printmaker see the website www.brianrice.co.uk; on Evans's work see *Taking His Time: The Photography of Tony Evans* (London, 2000).
10 Alan Jackson, *Semi-Detached London, 1900–1939* (London, 1973), at pp. 319, 324.
11 J. M. Richards, *The Castles on the Ground* (London, 1973), p. 1.
12 Ibid., pp. 2–4.
13 Ibid., p. 6.
14 Ibid., pp. 8–9.
15 Ibid. The remaining 1946 images are between pp. 40 and 41, and facing p. 56; Piper's illustrations to the book are discussed by Rigby Graham in his essay on 'Book Illustrations' in the Tate exhibition catalogue for *John Piper* (London, 1983), pp. 22–3.
16 Richards, *Castles*, facing p. 24.
17 John Betjeman, 'Slough', in *Collected Poems* (London, 1974), pp. 22–4.
18 John Betjeman, 'Love is Dead', in *First and Last Loves* (London, 1952), p. 1.
19 Andy Medhurst, 'Negotiating the Gnome Zone: Versions of Suburbia in British Popular Culture', in *Visions of Suburbia*, ed. Silverstone, pp. 240–68.
20 For the script of *Metro-land* see John Betjeman, 'Metro-Land', in *Coming Home: An Anthology of Prose* (London, 1997), pp. 444–65, at p. 465.
21 *Metro-Land* is discussed in Bevis Hillier, *Betjeman: The Bonus of Laughter* (London, 2004), pp. 330–53.
22 Betjeman, 'Metro-Land', p. 459.
23 Ibid., p. 457.
24 Ibid., p. 463.
25 Ibid., pp. 454–5.
26 Ibid., p. 460.
27 R. E. Pahl, *Urbs in rure: The Metropolitan Fringe in Hertfordshire* (London, 1965); the book was based on Pahl's London School of Economics doctoral thesis and carried a preface signed 'Royston, Hertfordshire'.
28 Ibid., pp. 9–10.
29 Ibid., p. 13.
30 Ibid., p. 41.
31 Ibid., p. 45.
32 R. E. Pahl, 'The Two Class Village', *New Society*, LXXIV (27 February 1964), pp. 7–9.
33 Pahl, *Urbs in rure*, p. 27.
34 Ibid., p. 33.

35 Ibid., p. 73.
36 Ibid., pp. 14, 25.
37 For a work complementing Pahl's analysis fifty years on see John Grindrod, *Outskirts: Living Life on the Edge of the Green Belt* (London, 2017). Grindrod reflects on the Green Belt, covering 13 per cent of England, having grown up on what felt like 'the last road in London', beyond Croydon, with fields and woods across from a council maisonette. Grindrod offers an upper-working-class social story of metropolitan suburbia to set alongside Tracey Thorn's middle-class variant in *Another Planet*. Grindrod also produces the Dirty Modern Scoundrel blog at www.dirtymodernscoundrel.blogspot.com.
38 Nicholas Taylor, *The Village in the City* (London, 1973), p. 7.
39 Ibid., pp. 23–4.
40 Ibid., p. 190.
41 Ibid., p. 198.
42 Reyner Banham, Paul Barker, Peter Hall and Cedric Price, 'Non-Plan: An Experiment in Freedom', *New Society*, XIII (20 March 1969), pp. 435–43; Paul Barker, *The Freedoms of Suburbia* (London, 2009); Paul Barker, 'Non-Plan Revisited: Or the Real Way Cities Grow', *Journal of Design History*, XII (1999), pp. 95–110; Peter Hall, *London 2000* (London, 1963).
43 Banham, Barker, Hall and Price, 'Non-Plan', pp. 437–8.
44 Ibid., p. 438.
45 *New Society*, XIII (27 March 1969).
46 *New Society*, XIII (3 April 1969).
47 *New Society*, XIII (17 April 1969).
48 David Gilbert and Rebecca Preston, '"Stop being so English": Suburban Modernity and National Identity in the Twentieth Century', in *Geographies of British Modernity*, ed. David Gilbert, David Matless and Brian Short (Oxford, 2003), pp. 187–203.
49 Quoted in Matthew Francis, '"A Crusade to Enfranchise the Many": Thatcherism and the "Property-Owning Democracy"', *Twentieth Century British History*, XXIII (2012), pp. 275–97, at p. 295; Gilbert and Preston, '"Stop being so English"', pp. 196–7.
50 John Major, *John Major: The Autobiography* (London, 1999); Gilbert and Preston, '"Stop being so English"', pp. 197–9.
51 The text of the speech is available on Major's website at www.johnmajor.co.uk.
52 George Orwell, 'The Lion and the Unicorn: Socialism and the English Genius', in *The Collected Essays, Journalism and Letters of George Orwell*, vol. II (London, 1968), pp. 56–109, at p. 57.
53 Ibid., p. 59.
54 Ibid., p. 57.
55 Ibid., p. 77.
56 Medhurst, 'Negotiating the Gnome Zone'; Andy Medhurst, *A National Joke: Popular Comedy and English Cultural Identities* (London, 2007).
57 Nobbs, *Reginald Perrin*, p. 5; see also Richard Webber, *The Life and Legacy of Reginald Perrin: A Celebration* (London, 1996).
58 Medhurst, 'Negotiating the Gnome Zone', p. 254.

59 *The Good Life* is discussed in the companion volume to this book, *England's Green*, for its portrayal of environmentalist self-sufficiency in suburbia.
60 Medhurst, 'Negotiating the Gnome Zone', pp. 257–8.
61 Stephen Potter, *One-Upmanship* (Harmondsworth, [1952] 1962).
62 Martin Parr, *The Cost of Living* (Manchester, 1989).
63 Martin Parr, *Think of England* (London, 2000); Val Williams, *Martin Parr* (London, 2002).
64 Pierre Bourdieu, *Distinction: A Social Critique of the Judgement of Taste* (London, 1984).
65 Parr, *Cost of Living*, back cover blurb.
66 Guy Ortolano, *Thatcher's Progress: From Social Democracy to Market Liberalism through an English New Town* (Cambridge, 2019), p. 132.
67 Raphael Samuel, 'The Return to Brick', in *Theatres of Memory* (London, 1994), pp. 119–35; Samuel notes the Redland 'Olde English Range', p. 123.
68 Banham, Barker, Hall and Price, 'Non-Plan', p. 436; Ortolano, *Thatcher's Progress*, p. 72. On Milton Keynes see also Mark Clapson, *A Social History of Milton Keynes: Middle England/Edge City* (London, 2004); Lauren Piko, *Milton Keynes in British Culture: Imagining England* (London, 2019).
69 Ortolano, *Thatcher's Progress*, p. 3.
70 Ruth Finnegan, *The Hidden Musicians: Music-Making in an English Town* (Cambridge, 1989); Milton Keynes is also the basis for Ruth Finnegan, *Tales of the City: A Study of Narrative and Urban Life* (Cambridge, 1998).
71 Rasmussen is quoted in Ortolano, *Thatcher's Progress*, p. 185, from Derek Walker, *The Architecture and Planning of Milton Keynes* (London, 1982).
72 W. G. Hoskins, *Midland England* (London, 1949), p. vi; David Matless, *Landscape and Englishness* (London, 1998; rev. edn 2016), also reproduces the image of Milton Keynes from *Midland England*.
73 Patrick Wright, 'An Encroachment Too Far', in *Town and Country*, ed. Anthony Barnett and Roger Scruton (London, 1998), pp. 18–33.
74 Mark Hallett, ed., *George Shaw: A Corner of a Foreign Field* (London, 2018), including an interview of Shaw by Jeremy Deller; Laurence Sillars, ed., *George Shaw: The Sly and Unseen Day* (Gateshead, 2011); Ian Waites, '"Places Where I Forgot Things"; Memory, Identity and the British Council Estate in the Paintings of George Shaw', *Cultural Politics*, IX (2013), pp. 357–70. See also Waites's own prose and photographic account of an estate in Gainsborough, Lincolnshire, paralleling Tile Hill; Ian Waites, *Middlefield: A Postwar Council Estate in Time* (Axminster, 2017).
75 Nicholas Alfrey, Stephen Daniels and Martin Postle, *Art of the Garden* (London, 2004), pp. 214–15.
76 Nikolaus Pevsner and Alexandra Wedgwood, *Warwickshire* (Harmondsworth, 1966), p. 281.
77 Hallett, *George Shaw*, p. 166.
78 George Shaw, *My Back to Nature* (London, 2016).
79 Ibid., p. 69.

80 Hallett, *George Shaw*, p. 313.
81 George Shaw, lecture delivered at Nottingham Trent University, 19 November 2010.
82 Hallett, *George Shaw*, pp. 262, 321.
83 Ibid., p. 316.
84 Ibid., p. 318.
85 John Myers, *Middle England* (Birmingham, 2011); see also John Myers, *The World Is Not Beautiful* (Manchester, 2017).
86 Tony Williams, *The Midlands* (Rugby, 2014), pp. 9–10. I am grateful to Tony for his permission to quote his work here.
87 Carolyn Steedman, *Landscape for a Good Woman* (London, 1986), p. 109.
88 Ibid., p. 103.
89 Ibid., p. 24.
90 Danny Dorling, 'Dying Quietly: English Suburbs and the Stiff Upper Lip', *Political Quarterly*, XC (2019), pp. 32–43, at p. 32.
91 Martin Newell, *Late Autumn Sunlight* (Colchester, 2001).

6 English Particulars

1 Stuart Jeffries, 'Gordon Murray', *The Guardian* (1 July 2016), p. 33.
2 Rachel Moseley, *Hand-Made Television: Stop-Frame Animation for Children in Britain, 1961–1974* (London, 2016), at pp. 33, 43, 52.
3 David Matless, 'The Agriculture Gallery: Displaying Modern Farming in the Science Museum', in *Histories of Technology, the Environment and Modern Britain*, ed. Jon Agar and Jacob Ward (London, 2018), pp. 101–22. The presentation of farming here and elsewhere in the period in considered in the companion volume to this book, *England's Green*.
4 Moseley, *Hand-Made Television*, Chapter Three.
5 Ibid., p. 18.
6 Jean Northam, 'Rehearsals in Citizenship: BBC Stop-Motion Animation Programmes for Young Children', *Journal for Cultural Research*, IX (2005), pp. 245–63.
7 Jeremy Dyson, Mark Gatiss, Steve Pemberton and Reece Shearsmith, *The League of Gentlemen: Scripts and That* (London, 2003), p. 52; Leon Hunt, *The League of Gentlemen* (London, 2008), especially Chapter Three, 'Local', pp. 39–74.
8 Dyson et al., *League of Gentlemen*, p. 84.
9 Sylvia Townsend Warner, *Lolly Willowes* (London, [1926] 1993), pp. 127–8; David Matless, *Landscape and Englishness* (London, 1998; rev. edn 2016), Chapter Two.
10 Katrina Navickas, 'Conflicts of Power, Landscape and Amenity in Debates over the British Super Grid in the 1950s', *Rural History*, XXX (2019), pp. 87–103.
11 Ian Nairn, 'Outrage', *Architectural Review*, CXVII (1955), pp. 361–40, at p. 365. On Nairn see Gillian Darley and David McKie, *Ian Nairn: Words in Place* (Nottingham, 2013).
12 David Matless, 'One Man's England: W. G. Hoskins and the English Culture of Landscape', *Rural History*, IV (1993), pp. 187–207; David Matless, 'Writing English Landscape History', *Anglia: Zeitschrift fur*

Englische Philologie, CXXVI (2008), pp. 295–311; Matthew Johnson, *Ideas of Landscape* (Oxford, 2007).
13 David Heathcote, *A Shell Eye on England: The Shell County Guides 1934–1984* (Faringdon, 2011).
14 W. G. Hoskins, *Rutland* (London, 1963), p. 7; Matless, *Landscape and Englishness*, Chapter Eight.
15 W. G. Hoskins, *Local History in England* (London, 1959), pp. 4–6.
16 W. G. Hoskins, *English Local History: The Past and the Future* (Leicester, 1966), p. 10.
17 Ibid., pp. 20–21.
18 W. G. Hoskins, *Provincial England* (London, 1963), frontispiece.
19 Raphael Samuel, *Theatres of Memory* (London, 1994), pp. 158–9.
20 W. G. Hoskins, *The Midland Peasant* (London, 1957), p. 282.
21 W. G. Hoskins, *Leicestershire* (London, 1970), pp. 111–12.
22 Samuel, *Theatres of Memory*.
23 Ronald Brunskill, *Traditional Buildings of Britain: An Introduction to Vernacular Architecture* (London, 1981), p. 14.
24 Essex County Council, *A Design Guide for Residential Areas* (Chelmsford, 1973), p. 5.
25 Ibid., p. 15.
26 Ibid., p. 111, p. 19.
27 Ibid., pp. 62–4.
28 Ibid., p. 94.
29 Ibid., p. 82.
30 Ian Nairn, 'Counter-Attack', *Architectural Review*, CXX (1956), pp. 352–440, at p. 361.
31 Essex County Council, *A Design Guide for Residential Areas* (Chelmsford, 1983), p. 3; Carl Bray, *New Villages: Case Studies, No. 2: South Woodham Ferrers* (Oxford, 1981).
32 A five-minute version of the original 23-minute 'A Riverside Country Town' film is available on the Essex Record Office website at www.essexrecordofficeblog.co.uk. The film is discussed in Gillian Darley, 'From Plotlands to New Towns', in *Radical Essex*, ed. Hayley Dixon and Joe Hill (Southend, 2018), pp. 101–21.
33 David Watkin, *The English Vision* (London, 1982), p. 199.
34 Dan Cruickshank, 'Shadows of the Past', *Architects' Journal*, CLXX (22 August 1979), pp. 378–9.
35 David Pearce, 'Making Places', *Building Design* (6 January 1978), pp. 8–9.
36 David Pearce, 'Return to Metroland', *Building Design* (13 January 1978), pp. 14–15.
37 Melville Dunbar, 'Forever Ambridge', *RIBA Journal*, LXXXVII (1980), p. 40.
38 Adrian Forty and Henry Moss, 'The Housing Style for Troubled Consumers: The Success of Pseudo-Vernacular', *Architectural Review*, CLXVII (1980), pp. 73–8.
39 Charles Holland, 'The Rise and Fall', in *Radical Essex*, ed. Dixon and Hill, pp. 69–100, at pp. 94–5.
40 Darley, 'From Plotlands to New Towns', p. 120; see also Gillian Darley, *Excellent Essex* (London, 2019).

41 Ronald Brunskill, *Traditional Buildings of Britain: An Introduction to Vernacular Architecture and Its Revival* (London, 2004), p. 198.
42 Samuel, *Theatres of Memory*, p. 131.
43 Sue Clifford and Angela King, *England in Particular* (London, 2006), p. 114.
44 Richard Mabey, *The Common Ground* (London, 1980); Richard Mabey, ed., *Second Nature* (London, 1984). Mabey's work is considered in detail in the companion volume to this book, *England's Green*.
45 On Common Ground's work see David Matless, 'Doing the English Village', in Paul Cloke, Marcus Doel, David Matless, Martin Phillips and Nigel Thrift, *Writing the Rural* (London, 1994), pp. 43–75; Jos Smith, *The New Nature Writing: Rethinking the Literature of Place* (London, 2017).
46 Sue Clifford and Angela King, *Holding Your Ground* (Aldershot, [1985] 1987), p. 2.
47 Common Ground, *Local Distinctiveness* (London, 1990 [leaflet]); Sue Clifford and Angela King, eds, *Local Distinctiveness: Place, Particularity and Identity* (London, 1993).
48 Clifford and King, *Holding Your Ground*, introduction, no pagination.
49 Common Ground, 'Mayday! Mayday!' (advertisement), *The Independent* (5 May 1990), p. 39.
50 Joanna Morland, *New Milestones: Sculpture, Community and the Land* (London, 1988), p. 24.
51 Fraser Harrison, 'England, Home and Beauty', in *Second Nature*, ed. Mabey, pp. 162–72, at p. 167.
52 Fraser Harrison, *The Living Landscape* (London, 1986), pp. 22, 26.
53 Mabey, *Second Nature*, p. x.
54 Common Ground's 2016 follow-up to *Second Nature*, Tim Dee's edited collection *Ground Work* (London, 2016), follows a similar track.
55 Sue Clifford and Angela King, eds, *From Place to PLACE: Maps and Parish Maps* (London, 1996); David Crouch and David Matless, 'Refiguring Geography: Parish Maps of Common Ground', *Transactions of the Institute of British Geographers*, XXI (1996), pp. 236–55; Patrick Devine-Wright, Jos Smith and Susana Batel, '"Positive Parochialism", Local Belonging and Ecological Concerns: Revisiting Common Ground's Parish Maps Project', *Transactions of the Institute of British Geographers*, XLIV (2019), pp. 407–21.
56 Jonathan Raban, *Coasting* (London, 1986), p. 176.
57 Gilbert White, *The Natural History of Selborne*, ed. Richard Mabey (London, 1977), introduction; quoted in Mabey, *Common Ground*, p. 38.
58 A contemporary equivalent literary experiment would be Adam Thorpe's novel *Ulverton* (London, 1992), where the local is made through distinctive modes of historical narration.
59 Common Ground, *The Parish Mapper* (London, 1988), p. 21.
60 Ibid., p. 24.
61 Devine-Wright et al., '"Positive Parochialism"'.
62 Clifford and King, *England in Particular*, pp. xiv–xv.
63 Ibid., p. ix.
64 Ibid., p. xii.

65 Ibid., p. xvi.
66 Ibid., p. 13.
67 Virginia Astley, 'A Poem for Apple Day. 21st October 2014', published on the *Caught by the River* website, www.caughtbytheriver.net, October 2014.
68 See the Scarthin Books website, www.scarthinbooks.com.
69 Robin Ravilious, *James Ravilious: A Life* (London, 2017).
70 Peter Hamilton, *An English Eye: The Photographs of James Ravilious* (Oxford, [1998] 2007), p. 20. On Massingham see Matless, *Landscape and Englishness*.
71 Alan Bennett, 'Foreword', in Hamilton, *An English Eye*, p. 7.
72 Hamilton, *An English Eye*, p. 13.
73 James Ravilious, *A Corner of England: North Devon Landscapes and People* (Tiverton, 1995).
74 Lewis, 'Where the Wild Things Went', p. 34.
75 James Ravilious, *The Heart of the Country* (London, 1980).
76 Peter Beacham and James Ravilious, *Down the Deep Lanes* (Oxford, 2000), pp. 11, 15.
77 Ted Hughes, 'Last Load', in *Collected Poems* (London, 2003), pp. 528–9.
78 Peter Beacham, *Devon Building* (Tiverton, 1990).
79 James Ravilious, *The Recent Past* (London, 2017).
80 Hamilton, *An English Eye*, p. 29.
81 Ibid., pp. 96–7.
82 Denis Hardy and Colin Ward, *Arcadia for All: The Legacy of a Makeshift Landscape* (London, 1984); Colin Ward, 'A Place in the Country', in *Second Nature*, ed. Mabey, pp. 198–206.
83 Clifford and King, *England in Particular*, pp. 60–61.
84 Matless, *Landscape and Englishness*, Chapter One.
85 Hardy and Ward, *Arcadia for All*, p. 225.
86 Pearce, 'Return to Metroland', p. 14.
87 Patrick Keiller, 'Rare Example of User Control', *Building Design* (27 January 1978), p. 9.
88 Terry Philpot, '"S Woodham Ferrers "Monument to Ambitious Planning"', *Building Design* (10 February 1978), p. 9.
89 Hardy and Ward, *Arcadia for All*, p. 161.
90 Stuart Rodger, 'This Is the End of the Line: A Dispatch from Ukipland', *New Statesman* (25 February 2016).
91 Robert Wyatt, quoted on the BBC website, 'Seaside Shangri-La Goes Upmarket', 13 December 2001, www.news.bbc.co.uk.
92 Jonathan Meades, 'First Shack', in *Museum without Walls* (London, 2012), pp. 325–8, at pp. 327–8.
93 Hilda Grieve, *The Great Tide* (Chelmsford, 1959), pp. 174–5.
94 On Eccles see David Matless, 'Next the Sea: Eccles and the Anthroposcenic', *Journal of Historical Geography*, LXII (2018), pp. 71–84.
95 Hilaire Belloc, 'On Inns', in *This and That and the Other* (New York, 1912), pp. 45–55, at pp. 45, 55; Christopher Hutt, *The Death of the English Pub* (London, 1973).
96 Richard Boston, *Beer and Skittles* (London, 1976), pp. 13, 105; Laura Hadland, *50 Years of CAMRA* (St Albans, 2021); Jessica Boak and Ray

Bailey, *Brew Britannia: The Strange Rebirth of British Beer* (London, 2017).
97 Lincoln Allison, 'The English Cultural Movement', *New Society* (16 February 1978); Lincoln Allison, *Condition of England: Essays and Impressions* (London, 1981).
98 Ian Nairn, 'The Best Beers of Our Lives', *Sunday Times* (30 June 1974), pp. 33–4. I am indebted here to the research of Graham Reeks and his dissertation 'Authenticating Ale: Brewing Landscapes', written for the MA in Landscape and Culture at the University of Nottingham, 2001, and drawing on interviews with key members of CAMRA.
99 Boston, *Beer and Skittles*, p. 15.
100 Ibid., p. 84.
101 Hutt, *Death of the English Pub*, Chapter Eight.
102 Michael Jackson, *The English Pub* (London, 1976), p. 5.
103 Ibid., p. 29.
104 Ibid., p. 48.
105 Michael Jackson, *The World Guide to Beer* (London, 1977).
106 Jackson, *The English Pub*, p. 60.
107 Ibid., pp. 51–2.
108 Frank Baillie, *The Beer Drinker's Companion* (Newton Abbot, 1973).
109 *Good Beer Guide* (St Albans, 1978), p. 130.
110 Frances and Michael Holmes, *Norwich Pubs and Breweries Past and Present* (Norwich, 2015). The Golden Star was a free house from 1977 to 1984, when it was acquired by Greene King. The Star Brewery's 'Norfolk Nog' was later remade by Norfolk brewery Woodfordes, itself founded in 1981, and named CAMRA's Champion Beer of Britain in 1992.
111 Hutt, *Death of the English Pub*, p. 159.
112 Ibid., pp. 10–11.
113 Boston, *Beer and Skittles*, pp. 79, 94.
114 Philip Conford, *The Development of the Organic Network: Linking People and Themes, 1945–95* (Edinburgh, 2011), pp. 280–81.
115 *An Antidote to Indifference*, 11 (2015), 'A Beer Special'; details at www.caughtbytheriver.net.
116 Patrick Wright, 'Last Orders', *The Guardian* (9 April 2005).
117 Belloc, 'On Inns', pp. 46–7.
118 In 2021 British Sea Power, after two decades of music-making, dropped the 'British' from their name, wary at the associations that might gather in an era of renewed nationalism. Attention to their work would have quickly shown it to be far from nationalistic, but evocations of place, and of islandness, lent the group's work intrigue and nuance. The 'sea' aspect of British Sea Power's work will be discussed in the companion volume to *About England, England's Green*.
119 Paul Kingsnorth, *Real England: The Battle against the Bland* (London, 2008), pp. 18, 285.
120 Ibid., p. 27.
121 Ibid., p. 50.
122 Paul Moody, 'The Last of England', *An Antidote to Indifference*, 11 (2015), pp. 8–11, at p. 8–9.
123 Hutt, *Death of the English Pub*, p. 127.

124 Jackson, *The English Pub*, p. 164.
125 Ibid., p. 51.
126 Jonathan Moses's doctoral thesis includes insightful analysis of Wetherspoon's, and of the community pub movement: Jonathan Moses, 'The Politics of the British Public House, 1979–Present: Architecture, Authenticity and Everyday Enchantment', PhD thesis, University of London, 2020.
127 Caroline Graham, *The Killings at Badger's Drift* (London, 1987), pp. 39–40.
128 John Nettles, *Bergerac's Jersey* (London, 1988).
129 'Midsomer Murders Producer Suspended over Diversity Remarks', *The Guardian* (15 March 2011).
130 John Lowerson, 'The Mystical Geography of the English', in *The English Rural Community*, ed. Brian Short (London, 1992), pp. 152–74.
131 Peter Sallis, *Summer Wine and Other Stories* (London, 2006), p. ix.
132 Roy Clarke, *Gala Week* (London, 1986), p. 5.
133 Tim Dunn, *Model Villages* (Stroud, 2017), p. 35; David Matless, Brian Short and David Gilbert, 'Emblematic Landscapes of the British Modern', in *Geographies of British Modernity*, ed. David Gilbert, David Matless and Brian Short (Oxford, 2003), pp. 250–57.
134 Shaw discusses model villages in Lily Ford, '"A Humbrol Art": A Film about George Shaw', available on the Yale Center for British Art website: www.britishart.yale.edu.
135 Colin Falck, 'Model Village', *Times Literary Supplement* (10 September 2004).
136 Will Self, *Scale* (London, 1995).
137 Liam Bailey, *Forever England* (Stockport, 2006).
138 Colman also appeared in the 2001 film *Hot Fuzz*, which featured a specially constructed model village.
139 Dunn, *Model Villages*, pp. 29–30, at p. 36.
140 Ibid., p. 55.
141 *Merrivale* (Norwich, 1972). A new guide was issued for the remodelled village: *Merrivale Model Village* (Great Yarmouth, 2005).
142 See the BBC report 'Banksy Stable at Model Village Could Fetch "Seven Figures"', at www.bbc.co.uk, 10 January 2022; a report on the auction sale is at www.andersonandgarland.com.
143 *Merrivale* (1972), no page numbers.

7 English Heritage

1 Andrew Flack, 'Lions Loose on a Gentleman's Lawn: Animality, Authenticity and Automobility in the Emergence of the English Safari Park', *Journal of Historical Geography*, LIV (2016), pp. 38–49; see also Adrian Tinniswood, *Noble Ambitions: The Fall and Rise of the English Country House after World War II* (London, 2021), Chapter Eighteen, on Longleat and other safari parks. Tinniswood notes that the fencing for Longleat's safari park perimeter came from government surplus left over from defending military bases in Kenya during the Mau Mau conflict, p. 315.

References

2 David Nobbs, *The Fall and Rise of Reginald Perrin* (Harmondsworth, 1976), pp. 28–35.
3 John Walton and Jason Wood, eds, *The Making of a Cultural Landscape: The English Lake District as Tourist Destination, 1750–2010* (London, 2013).
4 On the 1994 Act see Keith Halfacree, 'Trespassing against the Rural Idyll: The Criminal Justice and Public Order Act 1994 and Access to the Countryside', in *Rights of Way*, ed. Charles Watkins (London, 1996), pp. 179–93.
5 Peter Mandler, *The Fall and Rise of the Stately Home* (New Haven, CT, 1997); Tinniswood, *Noble Ambitions*.
6 Sean Nixon, 'Trouble at the National Trust: Post-War Recreation, the Benson Report and the Rebuilding of a Conservation Organization in the 1960s', *Twentieth Century British History*, XXVI (2015), pp. 529–50.
7 Robin Fedden, *The Continuing Purpose* (London, 1968), p. 119.
8 Mandler, *Fall and Rise of the Stately Home*, p. 382.
9 Ibid., p. 381.
10 Mark Broughton, 'The Figure (and Disfigurement) in the Landscape: *The Go-Between*'s Picturesque', in *British Rural Landscapes on Film*, ed. Paul Newland (Manchester, 2016), pp. 86–102, at p. 87. Losey's first estate film, *The Gypsy and the Gentleman* (1958), also used location filming.
11 L. P. Hartley, *The Go-Between* (Harmondsworth, 1971), p. 7; Penguin had published the book from 1958; the 1971 reissue included a film still of Julie Christie on the cover.
12 Mandler, *Fall and Rise of the Stately Home*, p. 401.
13 Patrick Cormack, *Heritage in Danger* (London, 1976). Cormack also edited *Right Turn* (London, 1978), featuring essays by people who had moved to the political right: 'Eight Men Who Changed Their Minds'.
14 John Cornforth, quoted by Marcus Binney in Roy Strong, Marcus Binney and John Harris, *The Destruction of the Country House* (London, 1975), p. 186.
15 Strong, Binney and Harris, *The Destruction of the Country House*, p. 22.
16 Ibid., p. 187.
17 Ibid., p. 163.
18 Ibid., p. 100.
19 Ibid., p. 7.
20 Ibid., p. 9.
21 Ibid., p. 10.
22 Marcus Binney and Peter Burman, *Change and Decay: The Future of Our Churches* (London, 1977).
23 Howard Glennerster, 'Why Was a Wealth Tax for the UK Abandoned? Lessons for the Policy Process and Tackling Wealth Inequality', *Journal of Social Policy*, XLI (2012), pp. 233–49.
24 Mandler, *Fall and Rise of the Stately Home*, p. 407.
25 Cormack, *Heritage in Danger*, pp. 15, 64.
26 Ibid., pp. 10–11.
27 Ibid., p. 14.
28 Ibid., p. 163.

29 Glennerster, 'Wealth Tax'.
30 Select Committee on a Wealth Tax, *Session 1974–75*, vol. IV, *Appendices to Minutes of Evidence* (London, 1974), pp. 1451–56.
31 Select Committee on a Wealth Tax, *Appendices to Minutes of Evidence*, pp. 1448–50.
32 Cormack, *Heritage in Danger*, p. 79.
33 Ibid., p. 59.
34 Ibid., p. 75.
35 Mandler, *Fall and Rise of the Stately Home*, p. 411.
36 Patrick Wright, *On Living in an Old Country* (London, 1985), p. 45.
37 Patrick Wright, *A Journey through Ruins* (London, 1991), p. 90.
38 Wright, *On Living in an Old Country*, pp. 38–42.
39 John Martin Robinson, *The Latest Country Houses* (London, 1984), p. 6.
40 Ibid., p. 170.
41 Mandler, *Fall and Rise of the Stately Home*, p. 360; Robinson, *Latest Country Houses*, p. 6.
42 Mandler, *Fall and Rise of the Stately Home*, p. 415.
43 Henry Green, *Concluding* (Harmondsworth, 1964), p. 113.
44 Ibid., p. 169.
45 Ibid., p. 204.
46 Ibid., p. 62.
47 Lucian Randall and Chris Welch, *Ginger Geezer: The Life of Vivian Stanshall* (London, 2001).
48 A film version of *Sir Henry at Rawlinson End* was produced in 1980 by Charisma Films (the LP had appeared on Charisma Records), with Trevor Howard playing Sir Henry and Stanshall as the narrator and Hubert, made in black-and-white at Knebworth House. Sir Henry in minstrel blackface on a unicycle walks a line, as with other comic surrealism of the time such as Monty Python or Spike Milligan, between a critique of stereotypes (in a film where every character is a stereotype) and their deployment for easy laughs.
49 Vivian Stanshall and Ki Longfellow-Stanshall, *Stinkfoot: An English Comic Opera* (Rotterdam, 2003).
50 Colin Amery and Dan Cruickshank, *The Rape of Britain* (London, 1975); the book was praised by Patrick Cormack in Chapter Five of *Heritage in Danger*, on 'Urban Dignity and Decay'.
51 Amery and Cruickshank, *Rape of Britain*, p. 10.
52 Ibid., p. 13.
53 Ibid., p. 187.
54 David Matless, *Landscape and Englishness* (London, 1998; rev. edn 2016).
55 Amery and Cruickshank, *Rape of Britain*, pp. 10–11.
56 Ibid., p. 24.
57 Ibid., p. 56.
58 Ibid., pp. 86, 96.
59 Ibid., pp. 156–8.
60 Ibid., p. 189.
61 Ibid., p. 188.
62 Ibid., p. 7.
63 John Betjeman, 'Inexpensive Progress', in *Collected Poems*, pp. 354–6.

64 Mark Tewdr-Jones, '"Oh, the Planners Did Their Best": The Planning Films of John Betjeman', *Planning Perspectives*, XX (2005), pp. 389–411; Mark Tewdr-Jones, *Urban Reflections: Narratives of Place, Planning and Change* (London, 2011), Chapter Seven; Bevis Hillier, *Betjeman: The Bonus of Laughter* (London, 2004), pp. 183–203.
65 On the Kinks and the Village Green LP, and Ray Davies's England, see Andy Miller, *The Kinks Are the Village Green Preservation Society* (London, 2003); Mark Doyle, *The Kinks* (London, 2020); Keith Gildart, 'From "Dead End Streets" to "Shangri Las": Negotiating Social Class and Post-War Politics with Ray Davies and the Kinks', *Contemporary British History*, XXVI (2012), pp. 273–98.
66 On the nature state see Matthew Kelly, 'Conventional Thinking and the Fragile Birth of the Nature State in Post-War Britain', in *The Nature State: Rethinking the History of Conservation*, ed. W. Hardenberg, M. Kelly, C. Leal and E. Waklid (London, 2017), pp. 114–34.
67 Section 1 of the 1967 Civic Amenities Act, quoted in John Delafons, *Politics and Preservation: A Policy History of the Built Heritage, 1882–1996* (London, 1997), p. 96.
68 Ibid., p. 101.
69 Otto Saumarez Smith, 'Central Government and Town-Centre Redevelopment in Britain, 1959–1966', *Historical Journal*, LVIII (2015), pp. 217–44, at p. 241; Otto Saumarez Smith, *Boom Cities: Architect-Planners and the Politics of Radical Urban Renewal in 1960s Britain* (Oxford, 2019).
70 Otto Saumarez Smith, 'The Inner City Crisis and the End of Urban Modernism in 1970s Britain', *Twentieth Century British History*, XXVII (2016), pp. 578–98, at p. 584.
71 Department of the Environment, *What is Our Heritage? United Kingdom Achievements for European Architectural Heritage Year 1975* (London, 1975), pp. v–vi.
72 Ibid., p. xi.
73 Ibid., p. 114.
74 Ibid., p. 119.
75 Ibid., p. vi.
76 Ibid., pp. xii, 102.
77 Ibid., p. 102.
78 Ray Taylor, Margaret Cox and Ian Dickins, eds, *Britain's Planning Heritage* (London, 1975), p. ix.
79 Ibid., at pp. 9, 30, 77, 92, 100, 136, 162, 121; the West Burton power station is discussed further in Chapter Eight below.
80 Simon Gunn, 'The Rise and Fall of British Urban Modernism', *Journal of British Studies*, XLIX (2010), pp. 849–69, at p. 860.
81 James Stevens Curl, 'Review of John Gold, *The Practice of Modernism*', *Journal of Urban Design*, XIV (2009), pp. 399–402; James Stevens Curl, *The Erosion of Oxford* (Oxford, 1977); John Gold, *The Practice of Modernism: Modern Architects and Urban Transformation, 1954–1972* (Abingdon, 2007); on the complexities of urban modernism see also Alan Powers, *Britain: Modern Architectures in History* (London, 2006).

82 Saumarez Smith, 'Central Government and Town-Centre Redevelopment in Britain', pp. 220–21.
83 Ibid., p. 228.
84 Matless, *Landscape and Englishness*.
85 Guy Ortolano, 'Planning the Urban Future in 1960s Britain', *Historical Journal*, LIV (2011), pp. 477–507; Guy Ortolano, *Thatcher's Progress: From Social Democracy to Market Liberalism through an English New Town* (Cambridge, 2019), pp. 33–68.
86 Colin Buchanan, *Traffic in Towns: The Specially Shortened Edition of the Buchanan Report* (Harmondsworth, 1964), p. 243.
87 Colin Buchanan, *Mixed Blessing: The Motor in Britain* (London, 1958).
88 Simon Gunn, 'The Buchanan Report, Environment and the Problem of Traffic in 1960s Britain', *Twentieth Century British History*, XXII (2011), pp. 521–42, at p. 536.
89 Saumarez Smith, *Boom Cities*, p. 105.
90 Jane Jacobs, *The Death and Life of Great American Cities* (New York, 1961); Marshall Berman, *All That Is Solid Melts into Air* (New York, 1982).
91 Stephen Ward, 'Colin Buchanan's American Journey', *Town Planning Review*, LXXXVIII (2017), pp. 201–31.
92 Ortolano, 'Planning the Urban Future', p. 504; Ortolano, *Thatcher's Progress*.
93 Gold, *The Practice of Modernism*, pp. 276–80.
94 Gunn, 'The Rise and Fall of British Urban Modernism', p. 864.
95 Amery and Cruickshank, *The Rape of Britain*, p. 120.
96 Dick Taverne, *The Future of the Left: Lincoln and After* (London, 1974), p. 108.
97 Ibid., p. 157.
98 Amery and Cruickshank, *The Rape of Britain*, p. 188.
99 Raphael Samuel, *Theatres of Memory* (London, 1994), p. 292.
100 Sarah Mass, 'Commercial Heritage as Democratic Action: Historicizing the "Save the Market" Campaigns in Bradford and Chesterfield, 1969–76', *Twentieth Century British History*, XXIX (2018), pp. 459–84, at p. 463.
101 Ibid., pp. 460–61.
102 Ibid., p. 476; Amery and Cruickshank, *The Rape of Britain*, p. 58, notes the case, with the plan then still proposed.
103 Mass, 'Commercial Heritage as Democratic Action', p. 480.
104 Gunn, 'The Buchanan Report'.
105 Nicholas Taylor, *The Village in the City* (London, 1973), p. 19; Gold, *The Practice of Modernism*, pp. 274–6.
106 Taylor, *The Village in the City*, p. 64.
107 Ibid., p. 100.
108 Ibid., pp. 149, 215.
109 Ibid., p. 221.
110 Robert Goodman, *After the Planners* (Harmondsworth, 1972), p. 40.
111 Ibid., p. 11.
112 Ibid., pp. 217, 228, 238.
113 Ibid., p. 50.
114 Jonathan Raban, *Coasting* (London, 1986), pp. 194–5.
115 Robert Hewison, *The Heritage Industry* (London, 1987), p. 31. For an overview of longer-term heritage debates see Ben Cowell, *The Heritage Obsession: The Battle for England's Past* (Stroud, 2008).

References

116 Wright, *A Journey through Ruins*, Chapter Eighteen, 'Refounding the City with Prince Charles'.
117 The speech is reprinted in Charles Jencks, *The Prince, the Architects and New Wave Monarchy* (London, 1988), p. 43.
118 Maxwell Hutchinson, *The Prince of Wales: Right or Wrong? An Architect Replies* (London, 1989), p. 190.
119 HRH The Prince of Wales, *A Vision of Britain: A Personal View of Architecture* (London, 1989), back cover, also p. 153.
120 Ibid., p. 8.
121 Ibid., p. 9.
122 Ibid., p. 13.
123 Christopher Booker, *The Neophiliacs* (London, 1992).
124 Prince of Wales, *A Vision of Britain*, p. 53.
125 Ibid., pp. 138–9; Wright, *Journey through Ruins*, pp. 374–91; Patrick Wright, 'Re-Enchanting the Nation: Prince Charles and Architecture', *Modern Painters*, II/3 (1989), pp. 26–35.
126 Nikolaus Pevsner, *The Englishness of English Art* (London, 1956), p. 186; Matless, *Landscape and Englishness*; Jane M. Jacobs, *Edge of Empire: Postcolonialism and the City* (London, 1996), Chapter Three.
127 Prince of Wales, *A Vision of Britain*, p. 69.
128 The speech is reprinted in Jencks, *The Prince*, pp. 47–9.
129 Prince of Wales, *A Vision of Britain*, p. 21.
130 Ibid., p. 41.
131 Hewison, *Heritage Industry*, pp. 144, 139.
132 Ibid., p. 9.
133 Ibid., pp. 141, 9.
134 Ibid., pp. 141–2.
135 Ibid., p. 79.
136 Ibid., pp. 83–4.
137 Ibid., p. 144.
138 Robert Hewison, *John Ruskin: The Argument of the Eye* (London, 1976).
139 Cyril Joad, *A Charter for Ramblers* (London, 1934); the cartoon is reproduced in Matless, *Landscape and Englishness*, p. 78.
140 Hewison, *Heritage Industry*, p. 146.
141 Marcus Binney and Max Hanna, *Preservation Pays* (London, 1978), pp. 127–30.
142 Marcus Binney, *Our Vanishing Heritage* (London, 1984).
143 Marcus Binney and Kit Martin, *The Country House: To Be or Not To Be* (London, 1982), p. 9.
144 Ibid., p. 5.
145 Ibid., p. 9.
146 Stephen Daniels and David Matless, 'The New Nostalgia', *New Statesman and Society* (19 May 1989), pp. 40–41.
147 David Pearce, *Conservation Today* (London, 1989), p. 232.
148 Ibid., p. 228.
149 Ibid., p. 236; Billingsgate is discussed by Pearce on pp. 52–4.
150 David St John Thomas, *The Country Railway* (Newton Abbot, 1976), pp. 93–4.
151 Jeoffry Spence, *Surviving Steam Railways* (London, 1979), no page numbers.

152 Ibid.
153 Ibid. On steam railway culture see Richard Sykes, Alastair Austin, Mark Fuller, Taki Kinoshita and Andrew Shrimpton, 'Steam Attraction: Railways in Britain's National Heritage', *Journal of Transport History*, XVIII (1997), pp. 156–75.
154 Samuel, *Theatres of Memory*, p. 139.
155 On History Workshop see Raphael Samuel, 'History Workshop, 1966–80', in *People's History and Socialist Theory*, ed. Raphael Samuel (London, 1981), pp. 410–17; on Samuel see Kynan Gentry, '"The Pathos of Conservation": Raphael Samuel and the Politics of Heritage', *International Journal of Heritage Studies*, XXI (2015), pp. 561–76.
156 Samuel, *Theatres of Memory*, pp. 8, 5.
157 Ibid., p. 160.
158 Ibid., p. 25.
159 Ibid., p. 281.
160 Wright, *Journey through Ruins*, p. 373.
161 Samuel, *Theatres of Memory*, pp. 162, 303, 288.
162 Ibid., p. 292.
163 Ibid., p. 139.
164 *National Trust Magazine* (Spring 2019). See the related National Trust guidebook by Jenna Ashton, *People's Landscapes: Unearthing Passion and Protest* (Swindon, 2019), with a foreword by film director Mike Leigh.
165 Samuel, *Theatres of Memory*, p. 260; Patrick Wright and Tim Putnam, 'Sneering at the Theme Parks', *Block*, XV (1989), pp. 48–55, at p. 50.
166 Samuel, *Theatres of Memory*, p. 263; Paul Reas and Stuart Cosgrove, *Flogging a Dead Horse: Heritage Culture and Its Role in Post-Industrial Britain* (Manchester, 1993).
167 Raphael Samuel, 'People's History', in *People's History and Socialist Theory*, ed. Samuel, pp. xv–xxxix, at p. xxxi.
168 Pearce, *Conservation Today*, p. 78; Binney, *Our Vanishing Heritage*.
169 Hewison, *Heritage Industry*, p. 104.
170 Ibid., p. 89.
171 Samuel, *Theatres of Memory*, p. 157; Samuel's reference is to Walter Pickles, *Our Grimy Heritage* (Fontwell, 1971).
172 Michael Rix, 'Industrial Archaeology', *Amateur Historian*, II (1955), pp. 225–9.
173 Michael Rix, *Industrial Archaeology* (London, 1967), pp. 17–18.
174 Neil Cossons, 'Perspective', in *Perspectives on Industrial Archaeology*, ed. Neil Cossons (London, 2000), pp. 9–17, at p. 12; see also R. A. Buchanan, 'The Origins of Industrial Archaeology', in *Perspectives on Industrial Archaeology*, ed. Cossons, pp. 18–38; Marilyn Palmer, 'Forty Years of *Industrial Archaeology Review*: A Personal View', *Industrial Archaeology Review*, XL (2018), pp. 58–64.
175 Neil Cossons and Kenneth Hudson, *Industrial Archaeologists' Guide, 1969–70* (Newton Abbot, 1969), pp. 63–78.
176 Ibid., p. 24. In 2000 Barrie Trinder noted that the coal drop had yet to be re-erected at the Beamish Museum, still lying at the edge of a field; Barrie Trinder, 'Industrial Archaeology in the Twentieth-Century Context', in *Perspectives on Industrial Archaeology*, ed. Cossons, pp. 39–56.
177 Nikolaus Pevsner, *Shropshire* (Harmondsworth, 1958), pp. 155–6.

References

178 Neil Cossons and Harry Sowden, *Ironbridge: Landscape of Industry* (London, 1977), p. 84.
179 Ibid., p. 19.
180 Laura Carter, 'Rethinking Folk Culture in Twentieth-Century Britain', *Twentieth Century British History*, XXVIII (2017), pp. 543–69, at p. 545.
181 R. A. Buchanan, *Industrial Archaeology in Britain* (Harmondsworth, 1972), pp. 50, 63.
182 Ibid., p. 22.
183 Ibid., p. 19.
184 Ibid., pp. 20, 51.
185 Ibid., pp. 389–90; the Ironbridge/Stonehenge phrase is from Rix, *Industrial Archaeology*, p. 12.
186 David Smith, 'History of Factory in the East Midlands', *Survey*, XII/1 (1961), pp. 15–23.
187 David Smith, 'Milford Mills', *East Midland Geographer*, XXI (1964), p. 289. Smith's article was reproduced in the final retrospective issue of *East Midland Geographer*, XX/2 (1999), p. 48.
188 David Smith, *Industrial Archaeology of the East Midlands* (Dawlish, 1965), p. 15.
189 Ibid., p. 231; as noted in Chapter One the building has since been converted into flats.
190 Ibid., p. 191; quoted in Rix, *Industrial Archaeology*, p. 20.
191 Hadfield left the management of David & Charles in 1964, though he continued to work, writing and editing canal books for the firm. On Hadfield, including his work with Thomas, see Joseph Boughey, *Charles Hadfield: Canal Man and More* (Stroud, 1998). Hadfield was one of the founders of the Railway and Canal Historical Society in 1954; St John Thomas was a member from 1956.
192 Smith, *Industrial Archaeology of the East Midlands*, p. 200; the image is also reproduced in K. Swindell, 'The Cromford Cotton Mills', *East Midland Geographer*, XXIV (1964), pp. 461–9, an article itself reproduced in the final retrospective issue of *East Midland Geographer*, XX/2 (1999), pp. 60–69.
193 Smith, *Industrial Archaeology of the East Midlands*, p. 241.
194 Trinder, 'Industrial Archaeology in the Twentieth-Century Context', pp. 46–7.
195 Rix, *Industrial Archaeology*, pp. 20–21.
196 Neil Cossons, *The BP Book of Industrial Archaeology* (Newton Abbot, 1975), p. 12.
197 Susanne Seymour, Lowri Jones and Julia Feuer-Cotter, 'The Global Connections of Cotton in the Derwent Valley Mills in the Later Eighteenth and Early Nineteenth Centuries', in *The Industrial Revolution: Cromford, the Derwent Valley and the Wider World*, ed. Chris Wrigley (Cromford, 2015), pp. 150–70. Further details of the Global Cotton Connections project are given at the project website, www.globalcottonconnections.wordpress.com.
198 Jan Zalasiewicz, Colin Waters et al., 'The Working Group on the Anthropocene: Summary of Evidence and Interim Recommendations', *Anthropocene*, XIX (2017), pp. 55–60; David Matless, 'The Anthroposcenic',

Transactions of the Institute of British Geographers, XLII (2017), pp. 363–76; the connection of England and the Anthropocene will be considered further in the companion volume to this book, *England's Green*.

8 The English Modern

1 Details of the Jodrell Bank inscription are given on the UNESCO website at www.whc.unesco.org.
2 Sylvia Crowe, *The Landscape of Power* (London, 1958), p. 49.
3 Nikolaus Pevsner and Edward Hubbard, *Cheshire* (Harmondsworth, 1971), p. 249.
4 Marcus Binney, *Our Vanishing Heritage* (London, 1984), p. 199.
5 David Pearce, *Conservation Today* (London, 1989), p. 112.
6 Bridget Cherry, 'The "Pevsner 50": Nikolaus Pevsner and the Listing of Modern Buildings', *Transactions of the Ancient Monuments Society*, XLVI (2002), pp. 97–110.
7 Aidan While, 'The State and the Controversial Demands of Cultural Built Heritage: Modernism, Dirty Concrete, and Postwar Listing in England', *Environment and Planning D: Planning and Design*, XXXIV (2007), pp. 645–63.
8 Ruth Craggs, Hilary Geoghegan and Hannah Neate, 'Architectural Enthusiasm: Visiting Buildings with the Twentieth Century Society', *Environment and Planning D: Society and Space*, XXXI (2013), pp. 879–96.
9 Susannah Charlton and Elain Harwood, *100 Buildings, 100 Years* (London, 2014), p. 7.
10 Christine Hui Lan Manley, *Frederick Gibberd* (London, 2017).
11 Nigel Whiteley, 'Modern Architecture, Heritage and Englishness', *Architectural History*, XXXVIII (1995), pp. 220–37.
12 Royal Commission on the Historical Monuments of England and English Heritage, *A Change of Heart: English Architecture since the War; A Policy for Protection* (London, 1992).
13 Ibid., pp. 3–4.
14 On the history of this relationship see William Whyte, 'The Englishness of English Architecture: Modernism and the Making of a National International Style, 1927–1957', *Journal of British Studies*, XLVIII (2009), pp. 441–65.
15 Whiteley, 'Modern Architecture', p. 235.
16 Royal Commission, *A Change of Heart*, p. 11.
17 Elain Harwood, *England: A Guide to Post-War Listed Buildings* (London, 2003).
18 Ray Taylor, Margaret Cox and Ian Dickins, eds, *Britain's Planning Heritage* (London, 1975); Trevor Dannatt, *Modern Architecture in Britain* (London, 1959).
19 Harwood, *England*, p. 6.
20 John Pendlebury and Aidan While, 'Post-War Social Housing: Conservation and Regeneration', in *Modern Futures*, ed. Hannah Neate and Ruth Craggs (Axminster, 2016), pp. 127–36, at p. 135; Owen Hatherley, *The Ministry of Nostalgia* (London, 2016).
21 Royal Commission, *A Change of Heart*, p. 6; Harwood, *England*, p. 254.

22 Nikolaus Pevsner, *The Englishness of English Art* (Harmondsworth, 1964), p. 189. The first edition of *The Englishness of English Art* (London, 1956) did not mention Stevenage, but focused on the environs of St Paul's in London, the London County Council Roehampton estate and a model of Harlow new town, as examples of 'picturesque principles applied to urban conditions'. All examples were retained in 1964, but by then the Harlow model was replaced by a photograph of the completed Harlow market square.
23 Ibid., p. 192.
24 Aidan While, 'Modernism vs Urban Renaissance: Negotiating Post-War Heritage in English City Centres', *Urban Studies*, XLIII (2006), pp. 2399–419.
25 Aidan While and Malcolm Tait, 'Exeter and the Question of Thomas Sharp's Physical Legacy', *Planning Perspectives*, XXIV (2009), pp. 77–97; David Matless, 'Ages of English Design: Preservation, Modernism and Tales of Their History, 1926–1939', *Journal of Design History*, III (1990), pp. 203–12.
26 While, 'Modernism vs Urban Renaissance', p. 2416.
27 Harwood, *England*, p. 176.
28 Andrew Saint, *Towards a Social Architecture: The Role of School-Building in Post-War England* (London, 1987), pp. ix, 236.
29 Ibid., p. 238.
30 Ibid., p. 249; Saint's book also covers the development of CLASP building in Nottinghamshire (Consortium of Local Authorities' Special Programme, 1957, addressing subsidence issues) and the higher educational enactment of Hertfordshire principles by Johnson-Marshall at the University of York.
31 Ibid., p. 226.
32 Ibid., pp. 138–47.
33 Ibid., p. ix.
34 Ibid., pp. x, 235.
35 Martin Parr, *Boring Postcards* (London, 1999); follow-up volumes covered the USA and Germany. See also Joe Moran, *Reading the Everyday* (Abingdon, 2005), pp. 124–8.
36 Some of the humbler views in and of obscurer places still linger; thus black-and-white views of Silloth, Cumbria, were still available for purchase in newsagents there as originals, ten years after Parr's commemorative volume.
37 Hannah Neate and Ruth Craggs, eds, *Modern Futures* (Axminster, 2016); see also Waites, *Middlefield*.
38 Michael Gallagher, 'Architecture about Us', in *Modern Futures*, ed. Neate and Craggs, pp. 113–18, at p. 114.
39 Luke Bennett, 'Bunkerology: A Case Study in the Theory and Practice of Urban Exploration', *Environment and Planning D: Society and Space*, XXIX (2011), pp. 421–34.
40 Hatherley, *Ministry of Nostalgia*, pp. 98–113.
41 Ruth Craggs and Hannah Neate, 'Post-Colonial Careering and Urban Policy Mobility: Between Britain and Nigeria, 1945–1990', *Transactions of the Institute of British Geographers*, XLII (2017), pp. 44–57.

42 Pendlebury and While, 'Post-War Social Housing', p. 135.
43 Hatherley, *Ministry of Nostalgia*, pp. 14–22; Owen Hatherley, *Militant Modernism* (London, 2009); Owen Hatherley, *A Guide to the New Ruins of Great Britain* (London, 2010).
44 Owen Hatherley, *A New Kind of Bleak: Journeys through Urban Britain* (London, 2012), pp. 178, 188.
45 Ibid., pp. xxxiv–xxxv.
46 Hatherley, *Ministry of Nostalgia*, p. 11.
47 Lee was an Irish singer who had worked in London from the early 1950s and was known for singing the theme tunes of the children's programmes *White Horses* and *Rupert the Bear*. I am grateful to Hannah Neate for alerting me to Lee's 'The Town I Live In'.
48 XTC and Neville Farmer, *Song Stories*.
49 Phil Hubbard, 'Darren Hayman and the Secondary Modern's *Pram Town*', *Cultural Geographies*, XVII (2010), pp. 407–14.
50 Thomas Sharp, 'The English Village', in Ministry of Housing and Local Government, *Design in Town and Village* (London, 1953), pp. 1–19, image at p. 15. July Skies founder Antony Harding informed me that *Landscape and Englishness* had 'assisted with the inspiration' for *The Weather Clock*.
51 Nikolaus Pevsner, *North-East Norfolk and Norwich* (Harmondsworth, 1962), p. 19.
52 Timothy Mowl, *Stylistic Cold Wars: Betjeman versus Pevsner* (London, 2000), p. 115.
53 Ibid., p. 117.
54 Colin MacInnes, 'The Englishness of Dr Pevsner', in *England, Half English* (London, [1961] 1986), pp. 119–29, at p. 127; David Matless, 'Topographic Culture: Nikolaus Pevsner and the Buildings of England', *History Workshop Journal*, LIV (2002), pp. 73–99.
55 Susie Harries, *Nikolaus Pevsner: The Life* (London, 2011), p. 97.
56 Simon Bradley and Bridget Cherry, eds, *The Buildings of England: A Celebration* (London, 2001); Harries, *Nikolaus Pevsner*.
57 Nikolaus Pevsner, *The Leaves of Southwell* (Harmondsworth, 1945), p. 67; Matless, 'Topographic Culture', pp. 91–4.
58 David Matless, 'Votive Leaves', *Uniformagazine*, VII (2016), pp. 3–5.
59 Nikolaus Pevsner, *Northamptonshire* (Harmondsworth, 1961), pp. 65–6.
60 Nikolaus Pevsner and Bridget Cherry, *Northamptonshire* (Harmondsworth, 1973).
61 Nikolaus Pevsner, *Staffordshire* (Harmondsworth, 1974), p. 17.
62 Peter Merriman, *Driving Spaces: A Cultural–Historical Geography of England's M1 Motorway* (Oxford, 2007).
63 The first three stamps in 'British Bridges' showed 'Tarr Steps, Prehistoric', the 1733 Aberfeldy Bridge and the 1826 Menai Bridge.
64 Jonathan Glancey, 'A Bridge Too Far?', *Independent Magazine* (18 July 1992), pp. 24–31, at p. 30; Peter Merriman, 'Motorways, Modern Heritage and the British Landscape', in *The Good, the Bad and the Unbuilt: Handling the Heritage of the Recent Past*, ed. S. May, H. Orange and S. Penrose (Oxford, 2012), pp. 103–11.
65 Helen Jones, 'Buildings Designed to Advertise Fuel', *British Archaeology*, XXXVIII (1998), pp. 6–7.

References

66 Harry Peach and Noel Carrington, eds, *The Face of the Land* (London, 1930), p. 80; the image used is reproduced in Matless, *Landscape and Englishness*, p. 89.
67 John Newman, *West Kent and the Weald* (Harmondsworth, 1969), p. 144.
68 The listing criteria are given on the Historic England website at www.historicengland.org.uk.
69 Val Williams, *Martin Parr* (London, 2002), p. 347.
70 Reyner Banham, 'Big Brum Artwork', *New Society* (13 July 1972), pp. 4–5.
71 Parr, *Boring Postcards*.
72 J. G. Ballard, 'The Car, the Future', in *A User's Guide to the Millenium* (London, 1996), pp. 262–7, at p. 262.
73 Parr, *Boring Postcards*; on the Forton listing see the Historic England website: www.historicengland.org.uk.
74 Reyner Banham, 'Disservice Areas', *New Society* (23 May 1968), pp. 762–3, at p. 763.
75 The site is now known as Rivington, after rebuilding.
76 David Lawrence, *Always a Welcome: The Glove Compartment History of the Motorway Service Area* (Twickenham, 1999), p. 7.
77 Merriman, *Driving Spaces*; on road culture in the motorway age see also Joe Moran, *On Roads: A Hidden History* (London, 2009).
78 Iain Sinclair, *London Orbital* (London, 2002), p. 16.
79 For a different encounter with lands along the M25 motorway see naturalist Helen Macdonald's 2020 BBC documentary *The Hidden Wilds of the Motorway*, detailed at www.bbc.co.uk.
80 Martin Caiger-Smith, ed., *Julian Opie* (London, 1993), pp. 106–9.
81 Ibid., pp. 116–19.
82 The work is shown on Julian Opie's website at www.julianopie.com. The site also shows the 2002 works *I Dreamt I Was Driving My Car (Night)* and *I Dreamt I Was Driving My Car (Village)*.
83 Parr, *Boring Postcards*.
84 On anti-road building campaigns see Moran, *On Roads*, Chapter Seven; Derek Wall, *Earth First! and the Anti-Roads Movement* (Abingdon, 1999); George McKay, *Senseless Acts of Beauty: Cultures of Resistance since the Sixties* (London, 1996), Chapter Five.
85 John Tyme, *Motorways versus Democracy* (London, 1978), p. 15.
86 Ibid., p. 1.
87 Ibid., p. x.
88 Ibid., p. 36. On Tyme's tactics see Wall, *Earth First!*, pp. 30–32. Wall notes Tom Sharpe's 1975 comic novel *Blott on the Landscape* (London, 1975), adapted for television in 1985, as in part a satire on Tyme.
89 Tyme, *Motorways*, p. 105.
90 Ibid., p. 19.
91 Terry Coleman, 'John Tyme Inquiry', *New Society* (2 December 1976), pp. 453–4.
92 Moran, *On Roads*, p. 198.
93 Wall, *Earth First!*.
94 Moran, *On Roads*, pp. 214–18, 236–7.
95 Toby Butler and Graeme Miller, 'Linked: A Landmark in Sound, a Public Walk of Art', *Cultural Geographies*, XII (2005), pp. 77–88, at pp. 86–7.

96 Barbara Bryant, *Twyford Down: Roads, Campaigning and Environmental Law* (London, 1996).
97 McKay, *Senseless Acts*, p. 138; paganism and English landscape will be discussed further in the companion volume to this book, *England's Green*.
98 Ibid., p. 136.
99 Merrick, *Battle for the Trees* (Leeds, 1996), p. 5. The site map is reproduced here in keeping with Merrick's publisher godhaven ink's statement: 'all godhaven ink publications are anti-copyright. Help yourself to any or all of it', p. 2.
100 Ibid., pp. 43–4.
101 Julian Cope, *Interpreter*, sleeve notes.
102 Reproduced in Merrick, *Battle for the Trees*, p. 3.
103 Ibid., p. 114.
104 Ballard, 'The Car, the Future', p. 266; Moran, *On Roads*, pp. 253–4.
105 Moran, *On Roads*, p. 36.
106 Ibid., pp. 239–40; see also Tim Cole, *About Britain* (London, 2021), pp. 39–45.
107 Pevsner and Williamson, *Nottinghamshire*, p. 374. West Burton is the focus of recent work by Ian Waites, as part of a wider research project on 'Decommissioning the Twentieth Century', noted at https://landscapedecisions.org.
108 The image appears on Roger Palmer's website at www.rogerpalmer.info. It is also reproduced with insightful commentary in Nicholas Alfrey, *Trentside* (Nottingham, 2001), p. 74.
109 Crowe, *Landscape of Power*, p. 53.
110 Ibid., p. 90.
111 Cossons and Sowden, *Ironbridge*, p. 57.
112 Simon Roberts, *We English* (London, 2008), 'Commentary' section.

9 Concluding

1 Henry Green, *Concluding* (Harmondsworth, [1948] 1964), p. 5.

SELECT BIBLIOGRAPHY

Agyeman, Julian, 'Black People in a White Landscape: Social and Environmental Justice', *Built Environment*, XVI (1990) pp. 232–6
——, and Rachel Spooner, 'Ethnicity and the Rural Environment', in *Contested Countryside Cultures*, ed. Paul Cloke and Jo Little (London, 1997), pp. 197–217
Allison, Lincoln, *Condition of England: Essays and Impressions* (London, 1981)
Amery, Colin, and Dan Cruickshank, *The Rape of Britain* (London, 1975)
Aqui, Lindsay, Michael Kenny and Nick Pearce, '"The Empire of England": Enoch Powell, Sovereignty and the Constitution of the Nation', *Twentieth Century British History*, XXXII (2021), pp. 238–60
Astley, Virginia, *The English River: A Journey down the Thames in Poems and Photographs* (Hexham, 2018)
Aughey, Arthur, *The Politics of Englishness* (Manchester, 2007)
——, '"England Is the Country and the Country Is England": But What of the Politics?', in *Literature of an Independent England*, ed. Claire Westall and Michael Gardiner (Basingstoke, 2013), pp. 46–59
Bailey, Liam, *Forever England* (Stockport, 2006)
Ballard, J. G., 'The Car, the Future', in *A User's Guide to the Millenium* (London, 1996), pp. 262–7
Banham, Reyner, Paul Barker, Peter Hall and Cedric Price, 'Non-Plan: An Experiment in Freedom', *New Society*, XIII (20 March 1969), pp. 435–43
Barker, Paul, *The Freedoms of Suburbia* (London, 2009)
Barnett, Anthony, *Iron Britannia* (London, 1982)
Barrell, John, *The Idea of Landscape and the Sense of Place, 1730–1840: An Approach to the Poetry of John Clare* (Cambridge, 1972)
——, and John Bull, eds, *The Penguin Book of English Pastoral Verse* (Harmondsworth, 1974)
Beacham, Peter, and James Ravilious, *Down the Deep Lanes* (Oxford, 2000)
Beck, John, *Landscape as Weapon* (London, 2020)
Becker, Tobias, and Felix Fuhg, 'Writing Europe into British Cultural History: An Introduction', *Contemporary British History*, XXXV (2021), pp. 325–39
Bell, Julia, and Jackie Gay, eds, *England Calling* (London, 2001)

Belloc, Hilaire, 'On Inns', in *This and That and the Other* (New York, 1912), pp. 45–55
Beloff, Nora, *The General Says No: Britain's Exclusion from Europe* (Harmondsworth, 1963)
Berger, John, and Jean Mohr, *A Fortunate Man: The Story of a Country Doctor* (London, 1967)
Betjeman, John, *Collected Poems* (London, 1974)
—, 'Metro-Land', in *Coming Home: An Anthology of Prose* (London, 1997), pp. 444–65
Binney, Marcus, *Our Vanishing Heritage* (London, 1984)
—, and Max Hanna, *Preservation Pays* (London, 1978)
—, and Kit Martin, *The Country House: To Be or Not To Be* (London, 1982)
Blythe, Ronald, *Akenfield* (London, 1969)
Boston, Richard, *Beer and Skittles* (London, 1976)
Bracewell, Michael, *England Is Mine: Pop Life in Albion from Wilde to Goldie* (London, 1997)
Bradley, Simon, and Bridget Cherry, eds, *The Buildings of England: A Celebration* (London, 2001)
Bragg, Billy, *The Progressive Patriot* (London, 2006)
Bragg, Melvyn, *Speak for England* (London, 1976)
Bressey, Caroline, 'Cultural Archaeology and Historical Geographies of the Black Presence in Rural England', *Journal of Rural Studies*, XXV (2009), pp. 386–95
Broughton, Mark, 'The Figure (and Disfigurement) in the Landscape: *The Go-Between*'s Picturesque', in *British Rural Landscapes on Film*, ed. Paul Newland (Manchester, 2016), pp. 86–102
Brunskill, Ronald, *Traditional Buildings of Britain: An Introduction to Vernacular Architecture* (London, 1981)
Bryant, Barbara, *Twyford Down: Roads, Campaigning and Environmental Law* (London, 1996)
Bryson, Bill, ed., *Icons of England* (London, 2010)
Buchanan, Colin, *Traffic in Towns: The Specially Shortened Edition of the Buchanan Report* (Harmondsworth, 1964)
Buchanan, R. A., *Industrial Archaeology in Britain* (Harmondsworth, 1972)
Butler, Toby, and Graeme Miller, 'Linked: A Landmark in Sound, a Public Walk of Art', *Cultural Geographies*, XII (2005), pp. 77–88
Caiger-Smith, Martin, ed., *Julian Opie* (London, 1993)
Campaign to Protect Rural England, *Litter in Lockdown: A Study in Littering in the Time of Coronavirus* (London, 2020)
Carter, Laura, 'Rethinking Folk Culture in Twentieth-Century Britain', *Twentieth Century British History*, XXVIII (2017), pp. 543–69
Cherry, Bridget, 'The "Pevsner 50": Nikolaus Pevsner and the Listing of Modern Buildings', *Transactions of the Ancient Monuments Society*, XLVI (2002), pp. 97–110
Clifford, Sue, and Angela King, eds, *Local Distinctiveness: Place, Particularity and Identity* (London, 1993)
—, and —, eds, *From Place to PLACE: Maps and Parish Maps* (London, 1996)
—, and Angela King, *England in Particular* (London, 2006)
Cole, Tim, *About Britain* (London, 2021)

Colls, Robert, *Identity of England* (Oxford, 2002)
——, and Philip Dodd, *Englishness: Politics and Culture, 1880–1920* (London, [1986] 2014)
Conford, Philip, *The Development of the Organic Network: Linking People and Themes, 1945–95* (Edinburgh, 2011)
Cormack, Patrick, *Heritage in Danger* (London, 1976)
Cossons, Neil, *The BP Book of Industrial Archaeology* (Newton Abbot, 1975)
——, 'Perspective', in *Perspectives on Industrial Archaeology*, ed. Neil Cossons (London, 2000), pp. 9–17
——, and Kenneth Hudson, *Industrial Archaeologists' Guide, 1969–70* (Newton Abbot, 1969)
——, and Harry Sowden, *Ironbridge: Landscape of Industry* (London, 1977)
Cowell, Ben, *The Heritage Obsession: The Battle for England's Past* (Stroud, 2008)
Craggs, Ruth, Hilary Geoghegan and Hannah Neate, 'Architectural Enthusiasm: Visiting Buildings with the Twentieth Century Society', *Environment and Planning, D: Society and Space*, XXXI (2013), pp. 879–96
——, and Hannah Neate, 'Post-Colonial Careering and Urban Policy Mobility: Between Britain and Nigeria, 1945–1990', *Transactions of the Institute of British Geographers*, XLII (2017), pp. 44–57
Crouch, David, and David Matless, 'Refiguring Geography: Parish Maps of Common Ground', *Transactions of the Institute of British Geographers*, XXI (1996), pp. 236–55
Crowe, Sylvia, *The Landscape of Power* (London, 1958)
'Culture and the EU', *Times Literary Supplement* (3 June 2016), pp. 14–17
Daniels, Stephen, 'Marxism, Culture and the Duplicity of Landscape', in *New Models in Geography*, vol. II, ed. Richard Peet and Nigel Thrift (London, 1989), pp. 196–220
——, *Fields of Vision: Landscape Imagery and National Identity in England and the United States* (Cambridge, 1993)
——, and David Matless, 'The New Nostalgia', *New Statesman and Society* (19 May 1989), pp. 40–41
——, Patrick Keiller, Doreen Massey and Patrick Wright, 'To Dispel a Great Malady: *Robinson in Ruins*, the Future of Landscape and the Moving Image', *Tate Papers*, XVII (2012)
——, Ben Cowell and Lucy Veale, *Landscapes of the National Trust* (London, 2015)
Darley, Gillian, 'From Plotlands to New Towns', in *Radical Essex*, ed. Hayley Dixon and Joe Hill (Southend, 2018), pp. 101–21
——, *Excellent Essex* (London, 2019)
——, and David McKie, *Ian Nairn: Words in Place* (Nottingham, 2013)
Davie, Donald, *The Shires* (London, 1974)
Davies, William, 'Donald Davie and Englishness', *Review of English Studies*, LXX (2018), pp. 332–53
Delafons, John, *Politics and Preservation: A Policy History of the Built Heritage, 1882–1996* (London, 1997)
Department of the Environment, *What Is Our Heritage? United Kingdom Achievements for European Architectural Heritage Year 1975* (London, 1975)

Derounian, James Garo, *Another Country: Real Life beyond Rose Cottage* (London, 1993)
Devine-Wright, Patrick, Jos Smith and Susana Batel, '"Positive Parochialism", Local Belonging and Ecological Concerns: Revisiting Common Ground's Parish Maps Project', *Transactions of the Institute of British Geographers*, XLIV (2019), pp. 407–21
Dodd, Philip, *The Battle over Britain* (London, 1995)
Dodds, Klaus, 'Enframing the Falklands: Identity, Landscape, and the 1982 South Atlantic War', *Environment and Planning D: Society and Space*, XVI (1998), pp. 733–56
——, *Pink Ice: Britain and the South Atlantic Empire* (London, 2002)
Dorling, Danny, 'Dying Quietly: English Suburbs and the Stiff Upper Lip', *Political Quarterly*, XC (2019), pp. 32–43
——, and Sally Tomlinson, *Rule Britannia: Brexit and the End of Empire* (London, 2019)
Doyle, Mark, *The Kinks* (London, 2020)
Dresser, Madge, and Andrew Hann, eds, *Slavery and the British Country House* (London, 2013)
Dummett, Ann, *A Portrait of English Racism* (Harmondsworth, 1973)
Dunn, Tim, *Model Villages* (Stroud, 2017)
Dyson, Jeremy, Mark Gatiss, Steve Pemberton and Reece Shearsmith, *The League of Gentlemen: Scripts and That* (London, 2003)
Essex County Council, *A Design Guide for Residential Areas* (Chelmsford, 1973)
Finnegan, Ruth, *The Hidden Musicians: Music-Making in an English Town* (Cambridge, 1989)
Flack, Andrew, 'Lions Loose on a Gentleman's Lawn: Animality, Authenticity and Automobility in the Emergence of the English Safari Park', *Journal of Historical Geography*, LIV (2016), pp. 38–49
Foot, Paul, *The Rise of Enoch Powell* (Harmondsworth, 1969)
Ford, Robert, and Matthew Goodwin, *Revolt on the Right* (London, 2014)
Fowler, Corinne, *Green Unpleasant Land: Creative Responses to Rural England's Colonial Connections* (Leeds, 2020)
Francis, Matthew, '"A Crusade to Enfranchise the Many": Thatcherism and the "Property-Owning Democracy"', *Twentieth Century British History*, XXIII (2012), pp. 275–97
Fussell, Paul, *The Great War and Modern Memory* (Oxford, [1975] 2013)
Gardiner, Michael, 'Brexit and the Aesthetics of Anachronism', in Robert Eaglestone, *Brexit and Literature* (London, 2018), pp. 105–17
Gentry, Kynan, '"The Pathos of Conservation": Raphael Samuel and the Politics of Heritage, *International Journal of Heritage Studies*, XXI (2015), pp. 561–76
Gifford, Terry, *Pastoral* (London, 1999)
Gilbert, David, David Matless and Brian Short, eds, *Geographies of British Modernity* (Oxford, 2003)
Gilbert, David, and Rebecca Preston, '"Stop Being So English": Suburban Modernity and National Identity in the Twentieth Century', in *Geographies of British Modernity*, ed. David Gilbert, David Matless and Brian Short (Oxford, 2003), pp. 187–203

Gildart, Keith, 'From "Dead End Streets" to "Shangri Las": Negotiating Social Class and Post-War Politics with Ray Davies and the Kinks', *Contemporary British History*, XXVI (2012), pp. 273–98

Gilroy, Paul, 'The Peculiarities of the Black English', in *Small Acts* (London, 1993), pp. 49–62

—, *'There Ain't No Black in the Union Jack': The Cultural Politics of Race and Nation* (London, [1987] 2002)

—, *After Empire: Melancholia or Convivial Culture?* (London, 2004)

—, 'At the End of Black Boy Lane', in Ingrid Pollard, *Carbon Slowly Turning* (London, 2022), pp. 10–19

Glennerster, Howard, 'Why Was a Wealth Tax for the UK Abandoned? Lessons for the Policy Process and Tackling Wealth Inequality', *Journal of Social Policy*, XLI (2012), pp. 233–49

Gold, John, *The Practice of Modernism: Modern Architects and Urban Transformation, 1954–1972* (Abingdon, 2007)

Goodhart, David, *The Road to Somewhere* (London, 2017)

Goodman, Robert, *After the Planners* (Harmondsworth, 1972)

Graham, Caroline, *The Killings at Badger's Drift* (London, 1987)

Green, Henry, *Concluding* (Harmondsworth, [1948] 1964)

Grieve, Hilda, *The Great Tide* (Chelmsford, 1959)

Grindrod, John, *Outskirts: Living Life on the Edge of the Green Belt* (London, 2017)

Gunn, Simon, 'The Rise and Fall of British Urban Modernism', *Journal of British Studies*, XLIX (2010), pp. 849–69

—, 'The Buchanan Report, Environment and the Problem of Traffic in 1960s Britain', *Twentieth Century British History*, XXII (2011), pp. 521–42

Hadland, Laura, *50 Years of CAMRA* (St Albans, 2021)

Halfacree, Keith, 'Trespassing against the Rural Idyll: The Criminal Justice and Public Order Act 1994 and Access to the Countryside', in *Rights of Way*, ed. Charles Watkins (London, 1996), pp. 179–93

Hall, Stuart, 'The Great Moving Right Show', *Marxism Today* (January 1979), pp. 14–20

—, 'Whose Heritage? Unsettling "The Heritage", Re-Imagining the Post-Nation', *Third Text*, XLIX (1999), pp. 3–13

Hallett, Mark, ed., *George Shaw: A Corner of a Foreign Field* (London, 2018)

Hamilton, Peter, *An English Eye: The Photographs of James Ravilious* (Oxford, [1998] 2007)

Hardy, Denis, and Colin Ward, *Arcadia for All: The Legacy of a Makeshift Landscape* (London, 1984)

Harries, Susie, *Nikolaus Pevsner: The Life* (London, 2011)

Harrison, Fraser, *The Living Landscape* (London, 1986)

Harrison, Melissa, *Rain: Four Walks in English Weather* (London, 2016)

—, *All Among the Barley* (London, 2018)

—, *The Stubborn Light of Things* (London, 2020)

Harwood, Elain, *England: A Guide to Post-War Listed Buildings* (London, 2003)

Hatherley, Owen, *Militant Modernism* (London, 2009)

—, *A Guide to the New Ruins of Great Britain* (London, 2010)

—, *A New Kind of Bleak: Journeys through Urban Britain* (London, 2012)

—, *The Ministry of Nostalgia* (London, 2016)
Head, Dominic, *Modernity and the English Rural Novel* (Cambridge, 2017)
Heaney, Seamus, 'Englands of the Mind', in *Finders Keepers: Selected Prose, 1971–2001* (London, 2002), pp. 77–95
Heathcote, David, *A Shell Eye on England: The Shell County Guides, 1934–1984* (Faringdon, 2011)
Heffer, Simon, *Like the Roman: The Life of Enoch Powell* (London, 1998)
Henderson, Ailsa, Charlie Jeffery, Robert Liniera, Roger Scully, Daniel Wincott and Richard Wyn Jones, 'England, Englishness and Brexit', *Political Quarterly*, LXXXVII (2016), pp. 187–99
Henderson, Ailsa, and Richard Wyn Jones, *Englishness: The Political Force Transforming Britain* (Oxford, 2021)
Hewison, Robert, *The Heritage Industry* (London, 1987)
Hill, Geoffrey, *Mercian Hymns* (London, 1971)
—, *The Orchards of Syon* (London, 2002)
Hillier, Bevis, *Betjeman: The Bonus of Laughter* (London, 2004)
Hogg, Jonathan, *British Nuclear Culture* (London, 2016)
Hollows, Joanne, 'Enthusing about Green Peppers: The Europeanisation of British Food Culture in Post-War Britain, 1960–1975', *Contemporary British History*, XXXV (2021), pp. 392–416
Horne, Donald, *God Is an Englishman* (Harmondsworth, 1969)
Hoskins, W. G., *Midland England* (London, 1949)
—, *The Making of the English Landscape* (London, 1955)
—, *The Midland Peasant* (London, 1957)
—, *Local History in England* (London, 1959)
—, *Rutland* (London, 1963)
—, *English Local History: The Past and the Future* (Leicester, 1966)
—, *Leicestershire* (London, 1970)
HRH The Prince of Wales, *A Vision of Britain: A Personal View of Architecture* (London, 1989)
Hubbard, Phil, 'Darren Hayman and the Secondary Modern's *Pram Town*', *Cultural Geographies*, XVII (2010), pp. 407–14
—, *Borderland: Identity and Belonging at the Edge of England* (Manchester, 2022)
Hunt, Leon, *The League of Gentlemen* (London, 2008)
Hutchinson, Maxwell, *The Prince of Wales: Right or Wrong? An Architect Replies* (London, 1989)
Hutt, Christopher, *The Death of the English Pub* (London, 1973)
Huq, Rupa, *Making Sense of Suburbia through Popular Culture* (London, 2013)
—, 'Postcards from the Edge? Setting the Suburban Scene', *Political Quarterly*, XC (2019), pp. 6–14
Jackson, Alan, *Semi-Detached London, 1900–1939* (London, 1973)
Jackson, Michael, *The English Pub* (London, 1976)
Jencks, Charles, *The Prince, the Architects and New Wave Monarchy* (London, 1988)
Johnson, Linton Kwesi, 'Inglan is a Bitch', in *Selected Poems* (London, 2006), pp. 39–41
Keiller, Patrick, *Robinson in Space* (London, 1999)

―, 'Landscape and Cinematography', *Cultural Geographies*, XVI (2009), pp. 409–14
―, *The Possibility of Life's Survival on the Planet* (London, 2012)
―, *The View from the Train: Cities and Other Landscapes* (London, 2013)
Kennard, Peter, *Visual Dissent* (London, 2019)
Kenny, Michael, *The Politics of English Nationhood* (Oxford, 2014)
―, '"A Traditional English (Not British) Country Gentleman of the Radical Left": Understanding the Making and Unmaking of Edward Thompson's English Idiom', *Contemporary British History*, XXVIII (2014), pp. 494–516
Kingsnorth, Paul, *Real England: The Battle against the Bland* (London, 2008)
Kinsman, Phil, 'Landscape, Race and National Identity: The Photography of Ingrid Pollard', *Area*, XXVII (1995), pp. 300–310
―, 'Conflict and Co-Operation over Ethnic Minority Access to the Countryside: The Black Environment Network and the Countryside Commission', in *Rights of Way*, ed. Charles Watkins (London, 1996), pp. 162–78
Kovesi, Simon, *John Clare: Nature, Criticism and History* (London, 2017)
Larkin, Philip, *The Whitsun Weddings* (London, 1964)
―, *High Windows* (London, 1974)
―, *Further Requirements* (London, 2001)
Lawrence, David, *Always a Welcome: The Glove Compartment History of the Motorway Service Area* (Twickenham, 1999)
Light, Alison, *Forever England: Femininity, Literature and Conservatism between the Wars* (London, 1991)
Littler, Jo, and Roshi Naidoo, eds, *The Politics of Heritage: The Legacies of 'Race'* (Abingdon, 2005)
Lowerson, John, 'The Mystical Geography of the English', in *The English Rural Community*, ed. Brian Short (London, 1992), pp. 152–74
Mabey, Richard, *The Common Ground* (London, 1980)
―, ed., *Second Nature* (London, 1984)
MacInnes, Colin, 'The Englishness of Dr Pevsner', in *England, Half English* (London, [1961] 1986), pp. 119–29
McKay, George, *Senseless Acts of Beauty: Cultures of Resistance since the Sixties* (London, 1996)
Mandler, Peter, *The Fall and Rise of the Stately Home* (New Haven, CT, 1997)
―, *The English National Character* (New Haven, CT, 2006)
Mass, Sarah, 'Commercial Heritage as Democratic Action: Historicizing the "Save the Market" Campaigns in Bradford and Chesterfield, 1969–76', *Twentieth Century British History*, XXIX (2018), pp. 459–84
Matless, David, 'Ages of English Design: Preservation, Modernism and Tales of Their History, 1926–1939', *Journal of Design History*, III (1990), pp. 203–12
―, 'One Man's England: W. G. Hoskins and the English Culture of Landscape', *Rural History*, IV (1993), pp. 187–207
―, 'Doing the English Village', in *Writing the Rural*, ed. Paul Cloke, Marcus Doel, David Matless, Martin Phillips and Nigel Thrift (London, 1994), pp. 7–88
―, *Landscape and Englishness* (London, 1998; rev. edn 2016)

——, 'The Predicament of Englishness', *Scottish Geographical Journal*, CXVI (2000), pp. 79–86
——, 'Topographic Culture: Nikolaus Pevsner and the Buildings of England', *History Workshop Journal*, LIV (2002), pp. 73–99
——, 'Writing English Landscape History', *Anglia: Zeitschrift für Englische Philologie*, CXXVI (2008), pp. 295–311
——, 'Votive Leaves', *Uniformagazine*, VII (2016), pp. 3–5
——, 'At Ease', in Simon Roberts, *Merrie Albion: Landscape Studies of a Small Island* (Stockport, 2017) pp. 149–50
——, 'The Anthroposcenic', *Transactions of the Institute of British Geographers*, XLII (2017), pp. 363–76
——, 'The Agriculture Gallery: Displaying Modern Farming in the Science Museum', in *Histories of Technology, the Environment and Modern Britain*, ed. Jon Agar and Jacob Ward (London, 2018), pp. 101–22
——, 'Next the Sea: Eccles and the Anthroposcenic', *Journal of Historical Geography*, LXII (2018), pp. 71–84
——, Brian Short and David Gilbert, 'Emblematic Landscapes of the British Modern', in *Geographies of British Modernity*, ed. David Gilbert, David Matless and Brian Short (Oxford, 2003), pp. 250–57
Meades, Jonathan, *Filthy English* (London, 1984)
——, 'First Shack', in *Museum without Walls* (London, 2012), pp. 325–8
Medhurst, Andy, 'Negotiating the Gnome Zone: Versions of Suburbia in British Popular Culture', in *Visions of Suburbia*, ed. Roger Silverstone (London, 1997), pp. 240–68
——, *A National Joke: Popular Comedy and English Cultural Identities* (London, 2007)
Merrick, *Battle for the Trees* (Leeds, 1996)
Merriman, Peter, *Driving Spaces: A Cultural–Historical Geography of England's M1 Motorway* (Oxford, 2007)
——, 'Motorways, Modern Heritage and the British Landscape', in *The Good, the Bad and the Unbuilt: Handling the Heritage of the Recent Past*, ed. S. May, H. Orange and S. Penrose (Oxford, 2012), pp. 103–11
Miller, Andy, *The Kinks Are the Village Green Preservation Society* (London, 2003)
Moran, Joe, *Reading the Everyday* (Abingdon, 2005)
——, *On Roads: A Hidden History* (London, 2009)
Morden, Terry, 'The Pastoral and the Pictorial', *Ten:8*, XII (1983), pp. 18–25
Morland, Joanna, *New Milestones: Sculpture, Community and the Land* (London, 1988)
Moseley, Rachel, *Hand-Made Television: Stop-Frame Animation for Children in Britain, 1961–1974* (London, 2016)
Moses, Jonathan, 'The Politics of the British Public House, 1979–Present: Architecture, Authenticity and Everyday Enchantment', PhD thesis, University of London, 2020
Mowl, Timothy, *Stylistic Cold Wars: Betjeman versus Pevsner* (London, 2000)
Myers, John, *Middle England* (Birmingham, 2011)
Naipaul, V. S., *The Enigma of Arrival* (London, 1987)
Nairn, Ian, 'Outrage', *Architectural Review*, CXVII (1955), pp. 361–460

—, 'Counter-Attack', *Architectural Review*, CXX (1956), pp. 352–440
Nairn, Tom, *The Break-Up of Britain* (London, 1977)
Navickas, Katrina, 'Conflicts of Power, Landscape and Amenity in Debates over the British Super Grid in the 1950s', *Rural History*, XXX (2019), pp. 87–103
Neate, Hannah, and Ruth Craggs, eds, *Modern Futures* (Axminster, 2016)
Newell, Martin, *Late Autumn Sunlight* (Colchester, 2001)
Newman, John, *West Kent and the Weald* (Harmondsworth, 1969)
Nixon, Sean, 'Trouble at the National Trust: Post-War Recreation, the Benson Report and the Rebuilding of a Conservation Organization in the 1960s', *Twentieth Century British History*, XXVI (2015), pp. 529–50
Nobbs, David, *The Fall and Rise of Reginald Perrin* (Harmondsworth, 1976)
Norcup, Joanne, 'Geography Education, Grey Literature and the Geographical Canon', *Journal of Historical Geography*, XLIX (2015), pp. 61–74
Northam, Jean, 'Rehearsals in Citizenship: BBC Stop-Motion Animation Programmes for Young Children', *Journal for Cultural Research*, IX (2005), pp. 245–63
O'Brien, Sean, *Journeys to the Interior: Ideas of England in Contemporary Poetry* (Newcastle/Tarset, 2012)
O'Toole, Fintan, *Heroic Failure: Brexit and the Politics of Pain* (London, 2019)
Oliver, Paul, Ian Davis and Ian Bentley, *Dunroamin: The Suburban Semi and Its Enemies* (London, 1981)
Openshaw, Stan, and Philip Steadman, 'The Geography of Two Hypothetical Nuclear Attacks on Britain', *Area*, XV (1983), pp. 193–201
Openshaw, Stan, Philip Steadman and Owen Greene, *Doomsday: Britain after Nuclear Attack* (Oxford, 1983)
Ortolano, Guy, 'Planning the Urban Future in 1960s Britain', *Historical Journal*, LIV (2011), pp. 477–507
—, *Thatcher's Progress: From Social Democracy to Market Liberalism through an English New Town* (Cambridge, 2019)
Orwell, George, 'The Lion and the Unicorn: Socialism and the English Genius', in *The Collected Essays, Journalism and Letters of George Orwell*, vol. II (1968), pp. 56–109
Pahl, R. E., 'The Two Class Village', *New Society*, LXXIV (27 February 1964), pp. 7–9
—, *Urbs in rure: The Metropolitan Fringe in Hertfordshire* (London, 1965)
Parr, Martin, *The Cost of Living* (Manchester, 1989)
—, *Boring Postcards* (London, 1999)
—, *Think of England* (London, 2000)
Pearce, David, *Conservation Today* (London, 1989)
Perec, Georges, *Species of Spaces and Other Pieces* (London, 1997)
Pevsner, Nikolaus, *The Leaves of Southwell* (Harmondsworth, 1945)
—, *Nottinghamshire* (Harmondsworth, 1951)
—, *The Englishness of English Art* (London, 1956)
—, *Shropshire* (Harmondsworth, 1958)
—, *Northamptonshire* (Harmondsworth, 1961)
—, *North-East Norfolk and Norwich* (Harmondsworth, 1962)
—, *The Englishness of English Art* (Harmondsworth, 1964)

—, *Staffordshire* (Harmondsworth, 1974)
—, and Edward Hubbard, *Cheshire* (Harmondsworth, 1971)
—, and Bridget Cherry, *Northamptonshire* (Harmondsworth, 1973)
—, and Elizabeth Williamson, *Nottinghamshire* (Harmondsworth, 1979)
Piko, Lauren, *Milton Keynes in British Culture: Imagining England* (London, 2019)
Pollard, Ingrid, 'Pastoral Interludes', *Third Text*, VII (1989)
—, 'Another View', *Feminist Review*, XLV (1993), pp. 46–50
—, *Carbon Slowly Turning* (Milton Keynes, 2022)
Powell, Enoch, *Dancer's End and The Wedding Gift* (London, 1951)
—, *Freedom and Reality* (London, 1969)
Raban, Jonathan, *Coasting* (London, 1986)
Randall, Lucian, and Chris Welch, *Ginger Geezer: The Life of Vivian Stanshall* (London, 2001)
Ravilious, James, *A Corner of England: North Devon Landscapes and People* (Tiverton, 1995)
—, *The Recent Past* (London, 2017)
Ravilious, Robin, *James Ravilious: A Life* (London, 2017)
Readman, Paul, '"The Cliffs Are Not Cliffs": The Cliffs of Dover and National Identities in Britain, c.1750–c.1950', *History*, LCIX (2014), pp. 241–69
—, *Storied Ground: Landscape and the Shaping of English National Identity* (Cambridge, 2018)
Rice, Brian, and Tony Evans, *The English Sunrise* (London, 1972)
Richards, J. M., *The Castles on the Ground* (London, 1973)
Rix, Michael, 'Industrial Archaeology', *Amateur Historian*, II (1955), pp. 225–9
—, *Industrial Archaeology* (London, 1967)
Roberts, Simon, *We English* (London, 2008)
—, *Merrie Albion: Landscape Studies of a Small Island* (Stockport, 2017)
Robinson, Emily, *History, Heritage and Tradition in Contemporary British Politics* (Manchester, 2012)
—, 'Radical Nostalgia, Progressive Patriotism and Labour's "English Problem"', *Political Studies Review*, XIV (2016)
Robinson, John Martin, *The Latest Country Houses* (London, 1984)
Royal Commission on the Historical Monuments of England and English Heritage, *A Change of Heart: English Architecture since the War; A Policy for Protection* (London, 1992)
Saint, Andrew, *Towards a Social Architecture: The Role of School-Building in Post-War England* (London, 1987)
Samuel, Raphael, 'People's History', in *People's History and Socialist Theory*, ed. Raphael Samuel (London, 1981), pp. xv–xxxix
—, 'History Workshop, 1966–80', in *People's History and Socialist Theory*, ed. Raphael Samuel (London, 1981), pp. 410–17
—, ed., *Patriotism: The Making and Unmaking of British National Identity*, vol. I: *History and Politics* (London, 1989)
—, ed., *Patriotism: The Making and Unmaking of British National Identity*, vol. II: *Minorities and Outsiders* (London, 1989)
—, ed., *Patriotism: The Making and Unmaking of British National Identity*, vol. III: *National Fictions* (London, 1989)

―, *Theatres of Memory* (London, 1994)
Saumarez Smith, Otto, 'Central Government and Town-Centre Redevelopment in Britain, 1959–1966', *Historical Journal*, LVIII (2015), pp. 217–44
―, 'The Inner City Crisis and the End of Urban Modernism in 1970s Britain', *Twentieth Century British History*, XXVII (2016), pp. 578–98
―, *Boom Cities: Architect-Planners and the Politics of Radical Urban Renewal in 1960s Britain* (Oxford, 2019)
Saunders, Robert, *Yes to Europe! The 1975 Referendum and Seventies Britain* (Cambridge, 2018)
―, 'Brexit and Empire: "Global Britain" and the Myth of Imperial Nostalgia', *Journal of Imperial and Commonwealth History*, XLVIII (2020), pp. 1140–74
Savage, Jon, *England's Dreaming: Sex Pistols and Punk Rock* (London, 1991)
Schofield, Camilla, *Enoch Powell and the Making of Postcolonial Britain* (Cambridge, 2013)
Schwarz, Bill, *The White Man's World* (Oxford, 2011)
Scruton, Roger, *England: An Elegy* (London, 2000)
Searle, Adam, Jonathon Turnbull and Jamie Lorimer, 'After the Anthropause: Lockdown Lessons for More-Than-Human Geographies', *Geographical Journal*, CLXXXVII (2021), pp. 69–77
Seymour, Susanne, Lowri Jones and Julia Feuer-Cotter, 'The Global Connections of Cotton in the Derwent Valley Mills in the Later Eighteenth and Early Nineteenth Centuries', in *The Industrial Revolution: Cromford, the Derwent Valley and the Wider World*, ed. Chris Wrigley (Cromford, 2015), pp. 150–70
Shaw, George, *My Back to Nature* (London, 2016)
Sillars, Laurence, ed., *George Shaw: The Sly and Unseen Day* (Gateshead, 2011)
Silverstone, Roger, ed., *Visions of Suburbia* (London, 1997)
Smith, David, *Industrial Archaeology of the East Midlands* (Dawlish, 1965)
Snell, Keith, 'Ronald Blythe: "Just a Voice for His Time"', *Rural History*, XXXII (2021), pp. 3–22
Spence, Jeoffry, *Surviving Steam Railways* (London, 1979)
Steedman, Carolyn, *Landscape for a Good Woman* (London, 1986)
Strong, Roy, Marcus Binney and John Harris, *The Destruction of the Country House* (London, 1975)
Taylor, John, 'The Imaginary Landscape', *Ten:8*, XII (1983), pp. 2–13
―, *A Dream of England: Landscape, Photography and the Tourist's Imagination* (Manchester, 1995)
Taylor, Nicholas, *The Village in the City* (London, 1973)
Taylor, Ray, Margaret Cox and Ian Dickins, eds, *Britain's Planning Heritage* (London, 1975)
Tewdr-Jones, Mark, '"Oh, the Planners Did Their Best": The Planning Films of John Betjeman', *Planning Perspectives*, XX (2005), pp. 389–411
Thomas, David St John, *The Country Railway* (Newton Abbot, 1976)
Thompson, E. P., 'The Peculiarities of the English', in *The Poverty of Theory* (London, 1978), pp. 35–91
Thorn, Tracey, *Another Planet: A Teenager in Suburbia* (Edinburgh, 2019)

Tinniswood, Adrian, *Noble Ambitions: The Fall and Rise of the English Country House after World War II* (London, 2021)
Tolia-Kelly, Divya, 'Fear in Paradise: The Affective Registers of the English Lake District Landscape Re-Visited', *Senses and Society*, II (2007), pp. 329–51
——, *Landscape, Race and Memory: Material Ecologies of Citizenship* (London, 2010)
Trinder, Barrie, 'Industrial Archaeology in the Twentieth-Century Context', in *Perspectives on Industrial Archaeology*, ed. Neil Cossons (London, 2000), pp. 39–56
Tyme, John, *Motorways versus Democracy* (London, 1978)
Veldman, Meredith, *Fantasy, the Bomb, and the Greening of Britain: Romantic Protest, 1945–1980* (Cambridge, 1994)
Waites, Ian, '"Places Where I Forgot Things"; Memory, Identity and the British Council Estate in the Paintings of George Shaw', *Cultural Politics*, IX (2013), pp. 357–70
——, *Middlefield: A Postwar Council Estate in Time* (Axminster, 2017)
Wall, Christine, '"Nuclear Prospects": The Siting and Construction of Sizewell A Power Station, 1957–1966', *Contemporary British History*, XXXIII (2019), pp. 246–73
Wall, Derek, *Earth First! and the Anti-Roads Movement* (Abingdon, 1999)
Ward, Colin, 'A Place in the Country', in *Second Nature*, ed. Richard Mabey (London, 1984), pp. 198–206
Ward, Stephen, 'Colin Buchanan's American Journey', *Town Planning Review*, LXXXVIII (2017), pp. 201–31
Warner, Sylvia Townsend, *Lolly Willowes* (London, [1926] 1993)
Watkin, David, *The English Vision* (London, 1982)
Webster, Wendy, *Englishness and Empire, 1939–1965* (Oxford, 2005)
Weldon, Fay, 'Letter to Laura', in *Second Nature*, ed. Richard Mabey (London, 1984), pp. 67–73
Westall, Claire, and Michael Gardiner, eds, *Literature of an Independent England* (Basingstoke, 2013)
While, Aidan, 'Modernism vs Urban Renaissance: Negotiating Post-War Heritage in English City Centres', *Urban Studies*, XLIV (2006), pp. 2399–2419
——, 'The State and the Controversial Demands of Cultural Built Heritage: Modernism, Dirty Concrete, and Postwar Listing in England', *Environment and Planning D: Planning and Design*, XXXIV (2007), pp. 645–63
——, and Malcolm Tait, 'Exeter and the Question of Thomas Sharp's Physical Legacy', *Planning Perspectives*, XXIV (2009), pp. 77–97
Whipple, Amy, 'Revisiting the "Rivers of Blood" Controversy: Letters to Enoch Powell', *Journal of British Studies*, XLVIII (2009), pp. 717–35
Whiteley, Nigel, 'Modern Architecture, Heritage and Englishness', *Architectural History*, XXXVIII (1995), pp. 220–37
Whyte, William, 'The Englishness of English Architecture: Modernism and the Making of a National International Style, 1927–1957', *Journal of British Studies*, XLVIII (2009), pp. 441–65
Wiener, Martin, *English Culture and the Decline of the Industrial Spirit, 1850–1980* (Cambridge, 1981)

Select Bibliography

Williams, Raymond, *The Country and the City* (London, 1973)
Williams, Tony, *The Midlands* (Rugby, 2014)
Williams, Val, *Martin Parr* (London, 2002)
Wood, Michael, *In Search of the Dark Ages* (London, 1981)
——, *In Search of England* (London, 1999)
——, *The Story of England* (London, 2010)
Wootten, William, 'Rhetoric and Violence in Geoffrey Hill's *Mercian Hymns* and the Speeches of Enoch Powell', *Cambridge Quarterly*, XXIX (2000), pp. 1–15
Wright, Patrick, *On Living in an Old Country* (London, 1985)
——, 'Re-Enchanting the Nation: Prince Charles and Architecture', *Modern Painters*, II/3 (1989), pp. 26–35
——, *A Journey through Ruins* (London, 1991)
——, 'The Stain on St George's Flag', *The Guardian* (18 August 1993)
——, 'Last Orders', *The Guardian* (9 April 2005)
——, 'An Encroachment Too Far', in *Town and Country*, ed. Anthony Barnett and Roger Scruton (London, 1998), pp. 18–33
——, and Tim Putnam, 'Sneering at the Theme Parks', *Block*, XV (1989), pp. 48–55
XTC and Neville Farmer, *Song Stories* (London, 1998)
Zalasiewicz, Jan, Colin Waters et al., 'The Working Group on the Anthropocene: Summary of Evidence and Interim Recommendations', *Anthropocene*, XIX (2017), pp. 55–60

DISCOGRAPHY

Songs and music mentioned in *About England*, referenced here as individual singles, album tracks or (in italics) albums, as appropriate to their citation in the text.

Virginia Astley, *From Gardens Where We Feel Secure* (1983)
John Betjeman, *Banana Blush* (1974)
——, *Late Flowering Love* (1974)
——, *Sir John Betjeman's Britain* (1977)
Cilla Black, 'Alfie' (1966)
Black Box Recorder, 'The English Motorway System', from *The Facts of Life* (2000)
David Bowie, 'The Little Bombardier', from *David Bowie* (1967)
British Sea Power, 'Blackout', from *The Decline of British Sea Power* (2003)
The Clash, 'London Calling', from *London Calling* (1979)
——, 'Something about England', from *Sandinista* (1980)
Shirley and Dolly Collins, *Anthems in Eden* (1969)
Elvis Costello, 'Shipbuilding', from *Punch the Clock* (1983)
Crass, 'How Does It Feel to Be the Mother of a Thousand Dead?' (1982)
——, 'Sheep Farming in the Falklands' (1983)
Depeche Mode, 'New Life' (1981)
The Durutti Column, 'Sketch for Summer', from *The Return of the Durutti Column* (1980)
——, 'English Landscape Tradition', from *The Guitar and Other Machines* (1987)
Michael Flanders and Donald Swann, 'Slow Train' (1963)
P. J. Harvey, *Let England Shake* (2010)
Darren Hayman and The Secondary Modern, *Pram Town* (2009)
July Skies, *The Weather Clock* (2007)
——, *The Weather Clock* EP (2007)
The Kinks, 'Sunny Afternoon' (1966)
Jackie Lee, 'The Town I Live In' (1966)
Vera Lynn, 'I Love This Land' (1982)
Morrissey, 'Everyday is Like Sunday', from *Viva Hate* (1988)
——, 'Bengali in Platforms', from *Viva Hate* (1988)

Discography

The Move, 'Goodbye Blackberry Way' (1968)
National Youth Jazz Orchestra, *In CAMRA* (1977)
Martin Newell, 'Christmas in Suburbia', from *The Greatest Living Englishman* (1993)
Mike Oldfield, *Tubular Bells* (1973)
The Osmonds, 'Down by the Lazy River' (1972)
Right Hand Man, 'South Woodham Ferrers' (1981)
Paul Rubens, 'Your King and Country Want You' (1914)
Saint Etienne, 'Like a Motorway', from *Tiger Bay* (1994)
———, *Sound of Water* (2000)
———, 'Sweet Arcadia', from *Home Counties* (2017)
Sex Pistols, 'God Save the Queen', from *Never Mind the Bollocks Here's the Sex Pistols* (1977)
Siouxsie and the Banshees, 'Suburban Relapse', from *The Scream* (1978)
Vivian Stanshall, *Sir Henry at Rawlinson End* (1978)
Edwin Starr, 'War' (1970)
Ultramarine, *United Kingdoms* (1994)
Robert Wyatt, 'Shipbuilding' (1982)
———, *Shleep* (1997)
XTC, 'New Town Animal in a Furnished Cage', from *White Music* (1978)
———, *English Settlement* (1982)
———, *Mummer* (1983)
———, *Skylarking* (1986)
———, 'Chalkhills and Children', from *Oranges and Lemons* (1989)

FILMOGRAPHY

Films and television programmes mentioned in *About England*.

Cinema

Akenfield (1974), dir. Peter Hall
Aldermaston Pottery (1965), dir. Michael Darlow and Anthony Searle
Born Free (1966), dir. James Hill
Carry On . . . (1958–78), dir. Gerald Thomas
The Go-Between (1971), dir. Joseph Losey
The Gruffalo (2009), dir. Jakob Schuh and Max Lang
London (1994), dir. Patrick Keiller
London Orbital (2002), dir. Chris Petit
The Lord of the Rings (trilogy, 2001–3), dir. Peter Jackson
The Man with the Golden Gun (1974), dir. Guy Hamilton
Passport to Pimlico (1949), dir. Henry Cornelius
Radio On (1979), dir. Chris Petit
Robinson in Ruins (2010), dir. Patrick Keiller
Robinson in Space (1997), dir. Patrick Keiller
The Spirit of '45 (2013), dir. Ken Loach
This Is England (2006), dir. Shane Meadows
The Titfield Thunderbolt (1953), dir. Charles Crichton

Television

About Anglia (ITV), 1960–90
Abroad in Britain (BBC), 1990
Akenfield Revisited (BBC), 2004
Bergerac (BBC), 1981–91
Blackadder Goes Forth (BBC), 1989
Blott on the Landscape (BBC), 1985
Brideshead Revisited (ITV), 1981
Call My Bluff (BBC), 1965–88
Camberwick Green (BBC), 1966
Car Share (BBC), 2015–18

Chigley (BBC), 1969
Daktari (BBC), 1966–9
The Darling Buds of May (ITV), 1991–3
Ever Decreasing Circles (BBC), 1984–9
The Fall and Rise of Reginald Perrin (BBC), 1976–9
The Good Life (BBC), 1975–8
Heritage in Danger (ITV), 1979
In Search of the Dark Ages (BBC), 1979–81
Industrial Archaeology (BBC), 1965
Landscapes of England (BBC), 1976–8
Last of the Summer Wine (BBC), 1973–2010
The League of Gentlemen (BBC), 1999–2002
The Likely Lads (BBC), 1964–6
The Making of the English Landscape (BBC), 1972
Metro-land (BBC), 1973
Midsomer Murders (ITV), 1997–
One-Upmanship (BBC), 1976
Only Fools and Horses (BBC), 1981–91
The Pallisers (BBC), 1974
Play School (BBC), 1964–88
Porridge (BBC), 1974–7
Rising Damp (ITV), 1974–8
The Services (Channel 4), 1998
Spitting Image (ITV), 1984–96
Springwatch (BBC), 2020
The Story of England (BBC), 2010
Terry and June (BBC), 1979–87
To the Manor Born (BBC), 1979–81
Trumpton (BBC), 1967
Whatever Happened to the Likely Lads? (BBC), 1973–4
The Wombles (BBC), 1973–5
The World about Us (BBC), 1967–87

ACKNOWLEDGEMENTS

The School of Geography at the University of Nottingham has provided a supportive environment for my research since 1994, and work carried out by staff and research students in the Cultural and Historical Geography Research Group there has been a valuable source of ideas and critical reflection. Thanks to current and former colleagues within that group, including Stephen Daniels, Charles Watkins, Susanne Seymour, Mike Heffernan, Georgina Endfield, Steve Legg, Isla Forsyth, Gary Priestnall, Jake Hodder and David Beckingham. Also at Nottingham to Adam Swain and Andrew Leyshon for their support and research collaboration. Teaching on English landscape with Susanne Seymour has helped shape themes in *About England*, and undergraduate students on our course at Nottingham have contributed through their questions and insights. Students on the former MA in Landscape and Culture at Nottingham also brought critical perspectives alongside their original research, and all the PhD students I have supervised at Nottingham have been important in shaping the intellectual outlook of the book. Matthew Smallman-Raynor provided impeccable support as Head of School during the challenging years when this book was written. Beyond Nottingham I also acknowledge the support and collaboration of George Revill, Laura Cameron, David Crouch, David Gilbert, Brian Short, Mike Pearson and Colin Sackett. Staff in the Manuscripts and Special Collections department at Nottingham facilitated access to research papers, and the Hallward Library at the University, and Beeston Library, have also proved valuable sources of material. For support before, during and after the pandemic, thanks to the staff of Round Hill School, Beeston. My parents, Brian and Audrey Matless, have always given love and support, and Jo Norcup's companionship and curiosity have shaped *About England* in many ways. The book is dedicated to our son, Edwyn, who over the past ten years has given me a new appreciation of places near and far, and who never fails to delight.

PHOTO ACKNOWLEDGEMENTS

The author and publishers wish to express their thanks to the below sources of illustrative material and/or permission to reproduce it.

F. L. Attenborough: p. 144; © Beaford Arts, digitally scanned from a Beaford Archive negative: pp. 176, 177; © Sue Clifford and Angela King: p. 172; © Common Ground: p. 168; Crown Copyright: pp. 49, 226 (These images are licenced under the Open Government Licence 3.0); David and Charles Publishing: p. 246; J. H. Dowd: p. 27 left and right; © Essex County Council: pp. 162, 163; © Tony Evans: p. 122; Getty Images: p. 32 top (LOCOG); Google Earth: p. 143; © Lewis Heriz: p. 41; © John Hinde Archive/Mary Evans: pp. 203 bottom, 220; © Jarrold Publishing, Norwich: p. 197; © July Skies 2007: p. 265; © Patrick Keiller: p. 56; © Peter Kennard: p. 89; Mrs. J. MacRae: p. 275; David Matless: pp. 18, 20, 21 top and bottom, 22, 23, 115 top and bottom, 181, 203 top, 204, 292; Merrick: p. 280; © John Myers: pp. 149, 151; © Julian Opie/Courtesy of Alan Cristea Gallery: p. 274; © Chris Orr: pp. 237, 240; © Roger Palmer/Courtesy of the artist: p. 283; © Martin Parr/Magnum Photos: p. 141 top and bottom; The Photographic Greeting Card Co., London: p. 198; © The Piper Estate/DACS 2022: p. 124; © Simon Roberts/Courtesy of Flowers Gallery: pp. 29, 31, 77, 113, 285; Stamp design © Royal Mail Group Limited: p. 269; © Axel Scheffler 2016: p. 112; © George Shaw/Courtesy of Anthony Wilkinson Gallery, London: pp. 146, 147; © The Tolkien Estate Ltd 1937: p. 32 bottom; © University of Nottingham, Manuscripts and Special Collections, MS627: pp. 249, 250; Waddington's: p. 255 top and bottom; © Wembley Stadium Ltd, 1973: p. 110; © XTC/Virgin Records: p. 35.

INDEX

Page numbers in *italics* indicate illustrations

Abercrombie, Patrick 261
Afghanistan 77–8
Agyeman, Julian 66–7, 70
Aldermaston 84–6
Alfred the Great, King 34–6
Allison, Lincoln 182–3
Amery, Colin 214, 221–4, 228, 230–31, 235, 237
Anderson, Perry 85
Anglo-Saxon England 16, 34–9, 59, 128–9, 145
Anthropocene 91, 253, 281–2, 286–7, 290
Arcadia 13, 74, 163, 176–81, 189
Archers, The 66, 81, 165
architecture 119, 123, 128–9, 140, 162–6, 221–40
Ardizzone, Edward 186
Arkwright Society 251
Arkwright, Richard 250–53
Ashton, Bill 185
Astley, Virginia 47–8, 50, 173, 289
Atkinson, Conrad 170
Atkinson, Frank 247
Attenborough 16, 19, 21–4, *22*, *23*, 288
Attenborough, F. L. 144, *144*, 267
Australia 63, 73, 79

Bacton Gas Terminal 227
Bailey, Liam 196
Baillie, Frank 184
Ballard, J. G. 271, 282
Banham, Reyner 129–30, 270

Banksy 198
Barbuda 70–71
Barker, Paul 129
Barnes, William 173
Barnett, Anthony 80–81, 83, 85
Barnett, Corelli 44
Barrell, John 52–4, 57, 169
Basildon 131, 164, 166
Bates, H. E. 43
Bath 222–3, 227, 258
Bath, Marquess of 204
Beacham, Peter 175
Beaford Arts Centre 174
Beamish Open Air Museum 245–7
Beaulieu 208, 215
Beckenham 270
Beckinsale, Richard 19
Bedford, Duke of 210
beer 105, 133, 181–9, 224
Beeston 16–22, *18*, *20*, *21*, 24, 115–16, *115*, 248–50, *249*, 285, 288, 292–3, *292*
Beeston Civic Society 19–20, 22
Bekonscot 195–8
Bell, Julia 11–13
Bell, Steve 14
Belloc, Hilaire 182, 186–7
Beloff, Nora 108–9
Benge, Alfreda 178–9
Benn, Tony 109
Bennett, Alan 174
Bentley, Ian 121
Berger, John 50–52, 57, 169, 213

350

Index

Betjeman, John 54, 124–8, 146, 150, 192, 222–3, 228, 232, 235, 258, 267, 289
Bewes, Rodney 124
Bibury 48–50, 57
Binney, Marcus 210–11, 238–9, 257
Black Box Recorder 274
Black Environment Network 66–7
Blackadder Goes Forth 78–80
Blackburn Meadows power station 286
Blair, Tony 131, 150, 264
Blake, William 58, 161, 245
Blythe, Ronald 46–7, 52, 72–4, 79, 153, 174
Bolam, James 124
Booker, Christopher 235
Boston, Richard 182–5
Bourdieu, Pierre 139
Bowie, David 10
Bowles, Peter 217
Boyle, Danny 30, 78
Bracewell, Michael 47
Bradford 228, 230
Bragg, Melvyn 101
Brexit 58, 100–116, 148, 188
Brideshead Revisited 217–18, 290
Briers, Richard 111, 136
British National Party 58, 105–6
British Sea Power 186, 317
Brook, Richard 263
Broughton, Mark 209
Brunskill, Ronald 162, 166
brutalism 128, 259, 263
Bryson, Bill 33, 36
Buchanan, Angus 247–8
Buchanan, Colin 229–30, 279
Bull, John 52–3
Butlin's 220–21, *220*
Byrne, David 281

Caiger-Smith, Alan 86
Calix, Mira 78
Calke Abbey 215–16
Camberwick Green 155–7
Cameron, David 100, 106
Campaign for Nuclear Disarmament 84–9

Campaign to Protect Rural England 33, 93–4
Campaign for Real Ale 182–8
Cant, Brian 156–7
Carolgees, Bob 271–2
cars 50–51, 123–4, 126–8, 142, 229–30, 272
Carter, Laura 247
Caught by the River 173, 186
Chadwick, Helen 170
Cherry, Bridget 268
Chesterfield 231–2
Chesterton, G. K. 35, 101–2, 145, 186, 235
Chigley 155–6
Chilterns 189–93
Chilwell 19
Chorleywood 126–8, 150
Civic Trust 224, 272, 283
Clare, John 53–5, 57–8
Clarke, Roy 194–5
Clash, The 13–16
class 45, 50–57, 119, 126–8, 136, 139–40, 145, 192–3, 211–12
Clifford, Sue 167, 170–72
Codrington, Simon 70–71
Coleman, Terry 277
Collins, Dolly 74, 291
Collins, Shirley 74–5, 291
Colls, Robert 82–3
comedy 118–19, 134–9, 193–5, 216–17
Common Ground 86, 166–74, *168*, 172, 176, 180, 186, 290
Conquy, Wally 221
Conservation Areas 17, 224, 226
Conservatism 60, 83, 101, 131, 139, 152, 215–16
Conservative Party 45, 60–61, 104–9, 131–4, 208–9, 228, 237, 277
Constable, John 34, 48, 68, 80, 84, 88–9
consumption 139–52
Contemporary Issues in Geography and Education 88
Cook, Ian 88
cooling towers 167, 173, 245, 283–7
Cooper, Adrian 167, 186
Cope, Julian 279
Cormack, Patrick 209–15

Cornforth, John 210
Cornish, Vaughan 93–4
Cosgrove, Stuart 243
Cossons, Neil 245–7, 250, 252, 284
Costello, Elvis 82
Cotswolds 26, 28–9, 48–50, 57
Cottrell Boyce, Frank 30, 297, 305
Council for the Preservation of Rural England 93, 263
Council for the Protection of Rural England 58
country house 69–71, 132, 202–19, 228
Covent Garden 185, 231
Coventry 145–8, 227, 257, 261–2
COVID-19 pandemic 10, 16, 90–96, 100, 292
Cox, Margaret 227
Craggs, Ruth 263
Crass 81
cricket 22, 34, 132–2, 137–8, 186, 199
Crimean War 18–19
Cromford 173, 248, 250–53, 250, 289
Crowe, Sylvia 84, 254–6, 284–5
Cruickshank, Dan 164, 221–4, 228, 230–31, 235, 237
Cummins, Paul 78
Curl, James Stevens 228
Curtis, G.C.S. 162

Daniels, Stephen 52–3
Daniels, Wyn 58
Dannatt, Trevor 260
Darley, Gillian 166
Darling Buds of May, The 43–4
Darlow, Michael 86
Dartmouth, Countess of 225–6, 228
David & Charles, publisher 250
Davie, Donald 99–100
Davies, Peter 130
Davies, Ray 223–4
Davies, William 99
Davis, Ian 121
Deakin, Roger 167
Deller, Jeremy 79
Depeche Mode 164
Derounian, James Garo 66
Destruction of the Country House, 1875–1975, The 210–11, 216
devolution 37, 91, 96–101, 103, 290

Devon 174–6, 241, 250
Dickins, Ian 227
Didcot power station 286
Dodd, Philip 82–3
Doddington Park 70–71
Donaldson, Julia 112
Dooleys, The 164
Dorling, Danny 103, 152–3
Dorset 92–3, 100, 173, 235–6
Dowd, J. H. 26–7, 27
Drinkwater, John 26–7, 55
Drummond, Bill 279
Dublin, Dion 66
Dummett, Ann 63–4
Dunbar, Melville 162, 165
Dunn, Tim 196–7
Durdle Door 92–3
Durutti Column, The 15–16
Dyckhoff, Tom 267

Earth First! 277–8
Eccles 180–81
Edinburgh, Duke of 225–7
Edmonds, Noel 217
Egan, Peter 137
Elgar, Edward 30
Elizabeth II, Queen 31, 83, 95, 164, 269
empire 17, 33, 60–64, 66, 69–71, 127, 263, 290
 and Brexit 103, 114
 and English landscape 205, 278
Empson, William 53
enclosure 53–6
English Civil War 22–3, 277, 279
English Heritage 69–70, 206–7, 215, 258–9, 261, 269–70
enterprise 238–40, 244
Esher, Lord 214
Esmonde, John 136
Essex 162–6, 180
Essex Design Guide 162–6, *162*, *163*, 176
Europe 49, 102–16, 133, 231
 culture and heritage 99, 112, 226–7, 267–8
 'Tree Circles for Europe' 17, 24, 115–16, 293

Index

European Architectural Heritage
  Year 1975 224–6, 239, 259
Evans, Tony 121
Ever Decreasing Circles 136–9, 152

Faiers, Roy 57–8, 104
Falck, Colin 196
Falklands War 20, 45, 76, 80–83, 95–6
Fall and Rise of Reginald Perrin, The
  118–19, 135–6, 205
Farage, Nigel 105–8
farming 40–42, 57, 72–3, 104, 156, 289
fascism 40–42
Fedden, Robin 208
Field, The 104
Finnegan, Ruth 142
First World War 17–18, 72–6, 78–80,
  94, 102, 291
Fisher, Mark 55
Fisher, Roy 151
Flanders, Michael 85
Foot, Michael 76, 80, 85, 109
football 34, 97, 110–11, *110*
Ford, Robert 104–5
Forty, Adrian 165
Fowler, Corinne 68, 70
Francis, Matthew 131
Fuller, Peter 213
Fussell, Paul 74–5

Gallagher, Brian 252
Gallipoli 73, 79–80
Gardiner, Michael 101, 106
Garnett, Stephen 57
Gay, Jackie 11–13
gender 119–21, 187–8, 194
Geography Workshop 306
Gibberd, Frederick 223, 258, 286
Gibson, Sian 272
Gill, Dawn 88
Gilroy, Paul 65–6, 68, 95
Girouard, Mark 214, 221
Glancey, Jonathan 269
Glennerster, Howard 213
Global Cotton Connections project
  252
Go-Between, The 209
Goldfinger, Erno 258, 260
Goldsmith, James 277

Goldsworthy, Andy 167
Good Life, The 136, 216
Goodhart, David 106–7
Goodman, Robert 233
Goodwin, Matthew 104–5
Goodwood 210–12
Graham, Caroline 191
Great Yarmouth 197–9
Green, Henry 218, 288
Greene, Owen 87–8
Greenham Common 86–7
Greeves, Tom 171
Grindrod, John 311
Grist, Jennifer 130
Grove-White, Robin 214
Gruffalo, The 112, 114
Gunn, Simon 228–30

Hadfield, Charles 250
Hall, Peter (director) 47, 73–4
Hall, Peter (geographer and planner)
  129–30, 144
Hall, Stuart 59–60, 64–5
Hamilton, Peter 174
Hancock, Tony 58
Hanna, Max 238
Hardman, Michael 182
Hardy, Denis 176–8
Hardy, Thomas 48, 75, 147
Harlow 166, 223, 227, 258, 265–6
Harries, Susie 267
Harris, John 210
Harrison, Fraser 169
Harrison, Melissa 39–42, *41*, 45–6,
  57, 91–2
Harrod, Tanya 86
Hartley, L. P. 209
Harvey, P. J. 79–80, 102–3
Harwood, Elain 259–20, 262
Hatherley, Owen 263–5
Hayman, Darren 75, 265
Hazlehurst, Ronnie 195
Head, Dominic 68
Healey, Denis 211
Heaney, Seamus 99–100
Heath, Edward 104, 109–10
Heaton, Paul 187
Hecht, Gabrielle 84
Helmer, Roger 58

Help for Heroes 15, 78
Helpston 54–5
Henderson, Ailsa 10–11, 111
heritage 54–5, 67, 69–70, 173, 183, 202–66, 291
Heriz, Lewis 41–2, *41*
Heron, Patrick 214
Heseltine, Michael 45, 104, 132, 216, 237, 257
Hewison, Robert 234, 236–41, *237*, *240*, 243–4
Hill, Geoffrey 38–9, 59, 99, 151
Hillier, Bevis 126
Hislop, Ian 36
Historic Houses Association 208, 210–11
History Workshop 83, 98, 241
Hogg, Jonathan 84
Holland, Charles 166
Holmfirth 195
Home Internationals 97, 102, 290
Horne, Donald 44, 69–70, 289
Hoskins, W. G. 84, 88, 143–4, *144*, 60–61, 167, 175, 268
Housman, A. E. 60
Hudson, Kenneth 246, 250
Hughes, Ted 99, 175
Hutchinson, Maxwell 234
Hutt, Christopher 182–4, 187

icons, English 33–4, 36
industrial archaeology 243–52
industrial heritage 19, 206, 243–53
infra-ordinary 119, 122, 273, 289–90
intergenerational 121, 152–4
Iraq 78
Ireland 22–4, 36, 78, 101, 104, 110, 114, 148
Ireton, Henry 22–4, 288
Ironbridge 206–7, 245–8, 251, 284
Irons, Jeremy 217

Jackson, Alan 122
Jackson, Michael 183–4
Jackson, Peter 31
Jason, David 43
Jaywick 178, 180
Jenkins, Simon 111
Jenks, Jorian 42

Jennings, Humphrey 30, 297
'Jerusalem' (song) 30, 33, 278–9
Joad, Cyril 238, 241
Jodrell Bank 206, 254–6, *255*
Johns, Pat 170
Johnson-Marshall, Stirrat 262
Johnson, Boris 34, 90–91, 103
Johnson, Linton Kwezi 65
Jones, Terry 185
Joseph, Keith 45
Joyce, William 12
July Skies 265–6, *265*

Kay, Peter 271–2
Keefe, Verity-Jane 263
Keiller, Patrick 55–7, *56*, 178
Keith, Penelope 216
Kennard, Peter 88–9, *88*
Kennet, Lord 214, 224
Kenny, Michael 65, 85, 100
Khanna, Balraj 170
Kiberd, Declan 114
Kibworth, Leicestershire 37–8
King, Angela 167, 170–72
King's Lynn 226, *226*
Kingsnorth, Paul 186–7
Kinks, The 212, 223–4, 259
Kovesi, Simon 54–5

Labour Party 33, 101, 109, 129, 131, 207, 211–12, 228, 231–2
Lake District 67–8, 94, 206
Lancaster, Osbert 225
landscape 51–7, 69
Larbey, Bob 136
Larkin, Philip 54, 75, 99, 147
Last of the Summer Wine 193–5, 272
Lawrence, David 272
Le Pen, Jean-Marie 58
League of Gentlemen, The 157–9
Lee, Jackie 265
Lees-Milne, James 207, 209
Leicester 37, 70–71, 160–61
leisure 38–9, 65, 67–8, 92–4, 220
Lewis, Paul 52, 174
Lewty, Simon 170
Leyh, Liz 142
Liberal Democrats 109, 231

Index

Liberal Party 105, 109
Light, Alison 119–20
Lillyhall Industrial Estate, Workington 227
Limerick 22–3
Lincoln 230–32
Llewelyn-Bowen, Laurence 77
Loach, Ken 264
local, the 38–9, 155–76, 181–9, 290
lockdown 91–4
London 122, 125–9, 132, 234–6
Longleat 140, 202–5, *203*, *204*, 207–8, 289
Losey, Joseph 75, 209
Lowe, Arthur 58, 111
Lowerson, John 193
Lynn, Vera 82, 95

Mabey, Richard 167, 169–70, 185
McAlpine, Lord 237–8
McClure, Vicky 20
MacInnes, Colin 267
Macintosh, Duncan 130
McKay, George 278
Macmillan, Iain 183, 187
MacRae, Mrs J. 275, *275*
Major, John 105, 131–4, 153, 281
Mandler, Peter 13, 103, 207–9, 215–16, 218, 295
March, Earl of 211–12
marketplaces 231–2
Marples, Ernest 272–3
Martin, Kit 239
Martin, Tim 188–9
Mass, Sarah 231–2
Massey, Doreen 55
Massingham, H. J. 42, 50, 174
Matthews, Jeffrey 269, *269*, 281
May, Theresa 107, 112–13, 186
Meades, Jonathan 179–80, 298
Meadows, Shane 20, 148
Medhurst, Andy 125, 136–7
Mee, Arthur 75
Mentmore Towers 215
Mercia 36, 38–9, 59, 145, 151
Merrick 279–80, *280*
Merriman, Peter 269
Merrivale 197–9, *197*, *198*, 289
Metcalfe, John 15

Metro-land 125–8, 134, 146, 150
Midlands 10, 16, 33, 37–9, 144–51, 248
Midsomer Murders 189–94, 196–7, 290
migration 14–15, 59–63, 107–8, 230, 268
Miller, Graeme 278
Millson, Stuart 58
Milton Keynes 134, 140–45, *141*, 162, 229, 263, 289
Mirzoeff, Eddie 126
Mitchell, David 173
model village 195–9, *197*, *198*
modernism 17, 19, 24, 165–6, 222–3, 254–71
Mohr, Jean 50–51
monorails 220–21, *220*, 229
Montagu, Lord 215
Moody, Paul 187
Moore, Bobby 80, 110
Moore, Tom 95
Moran, Joe 277, 282
Morris, William 42, 45, 48, 50, 85, 242
Morris dancing 34, 74, 140, 184
Morrissey 296
Mortimer, John 217
Morton, H. V. 37
Moseley, Rachel 155–7
Moss, Henry 165
motorway 40, 48, 100, 128, 130, 229, 256, 268–82, *269*, 286
Mowl, Timothy 266–7
Murray, Gordon 155–6, 195
museums 238, 244–7
music 13–16, 34–6, 47–8, 74–5, 142, 153, 185, 193, 206–7, 219, 223–4, 265–6, 274, 281
Myers, John 148–51, *149*, *151*
mysticism 193

Naipaul, V. S. 68–9
Nairn, Ian 159–60, 163, 183, 186
Nairn, Tom 97–8, 101
Nash, David 170
Nash, Paul 286
National Health Service 31, 94–6, 292
National Trust 50, 70, 132, 140, 206–10, 215–16, 237, 242, 258

nature 40, 56–7, 169, 179
Navickas, Katrina 159
Neate, Hannah 263
Nettles, John 192
New Society 127, 129–30, 277
new towns 140–43, 263, 265
Newbolt, Henry 137
Newbury 229, 279–80, *280*
Newell, Martin 153
Newley, Anthony 10
Newman, John 270
Nobbs, David 118, 135, 205
'Non-Plan: An Experiment in Freedom' 129–30, 142
Norris, Rufus 79
Northam, Jean 157
Northern Ireland 97, 99, 101
Norwich 184, 208, 229
nostalgia 264–5
Nottinghamshire 16–24, 100, 171, 267–8, 283–6
nuclear power 83–4, 263
nuclear weapons 14, 83–9, *88*, 253, 263–4

O'Brien, Sean 111
Offa, King 38–9, 59, 62
Oldfield, Mike 31, 219
Oliver, Paul 121, 214
Olympics 2008 34
Olympics 2012 30–34, *31*, *32*, 95, 289, 291
Openshaw, Stan 87–8
Opie, Julian 273–4, *274*
Orr, Chris 236–7, *237*, 240–41, *240*
Ortolano, Guy 142, 230
Orwell, George 133–4, 153, 188
O'Toole, Fintan 103, 114
Owen, Bill 194
Owen, Wilfred 78–9
Oxfordshire 47–8, 55–6, 191

Packham, Chris 91
Pahl, Ray 127–8
Palmer, John 233
Palmer, Roger 283–4, *283*
Parish Maps 169–71
Parker, Jim 125, 192–3

Parr, Martin 139–44, *141*, 152, 162, 262–3, 270–71, 275, *275*
Partridge, Andy 36, 153
passport, UK 48–9, *49*
pastoral 15–16, 40–41, 43–71, 92, 174–7, 189, 290
and music 47–8, 193, 195
and war 74, 81, 85–6
Paternoster Square 236
patriotism 61, 72, 82–5, 148
Pearce, David 165, 177–8, 211, 239–40, 244, 257
Pendlebury, John 260, 264
Perec, Georges 118–19, 147
Petit, Chris 273
petrol stations 270
Pevsner, Nikolaus 17, 19, 76, 146, 236, 246–7, 256–7, 260–61, 266–9, 283
Phelps, Richard 263
Philpot, Terry 178
photography 28–31, 121–2, 139–44, 148–51, 183, 262, 275, 284–5
Pick, Frank 263
Pinter, Harold 209
Piper, John 56, 123–4, *124*
Piper, Tom 78
planning 223–5, 227–33
Plas, Annemarie 94
plotlands 176–81
Plymouth 227, 261, 264
Pollard, Ingrid 67–8
Pooley, Fred 229
postcolonial 61–2, 127, 205, 227, 277
Potter, Stephen 138
Powell, Enoch 59–63, 66, 71, 98, 104–5, 109, 205, 290
power stations 260, 283–7
Previn, Andre 82
Price, Cedric 129
Priestley, J. B. 264
Prince of Wales 33, 221, 223, 234–7, 239, 242
public art 16, 19–21, 168–9
pubs 18–19, 37, 46, 102, 105–6, 181–9, 290

Raban, Jonathan 81–2, 170, 233–4
race 57–71, 95, 102, 108, 126, 148, 186, 192

Index

Ramsey, Robert 22
Rasmussen, Steen Eiler 179
Ratcliffe-on-Soar power station 284–6, 289
Reas, Paul 243
Rebanks, James 53
Redgrave, Vanessa 55
remembrance 75–8, 291
Reilly, Vini 15, 296
Rice, Brian 121
Richards, E. P. 93
Richards, J. M. 122–4
'Right to Buy' housing policy 131–2, 142, 145
Rising Damp 20, 135
Rix, Michael 245, 249, 251–2
road protests 275–81, *275*, *280*
Roberts, Simon 27–31, *29*, *31*, 65, 76–8, *77*, 112–13, *113*, 284–6, *285*
Robinson, John Martin 216
Romain, John 96
Ronan Point 230, 232
Rossiter, Leonard 118, 135, 138
Round Hill Primary School 249
Rubens, Paul 79
Ruskin, John 238, 242

safari parks 202–5
Saint, Andrew 259, 261–2, 269–70
Saint Etienne 179, 274
St George's flag 20, 148, 181, 208
Sallis, Peter 194–5
Samuel, Raphael 83–4, 140, 161–2, 166, 231, 241–5
Sandys, Duncan 224
Saumarez Smith, Otto 224–5, 228–9
Saunders, Robert 103
Savage, Jon 12
Savary, Peter de 82
SAVE Britain's Heritage 211, 238–9, 244, 257
Scarthin Books 173
Scheffler, Axel 112, *112*
Schofield, Camilla 62
Schumacher, E. F. 185
Schwarz, Bill 62–3
Scofield, Paul 55
Scotland 13, 17, 33, 97–8, 103–4, 106–7, 109

Scott, Terry 138
Scott, Walter 17
Scottish National Party 100, 109
Scruton, Roger 101
Searle, Anthony 86
Second World War 9–10, 14, 18, 82, 94–6, 215, 236, 291–2
Self, Will 196
Sex Pistols 12
Shaftesbury 140, 167
Shakespeare, William 30
Shand, Garrow 73–4
Shankland, Graeme 229
Sharp, Thomas 261, 266
Shaw, George 145–50, *146*, *147*, 152, 196, 262
Sherman, Alfred 130
Siouxsie and the Banshees 120
Sked, Alan 105
Skegness 220, *220*
Simmons, Jack 245, 247
Sinclair, Iain 54, 273
slavery 69–71, 252–3
Sledmere 76
Smith, David 248–51, *249*, *250*
Smith, Paul 19
social democracy 264–5
Society for the Preservation of Beers from the Wood 182
South Woodham Ferrers 164–6, 177–8, 180, 211, 289
Southwell 267–8
Sowden, Harry 247, 284
Spandler, Brenda 88
Spence, Jeoffry 241
Spence, Peter 216–17
Spencer, Earl 225–6, *226*
Spencer, Stanley 82
Spitalfields 221, 242
Spitfire 33, 96
Springwatch 91
Standard, Sidney 20
Stanshall, Vivian 219
Starmer, Keir 95
Starr, Edwin 19
Steadman, Philip 87–8
steam railways 156, 240–41, 243
Steedman, Carolyn 152–3
Stevenage 260, 262

Stonehenge 33–4, 140, 206–7, 268
Stourbridge 148–50
Strong, Roy 210–12, 215
suburbia 16–17, 22–4, 38, 118–54, 160, 163, 216–17, 228
Suffolk 40–42, 46–7, 72–4, 157
Swann, Donald 85
Sykes, Mark 76

Talking Heads 281
Taverne, Dick 231
Tayler & Green, architects 263, 266
Taylor, Nicholas 128–9, 232–3
Taylor, Ray 227
Tebay services 272
Tebbit, Norman 104
television 7, 20, 118–20, 134–9, 189–95, 216–18, 223, 235
Terry, Quinlan 216, 237–8
Thames, River 29–30, 48, 235
Thatcher, Margaret 45, 59, 80–81, 83, 98, 131–2, 152, 215, 273
Thatcherism 12, 130, 233, 264
Thirties Society 257
This England 57–9, 148, 191, 289
Thomas, David St John 241, 250
Thomas, Simon 168–9
Thompson, E. P. 56, 65, 85, 89
Thorn, Tracey 120–21
Thornton, Frank 194
Thornton, Peter 210
Tidy, Bill 185
Times Literary Supplement 111, 114
Titfield Thunderbolt, The 85
To the Manor Born 216–18
Tolkien, J.R.R. 31–3, *32*, 84, 147, 164
Tomlinson, Sally 103
Tower of London 78
townscape 220–33
Trent, River 16–17, 21–3, 185, 283–4, 288
Trevor-Roper, Hugh 226–7
True-May, Brian 192
Trumpton 155–7, 160, 181, 195, 198, 289
Twentieth Century Society 258, 270
Twyford Down 278–9, 282, 289
Tyme, John 276–8

Uffington white horse 35–6
Ultramarine 206–7
United Kingdom Independence Party (UKIP) 58, 104–8, 178
urban redevelopment 60, 221–3, 228–36

Vaughan Williams, Ralph 173
Veldman, Meredith 84–5
vernacular architecture 160–68, 232–3
Victoria and Albert Museum 210–11, 218, 235, 267
village, English 46–50, 86, 106, 127–8, 138, 142–4, 223–4

Wailes, Rex 244–5
Waites, Ian 263, 312, 330
Wales 33, 59, 66, 97–8, 101, 104, 111
Wall, Derek 277
war memorials 17–19, 24, 74–6
Ward, Colin 176–8
Warner, Sylvia Townsend 40, 159
Watkin, David 164
Waugh, Evelyn 217
Wealth Tax 209–14
Webster, Wendy 107
Weldon, Fay 86–7
Wembley Stadium 90, 110–11
Wesker, Arnold 214
Westall, Claire 101
West Burton power station 227, 283–4, 286
Wetherspoon, J. D. 188–9
Whatever Happened to the Likely Lads? 124, 144, 147
white cliffs 95, 112–13, *112*, *113*
whiteness 62–5
Whiteley, Nigel 259
Wiener, Martin 44–5, 237, 289
Wilde, Brian 194
Willats, Stephen 170
Williams, Owen 17, 268–70
Williams, Raymond 51–3, 57, 169
Williams, Tony 150–51
Williams, Val 270
Williamson, Elizabeth 283–4
Williamson, Henry 41–2

Wilson, Harold 109
Wilton, Penelope 137
Windrush, ss *Empire* 31, 33, 59
Windscale 84
Woburn 208, 210
Wombles, The 175–6
Wood, Michael 36–8, 70–71
Wood, Roy 180
Woolf, Virginia 113
Wootten, William 59

Wootton Bassett 77–8, *77*
World Heritage Sites 206, 247, 251
Wright, Patrick 55, 58, 76, 82–3, 101, 145, 215, 242–3
Wyatt, Robert 82, 178–9, 207
Wyn Jones, Richard 10–11

XTC 34–6, *35*, 153, 265, 281

Zabou 19